ROUTLEDGE
STUDENT STATUTES

Evidence Statutes
2009–2010

Designed specifically for students, and responding to current market feedback, Routledge Student Statutes offers a comprehensive collection of statutory provisions un-annotated and therefore ideal for LLB and GDL course and exam use. In addition, an accompanying website offers extensive guidance on how to use and interpret statutes, providing valuable tutorial and exam preparation.

The Routledge Student Statutes series collects together, in each volume, all the legislation students need to pass their exams so it is comprehensive, clearly presented, and easy to access.

Routledge Student Statutes provide extensive innovative features, vital in aiding LLB and GDL learning:

- Comprehensive content, with legislation carefully selected to match the common curriculum
- Written by leading experts in each field so students can feel confident in the experience and judgement behind each selection
- Un-annotated, making the series ideal for both course and exam use
- Each title contains alphabetical, chronological and thematic contents listings and is fully indexed making it easy to navigate
- A free Companion Website providing students with extra guidance and testing on how to use and interpret statutes
- Updated annually to incorporate all of the latest legislation covered in UK law syllabi
- Highly competitive price makes Routledge Student Statutes the statutes series of choice

Claire McGourlay is Lecturer in Law at the University of Sheffield.

ROUTLEDGE STUDENT STATUTES

Designed specifically for students, and responding to current market feedback, Routledge Student Statutes offers a comprehensive collection of statutory provisions un-annotated and therefore ideal for LLB and GDL course and exam use. The accompanying website offers extensive guidance on how to use and interpret statutes, providing valuable tutorial and exam preparation.

Titles in the series:

Company Law Statutes 2009–2010
  MARC MOORE

Contract, Tort and Restitution Statutes 2009–2010
  JAMES DEVENNEY AND HOWARD JOHNSON

Criminal Law Statutes 2009–2010
  JONATHAN HERRING

Employment Law Statutes 2009–2010
  JANICE NAIRNS

European Union Legislation 2009–2010
  JEFF KENNER

Evidence Statutes 2009–2010
  CLAIRE MCGOURLAY

Family Law Statutes 2009–2010
  PHIL BATES

International Trade Law Statutes and Conventions 2009–2010
  INDIRA CARR AND RICHARD KIDNER

Property Law Statutes 2009–2010
  RUSSELL HEWITSON

Public Law and Human Rights 2009–2010
  PAUL BEHRENS

www.routledgelaw.com/statutes/

ROUTLEDGE
STUDENT STATUTES

Evidence Statutes
2009–2010

CLAIRE McGOURLAY
Lecturer in Law,
University of Sheffield

Routledge
Taylor & Francis Group

LONDON AND NEW YORK

First published 2010 by Routledge
2 Park Square, Milton Park, Abingdon, Oxon, OX14 4RN

Simultaneously published in the USA and Canada
by Routledge
270 Madison Ave, New York, NY 10016

Routledge is an imprint of the Taylor & Francis Group, an informa business

© 2010 Routledge

Typeset in Sabon by RefineCatch Limited, Bungay, Suffolk
Printed and bound in Great Britain by TJ International Ltd, Padstow, Cornwall

British Library Cataloguing in Publication Data
A catalogue record for this book is available from the British Library

Library of Congress Cataloging in Publication Data
Evidence statutes 2009–2010 / [compiled by] Claire McGourlay.
    p. cm.
  1. Evidence (Law—England.   I. McGourlay, Claire.
  KD7499.6.E94 2009
  347.42′06—dc22

                                        2009025094

Parliamentary material is reproduced with the permission of the
Controller of HMSO on behalf of Parliament.

ISBN10: 0–415–45839–0 (pbk)
ISBN13: 978–0–415–45839–9 (pbk)

Contents

PREFACE

This is the first edition of *Evidence Statutes*. In creating this book, I hope to provide a statute book that students will find accessible and easy to navigate. This book also improves the pedagogical value for the student through the addition of alphabetical, chronological and thematic contents listings and a free Companion Website providing students with extra guidance and testing on how to use and interpret statutes

I have concentrated on those topics that tend to feature commonly on Evidence courses and I believe I have selected the most pertinent parts of the statutory material available.

Amendments, insertions repeals or substitutions have been included in the text but there is only a note made at the end of that particular Act if this occurred after 2007. In addition where a commencement date is known, and it is after 1 June 2009 but on or before 31 December 2009, the amendment has been made and a note added at the end of the Act in question. If a commencement date is known but it is on or after the following 1 January (2010), no change has been made to the text but a note has been added at the end of the Act. Any amendment for which, at 1 June 2009, a commencement date had not been fixed has been excluded.

On a final note, I wish to express my sincere gratitude to Fiona Kinnear and Rebecca Slorach at Routledge-Cavendish for overseeing the preparation and production of this text, Abigail Pearce-Dyke a former student, who gave invaluable feedback on this first edition and Roger George at Bristol University for stepping in at the last minute to do the indexes on this book. I am also grateful for the support of my husband Jamie and my two children Abigail and Owen who suffered in almost silence whilst mum was working.

As the author, I accept full responsibility for any errors or omissions in the text and would be grateful for any suggestions for future editions.

All statutes are up to date as of June 1st 2009.

WITNESSES ACT 1806
(c. 37)

1 Witnesses cannot refuse to answer question tended to establish their indebtedness, etc.

A witness cannot by law refuse to answer a question relevant to the matter in issue, the answering of which has no tendency to accuse himself or to expose him to penalty or forfeiture of any nature whatsoever, by reason only or on the sole ground that the answering of such question may establish or tend to establish that he owes a debt, or is otherwise subject to a civil suit either at the instance of his Majesty or of any other person or persons.

CRIMINAL PROCEDURE ACT 1865
(c. 18)

3 How far witness may be discredited by the party producing

A party producing a witness shall not be allowed to impeach his credit by general evidence of bad character; but he may, in case the witness shall in the opinion of the judge prove adverse, contradict him by other evidence, or, by leave of the judge, prove that he has made at other times a statement inconsistent with his present testimony; but before such last-mentioned proof can be given the circumstances of the supposed statement, sufficient to designate the particular occasion, must be mentioned to the witness, and he must be asked whether or not he has made such statement.

4 As to proof of contradictory statements of adverse witness

If a witness, upon cross-examination as to a former statement made by him relative to the subject matter of the indictment or proceeding, and inconsistent with his present testimony, does not distinctly admit that he has made such statement, proof may be given that he did in fact make it; but before such proof can be given the circumstances of the supposed statement, sufficient to designate the particular occasion, must be mentioned to the witness, and he must be asked whether or not he has made such statement.

5 Cross-examinations as to previous statements in writing

A witness may be cross-examined as to previous statements made by him in writing, or reduced into writing, relative to the subject matter of the indictment or proceeding, without such writing being shown to him; but if it is intended to contradict such witness by the writing, his attention must, before such contradictory proof can be given, be called to those parts of the writing which are to be used for the purpose of so contradicting him: Provided always, that it shall be competent for the judge, at any time during the trial, to require the production of the writing for his inspection, and he may thereupon make such use of it for the purposes of the trial as he may think fit.

Bankers' Book Evidence Act 1879

(c. 11)

3 Mode of proof of entries in bankers' books

Subject to the provisions of this Act, a copy of any entry in a banker's book shall in all legal proceedings be received as primâ facie evidence of such entry, and of the matters, transactions, and accounts therein recorded.

4 Proof that book is a banker's book

A copy of an entry in a banker's book shall not be received in evidence under this Act unless it be first proved that the book was at the time of the making of the entry one of the ordinary books of the bank, and that the entry was made in the usual and ordinary course of business, and that the book is in the custody or control of the bank.

Such proof may be given by a partner or officer of the bank, and may be given orally or by an affidavit sworn before any commissioner or person authorised to take affidavits.

5 Verification of copy

A copy of an entry in a banker's book shall not be received in evidence under this Act unless it be further proved that the copy has been examined with the original entry and is correct.

Such proof shall be given by some person who has examined the copy with the original entry, and may be given either orally or by an affidavit sworn before any commissioner or person authorised to take affidavits.

6 Case in which banker, &c. not compellable to produce book, &c.

A banker or officer of a bank shall not, in any legal proceeding to which the bank is not a party, be compellable to produce any banker's book the contents of which can be proved under this Act, or under the Civil Evidence (Scotland)Act 1988 or Schedule 8 to the Criminal Procedure (Scotland) Act 1995 or Schedule 3 to the Prisoners and Criminal Proceedings (Scotland) Act 1993 or to appear as a witness to prove the matters, transactions, and accounts therein recorded, unless by order of a judge made for special cause.

9 Interpretation of "bank," "banker," and "bankers' books"

In this Act the expressions "bank" and "banker" mean any person, persons, partnership, or company carrying on the business of bankers and having duly made a return to the Commissioners of Inland Revenue, and also any savings bank certified under the Acts relating to savings banks, and also any post office savings bank.

The fact of any such bank having duly made a return to the Commissioners of Inland Revenue may be proved in any legal proceeding by production of a copy of its return verified by the affidavit of a partner or officer of the bank, or by the production of a copy of a newspaper purporting to contain a copy of such return published by the Commissioners of Inland Revenue; the fact that any such savings bank is certified under the Acts relating to savings banks may be proved by an office or examined copy of its certificate; the fact that any such bank is a post office savings bank may be proved by a certificate purporting to be under the hand of Her Majesty's Postmaster-General or one of the secretaries of the Post Office.

Expressions in this Act relating to "bankers' books" include ledgers, day books, cash books, account books, and all other books used in the ordinary business of the bank.

CRIMINAL EVIDENCE ACT 1898
(c. 36)

1   Competency of witnesses in criminal cases

Every person charged with an offence, and the wife or husband, as the case may be, of the person so charged, shall be a competent witness for the defence at every stage of the proceedings, whether the person so charged is charged solely or jointly with any other person. Provided as follows:—

(1) A person charged in criminal proceedings shall not be called as a witness in the proceedings except upon his own application:

    (c) The wife or husband of the person charged shall not, save as in this Act mentioned, be called as a witness in pursuance of this Act except upon the application of the person so charged:

    (d) Nothing in this Act shall make a husband compellable to disclose any communication made to him by his wife during the marriage, or a wife compellable to disclose any communication made to her by her husband during the marriage:

(2) A person charged in criminal proceedings who is called as a witness in the proceedings may be asked any question in cross-examination notwithstanding that it would tend to criminate him as to any offence with which he is charged in the proceedings:

(3) A person charged in criminal proceedings who is called as a witness in the proceedings shall not be asked, and if asked shall not be required to answer, any question tending to show that he has committed or been convicted of or been charged with any offence other than one with which he is then charged, or is of bad character, unless—

    (i) the proof that he has committed or been convicted of such other offence is admissible evidence to show that he is guilty of an offence with which he is then charged; or

    (ii) he has personally or by his advocate asked questions of the witnesses for the prosecution with a view to establish his own good character, or has given evidence of his good character, or the nature or conduct of the defence is such as to involve imputations on the character of the prosecutor or the witnesses for the prosecution; or the deceased victim of the alleged crime; or

    (iii) he has given evidence against any other person charged in the same proceedings:

(4) Every person charged in criminal proceedings who is called as a witness in the proceedings shall, unless otherwise ordered by the court, give his evidence from the witness box or other place from which the other witnesses give their evidence:

Perjury Act 1911
(c. 6)

13 Corroboration

A person shall not be liable to be convicted of any offence against this Act, or of any offence declared by any other Act to be perjury or subornation of perjury, or to be punishable as perjury or subornation of perjury, solely upon the evidence of one witness as to the falsity of any statement alleged to be false.

14 Proof of certain proceedings on which perjury is assigned

On a prosecution—

(a) for perjury alleged to have been committed on the trial of an indictment for misdemeanour; or

(b) for procuring or suborning the commission of perjury on any such trial,

the fact of the former trial shall be sufficiently proved by the production of a certificate containing the substance and effect (omitting the formal parts) of the indictment and trial purporting to be signed by the clerk of the court, or other person having the custody of the records of the court where the indictment was tried, or by the deputy of that clerk or other person, without proof of the signature or official character of the clerk or person appearing to have signed the certificate.

LAW OF PROPERTY ACT 1925
(c. 20)

184   Presumption of survivorship in regard to claims to property

In all cases where, after the commencement of this Act, two or more persons have died in circumstances rendering it uncertain which of them survived the other or others, such deaths shall (subject to any order of the court), for all purposes affecting the title to property, be presumed to have occurred in order of seniority, and accordingly the younger shall be deemed to have survived the elder.

CHILDREN AND YOUNG PERSONS ACT 1933
(c. 12)

42—Extension of power to take deposition of child or young person

(1) Where a justice of the peace is satisfied by the evidence of a duly qualified medical practitioner that the attendance before a court of any child or young person in respect of whom any of the offences mentioned in the First Schedule to this Act is alleged to have been committed would involve serious danger to his life or health, the justice may taken in writing the deposition of the child or young person on oath, and shall thereupon subscribe the deposition and add thereto a statement of his reason for taking it and of the day when and place where it was taken, and of the names of the persons (if any) present at the taking thereof.

(2) The justice taking any such deposition shall transmit it with his statement—
   (a) if the deposition relates to an offence for which any accused person is already [sent]for trial, to the proper officer of the court for the trial at which the accused person has been sent; and
   (b) in any other case, to the [proper officer] of the court before which proceedings are pending in respect of the offence.

43   Admission of deposition of child or young person in evidence

Where, in any proceedings in respect of any of the offences mentioned in the First Schedule of this Act, the court is satisfied by the evidence of a duly qualified medical practitioner that the attendance before the court of any child or young person in respect of whom the offence is alleged to have been committed would involve serious danger to his life or health, any deposition of the child or young person taken under the Indictable Offences Act 1848, or this Part of this Act, shall be admissible in evidence either for or against the accused person without further proof thereof if it purports to be signed by the justice by or before whom it purports to be taken:

Provided that the deposition shall not be admissible in evidence against the accused person unless it is proved that reasonable notice of the intention to take the deposition has been served upon him and that he or his counsel or solicitor had, or might have had if he had chosen to be present, an opportunity of cross-examining the child or young person making the deposition.

50   Age of criminal responsibility

It shall be conclusively presumed that no child under the age of ten years can be guilty of any offence.

Prevention of Crime Act 1953
(c. 14)

1—Prohibition of the carrying of offensive weapons without lawful authority or reasonable excuse

(1) Any person who without lawful authority or reasonable excuse, the proof whereof shall lie on him, has with him in any public place any offensive weapon shall be guilty of an offence, and shall be liable—
  (a) on summary conviction, to imprisonment for a term not exceeding six months or a fine not exceeding the prescribed sum or both;
  (b) on conviction on indictment, to imprisonment for a term not exceeding [four] years or a fine, or both.

(2) Where any person is convicted of an offence under subsection (1) of this section the court may make an order for the forfeiture or disposal of any weapon in respect of which the offence was committed.

(4) In this section "public place" includes any highway and any other premises or place to which at the material time the public have or are permitted to have access, whether on payment or otherwise; and "offensive weapon" means any article made or adapted for use for causing injury to the person, or intended by the person having it with him for such use by him or by some other person.

HOMICIDE ACT 1957
(c. 11)

2—Persons suffering from diminished responsibility

(1) Where a person kills or is a party to the killing of another, he shall not be convicted of murder if he was suffering from such abnormality of mind (whether arising from a condition of arrested or retarded development of mind or any inherent causes or induced by disease or injury) as substantially impaired his mental responsibility for his acts and omissions in doing or being a party to the killing.

(2) On a charge of murder, it shall be for the defence to prove that the person charged is by virtue of this section not liable to be convicted of murder.

(3) A person who but for this section would be liable, whether as principal or as accessory, to be convicted of murder shall be liable instead to be convicted of manslaughter.

(4) The fact that one party to a killing is by virtue of this section not liable to be convicted of murder shall not affect the question whether the killing amounted to murder in the case of any other party to it.

CRIMINAL JUSTICE ACT 1967
(c. 80)

9—Proof by written statement

(1) In any criminal proceedings, other than committal proceedings, a written statement by any person shall, if such of the conditions mentioned in the next following subsection as are applicable are satisfied, be admissible as evidence to the like extent as oral evidence to the like effect by that person.

(2) The said conditions are—

    (a) the statement purports to be signed by the person who made it;

    (b) the statement contains a declaration by that person to the effect that it is true to the best of his knowledge and belief and that he made the statement knowing that, if it were tendered in evidence, he would be liable to prosecution if he wilfully stated in it anything which he knew to be false or did not believe to be true;

    (c) before the hearing at which the statement is tendered in evidence, a copy of the statement is served, by or on behalf of the party proposing to tender it, on each of the other parties to the proceedings; and

    (d) none of the other parties or their solicitors, within seven days from the service of the copy of the statement, serves a notice on the party so proposing objecting to the statement being tendered in evidence under this section:

Provided that the conditions mentioned in paragraphs (c) and (d) of this subsection shall not apply if the parties agree before or during the hearing that the statement shall be so tendered.

(3) The following provisions shall also have effect in relation to any written statement tendered in evidence under this section, that is to say—

    (a) if the statement is made by a person under the age of eighteen, it shall give his age;

    (b) if it is made by a person who cannot read it, it shall be read to him before he signs it and shall be accompanied by a declaration by the person who so read the statement to the effect that it was so read; and

    (c) if it refers to any other document as an exhibit, the copy served on any other party to the proceedings under paragraph (c) of the last foregoing subsection shall be accompanied by a copy of that document or by such information as may be necessary in order to enable the party on whom it is served to inspect that document or a copy thereof.

(4) Notwithstanding that a written statement made by any person may be admissible as evidence by virtue of this section—

    (a) the party by whom or on whose behalf a copy of the statement was served may call that person to give evidence; and

    (b) the court may, of its own motion or on the application of any party to the proceedings, require that person to attend before the court and give evidence.

(5) An application under paragraph (b) of the last foregoing subsection to a court other than a magistrates' court may be made before the hearing and on any such application the powers of the court shall be exercisable by a puisne judge of the High Court, a Circuit judge or Recorder sitting alone.

(6) So much of any statement as is admitted in evidence by virtue of this section shall, unless the court otherwise directs, be read aloud at the hearing and where the court so directs an account shall be given orally of so much of any statement as is not read aloud.

(7) Any document or object referred to as an exhibit and identified in a written statement tendered in evidence under this section shall be treated as if it had been produced as an exhibit and identified in court by the maker of the statement.

(8) A document required by this section to be served on any person may be served—

    (a) by delivering it to him or to his solicitor; or

    (b) by addressing it to him and leaving it at his usual or last known place of abode or place of business or by addressing it to his solicitor and leaving it at his office; or

    (c) by sending it in a registered letter or by the recorded delivery service or by first class post addressed to him at his usual or last known place of abode or place of business or addressed to his solicitor at his office; or

    (d) in the case of a body corporate, by delivering it to the secretary or clerk of the body at its registered or principal office or sending it in a registered letter or by the recorded delivery service or by first class post addressed to the Secretary or clerk of that body at that office; and in paragraph (d) of this subsection references to the secretary, in relation to a limited liability partnership, are to any designated member of the limited liability partnership.

10—Proof by formal admission

(1) Subject to the provisions of this section, any fact of which oral evidence may be given in any criminal proceedings may be admitted for the purpose of those proceedings by or on behalf of the prosecutor or

defendant, and the admission by any party of any such fact under this section shall as against that party be conclusive evidence in those proceedings of the fact admitted.

(2) An admission under this section—

    (a) may be made before or at the proceedings;

    (b) if made otherwise than in court, shall be in writing;

    (c) if made in writing by an individual, shall purport to be signed by the person making it and, if so made by a body corporate, shall purport to be signed by a director or manager, or the secretary or clerk, or some other similar officer of the body corporate;

    (d) if made on behalf of a defendant who is an individual, shall be made by his counsel or solicitor;

    (e) if made at any state before the trial by a defendant who is an individual, must be approved by his counsel or solicitor (whether at the time it was made or subsequently) before or at the proceedings in question.

(3) An admission under this section for the purpose of proceedings relating to any matter shall be treated as an admission for the purpose of any subsequent criminal proceedings relating to that matter (including any appeal or retrial).

(4) An admission under this section may with the leave of the court be withdrawn in the proceedings for the purpose of which it is made or any subsequent criminal proceedings relating to the same matter.

CIVIL EVIDENCE ACT 1968
(c. 64)

11—Convictions as evidence in civil proceedings.

(1) In any civil proceedings the fact that a person has been convicted of an offence by or before any court in the United Kingdom or by a court-martial there or elsewhere shall (subject to subsection (3) below) be admissible in evidence for the purpose of proving, where to do so is relevant to any issue in those proceedings, that he committed that offence, whether he was so convicted upon a plea of guilty or otherwise and whether or not he is a party to the civil proceedings; but no conviction other than a subsisting one shall be admissible in evidence by virtue of this section.

(2) In any civil proceedings in which by virtue of this section a person is proved to have been convicted of an offence by or before any court in the United Kingdom or by a court-martial there or elsewhere—
   (a) he shall be taken to have committed that offence unless the contrary is proved; and
   (b) without prejudice to the reception of any other admissible evidence for the purpose of identifying the facts on which the conviction was based, the contents of any document which is admissible as evidence of the conviction, and the contents of the information, complaint, indictment or charge-sheet on which the person in question was convicted, shall be admissible in evidence for that purpose.

(3) Nothing in this section shall prejudice the operation of section 13 of this Act or any other enactment whereby a conviction or a finding of fact in any criminal proceedings is for the purposes of any other proceedings made conclusive evidence of any fact.

(4) Where in any civil proceedings the contents of any document are admissible in evidence by virtue of subsection (2) above, a copy of that document, or of the material part thereof, purporting to be certified or otherwise authenticated by or on behalf of the court or authority having custody of that document shall be admissible in evidence and shall be taken to be a true copy of that document or part unless the contrary is shown.

(5) Nothing in any of the following enactments, that is to say—
   (a) section 14 of the Powers of Criminal Courts (Sentencing) Act 2000 (under which a conviction leading to discharge is to be disregarded except as therein mentioned);

(b) section 191 of the Criminal Procedure (Scotland) Act 1975 (which makes similar provision in respect of convictions on indictment in Scotland); and

(c) section 8 of the Probation Act (Northern Ireland) 1950 (which corresponds to the said section 12) or any corresponding enactment of the Parliament of Northern Ireland for the time being in force,

shall affect the operation of this section; and for the purposes of this section any order made by a court of summary jurisdiction in Scotland under section 383 or section 384 of the said Act of 1975 shall be treated as a conviction.

(6) In this section "court-martial" means a court-martial constituted under the Army Act 1955, the Air Force Act 1955 or the Naval Discipline Act 1957 and in relation to a court-martial "conviction" means a finding of guilty which is, or falls to be treated as, the finding of the court, and "conviction" shall be construed accordingly.

12—Findings of adultery and paternity as evidence in civil proceedings.

(1) In any civil proceedings—
(a) the fact that a person has been found guilty of adultery in any matrimonial proceedings; and

(b) the fact that a person has been found to be the father of a child in relevant proceedings before any court in England and Wales or has been adjudged to be the father of a child in affiliation proceedings before any court in the United Kingdom;

shall (subject to subsection (3) below) be admissible in evidence for the purpose of proving, where to do so is relevant to any issue in those civil proceedings, that he committed the adultery to which the finding relates or, as the case may be, is (or was) the father of that child, whether or not he offered any defence to the allegation of adultery or paternity and whether or not he is a party to the civil proceedings; but no finding or adjudication other than a subsisting one shall be admissible in evidence by virtue of this section.

(2) In any civil proceedings in which by virtue of this section a person is proved to have been found guilty of adultery as mentioned in subsection (1)(a) above or [to have been found or adjudged]to be the father of a child as mentioned in subsection (1)(b) above—
(a) he shall be taken to have committed the adultery to which the finding relates or, as the case may be, to be (or have been) the father of that child, unless the contrary is proved; and

(b) without prejudice to the reception of any other admissible evidence for the purpose of identifying the facts on which the finding or adjudication was based, the contents of any document which was before the court, or which contains any pronouncement of the court, in the [other proceedings]in question shall be admissible in evidence for that purpose.

(3) Nothing in this section shall prejudice the operation of any enactment whereby a finding of fact in any matrimonial or affiliation proceedings is for the purposes of any other proceedings made conclusive evidence of any fact.

(4) Subsection (4) of section 11 of this Act shall apply for the purposes of this section as if the reference to subsection (2) were a reference to subsection (2) of this section.

(5) In this section—

"matrimonial proceedings" means any matrimonial cause in the High Court or a county court in England and Wales or in the High Court in Northern Ireland, any consistorial action in Scotland, or any appeal arising out of any such cause or action;

'relevant proceedings' means—

(a) proceedings on a complaint under section 42 of the National Assistance Act 1948 or section 26 of the Social Security Act 1986;

(b) proceedings under the Children Act 1989;

(c) proceedings which would have been relevant proceedings for the purposes of this section in the form in which it was in force before the passing of the Children Act 1989

"affiliation proceedings" means, in relation to Scotland, any action of affiliation and aliment;

and in this subsection "consistorial action" does not include an action of aliment only between husband and wife raised in the Court of Session or an action of interim aliment raised in the sheriff court.

13—Conclusiveness of convictions for purposes of defamation actions.

(1) In an action for libel or slander in which the question whether the plaintiff did or did not commit a criminal offence is relevant to an issue arising in the action, proof that, at the time when that issue falls to be determined, he stands convicted of that offence shall be conclusive evidence that he committed that offence; and his conviction thereof shall be admissible in evidence accordingly.

(2) In any such action as aforesaid in which by virtue of this section the plaintiff is proved to have been convicted of an offence, the contents of any document which is admissible as evidence of the conviction, and the contents of the information, complaint, indictment or charge-sheet on which [he] was convicted, shall, without prejudice to the reception of any other admissible evidence for the purpose of identifying the facts on which the conviction was based, be admissible in evidence for the purpose of identifying those facts.

(2A)   In the case of an action for libel or slander in which there is more than one plaintiff—

(a)   the references in subsections (1) and (2) above to the plaintiff shall be construed as references to any of the plaintiffs, and

(b)   proof that any of the plaintiffs stands convicted of an offence shall be conclusive evidence that he committed that offence so far as that fact is relevant to any issue arising in relation to his cause of action or that of any other plaintiff.

(3)   For the purposes of this section a person shall be taken to stand convicted of an offence if but only if there subsists against him a conviction of that offence by or before a court in the United Kingdom or by a court-martial there or elsewhere.

(4)   Subsections (4) to (6) of section 11 of this Act shall apply for the purposes of this section as they apply for the purposes of that section, but as if in the said subsection (4) the reference to subsection (2) were a reference to subsection (2) of this section.

(5)   The foregoing provisions of this section shall apply for the purposes of any action begun after the passing of this Act, whenever the cause of action arose, but shall not apply for the purposes of any action begun before the passing of this Act or any appeal or other proceedings arising out of any such action.

14—Privilege against incrimination of self or spouse or civil partner.

(1)   The right of a person in any legal proceedings other than criminal proceedings to refuse to answer any question or produce any document or thing if to do so would tend to expose that person to proceedings for an offence or for the recovery of a penalty—

(a)   shall apply only as regards criminal offence under the law of any part of the United Kingdom and penalties provided for by such law; and

(b)   shall include a like right to refuse to answer any question or produce any document or thing if to do so would tend to expose the [spouse or civil partner] of that person to proceedings for any such criminal offence or for the recovery of any such penalty.

(2)   In so far as any existing enactment conferring (in whatever words) powers of inspection or investigation confers on a person (in whatever words) any right otherwise than in criminal proceedings to refuse to answer any question or give any evidence tending to incriminate that person, subsection (1) above shall apply to that right as it applies to the right described in that subsection; and every such existing enactment shall be construed accordingly.

(3)   In so far as any existing enactment provides (in whatever words) that in any proceedings other than criminal proceedings a person shall not be excused from answering any question or giving any evidence on the

ground that to do so may incriminate that person, that enactment shall be construed as providing also that in such proceedings a person shall not be excused from answering any question or giving any evidence on the ground that to do so may incriminate the husband or wife of that person.

(4) Where any existing enactment (however worded) that—
   (a) confers powers of inspection or investigation; or

   (b) provides as mentioned in subsection (3) above,

   further provides (in whatever words) that any answer or evidence given by a person shall not be admissible in evidence against that person in any proceedings or class of proceedings (however described, and whether criminal or not), that enactment shall be construed as providing also that any answer or evidence given by that person shall not be admissible in evidence against the husband or wife of that person in the proceedings or class of proceedings in question.

(5) In this section "existing enactment" means any enactment passed before this Act; and the references to giving evidence are references to giving evidence in any manner, whether by furnishing information, making discovery, producing documents or otherwise.

16—Abolition of certain privileges.

(1) The following rules of law are hereby abrogated except in relation to criminal proceedings, that is to say—
   (a) the rule whereby, in any legal proceedings, a person cannot be compelled to answer any question or produce any document or thing if to do so would tend to expose him to a forfeiture; and

   (b) the rule whereby, in any legal proceedings, a person other than a party to the proceedings cannot be compelled to produce any deed or other document relating to his title to any land.

(2) The rule of law whereby, in any civil proceedings, a party to the proceedings cannot be compelled to produce any document relating solely to his own case and in no way tending to impeach that case or support the case of any opposing party is hereby abrogated.

(5) A witness in any proceedings instituted in consequence of adultery, whether a party to the proceedings or not, shall not be excused from answering any question by reason that it tends to show that he or she has been guilty of adultery; and accordingly the proviso to section 3 of the Evidence Further Amendment Act 1869 and, in section 43(2) of the Matrimonial Causes Act 1965, the words from "but" to the end of the subsection shall cease to have effect.

CRIMINAL APPEAL ACT 1968
(c. 19)

1—Right of appeal.

(1) [Subject to subsection (3) below a person convicted of an offence on indictment may appeal to the Court of Appeal against his conviction.

(2) An appeal under this section lies only—
    (a) with the leave of the Court of Appeal; or
    (b) if, within 28 days from the date of the conviction, the judge of the court of trial grants a certificate that the case is fit for appeal.

(3) Where a person is convicted before the Crown Court of a scheduled offence it shall not be open to him to appeal to the Court of Appeal against the conviction on the ground that the decision of the court which sent him to the Crown Court for trial as to the value involved was mistaken.

(4) In subsection (3) above "scheduled offence" and "the value involved" have the same meanings as they have in section 22 of the Magistrates' Courts Act 1980 (certain offences against property to be tried summarily if value of property or damage is small).

22—Right of appellant to be present.

(1) Except as provided by this section, an appellant shall be entitled to be present, if he wishes it, on the hearing of his appeal, although he may be in custody.

(2) A person in custody shall not be entitled to be present—
    (a) where his appeal is on some ground involving a question of law alone; or
    (b) on an application by him for leave to appeal; or
    (c) on any proceedings preliminary or incidental to an appeal; or
    (d) where he is in custody in consequence of a verdict of not guilty by reason of insanity or of a finding of disability,

unless the Court of Appeal give him leave to be present.

(3) The power of the Court of Appeal to pass sentence on a person may be exercised although he is for any reason not present.

(4) The Court of Appeal may give a live link direction in relation to a hearing at which the appellant is expected to be in custody but is entitled to be present (by virtue of subsection (1) or leave given under subsection (2)) at any time before the beginning of that hearing.

(5) For this purpose—

   (a) a "live link direction" is a direction that the appellant (if he is being held in custody at the time of the hearing) is to attend the hearing through a live link from the place at which he is held; and

   (b) "live link" means an arrangement by which the appellant is able to see and hear, and to be seen and heard by, the Court of Appeal (and for this purpose any impairment of eyesight or hearing is to be disregarded).

(6) The Court of Appeal—

   (a) must not give a live link direction unless the parties to the appeal have had the opportunity to make representations about the giving of such a direction; and

   (b) may rescind a live link direction at any time before or during any hearing to which it applies (whether of its own motion or on the application of a party).

23—Evidence

(1) For the purposes of an appeal, or an application for leave to appeal, under this Part of this Act the Court of Appeal may, if they think it necessary or expedient in the interests of justice—

   (a) order the production of any document, exhibit or other thing connected with the proceedings, the production of which appears to them necessary for the determination of the case;

   (b) order any witness to attend for examination and be examined before the Court (whether or not he was called in the proceedings from which the appeal lies); and

   (c) receive any evidence which was not adduced in the proceedings from which the appeal lies.

(1A) The power conferred by subsection (1)(a) may be exercised so as to require the production of any document, exhibit or other thing mentioned in that subsection to—

   (a) the Court;

   (b) the appellant;

   (c) the respondent.

(2) The Court of Appeal shall, in considering whether to receive any evidence, have regard in particular to—

   (a) whether the evidence appears to the Court to be capable of belief;

   (b) whether it appears to the Court that the evidence may afford any ground for allowing the appeal;

   (c) whether the evidence would have been admissible in the proceedings from which the appeal lies on an issue which is the subject of the appeal; and

(d) whether there is a reasonable explanation for the failure to adduce the evidence in those proceedings.

(3) Subsection (1)(c) above applies to any evidence of a witness (including the appellant) who is competent but not compellable

(4) For the purposes of an appeal, or an application for leave to appeal, under this Part of this Act, the Court of Appeal may, if they think it necessary or expedient in the interests of justice, order the examination of any witness whose attendance might be required under subsection (1)(b) above to be conducted, in manner provided by rules of court, before any judge or officer of the Court or other person appointed by the Court for the purpose, and allow the admission of any depositions so taken as evidence before the Court.

(5) A live link direction under section 22(4) does not apply to the giving of oral evidence by the appellant at any hearing unless that direction, or any subsequent direction of the court, provides expressly for the giving of such evidence through a live link.

(6) In this section, "respondent" includes a person who will be a respondent if leave to appeal is granted.

Words inserted by Criminal Justice and Immigration Act 2008 c. 4 Sch.8(1) para.10(2) (July 14, 2008);Substituted by Criminal Justice and Immigration Act 2008 c. 4 Sch.8(1) para.10(3) (July 14, 2008);Added by Criminal Justice and Immigration Act 2008 c. 4 Sch.8(1) para.10(4) (July 14, 2008);Words inserted by Criminal Justice and Immigration Act 2008 c. 4 Sch.8(1) para.10(5) (July 14, 2008);Added by Criminal Justice and Immigration Act 2008 c. 4 Sch.8(1) para.10(6) (July 14, 2008).

THEFT ACT 1968
(c. 60)

25—Going equipped for stealing, etc.

(1) A person shall be guilty of an offence if, when not at his place of abode, he has with him any article for use in the course of or in connection with any burglary or theft.

(2) A person guilty of an offence under this section shall on conviction on indictment be liable to imprisonment for a term not exceeding three years.

(3) Where a person is charged with an offence under this section, proof that he had with him any article made or adapted for use in committing a burglary or theft shall be evidence that he had it with him for such use.

(5) For purposes of this section an offence under section 12(1) of this Act of taking a conveyance shall be treated as theft.

27—Evidence and procedure on charge of theft or handling stolen goods

(1) Any number of persons may be charged in one indictment, with reference to the same theft, with having at different times or at the same time handled all or any of the stolen goods, and the persons so charged may be tried together.

(2) On the trial of two or more persons indicted for jointly handling any stolen goods the jury may find any of the accused guilty if the jury are satisfied that he handled all or any of the stolen goods, whether or not he did so jointly with the other accused or any of them.

(3) Where a person is being proceeded against for handling stolen goods (but not for any offence other than handling stolen goods), then at any stage of the proceedings, if evidence has been given of his having or arranging to have in his possession the goods the subject of the charge, or of his undertaking or assisting in, or arranging to undertake or assist in, their retention, removal, disposal or realisation, the following evidence shall be admissible for the purpose of proving that he knew or believed the goods to be stolen goods:—

    (a) evidence that he has had in his possession, or has undertaken or assisted in the retention, removal, disposal or realisation of, stolen goods from any theft taking place not earlier than twelve months before the offence charged; and

    (b) provided that seven days' notice in writing has been given to him of the intention to prove the conviction evidence that he has within the five years preceding the date of the offence charged been convicted of theft or of handling stolen goods.

(4) In any proceedings for the theft of anything in the course of transmission (whether by post or otherwise), or for handling stolen goods from such a theft, a statutory declaration made by any person that he despatched or received or failed to receive any goods or postal packet, or that any goods or postal packet when despatched or received by him were in a particular state or condition, shall be admissible as evidence of the facts stated in the declaration, subject to the following conditions:—

    (a) a statutory declaration shall only be admissible where and to the extent to which oral evidence to the like effect would have been admissible in the proceedings; and

    (b) a statutory declaration shall only be admissible if at least seven days before the hearing or trial a copy of it has been given to the person charged, and he has not, at least three days before the hearing or trial or within such further time as the court may in special circumstances allow, given the prosecutor written notice requiring the attendance at the hearing or trial of the person making the declaration.

(4A) Where the proceedings mentioned in subsection (4) above are proceedings before a magistrates' court inquiring into an offence as examining justices that subsection shall have effect with the omission of the words from "subject to the following conditions" to the end of the subsection.

(5) This section is to be construed in accordance with section 24 of this Act; and in subsection (3)(b) above the reference to handling stolen goods shall include any corresponding offence committed before the commencement of this Act.

31—Effect on civil proceedings and rights

(1) A person shall not be excused, by reason that to do so may incriminate that person or the spouse or civil partner of that person of an offence under this Act—

    (a) from answering any question put to that person in proceedings for the recovery or administration of any property, for the execution of any trust or for an account of any property or dealings with property; or

    (b) from complying with any order made in any such proceedings;

but no statement or admission made by a person in answering a question put or complying with an order made as aforesaid shall, in proceedings for an offence under this Act, be admissible in evidence against that person or (unless they married or became civil partners after the making of the statement or admission) against the spouse or civil partner of that person.

(2) Notwithstanding any enactment to the contrary, where property has been stolen or obtained by fraud or other wrongful means, the title to that or any other property shall not be affected by reason only of the conviction of the offender.

Family Law Reform Act 1969
(c. 46)

20—Power of court to require use of blood tests

(1) In any civil proceedings in which the parentage of any person falls to be determined, the court may, either of its own motion or on an application by any party to the proceedings, give a direction—

  (a) for the use of scientific tests to ascertain whether such tests show that a party to the proceedings is or is not the father or mother of that person; and

  (b) for the taking, within a period specified in the direction, of bodily samples from all or any of the following, namely, that person, any party who is alleged to be the father or mother of that person and any other party to the proceedings;

and the court may at any time revoke or vary a direction previously given by it under this subsection.

(1A) Tests required by a direction under this section may only be carried out by a body which has been accredited for the purposes of this section by–

  (a) the Lord Chancellor, or

  (b) a body appointed by him for the purpose.

(2) The individual carrying out scientific tests in pursuance of a direction under subsection (1) [("the tester")] above shall make to the court a report in which he shall state—

  (a) the results of the tests;

  (b) whether any party to whom the report relates is or is not excluded by the results from being the father or mother of the person whose parentage is to be determined; and

  (c) in relation to any party who is not so excluded, the value, if any, of the results in determining whether that party is the father or mother of that person;

and the report shall be received by the court as evidence in the proceedings of the matters stated in it.

(2A) Where the proceedings in which the parentage of any person falls to be determined are proceedings on an application under section 55A or 56 of the Family Law Act 1986, any reference in subsection (1) or (2) of this section to any party to the proceedings shall include a reference to any person named in the application.

(3) A report under subsection (2) of this section shall be in the form prescribed by regulations made under section 22 of this Act.

(4) Where a report has been made to a court under subsection (2) of this section, any party may, with the leave of the court, or shall, if the court so directs, obtain form the tester a written statement explaining or amplifying any statement made in the report, and that statement shall be deemed for the purposes of this section (except subsection (3) thereof) to form part of the report made to the court.

(5) Where a direction is given under this section in any proceedings, a party to the proceedings, unless the court otherwise directs, shall not be entitled to call as a witness the tester, or any other person by whom any thing necessary for the purpose of enabling those tests to be carried out was done, unless within fourteen days after receiving a copy of the report he serves notice on the other parties to the proceedings, or on such of them as the court may direct, of his intention to call the tester or that other person; and where the tester or any such person is called as a witness the party who called him shall be entitled to cross-examine him.

(6) Where a direction is given under this section the party on whose application the direction is given shall pay the cost of taking and testing bodily samples for the purpose of giving effect to the direction (including any expenses reasonably incurred by any person in taking any steps required of him for the purpose), and of making a report to the court under this section, but the amount paid shall be treated as costs incurred by him in the proceedings.

23—Failure to comply with direction for taking blood tests

(1) Where a court gives a direction under section 20 of this Act and any person fails to take any step required of him for the purpose of giving effect to the direction, the court may draw such inferences, if any, from that fact as appear proper in the circumstances.

(2) Where in any proceedings in which the [parentage]of any person falls to be determined by the court hearing the proceedings there is a presumption of law that that person is legitimate, then if—

   (a) a direction is given under section 20 of this Act in those proceedings, and

   (b) any party who is claiming any relief in the proceedings and who for the purpose of obtaining that relief is entitled to rely on the presumption fails to take any step required of him for the purpose of giving effect to the direction.

the court may adjourn the hearing for such period as it thinks fit to enable that party to take that step, and if at the end of that period he has failed without reasonable cause to take it the court may, without prejudice to subsection (1) of this section, dismiss his claim for relief notwithstanding the absence of evidence to rebut the presumption.

(3) Where any person named in a direction under section 20 of this Act fails to consent to the taking of a [bodily sample] from himself or from any person named in the direction of whom he has the care and control, he shall be deemed for the purposes of this section to have failed to take a step required of him for the purpose of giving effect to the direction.

PART IV
MISCELLANEOUS AND GENERAL

26 Rebuttal of presumption as to legitimacy and illegitimacy

Any presumption of law as to the legitimacy or illegitimacy of any person may in any civil proceedings be rebutted by evidence which shows that it is more probable than not that that person is illegitimate or legitimate, as the case may be, and it shall not be necessary to prove that fact beyond reasonable doubt in order to rebut the presumption.

Misuse of Drugs Act 1971
(c. 38)

5—Restriction of possession of controlled drugs

(1) Subject to any regulations under section 7 of this Act for the time being in force, it shall not be lawful for a person to have a controlled drug in his possession.

(2) Subject to section 28 of this Act and to subsection (4) below, it is an offence for a person to have a controlled drug in his possession in contravention of subsection (1) above.

(3) Subject to section 28 of this Act, it is an offence for a person to have a controlled drug in his possession, whether lawfully or not, with intent to supply it to another in contravention of section 4(1) of this Act.

(4) In any proceedings for an offence under subsection (2) above in which it is proved that the accused had a controlled drug in his possession, it shall be a defence for him to prove—

    (a) that, knowing or suspecting it to be a controlled drug, he took possession of it for the purpose of preventing another from committing or continuing to commit an offence in connection with that drug and that as soon as possible after taking possession of it he took all such steps as were reasonably open to him to destroy the drug or to deliver it into the custody of a person lawfully entitled to take custody of it; or

    (b) that, knowing or suspecting it to be a controlled drug, he took possession of it for the purpose of delivering it into the custody of a person lawfully entitled to take custody of it and that as soon as possible after taking possession of it he took all such steps as were reasonably open to him to deliver it into the custody of such a person.

(5) Subsection (4) above shall apply in the case of proceedings for an offence under section 19(1) of this Act consisting of an attempt to commit an offence under subsection (2) above as it applies in the case of proceedings for an offence under subsection (2), subject to the following modifications, that is to say—

    (a) for the references to the accused having in his possession, and to his taking possession of, a controlled drug there shall be substituted respectively references to his attempting to get, and to his attempting to take, possession of such a drug; and

(b) in paragraphs (a) and (b) the words from "and that as soon as possible" onwards shall be omitted.

(6) Nothing in subsection (4) or (5) above shall prejudice any defence which it is open to a person charged with an offence under this section to raise apart from that subsection.

CIVIL EVIDENCE ACT 1972
(c. 30)

2—Rules of court with respect to expert reports and oral expert evidence

(3) Notwithstanding any enactment or rule of law by virtue of which documents prepared for the purpose of pending or contemplated civil proceedings or in connection with the obtaining or giving of legal advice are in certain circumstances privileged from disclosure provision may be made by rules of court—

    (a) for enabling the court in any civil proceedings to direct, with respect to medical matters or matters of any other class which may be specified in the direction, that the parties or some of them shall each by such date as may be so specified (or such later date as may be permitted or agreed in accordance with the rules) disclose to the other or others in the form of one or more expert reports the expert evidence on matters of that class which he proposes to adduce as part of his case at the trial; and

    (b) for prohibiting a party who fails to comply with a direction given in any such proceedings under rules of court made by virtue of paragraph (a) above from adducing in evidence [. . .], except with the leave of the court, any statement (whether of fact or opinion) contained in any expert report whatsoever in so far as that statement deals with matters of any class specified in the direction.

(4) Provision may be made by rules of court as to the conditions subject to which oral expert evidence may be given in civil proceedings.

(5) Without prejudice to the generality of subsection (4) above, rules of court made in pursuance of that subsection may make provision for prohibiting a party who fails to comply with a direction given as mentioned in subsection (3)(b) above from adducing, except with the leave of the court, any oral expert evidence whatsoever with respect to matters of any class specified in the direction.

(6) Any rules of court made in pursuance of this section may make different provision for different classes of cases, for expert reports dealing with matters of different classes, and for other different circumstances.

(7) References in this section to an expert report are references to a written report by a person dealing wholly or mainly with matters on which he is (or would if living be) qualified to give expert evidence.

3—Admissibility of expert opinion and certain expressions of non-expert opinion

(1) Subject to any rules of court made in pursuance of this Act, where a person is called as a witness in any civil proceedings, his opinion on any relevant matter on which he is qualified to give expert evidence shall be admissible in evidence.

(2) It is hereby declared that where a person is called as a witness in any civil proceedings, a statement of opinion by him on any relevant matter on which he is not qualified to give expert evidence, if made as a way of conveying relevant facts personally perceived by him, is admissible as evidence of what he perceived.

(3) In this section "relevant matter" includes an issue in the proceedings in question.

4—Evidence of foreign law

(1) It is hereby declared that in civil proceedings a person who is suitably qualified to do so on account of his knowledge or experience is competent to give expert evidence as to the law of any country or territory outside the United Kingdom, or of any part of the United Kingdom other than England and Wales, irrespective of whether he has acted or is entitled to act as a legal practitioner there.

(2) Where any question as to the law of any country or territory outside the United Kingdom, or of any part of the United Kingdom other than England and Wales, with respect to any matter has been determined (whether before or after the passing of this Act) in any such proceedings as are mentioned in subsection (4) below, then in any civil proceedings (not being proceedings before a court which can take judicial notice of the law of that country, territory or part with respect to that matter)—

    (a) any finding made or decision given on that question in the first-mentioned proceedings shall, if reported or recorded in citable form, be admissible in evidence for the purpose of proving the law of that country, territory or part with respect to that matter; and

    (b) if that finding or decision, as so reported or recorded, is adduced for that purpose, the law of that country, territory or part with respect to that matter shall be taken to be in accordance with that finding or decision unless the contrary is proved:

Provided that paragraph (b) above shall not apply in the case of a finding or decision which conflicts with another finding or decision on the same question adduced by virtue of this subsection in the same proceedings.

(3) Except with the leave of the court, a party to any civil proceedings shall not be permitted to adduce any such finding or decision as is mentioned in subsection (2) above by virtue of that subsection unless he has in accordance with rules of court given to every other party to the proceedings notice that he intends to do so.

(4) The proceedings referred to in subsection (2) above are the following, whether civil or criminal, namely—

(a) proceedings at first instance in any of the following courts, namely the High Court, the Crown Court, a court of quarter sessions, the Court of Chancery of the county palatine of Lancaster and the Court of Chancery of the county palatine of Durham;

(b) appeals arising out of any such proceedings as are mentioned in paragraph (a) above;

(c) proceedings before the Judicial Committee of the Privy Council on appeal (whether to Her Majesty in Council or to the Judicial Committee as such) from any decision of any court outside the United Kingdom.

(5) For the purposes of this section a finding or decision on any such question as is mentioned in subsection (2) above shall be taken to be reported or recorded in citable from it, but only it, it is reported or recorded in writing in a report, transcript or other document which, if that question had been a question as to the law of England and Wales, could be cited as an authority in legal proceedings in England and Wales.

5—Interpretation, application to arbitrations etc. and savings

(1) In this Act 'civil proceedings' means civil proceedings, before any tribunal, in relation to which the strict rules of evidence apply, whether as a matter of law or by agreement of the parties; and references to 'the court' shall be construed accordingly.

(2) The rules of court made for the purposes of the application of sections 2 and 4 of this Act to proceedings in the High Court apply, except in so far as their application is excluded by agreement, to proceedings before tribunals other than the ordinary courts of law, subject to such modifications as may be appropriate.

Any question arising as to what modifications are appropriate shall be determined, in default of agreement, by the tribunal.

(3) Nothing in this Act shall prejudice—

(a) any power of a court, in any civil proceedings, to exclude evidence (whether by preventing questions from being put or otherwise) at its discretion; or

(b) the operation of any agreement (whenever made) between the parties to any civil proceedings as to the evidence which is to be admissible (whether generally or for any particular purpose) in those proceedings.

MATRIMONIAL CAUSES ACT 1973
(c. 18)

PART I
DIVORCE, NULLITY AND OTHER MATRIMONIAL SUITS

Other matrimonial suits

19—Presumption of death and dissolution of marriage

(1) Any married person who alleges that reasonable grounds exist for supposing that the other party to the marriage is dead may, present a petition to the court to have it presumed that the other party is dead and to have the marriage dissolved, and the court may, if satisfied that such reasonable grounds exist, grant a decree of presumption of death and dissolution of the marriage.

(3) In any proceedings under this section the fact that for a period of seven years or more the other party to the marriage has been continually absent from the petitioner and the petitioner has no reason to believe that the other party has been living within that time shall be evidence that the other party is dead until the contrary is proved.

(4) Sections 1(5), 8 and 9 above shall apply to a petition and a decree under this section as they apply to a petition for divorce and a decree of divorce respectively.

(6) It is hereby declared that neither collusion nor any other conduct on the part of the petitioner which has at any time been a bar to relief in matrimonial proceedings constitutes a bar to the grant of a decree under this section.

PART IV
MISCELLANEOUS AND SUPPLEMENTAL

48—Evidence

(1) The evidence of a husband or wife shall be admissible in any proceedings to prove that marital intercourse did or did not take place between them during any period.

(2) In any proceedings for nullity of marriage, evidence on the question of sexual capacity shall be heard in camera unless in any case the judge is satisfied that in the interests of justice any such evidence ought to be heard in open court.

Rehabilitation of Offenders Act 1974
(c. 53)

4—Effect of rehabilitation

(1) Subject to sections 7 and 8 below, a person who has become a rehabilitated person for the purposes of this Act in respect of a conviction shall be treated for all purposes in law as a person who has not committed or been charged with or prosecuted for or convicted of or sentenced for the offence or offences which were the subject of that conviction; and, notwithstanding the provisions of any other enactment or rule of law to the contrary, but subject as aforesaid—

   (a) no evidence shall be admissible in any proceedings before a judicial authority exercising its jurisdiction or functions in Great Britain to prove that any such person has committed or been charged with or prosecuted for or convicted of or sentenced for any offence which was the subject of a spent conviction; and

   (b) a person shall not, in any such proceedings, be asked, and, if asked, shall not be required to answer, any question relating to his past which cannot be answered without acknowledging or referring to a spent conviction or spent convictions or any circumstances ancillary thereto.

(2) Subject to the provisions of any order made under subsection (4) below, where a question seeking information with respect to a person's previous convictions, offences, conduct or circumstances is put to him or to any other person otherwise than in proceedings before a judicial authority—

   (a) the question shall be treated as not relating to spent convictions or to any circumstances ancillary to spent convictions, and the answer thereto may be framed accordingly; and

   (b) the person questioned shall not be subjected to any liability or otherwise prejudiced in law by reason of any failure to acknowledge or disclose a spent conviction or any circumstances ancillary to a spent conviction in his answer to the question.

(3) Subject to the provisions of any order made under subsection (4) below,—

   (a) any obligation imposed on any person by any rule of law or by the provisions of any agreement or arrangement to disclose any matters to any other person shall not extend to requiring him to disclose a spent conviction or any circumstances ancillary to a spent conviction (whether the conviction is his own or another's); and

(b)   a conviction which has become spent or any circumstances ancillary thereto, or any failure to disclose a spent conviction or any such circumstances, shall not be a proper ground for dismissing or excluding a person from any office, profession, occupation or employment, or for prejudicing him in any way in any occupation or employment.

(4)   The Secretary of State may by order—

(a)   make such provision as seems to him appropriate for excluding or modifying the application of either or both of paragraphs (a) and (b) of subsection (2) above in relation to questions put in such circumstances as may be specified in the order;

(b)   provide for such exceptions from the provisions of subsection (3) above as seem to him appropriate, in such cases or classes of case, and in relation to convictions of such a description, as may be specified in the order.

(5)   For the purposes of this section and section 7 below any of the following are circumstances ancillary to a conviction, that is to say—

(a)   the offence or offences which were the subject of that conviction;

(b)   the conduct constituting that offence or those offences; and

(c)   any process or proceedings preliminary to that conviction, any sentence imposed in respect of that conviction, any proceedings (whether by way of appeal or otherwise) for reviewing that conviction or any such sentence, and anything done in pursuance of or undergone in compliance with any such sentence.

(6)   For the purposes of this section and section 7 below "proceedings before a judicial authority" includes, in addition to proceedings before any of the ordinary courts of law, proceedings before any tribunal, body or person having power—

(a)   by virtue of any enactment, law, custom or practice;

(b)   under the rules governing any association, institution, profession, occupation or employment; or

(c)   under any provision of an agreement providing for arbitration with respect to questions arising thereunder;

to determine any question affecting the rights, privileges, obligations or liabilities of any person, or to receive evidence affecting the determination of any such question.

7—Limitations on rehabilitation under this Act, etc.

(1)   Nothing in section 4(1) above shall affect—

(a)   any right of Her Majesty, by virtue of Her Royal prerogative or otherwise, to grant a free pardon, to quash any conviction or sentence, or to commute any sentence;

(b)   the enforcement by any process or proceedings of any fine or other sum adjudged to be paid by or imposed on a spent conviction;

(c)   the issue of any process for the purpose of proceedings in respect of any breach of a condition or requirement applicable to a sentence imposed in respect of a spent conviction; or

(d)   the operation of any enactment by virtue of which, in consequence of any conviction, a person is subject, otherwise than by way of sentence, to any disqualification, disability, prohibition or other penalty the period of which extends beyond the rehabilitation period applicable in accordance with section 6 above to the conviction.

(2)   Nothing in section 4(1) above shall affect the determination of any issue, or prevent the admission or requirement of any evidence, relating to a person's previous convictions or to circumstances ancillary thereto—

(a)   in any criminal proceedings before a court in Great Britain (including any appeal or reference in a criminal matter);

(b)   in any service disciplinary proceedings or in any proceedings on appeal from any service disciplinary proceedings;

(bb) in any proceedings under Part 2 of the Sexual Offences Act 2003, or on appeal from any such proceedings;

(c)   in any proceedings relating to parental responsibilities or parental rights (within the meaning of section 1(3) and section 2(4) respectively of the Children (Scotland) Act 1995), guardianship, adoption or the provision by any person of accommodation, care or schooling for children under the age of 18 years;

(cc) in any proceedings under Part II of the Children (Scotland) Act 1995;

(d)   in any care proceedings under section 1 of the Powers of Criminal Courts (Sentencing) Act 2000 or on appeal from any such proceedings, or in any proceedings relating to the variation or discharge of a care order or supervision order under that Act;

(f)   in any proceedings in which he is a party or a witness, provided that, on the occasion when the issue or the admission or requirement of the evidence falls to be determined, he consents to the determination of the issue or, as the case may be, the admission or requirement of the evidence notwithstanding the provisions of section 4(1).

(3)   If at any stage in any proceedings before a judicial authority in Great Britain (not being proceedings to which, by virtue of any of paragraphs (a) to (e) of subsection (2) above or of any order for the time being in force under subsection (4) below, section 4(1) above has no application, or proceedings to which section 8 below applies) the authority is satisfied, in the light of any considerations which appear to it to be relevant (including any evidence which has been or may thereafter be put before it), that justice cannot be done in the case except by admitting or requiring evidence relating to a person's spent convictions or to

circumstances ancillary thereto, that authority may admit or, as the case may be, require the evidence in question notwithstanding the provisions of subsection (1) of section 4 above, and may determine any issue to which the evidence relates in disregard, so far as necessary, of those provisions.

(4) The Secretary of State may by order exclude the application of section 4(1) above in relation to any proceedings specified in the order (other than proceedings to which section 8 below applies) to such extent and for such purposes as may be so specified.

(5) No order made by a court with respect to any person otherwise than on a conviction shall be included in any list or statement of that person's previous convictions given or made to any court which is considering how to deal with him in respect of any offence.

Oaths Act 1978
(c. 19)

PART I
ENGLAND, WALES AND NORTHERN IRELAND

1—Manner of administration of oaths

(1) Any oath may be administered and taken in England, Wales or Northern Ireland in the following form and manner:—

   The person taking the oath shall hold the New Testament, or, in the case of a Jew, the Old Testament, in his uplifted hand, and shall say or repeat after the officer administering the oath the words "I swear by Almighty God that . . .", followed by the words of the oath prescribed by law.

(2) The officer shall (unless the person about to take the oath voluntarily objects thereto, or is physically incapable of so taking the oath) administer the oath in the form and manner aforesaid without question.

(3) In the case of a person who is neither a Christian nor a Jew, the oath shall be administered in any lawful manner.

(4) In this section "officer" means any person duly authorised to administer oaths.

5—Making of solemn affirmations

(1) Any person who objects to being sworn shall be permitted to make his solemn affirmation instead of taking an oath.

(2) Subsection (1) above shall apply in relation to a person to whom it is not reasonably practicable without inconvenience or delay to administer an oath in the manner appropriate to his religious belief as it applies in relation to a person objecting to be sworn.

(3) A person who may be permitted under subsection (2) above to make his solemn affirmation may also be required to do so.

(4) A solemn affirmation shall be of the same force and effect as an oath.

Magistrates' Courts Act 1980
(c. 43)

PART I
CRIMINAL JURISDICTION AND PROCEDURE

Committal proceedings

5A—Evidence which is admissible

(1) Evidence falling within subsection (2) below, and only that evidence, shall be admissible by a magistrates' court inquiring into an offence as examining justices.

(2) Evidence falls within this subsection if it—
  (a) is tendered by or on behalf of the prosecutor, and
  (b) falls within subsection (3) below.

(3) The following evidence falls within this subsection—
  (a) written statements complying with section 5B below;
  (b) the documents or other exhibits (if any) referred to in such statements;
  (c) depositions complying with section 5C below;
  (d) the documents or other exhibits (if any) referred to in such depositions;
  (e) statements complying with section 5D below;
  (f) documents falling within section 5E below.

(4) In this section "document" means anything in which information of any description is recorded.

5B—Written statements

(1) For the purposes of section 5A above a written statement complies with this section if—
  (a) the conditions falling within subsection (2) below are met, and
  (b) such of the conditions falling within subsection (3) below as apply are met.

(2) The conditions falling within this subsection are that—
  (a) the statement purports to be signed by the person who made it;
  (b) the statement contains a declaration by that person to the effect that it is true to the best of his knowledge and belief and that he made the statement knowing that, if it were tendered in evidence, he would be

liable to prosecution if he wilfully stated in it anything which he knew to be false or did not believe to be true;

(c)   before the statement is tendered in evidence a copy of the statement is given, by or on behalf of the prosecutor, to each of the other parties to the proceedings.

(3)   The conditions falling within this subsection are that—

(a)   if the statement is made by a person under 18 years old, it gives his age;

(b)   if it is made by a person who cannot read it, it is read to him before he signs it and is accompanied by a declaration by the person who so read the statement to the effect that it was so read;

(c)   if it refers to any other document as an exhibit, the copy given to any other party to the proceedings under subsection (2)(c) above is accompanied by a copy of that document or by such information as may be necessary to enable the party to whom it is given to inspect that document or a copy of it.

(4)   So much of any statement as is admitted in evidence by virtue of this section shall, unless the court commits the accused for trial by virtue of section 6(2) below or the court otherwise directs, be read aloud at the hearing; and where the court so directs an account shall be given orally of so much of any statement as is not read aloud.

(5)   Any document or other object referred to as an exhibit and identified in a statement admitted in evidence by virtue of this section shall be treated as if it had been produced as an exhibit and identified in court by the maker of the statement.

(6)   In this section "document" means anything in which information of any description is recorded.

5C—Depositions

(1)   For the purposes of section 5A above a deposition complies with this section if—

(a)   a copy of it is sent to the prosecutor under section 97A(9) below,

(b)   the condition falling within subsection (2) below is met, and

(c)   the condition falling within subsection (3) below is met, in a case where it applies.

(2)   The condition falling within this subsection is that before the magistrates' court begins to inquire into the offence concerned as examining justices a copy of the deposition is given, by or on behalf of the prosecutor, to each of the other parties to the proceedings.

(3)   The condition falling within this subsection is that, if the deposition refers to any other document as an exhibit, the copy given to any other party to the proceedings under subsection (2) above is accompanied by a copy of that document or by such information as may be necessary to

enable the party to whom it is given to inspect that document or a copy of it.

(4) So much of any deposition as is admitted in evidence by virtue of this section shall, unless the court commits the accused for trial by virtue of section 6(2) below or the court otherwise directs, be read aloud at the hearing; and where the court so directs an account shall be given orally of so much of any deposition as is not read aloud.

(5) Any document or other object referred to as an exhibit and identified in a deposition admitted in evidence by virtue of this section shall be treated as if it had been produced as an exhibit and identified in court by the person whose evidence is taken as the deposition.

(6) In this section "document" means anything in which information of any description is recorded.

5D—Statements

(1) For the purposes of section 5A above a statement complies with this section if the conditions falling within subsections (2) to (4) below are met.

(2) The condition falling within this subsection is that, before the committal proceedings begin, the prosecutor notifies the magistrates' court and each of the other parties to the proceedings that he believes—
  (a) that the statement might by virtue of section 23 or 24 of the Criminal Justice Act 1988 (statements in certain documents) be admissible as evidence if the case came to trial, and
  (b) that the statement would not be admissible as evidence otherwise than by virtue of section 23 or 24of that Act if the case came to trial.

(3) The condition falling within this subsection is that—
  (a) the prosecutor's belief is based on information available to him at the time he makes the notification,
  (b) he has reasonable grounds for his belief, and
  (c) he gives the reasons for his belief when he makes the notification.

(4) The condition falling within this subsection is that when the court or a party is notified as mentioned in subsection (2) above a copy of the statement is given, by or on behalf of the prosecutor, to the court or the party concerned.

(5) So much of any statement as is in writing and is admitted in evidence by virtue of this section shall, unless the court commits the accused for trial by virtue of section 6(2) below or the court otherwise directs, be read aloud at the hearing; and where the court so directs an account shall be given orally of so much of any statement as is not read aloud.

5E—Other documents

(1) The following documents fall within this section—

(a)   any document which by virtue of any enactment is evidence in proceedings before a magistrates' court inquiring into an offence as examining justices;

(b)   any document which by virtue of any enactment is admissible, or may be used, or is to be admitted or received, in or as evidence in such proceedings;

(c)   any document which by virtue of any enactment may be considered in such proceedings;

(d)   any document whose production constitutes proof in such proceedings by virtue of any enactment;

(e)   any document by the production of which evidence may be given in such proceedings by virtue of any enactment.

(2)   In subsection (1) above—
  (a)   references to evidence include references to prima facie evidence;
  (b)   references to any enactment include references to any provision of this Act.

(3)   So much of any document as is admitted in evidence by virtue of this section shall, unless the court commits the accused for trial by virtue of section 6(2) below or the court otherwise directs, be read aloud at the hearing; and where the court so directs an account shall be given orally of so much of any document as is not read aloud.

(4)   In this section "document" means anything in which information of any description is recorded.

5F—Proof by production of copy

(1)   Where a statement, deposition or document is admissible in evidence by virtue of section 5B, 5C, 5D or 5E above it may be proved by the production of—
  (a)   the statement, deposition or document, or
  (b)   a copy of it or the material part of it.

(2)   Subsection (1)(b) above applies whether or not the statement, deposition or document is still in existence.

(3)   It is immaterial for the purposes of this section how many removes there are between a copy and the original.

(4)   In this section "copy", in relation to a statement, deposition or document, means anything onto which information recorded in the statement, deposition or document has been copied, by whatever means and whether directly or indirectly."

6—Discharge or committal for trial

(1)   A magistrates' court inquiring into an offence as examining justices shall on consideration of the evidence—

(a) commit the accused for trial if it is of opinion that there is sufficient evidence to put him on trial by jury for any indictable offence;

(b) discharge him if it is not of that opinion and he is in custody for no other cause than the offence under inquiry;

but the preceding provisions of this subsection have effect subject to the provisions of this and any other Act relating to the summary trial of indictable offences.

(2) If a magistrates' court inquiring into an offence as examining justices is satisfied that all the evidence tendered by or on behalf of the prosecutor falls within section 5A(3) above, it may commit the accused for trial for the offence without consideration of the contents of any statements, depositions or other documents, and without consideration of any exhibits which are not documents, unless—

(a) the accused or one of the accused has no legal representative acting for him in the case, or

(b) a legal representative for the accused or one of the accused, as the case may be, has requested the court to consider a submission that there is insufficient evidence to put that accused on trial by jury for the offence;

and subsection (1) above shall not apply to a committal for trial under this subsection.

(3) Subject to section 4 of the Bail Act 1976 and section 41 below, the court may commit a person for trial—

(a) in custody, that is to say, by committing him to custody there to be safety kept until delivered in due course of law, or

(b) on bail in accordance with the Bail Act 1976, that is to say, by directing him to appear before the Crown Court for trial;

and where his release on bail is conditional on his providing one or more surety or sureties and, in accordance with section 8(3) of the Bail Act 1976, the court fixes the amount in which the surety is to be bound with a view to his entering into his recognizance subsequently in accordance with subsections (4) and (5) or (6) of that section the court shall in the meantime commit the accused to custody in accordance with paragraph (a) of this subsection.

(4) Where the court has committed a person to custody in accordance with paragraph (a) of subsection (3) above, then, if that person is in custody for no other cause, the court may, at any time before his first appearance before the Crown Court, grant him bail in accordance with the Bail Act 1976 subject to a duty to appear before the Crown Court for trial.

(5) Where a magistrates' court acting as examining justices commits any person for trial or determines to discharge him, the [designated officer for] the court shall, on the day on which the committal proceedings are concluded or the next day, cause to be displayed in a part of the court house to which the public have access a notice—

(a) in either case giving that person's name, address, and age (if known);

(b) in a case where the court so commits him, stating the charge or charges on which he is committed and the court to which he is committed;

(c) in a case where the court determines to discharge him, describing the offence charged and stating that it has so determined;

but this subsection shall have effect subject to [section 4 of the Sexual Offences (Amendment) Act 1976 (anonymity of complainant in rape etc. cases)].

(6) A notice displayed in pursuance of subsection (5) above shall not contain the name or address of any person under [the age of 18 years] unless the justices in question have stated that in their opinion he would be mentioned in the notice apart from the preceding provisions of this subsection and should be mentioned in it for the purpose of avoiding injustice to him.

98 Evidence on oath

Subject to the provisions of any enactment or rule of law authorising the reception of unsworn evidence, evidence given before a magistrates' court shall be given on oath.

101   Onus of proving exceptions, etc.

Where the defendant to an information or complaint relies for his defence on any exception, exemption, proviso, excuse or qualification, whether or not it accompanies the description of the offence or matter of complaint in the enactment creating the offence or on which the complaint is founded, the burden of proving the exception, exemption, proviso, excuse or qualification shall be on him; and this notwithstanding that the information or complaint contains an allegation negativing the exception, exemption, proviso, excuse or qualification.

103—Evidence of persons under 14 in committal proceedings for assault, sexual offences etc.

(1) In any proceedings before a magistrates' court inquiring as examining justices into an offence to which this section applies, a statement made in writing by or taken in writing from a child shall be admissible in evidence of any matter.

(2) This section applies—
(a) to an offence which involves an assault, or injury or a threat of injury to, a person;
(b) to an offence under section 1 of the Children and Young Persons Act 1933 (cruelty to persons under 16);

(c) to an offence under the Sexual Offences Act 1956, the Protection of Children Act 1978 or Part 1 of the Sexual Offences Act 2003; and

(d) to an offence which consists of attempting or conspiring to commit, or of aiding, abetting, counselling, procuring or inciting the commission of, an offence falling within paragraph (a), (b) or (c) above.

(5) In this section 'child' has the same meaning as in section 53 of the Criminal Justice Act 1991.

CONTEMPT OF COURT ACT 1981
(c. 49)

Other aspects of law and procedure

10 Sources of information

No court may require a person to disclose, nor is any person guilty of contempt of court for refusing to disclose, the source of information contained in a publication for which he is responsible, unless it be established to the satisfaction of the court that disclosure is necessary in the interests of justice or national security or for the prevention of disorder or crime.

SUPREME COURT ACT 1981
(c. 54)

PART III
PRACTICE AND PROCEDURE

Chapter 006
THE HIGH COURT

Mode of conducting business

69—Trial by jury

(5) Where for the purpose of disposing of any action or other matter which is being tried in the High Court by a judge with a jury it is necessary to ascertain the law of any other country which is applicable to the facts of the case, any question as to the effect of the evidence given with respect to that law shall, instead of being submitted to the jury, be decided by the judge.

72—Withdrawal of privilege against incrimination of self or spouse in certain proceedings.

(1) In any proceedings to which this subsection applies a person shall not be excused, by reason that to do so would tend to expose that person, or his or her spouse or civil partner, to proceedings for a related offence or for the recovery of a related penalty—

    (a) from answering any questions put to that person in the first-mentioned proceedings; or

    (b) from complying with any order made in those proceedings.

(2) Subsection (1) applies to the following civil proceedings in the High Court, namely—

    (a) proceedings for infringement of rights pertaining to any intellectual property or for passing off;

    (b) proceedings brought to obtain disclosure of information relating to any infringement of such rights or to any passing off; and

    (c) proceedings brought to prevent any apprehended infringement of such rights or any apprehended passing off.

(3) Subject to subsection (4), no statement or admission made by a person—

    (a) in answering a question put to him in any proceedings to which subsection (1) applies; or

(b)   in complying with any order made in any such proceedings,

shall, in proceedings for any related offence or for the recovery of any related penalty, be admissible in evidence against that person or (unless they [married or became civil partners after the making of the statement or admission) against the spouse or civil partner] of that person.

(4)   Nothing in subsection (3) shall render any statement or admission made by a person as there mentioned inadmissible in evidence against that person in proceedings for perjury or contempt of court.

(5)   In this section—

"intellectual property" means any patent, trade mark, copyright, [design right], registered design, technical or commercial information or other intellectual property;

"related offence", in relation to any proceedings to which subsection (1) applies, means —

(a)   in the case of proceedings within subsection (2)(a) or (b)—

(i)   any offence committed by or in the course of the infringement or passing off to which those proceedings relate; or

(ii)   any offence not within sub-paragraph (i) committed in connection with that infringement or passing off, being an offence involving fraud or dishonesty;

(b)   in the case of proceedings within subsection (2)(c), any offence revealed by the facts on which the plaintiff relies in those proceedings;

"related penalty", in relation to any proceedings to which subsection (1) applies means —

(a)   in the case of proceedings within subsection (2)(a) or (b), any penalty incurred in respect of anything done or omitted in connection with the infringement or passing off to which those proceedings relate;

(b)   in the case of proceedings within subsection (2)(c), any penalty incurred in respect of any act or omission revealed by the facts on which the plaintiff relies in those proceedings.

(6)   Any reference in this section to civil proceedings in the High Court of any description includes a reference to proceedings on appeal arising out of civil proceedings in the High Court of that description.

CRIMINAL JUSTICE ACT 1982
(c. 48)

PART V
MISCELLANEOUS

Unsworn statements

72—Abolition of right of accused to make unsworn statement.

(1) Subject to subsections (2) and (3) below, in any criminal proceedings the accused shall not be entitled to make a statement without being sworn, and accordingly, if he gives evidence, he shall do so [(subject to sections 55 and 56 of the Youth Justice and Criminal Evidence Act 1999)] on oath and be liable to cross-examination; but this section shall not affect the right of the accused, if not represented by counsel or a solicitor, to address the court or jury otherwise than on oath on any matter on which, if he were so represented, counsel or a solicitor could address the court or jury on his behalf.

(2) Nothing in subsection (1) above shall prevent the accused making a statement without being sworn—
   (a) if it is one which he is required by law to make personally; or
   (b) if he makes it by way of mitigation before the court passes sentence upon him.

Repealed by Statute Law (Repeals) Act 2008 c. 12 Sch.1(3) para.1 (July 21, 2008)

POLICE AND CRIMINAL EVIDENCE ACT 1984

(c. 60)

PART I
POWERS TO STOP AND SEARCH

1—Power of constable to stop and search persons, vehicles etc.

(1) A constable may exercise any power conferred by this section—
 (a) in any place to which at the time when he proposes to exercise the power the public or any section of the public has access, on payment or otherwise, as of right or by virtue of express or implied permission; or
 (b) in any other place to which people have ready access at the time when he proposes to exercise the power but which is not a dwelling.

(2) Subject to subsection (3) to (5) below, a constable—
 (a) may search—

  (i) any person or vehicle;

  (ii) anything which is in or on a vehicle,

for stolen or prohibited articles, any article to which subsection (8A) below applies or any firework to which subsection (8B) below applies; and

  (b) may detain a person or vehicle for the purpose of such a search.

(3) This section does not give a constable power to search a person or vehicle or anything in or on a vehicle unless he has reasonable grounds for suspecting that he will find stolen or prohibited articles or, any article to which subsection (8A) below applies or any firework to which subsection (8B) below applies.

(4) If a person is in a garden or yard occupied with and used for the purposes of a dwelling or on other land so occupied and used, a constable may not search him in the exercise of the power conferred by this section unless the constable has reasonable grounds for believing—
  (a) that he does not reside in the dwelling; and
  (b) that he is not in the place in question with the express or implied permission of a person who resides in the dwelling.

(5) If a vehicle is in a garden or yard occupied with and used for the purposes of a dwelling or on other land so occupied and used, a constable may not search the vehicle or anything in or on it in the exercise of the power conferred by this section unless he has reasonable grounds for believing—
  (a) that the person in charge of the vehicle does not reside in the dwelling; and
  (b) that the vehicle is not in the place in question with the express or implied permission of a person who resides in the dwelling.

(6) If in the course of such a search a constable discovers an article which he has reasonable grounds for suspecting to be a stolen or prohibited article, an article to which subsection (8A) below applies or a firework to which subsection (8B) below applies, he may seize it.

(7) An article is prohibited for the purposes of this Part of this Act if it is—
  (a) an offensive weapon; or
  (b) an article—
    (i) made or adapted for use in the course of or in connection with an offence to which this sub-paragraph applies; or
    (ii) intended by the person having it with him for such use by him or by some other person.

(8) The offences to which subsection (7)(b)(i) above applies are—
  (a) burglary;
  (b) theft;
  (c) offences under section 12 of the Theft Act 1968 (taking motor vehicle or other conveyance without authority);

(d)   fraud (contrary to section 1 of the Fraud Act 2006)

(e)   offences under section 1 of the Criminal Damage Act 1971 (destroying or damaging property).

(8A)   This subsection applies to any article in relation to which a person has committed, or is committing or is going to commit an offence under section 139 of the Criminal Justice Act 1988.

(8B)   This subsection applies to any firework which a person possesses in contravention of a prohibition imposed by fireworks regulations.

(8C)   In this section—

(a)   "firework" shall be construed in accordance with the definition of "fireworks" in section 1(1) of the Fireworks Act 2003; and

(b)   "fireworks regulations" has the same meaning as in that Act.

(9)   In this Part of this Act "offensive weapon" means any article—

(a)   made or adapted for use for causing injury to persons; or

(b)   intended by the person having it with him for such use by him or by some other person.

2—Provisions relating to search under section 1 and other powers

(1)   A constable who detains a person or vehicle in the exercise—

(a)   of the power conferred by section 1 above; or

(b)   of any other power—

    (i)   to search a person without first arresting him; or

    (ii)   to search a vehicle without making an arrest,

need not conduct a search if it appears to him subsequently—

    (i)   that no search is required; or

    (ii)   that a search is impracticable.

(2)   If a constable contemplates a search, other than a search of an unattended vehicle, in the exercise—

(a)   of the power conferred by section 1 above; or

(b)   of any other power, except the power conferred by section 6 below and the power conferred by section 27(2) of the Aviation Security Act 1982—

    (i)   to search a person without first arresting him; or

    (ii)   to search a vehicle without making an arrest,

it shall be his duty, subject to subsection (4) below, to take reasonable steps before he commences the search to bring to the attention of the appropriate person—

    (i)   if the constable is not in uniform, documentary evidence that he is a constable; and

    (ii)   whether he is in uniform or not, the matters specified in subsection (3) below;

and the constable shall not commence the search until he has performed that duty.

(3) The matters referred to in subsection (2)(ii) above are—

    (a) the constable's name and the name of the police station to which he is attached;

    (b) the object of the proposed search;

    (c) the constable's grounds for proposing to make it; and

    (d) the effect of section 3(7) or (8) below, as may be appropriate.

(4) A constable need not bring the effect of section 3(7) or (8) below to the attention of the appropriate person if it appears to the constable that it will not be practicable to make the record in section 3(1) below.

(5) In this section "the appropriate person" means —

    (a) if the constable proposes to search a person, that person; and

    (b) if he proposes to search a vehicle, or anything in or on a vehicle, the person in charge of the vehicle.

(6) On completing a search of an unattended vehicle or anything in or on such a vehicle in the exercise of any such power as is mentioned in subsection (2) above a constable shall leave a notice—

    (a) stating that he has searched it;

    (b) giving the name of the police station to which he is attached;

    (c) stating that an application for compensation for any damage caused by the search may be made to that police station; and

    (d) stating the effect of section 3(8) below.

(7) The constable shall leave the notice inside the vehicle unless it is not reasonably practicable to do so without damaging the vehicle.

(8) The time for which a person or vehicle may be detained for the purposes of such a search is such time as is reasonably required to permit a search to be carried out either at the place where the person or vehicle was first detained or nearby.

(9) Neither the power conferred by section 1 above nor any other power to detain and search a person without first arresting him or to detain and search a vehicle without making an arrest is to be construed—

    (a) as authorising a constable to require a person to remove any of his clothing in public other than an outer coat, jacket or gloves; or

    (b) as authorising a constable not in uniform to stop a vehicle.

(10) This section and section 1 above apply to vessels, aircraft and hovercraft as they apply to vehicles.

3—Duty to make records concerning searches

(1) Where a constable has carried out a search in the exercise of any such power as is mentioned in section 2(1) above, other than a search—

(a)   under section 6 below; or

(b)   under section 27(2) of the Aviation Security Act 1982,

he shall make a record of it in writing unless it is not practicable to do so.

(2)   If—

(a)   a constable is required by subsection (1) above to make a record of a search; but

(b)   it is not practicable to make the record on the spot,

he shall make it as soon as practicable after the completion of the search.

(3)   The record of a search of a person shall include a note of his name, if the constable knows it, but a constable may not detain a person to find out his name.

(4)   If a constable does not know the name of a person whom he has searched, the record of the search shall include a note otherwise describing that person.

(5)   The record of a search of a vehicle shall include a note describing the vehicle.

(6)   The record of a search of a person or a vehicle—

(a)   shall state—

(i)   the object of the search;

(ii)   the grounds for making it;

(iii) the date and time when it was made;

(iv) the place where it was made;

(v)   whether anything, and if so what, was found;

(vi) whether any, and if so what, injury to a person or damage to property appears to the constable to have resulted from the search; and

(b)   shall identify the constable making it.

(7)   If a constable who conducted a search of a person made a record of it, the person who was searched shall be entitled to a copy of the record if he asks for one before the end of the period specified in subsection (9) below.

(8)   If—

(a)   the owner of a vehicle which has been searched or the person who was in charge of the vehicle at the time when it was searched asks for a copy of the record of the search before the end of the period specified in subsection (9) below; and

(b)   the constable who conducted the search made a record of it,

the person who made the request shall be entitled to a copy.

(9)   The period mentioned in subsections (7) and (8) above is the period of 12 months beginning with the date on which the search was made.

(10)   The requirements imposed by this section with regard to records of searches of vehicles shall apply also to records of searches of vessels, aircraft and hovercraft.

4—Road checks

(1) This section shall have effect in relation to the conduct of road checks by police officers for the purpose of ascertaining whether a vehicle is carrying—

(a)   a person who has committed an offence other than a road traffic offence or a vehicle excise offence;

(b)   a person who is a witness to such an offence;

(c)   a person intending to commit such an offence; or

(d)   a person who is unlawfully at large.

(2) For the purposes of this section a road check consists of the exercise in a locality of the power conferred by section 163 of the Road Traffic Act 1988 in such a way as to stop during the period for which its exercise in that way in that locality continues all vehicles or vehicles selected by any criterion.

(3) Subject to subsection (5) below, there may only be such a road check if a police officer of the rank of superintendent or above authorises it in writing.

(4) An officer may only authorise a road check under subsection (3) above—

(a)   for the purpose specified in subsection (1)(a) above, if he has reasonable grounds—

(i)   for believing that the offence is an indictable offence; and

(ii) for suspecting that the person is, or is about to be, in the locality in which vehicles would be stopped if the road check were authorised;

(b)   for the purpose specified in subsection (1)(b) above, if he has reasonable grounds for believing that the offence is an indictable offence;

(c)   for the purpose specified in subsection (1)(c) above, if he has reasonable grounds—

(i)   for believing that the offence would be an indictable offence; and

(ii) for suspecting that the person is, or is about to be, in the locality in which vehicles would be stopped if the road check were authorised;

(d)   for the purpose specified in subsection (1)(d) above, if he has reasonable grounds for suspecting that the person is, or is about to be, in that locality.

(5) An officer below the rank of superintendent may authorise such a road check if it appears to him that it is required as a matter of urgency for one of the purposes specified in subsection (1) above.

(6) If an authorisation is given under subsection (5) above, it shall be the duty of the officer who gives it—

(a) to make a written record of the time at which he gives it; and

(b) to cause an officer of the rank of superintendent or above to be informed that it has been given.

(7) The duties imposed by subsection (6) above shall be performed as soon as it is practicable to do so.

(8) An officer to whom a report is made under subsection (6) above may, in writing, authorise the road check to continue.

(9) If such an officer considers that the road check should not continue, he shall record in writing—

(a) the fact that it took place; and

(b) the purpose for which it took place.

(10) An officer giving an authorisation under this section shall specify the locality in which vehicles are to be stopped.

(11) An officer giving an authorisation under this section, other than an authorisation under subsection (5) above—

(a) shall specify a period, not exceeding seven days, during which the road check may continue; and

(b) may direct that the road check—

(i) shall be continuous; or

(ii) shall be conducted at specified times,

during that period.

(12) If it appears to an officer of the rank of superintendent or above that a road check ought to continue beyond the period for which it has been authorised he may, from time to time, in writing specify a further period, not exceeding seven days, during which it may continue.

(13) Every written authorisation shall specify—

(a) the name of the officer giving it;

(b) the purpose of the road check; and

(c) the locality in which vehicles are to be stopped.

(14) The duties to specify the purposes of a road check imposed by subsections (9) and (13) above include duties to specify any relevant indictable offence.

(15) Where a vehicle is stopped in a road check, the person in charge of the vehicle at the time when it is stopped shall be entitled to obtain a written statement of the purpose of the road check if he applies for such a statement not later than the end of the period of twelve months from the day on which the vehicle was stopped.

(16)   Nothing in this section affects the exercise by police officers of any power to stop vehicles for purposes other than those specified in subsection (1) above.

PART II
POWERS OF ENTRY, SEARCH AND SEIZURE

Search warrants

8—Power of justice of the peace to authorise entry and search of premises

(1)   If on an application made by a constable a justice of the peace is satisfied that there are reasonable grounds for believing—
   (a)   that an indictable offence has been committed; and
   (b)   that there is material on premises [mentioned in subsection (1A) below which is likely to be of substantial value (whether by itself or together with other material) to the investigation of the offence; and
   (c)   that the material is likely to be relevant evidence; and
   (d)   that it does not consist of or include items subject to legal privilege, excluded material or special procedure material; and
   (e)   that any of the conditions specified in subsection (3) below applies in relation to each set of premises specified in the application,

he may issue a warrant authorising a constable to enter and search the premises.

(1A)   The premises referred to in subsection (1)(b) above are—
   (a)   one or more sets of premises specified in the application (in which case the application is for a "specific premises warrant"); or
   (b)   any premises occupied or controlled by a person specified in the application, including such sets of premises as are so specified (in which case the application is for an "all premises warrant").

(1B)   If the application is for an all premises warrant, the justice of the peace must also be satisfied—
   (a)   that because of the particulars of the offence referred to in paragraph (a) of subsection (1) above, there are reasonable grounds for believing that it is necessary to search premises occupied or controlled by the person in question which are not specified in the application in order to find the material referred to in paragraph (b) of that subsection; and
   (b)   that it is not reasonably practicable to specify in the application all the premises which he occupies or controls and which might need to be searched.

(1C)   The warrant may authorise entry to and search of premises on more than one occasion if, on the application, the justice of the peace is satisfied that it is necessary to authorise multiple entries in order to achieve the purpose for which he issues the warrant.

(1D)   If it authorises multiple entries, the number of entries authorised may be unlimited, or limited to a maximum.

(2)   A constable may seize and retain anything for which a search has been authorised under subsection (1) above.

(3)   The conditions mentioned in subsection (1)(e) above are—

(a)   that it is not practicable to communicate with any person entitled to grant entry to the premises;

(b)   that it is practicable to communicate with a person entitled to grant entry to the premises but it is not practicable to communicate with any person entitled to grant access to the evidence;

(c)   that entry to the premises will not be granted unless a warrant is produced;

(d)   that the purpose of a search may be frustrated or seriously prejudiced unless a constable arriving at the premises can secure immediate entry to them.

(4)   In this Act "relevant evidence", in relation to an offence, means anything that would be admissible in evidence at a trial for the offence.

(5)   The power to issue a warrant conferred by this section is in addition to any such power otherwise conferred.

(6)   This section applies in relation to a relevant offence (as defined in section 28D(4) of the Immigration Act 1971) as it applies in relation to an indictable offence.

(7)   Section 4 of the Summary Jurisdiction (Process) Act 1881 (execution of process of English courts in Scotland) shall apply to a warrant issued on the application of an officer of Revenue and Customs under this section by virtue of section 114 below.

9—Special provisions as to access

(1)   A constable may obtain access to excluded material or special procedure material for the purposes of a criminal investigation by making an application under Schedule 1 below and in accordance with that Schedule.

(2)   Any Act (including a local Act) passed before this Act under which a search of premises for the purposes of a criminal investigation could be authorised by the issue of a warrant to a constable shall cease to have effect so far as it relates to the authorisation of searches—

(a)   for items subject to legal privilege; or

(b)   for excluded material; or

(c)   for special procedure material consisting of documents or records other than documents.

(2A) Section 4 of the Summary Jurisdiction (Process) Act 1881 (c. 24) (which includes provision for the execution of process of English courts in Scotland) and section 29 of the Petty Sessions (Ireland) Act 1851 (c. 93) (which makes equivalent provision for execution in Northern Ireland) shall each apply to any process issued by a circuit judge under Schedule 1 to this Act as it applies to process issued by a magistrates' court under the Magistrates' Courts Act 1980 (c. 43).

10—Meaning of "items subject to legal privilege"

(1) Subject to subsection (2) below, in this Act "items subject to legal privilege" means—
  (a) communications between a professional legal adviser and his client or any person representing his client made in connection with the giving of legal advice to the client;
  (b) communications between a professional legal adviser and his client or any person representing his client or between such an adviser or his client or any such representative and any other person made in connection with or in contemplation of legal proceedings and for the purposes of such proceedings; and
  (c) items enclosed with or referred to in such communications and made—
    (i) in connection with the giving of legal advice;
    or
    (ii) in connection with or in contemplation of legal proceedings and for the purposes of such proceedings,
when they are in the possession of a person who is entitled to possession of them.

(2) Items held with the intention of furthering a criminal purpose are not items subject to legal privilege.

11—Meaning of "excluded material"

(1) Subject to the following provisions of this section, in this Act "excluded material" means—
  (a) personal records which a person has acquired or created in the course of any trade, business, profession or other occupation or for the purposes of any paid or unpaid office and which he holds in confidence;
  (b) human tissue or tissue fluid which has been taken for the purposes of diagnosis or medical treatment and which a person holds in confidence;
  (c) journalistic material which a person holds in confidence and which consists—

(i)   of documents; or

(ii) of records other than documents.

(2) A person holds material other than journalistic material in confidence for the purposes of this section if he holds it subject—

(a) to an express or implied undertaking to hold it in confidence; or

(b) to a restriction on disclosure or an obligation of secrecy contained in any enactment, including an enactment contained in an Act passed after this Act.

(3) A person holds journalistic material in confidence for the purposes of this section if—

(a) he holds it subject to such an undertaking, restriction or obligation; and

(b) it has been continuously held (by one or more persons) subject to such an undertaking, restriction or obligation since it was first acquired or created for the purposes of journalism.

12   Meaning of "personal records"

In this Part of this Act "personal records" means documentary and other records concerning an individual (whether living or dead) who can be identified from them and relating—

(a) to his physical or mental health;

(b) to spiritual counselling or assistance given or to be given to him; or

(c) to counselling or assistance given or to be given to him, for the purposes of his personal welfare, by any voluntary organisation or by any individual who—

(i)   by reason of his office or occupation has responsibilities for his personal welfare; or

(ii) by reason of an order of a court has responsibilities for his supervision.

13—Meaning of "journalistic material"

(1) Subject to subsection (2) below, in this Act "journalistic material" means material acquired or created for the purposes of journalism.

(2) Material is only journalistic material for the purposes of this Act if it is in the possession of a person who acquired or created it for the purposes of journalism.

(3) A person who receives material from someone who intends that the recipient shall use it for the purposes of journalism is to be taken to have acquired it for those purposes.

14—Meaning of "special procedure material"

(1) In this Act "special procedure material" means —

    (a) material to which subsection (2) below applies; and

    (b) journalistic material, other than excluded material.

(2) Subject to the following provisions of this section, this subsection applies to material, other than items subject to legal privilege and excluded material, in the possession of a person who—

    (a) acquired or created it in the course of any trade, business, profession or other occupation or for the purpose of any paid or unpaid office; and

    (b) holds it subject—

        (i) to an express or implied undertaking to hold it in confidence; or

        (ii) to a restriction or obligation such as is mentioned in section]11(2)(b) above.

(3) Where material is acquired—

    (a) by an employee from his employer and in the course of his employment; or

    (b) by a company from an associated company,

it is only special procedure material if it was special procedure material immediately before the acquisition.

(4) Where material is created by an employee in the course of his employment, it is only special procedure material if it would have been special procedure material had his employer created it.

(5) Where material is created by a company on behalf of an associated company, it is only special procedure material if it would have been special procedure material had the associated company created it.

(6) A company is to be treated as another's associated company for the purposes of this section if it would be so treated under section 302 of the Income and Corporation Taxes Act 1970.

15—Search warrants—safeguards

(1) This section and section 16 below have effect in relation to the issue to constables under any enactment, including an enactment contained in an Act passed after this Act, of warrants to enter and search premises; and an entry on or search of premises under a warrant is unlawful unless it complies with this section and section 16 below.

(2) Where a constable applies for any such warrant, it shall be his duty—

    (a) to state—

        (i) the ground on which he makes the application;

        (ii) the enactment under which the warrant would be issued; and

        (iii) if the application is for a warrant authorising entry and search on more than one occasion, the ground on which he applies for such a warrant, and whether he seeks a warrant authorising an unlimited number of entries, or (if not) the maximum number of entries desired;

(b)   to specify the matters set out in subsection (2A) below; and

(c)   to identify, so far as is practicable, the articles or persons to be sought.

(2A)   The matters which must be specified pursuant to subsection (2)(b) above are—

(a)   if the application relates to one or more sets of premises specified in the application, each set of premises which it is desired to enter and search;

(b)   [if the application relates to any premises occupied or controlled by a person specified in the application–

(i)   as many sets of premises which it is desired to enter and search as it is reasonably practicable to specify;

(ii)   the person who is in occupation or control of those premises and any others which it is desired to enter and search;

(iii) why it is necessary to search more premises than those specified under sub-paragraph (i); and

(iv) why it is not reasonably practicable to specify all the premises which it is desired to enter and search.

(3)   An application for such a warrant shall be made ex parte and supported by an information in writing.

(4)   The constable shall answer on oath any question that the justice of the peace or judge hearing the application asks him.

(5)   A warrant shall authorise an entry on one occasion only unless it specifies that it authorises multiple entries.

(5A)   If it specifies that it authorises multiple entries, it must also specify whether the number of entries authorised is unlimited, or limited to a specified maximum.

(6)   A warrant—

(a)   shall specify—

(i)   the name of the person who applies for it;

(ii)   the date on which it is issued;

(iii) the enactment under which it is issued; and

(iv) each set of premises to be searched, or (in the case of an all premises warrant) the person who is in occupation or control of premises to be searched, together with any premises under his occupation or control which can be specified and which are to be searched; and

(b)   shall identify, so far as is practicable, the articles or persons to be sought.

(7) Two copies shall be made of a warrant which specifies only one set of premises and does not authorise multiple entries; and as many copies as are reasonably required may be made of any other kind of warrant.

(8) The copies shall be clearly certified as copies.

16—Execution of warrants

(1) A warrant to enter and search premises may be executed by any constable.

(2) Such a warrant may authorise persons to accompany any constable who is executing it.

(2A) A person so authorised has the same powers as the constable whom he accompanies in respect of—

(a) the execution of the warrant, and

(b) the seizure of anything to which the warrant relates.

(2B) But he may exercise those powers only in the company, and under the supervision, of a constable.

(3) Entry and search under a warrant must be within three months from the date of its issue.

(3A) If the warrant is an all premises warrant, no premises which are not specified in it may be entered or searched unless a police officer of at least the rank of inspector has in writing authorised them to be entered.

(3B) No premises may be entered or searched for the second or any subsequent time under a warrant which authorises multiple entries unless a police officer of at least the rank of inspector has in writing authorised that entry to those premises.

(4) Entry and search under a warrant must be at a reasonable hour unless it appears to the constable executing it that the purpose of a search may be frustrated on an entry at a reasonable hour.

(5) Where the occupier of premises which are to be entered and searched is present at the time when a constable seeks to execute a warrant to enter and search them, the constable—

(a) shall identify himself to the occupier and, if not in uniform, shall produce to him documentary evidence that he is a constable;

(b) shall produce the warrant to him; and

(c) shall supply him with a copy of it.

(6) Where—

(a) the occupier of such premises is not present at the time when a constable seeks to execute such a warrant; but

(b) some other person who appears to the constable to be in charge of the premises is present,

subsection (5) above shall have effect as if any reference to the occupier were a reference to that other person.

(7) If there is no person present who appears to the constable to be in charge of the premises, he shall leave a copy of the warrant in a prominent place on the premises.

(8) A search under a warrant may only be a search to the extent required for the purpose for which the warrant was issued.

(9) A constable executing a warrant shall make an endorsement on it stating—

   (a) whether the articles or persons sought were found; and

   (b) whether any articles were seized, other than articles which were sought,

and, unless the warrant is a warrant specifying one set of premises only, he shall do so separately in respect of each set of premises entered and searched, which he shall in each case state in the endorsement.

(10)   A warrant shall be returned to the appropriate person mentioned in subsection (10A) below—

   (a) when it has been executed; or

   (b) in the case of a specific premises warrant which has not been executed, or an all premises warrant, or any warrant authorising multiple entries, upon the expiry of the period of three months referred to in subsection (3) above or sooner.

(10A)   The appropriate person is—

   (a) if the warrant was issued by a justice of the peace, the designated officer for the local justice area in which the justice was acting when he issued the warrant;

   (b) if it was issued by a judge, the appropriate officer of the court from which he issued it.

(11)   A warrant which is returned under subsection (10) above shall be retained for 12 months from its return—

   (a) by the designated officer for the local justice area, if it was returned under paragraph (i) of that subsection; and

   (b) by the appropriate officer, if it was returned under paragraph (ii).

(12)   If during the period for which a warrant is to be retained the occupier of premises to which it relates asks to inspect it, he shall be allowed to do so.

17—Entry for purpose of arrest etc.

(1) Subject to the following provisions of this section, and without, prejudice to any other enactment, a constable may enter and search any premises for the purpose—

   (a) of executing—

      (i) a warrant of arrest issued in connection with or arising out of criminal proceedings; or

      (ii) a warrant of commitment issued under section 76 of the Magistrates' Courts Act 1980;

(b) of arresting a person for an indictable offence;

(c) of arresting a person for an offence under—

    (i) section 1 (prohibition of uniforms in connection with political objects) of the Public Order Act 1936;

    (ii) any enactment contained in sections 6 to 8 or 10 of the Criminal Law Act 1977 (offences relating to entering and remaining on property);

    (iii) section 4 of the Public Order Act 1986 (fear or provocation of violence);

    (iiia) section 4 (driving etc. when under influence of drink or drugs) or 163 (failure to stop when required to do so by constable in uniform) of the Road Traffic Act 1988;

    (iiib) section 27 of the Transport and Works Act 1992 (which relates to offences involving drink or drugs);

    (iv) section 76 of the Criminal Justice and Public Order Act 1994 (failure to comply with interim possession order);

    (v) any of sections 4, 5, 6(1) and (2), 7 and 8(1) and (2) of the Animal Welfare Act 2006 (offences relating to the prevention of harm to animals);".

(ca) of arresting, in pursuance of section 32(1A) of the Children and Young Persons Act 1969, any child or young person who has been remanded or committed to local authority accommodation under section 23(1) of that Act;

(caa) of arresting a person for an offence to which section 61 of the Animal Health Act 1981 applies;

(cb) of recapturing any person who is, or is deemed for any purpose to be, unlawfully at large while liable to be detained—

    (i) in a prison, remand centre, young offender institution or secure training centre, or

    (ii) in pursuance of [section 92 of the Powers of Criminal Courts (Sentencing) Act 2000] (dealing with children and young persons guilty of grave crimes), in any other place;

(d) of recapturing [any person whatever] who is unlawfully at large and whom he is pursuing; or

(e) of saving life or limb or preventing serious damage to property.

(2) Except for the purpose specified in paragraph (e) of subsection (1) above, the powers of entry and search conferred by this section—

(a) are only exercisable if the constable has reasonable grounds for believing that the person whom he is seeking is on the premises; and

(b) are limited, in relation to premises consisting of two or more separate dwellings, to powers to enter and search—

(i) any parts of the premises which the occupiers of any dwelling comprised in the premises use in common with the occupiers of any other such dwelling; and

(ii) any such dwelling in which the constable has reasonable grounds for believing that the person whom he is seeking may be.

(3) The powers of entry and search conferred by this section are only exercisable for the purposes specified in subsection (1)(c)(ii) [or (iv)] above by a constable in uniform.

(4) The power of search conferred by this section is only a power to search to the extent that is reasonably required for the purpose for which the power of entry is exercised.

(5) Subject to subsection (6) below, all the rules of common law under which a constable has power to enter premises without a warrant are hereby abolished.

(6) Nothing in subsection (5) above affects any power of entry to deal with or prevent a breach of the peace.

18—Entry and search after arrest

(1) Subject to the following provisions of this section, a constable may enter and search any premises occupied or controlled by a person who is under arrest for an [indictable] offence, if he has reasonable grounds for suspecting that there is on the premises evidence, other than items subject to legal privilege, that relates—
(a) to that offence; or
(b) to some other [indictable] offence which is connected with or similar to that offence.

(2) A constable may seize and retain anything for which he may search under subsection (1) above.

(3) The power to search conferred by subsection (1) above is only a power to search to the extent that is reasonably required for the purpose of discovering such evidence.

(4) Subject to subsection (5) below, the powers conferred by this section may not be exercised unless an officer of the rank of inspector or above has authorised them in writing.

(5) A constable may conduct a search under subsection (1)—
(a) before the person is taken to a police station or released on bail under section 30A, and
(b) without obtaining an authorisation under subsection (4),
if the condition in subsection (5A) is satisfied.

(5A) The condition is that the presence of the person at a place (other than a police station) is necessary for the effective investigation of the offence.

(6) If a constable conducts a search by virtue of subsection (5) above, he shall inform an officer of the rank of inspector or above that he has made the search as soon as practicable after he has made it.

(7) An officer who—

   (a) authorises a search; or

   (b) is informed of a search under subsection (6) above, shall make a record in writing—

      (i) of the grounds for the search; and

      (ii) of the nature of the evidence that was sought.

(8) If the person who was in occupation or control of the premises at the time of the search is in police detention at the time the record is to be made, the officer shall make the record as part of his custody record.

19—General power of seizure etc.

(1) The powers conferred by subsections (2), (3) and (4) below are exercisable by a constable who is lawfully on any premises.

(2) The constable may seize anything which is on the premises if he has reasonable grounds for believing—

   (a) that it has been obtained in consequence of the commission of an offence; and

   (b) that it is necessary to seize it in order to prevent it being concealed, lost, damaged, altered or destroyed.

(3) The constable may seize anything which is on the premises if he has reasonable grounds for believing—

   (a) that it is evidence in relation to an offence which he is investigating or any other offence; and

   (b) that it is necessary to seize it in order to prevent the evidence being concealed, lost, altered or destroyed.

(4) The constable may require any information which is [stored in any electronic form] and is accessible from the premises to be produced in a form in which it can be taken away and in which it is visible and legible [or from which it can readily be produced in a visible and legible form] if he has reasonable grounds for believing—

   (a) that—

      (i) it is evidence in relation to an offence which he is investigating or any other offence; or

      (ii) it has been obtained in consequence of the commission of an offence; and

   (b) that it is necessary to do so in order to prevent it being concealed, lost, tampered with or destroyed.

(5) The powers conferred by this section are in addition to any power otherwise conferred.

(6) No power of seizure conferred on a constable under any enactment (including an enactment contained in an Act passed after this Act) is to be taken to authorise the seizure of an item which the constable exercising the power has reasonable grounds for believing to be subject to legal privilege.

20—Extension of powers of seizure to computerised information

(1) Every power of seizure which is conferred by an enactment to which this section applies on a constable who has entered premises in the exercise of a power conferred by an enactment shall be construed as including a power to require any information [stored in any electronic form] and accessible from the premises to be produced in a form in which it can be taken away and in which it is visible and legible [or from which it can readily be produced in a visible and legible form].

(2) This section applies—

(a) to any enactment contained in an Act passed before this Act;

(b) to sections 8 and 18 above;

(c) to paragraph 13 of Schedule 1 to this Act; and

(d) to any enactment contained in an Act passed after this Act.

21—Access and copying

(1) A constable who seizes anything in the exercise of a power conferred by any enactment, including an enactment contained in an Act passed after this Act, shall, if so requested by a person showing himself—

(a) to be the occupier of premises on which it was seized; or

(b) to have had custody or control of it immediately before the seizure,

provide that person with a record of what he seized.

(2) The officer shall provide the record within a reasonable time from the making of the request for it.

(3) Subject to subsection (8) below, if a request for permission to be granted access to anything which—

(a) has been seized by a constable; and

(b) is retained by the police for the purpose of investigating an offence,

is made to the officer in charge of the investigation by a person who had custody or control of the thing immediately before it was so seized or by someone acting on behalf of such a person, the officer shall allow the person who made the request access to it under the supervision of a constable.

(4) Subject to subsection (8) below, if a request for a photograph or copy of any such thing is made to the officer in charge of the investigation by a person who had custody or control of the thing immediately before it was so seized, or by someone acting on behalf of such a person, the officer shall—

    (a) allow the person who made the request access to it under the supervision of a constable for the purpose of photographing or copying it; or

    (b) photograph or copy it, or cause it to be photographed or copied.

(5) A constable may also photograph or copy, or have photographed or copied, anything which he has power to seize, without a request being made under subsection (4) above.

(6) Where anything is photographed or copied under subsection (4)(b) above, the photograph or copy shall be supplied to the person who made the request.

(7) The photograph or copy shall be so supplied within a reasonable time from the making of the request.

(8) There is no duty under this section to grant access to, or to supply a photograph or copy of, anything if the officer in charge of the investigation for the purposes of which it was seized has reasonable grounds for believing that to do so would prejudice—

    (a) that investigation;

    (b) the investigation of an offence other than the offence for the purposes of investigating which the thing was seized; or

    (c) any criminal proceedings which may be brought as a result of—

        (i) the investigation of which he is in charge; or

        (ii) any such investigation as is mentioned in paragraph (b) above.

(9) The references to a constable in subsections (1), (2), (3)(a) and (5) include a person authorised under section 16(2) to accompany a constable executing a warrant.

22—Retention

(1) Subject to subsection (4) below, anything which has been seized by a constable or taken away by a constable following a requirement made by virtue of section 19 or 20 above may be retained so long as is necessary in all the circumstances.

(2) Without prejudice to the generality of subsection (1) above—

    (a) anything seized for the purposes of a criminal investigation may be retained, except as provided by subsection (4) below—

        (i) for use as evidence at a trial for an offence; or

        (ii) for forensic examination or for investigation in connection with an offence; and

    (b) anything may be retained in order to establish its lawful owner, where there are reasonable grounds for believing that it has been obtained in consequence of the commission of an offence.

(3) Nothing seized on the ground that it may be used—

    (a) to cause physical injury to any person;

(b) to damage property;

(c) to interfere with evidence; or

(d) to assist in escape from police detention or lawful custody,

may be retained when the person from whom it was seized is no longer in police detention or the custody of a court or is in the custody of a court but has been released on bail.

(4) Nothing may be retained for either of the purposes mentioned in subsection (2)(a) above if a photograph or copy would be sufficient for that purpose.

(5) Nothing in this section affects any power of a court to make an order under section 1 of the Police (Property) Act 1897.

(6) This section also applies to anything retained by the police under section 28H(5) of the Immigration Act 1971.

(7) The reference in subsection (1) to anything seized by a constable includes anything seized by a person authorised under section 16(2) to accompany a constable executing a warrant.

23 Meaning of "premises" etc.

In this Act—

"premises" includes any place and, in particular, includes—

(a) any vehicle, vessel, aircraft or hovercraft;

(b) any offshore installation;

(ba) any renewable energy installation;

(c) any tent or movable structure;

"offshore installation" has the meaning given to it by section 1 of the Mineral Workings (Offshore Installations) Act 1971.

'renewable energy installation' has the same meaning as in Chapter 2 of Part 2 of the Energy Act 2004.

PART III
ARREST

24 Arrest without warrant: constables

(1) A constable may arrest without a warrant—
(a) anyone who is about to commit an offence;

(b) anyone who is in the act of committing an offence;

(c) anyone whom he has reasonable grounds for suspecting to be about to commit an offence;

(d) anyone whom he has reasonable grounds for suspecting to be committing an offence.

(2) If a constable has reasonable grounds for suspecting that an offence has been committed, he may arrest without a warrant anyone whom he has reasonable grounds to suspect of being guilty of it.

(3) If an offence has been committed, a constable may arrest without a warrant—

(a) anyone who is guilty of the offence;

(b) anyone whom he has reasonable grounds for suspecting to be guilty of it.

(4) But the power of summary arrest conferred by subsection (1), (2) or (3) is exercisable only if the constable has reasonable grounds for believing that for any of the reasons mentioned in subsection (5) it is necessary to arrest the person in question.

(5) The reasons are—

(a) to enable the name of the person in question to be ascertained (in the case where the constable does not know, and cannot readily ascertain, the person's name, or has reasonable grounds for doubting whether a name given by the person as his name is his real name);

(b) correspondingly as regards the person's address;

(c) to prevent the person in question—

(i) causing physical injury to himself or any other person;

(ii) suffering physical injury;

(iii) causing loss of or damage to property;

(iv) committing an offence against public decency (subject to subsection (6)); or

(v) causing an unlawful obstruction of the highway;

(d) to protect a child or other vulnerable person from the person in question;

(e) to allow the prompt and effective investigation of the offence or of the conduct of the person in question;

(f) to prevent any prosecution for the offence from being hindered by the disappearance of the person in question.

(6) Subsection (5)(c)(iv) applies only where members of the public going about their normal business cannot reasonably be expected to avoid the person in question.

24A   Arrest without warrant: other persons

(1) A person other than a constable may arrest without a warrant—

(a) anyone who is in the act of committing an indictable offence;

(b) anyone whom he has reasonable grounds for suspecting to be committing an indictable offence.

(2) Where an indictable offence has been committed, a person other than a constable may arrest without a warrant—

(a)   anyone who is guilty of the offence;

(b)   anyone whom he has reasonable grounds for suspecting to be guilty of it.

(3) But the power of summary arrest conferred by subsection (1) or (2) is exercisable only if—

(a)   the person making the arrest has reasonable grounds for believing that for any of the reasons mentioned in subsection (4) it is necessary to arrest the person in question; and

(b)   it appears to the person making the arrest that it is not reasonably practicable for a constable to make it instead.

(4) The reasons are to prevent the person in question—

(a)   causing physical injury to himself or any other person;

(b)   suffering physical injury;

(c)   causing loss of or damage to property; or

(d)   making off before a constable can assume responsibility for him.

(5) This section does not apply in relation to an offence under Part 3 or 3A of the Public Order Act 1986.

26—Repeal of statutory powers of arrest without warrant or order

(1) Subject to subsection (2) below, so much of any Act (including a local Act) passed before this Act as enables a constable—

(a)   to arrest a person for an offence without a warrant; or

(b)   to arrest a person otherwise than for an offence without a warrant or an order of a court,

shall cease to have effect.

(2) Nothing in subsection (1) above affects the enactments specified in Schedule 2 to this Act.

28—Information to be given on arrest

(1) Subject to subsection (5) below, where a person is arrested, otherwise than by being informed that he is under arrest, the arrest is not lawful unless the person arrested is informed that he is under arrest as soon as is practicable after his arrest.

(2) Where a person is arrested by a constable, subsection (1) above applies regardless of whether the fact of the arrest is obvious.

(3) Subject to subsection (5) below, no arrest is lawful unless the person arrested is informed of the ground for the arrest at the time of, or as soon as is practicable after, the arrest.

(4) Where a person is arrested by a constable, subsection (3) above applies regardless of whether the ground for the arrest is obvious.

(5) Nothing in this section is to be taken to require a person to be informed—

(a) that he is under arrest; or

(b) of the ground for the arrest,

if it was not reasonably practicable for him to be so informed by reason of his having escaped from arrest before the information could be given.

29 Voluntary attendance at police station etc.

Where for the purpose of assisting with an investigation a person attends voluntarily at a police station or at any other place where a constable is present or accompanies a constable to a police station or any such other place without having been arrested—

(a) he shall be entitled to leave at will unless he is placed under arrest;

(b) he shall be informed at once that he is under arrest if a decision is taken by a constable to prevent him from leaving at will.

30—Arrest elsewhere than at police station

(1) Subsection (1A) applies where a person is, at any place other than a police station—

(a) arrested by a constable for an offence, or

(b) taken into custody by a constable after being arrested for an offence by a person other than a constable.

(1A)   The person must be taken by a constable to a police station as soon as practicable after the arrest.

(1B)   Subsection (1A) has effect subject to section 30A (release on bail) and subsection (7) (release without bail).

(2) Subject to subsections (3) and (5) below, the police station to which an arrested person is taken under [subsection (1A)] above shall be a designated police station.

(3) A constable to whom this subsection applies may take an arrested person to any police station unless it appears to the constable that it may be necessary to keep the arrested person in police detention for more than six hours.

(4) Subsection (3) above applies—

(a) to a constable who is working in a locality covered by a police station which is not a designated police station; and

(b) to a constable belonging to a body of constables maintained by an authority other than a police authority.

(5) Any constable may take an arrested person to any police station if—

(a) either of the following conditions is satisfied—

(i)   the constable has arrested him without the assistance of any other constable and no other constable is available to assist him;

> (ii) the constable has taken him into custody from a person other than a constable without the assistance of any other constable and no other constable is available to assist him; and
>
> (b) it appears to the constable that he will be unable to take the arrested person to a designated police station without the arrested person injuring himself, the constable or some other person.

(6) If the first police station to which an arrested person is taken after his arrest is not a designated police station, he shall be taken to a designated police station not more than six hours after his arrival at the first police station unless he is released previously.

(7) A person arrested by a constable at any place other than a police station must be released without bail if the condition in subsection (7A) is satisfied.

(7A) The condition is that, at any time before the person arrested reaches a police station, a constable is satisfied that there are no grounds for keeping him under arrest or releasing him on bail under section 30A.

(8) A constable who releases a person under subsection (7) above shall record the fact that he has done so.

(9) The constable shall make the record as soon as is practicable after the release.

(10) Nothing in subsection (1A) or in section 30A prevents a constable delaying taking a person to a police station or releasing him on bail if the condition in subsection (10A) is satisfied.

(10A) The condition is that the presence of the person at a place (other than a police station) is necessary in order to carry out such investigations as it is reasonable to carry out immediately.

(11) Where there is any such delay the reasons for the delay must be recorded when the person first arrives at the police station or (as the case may be) is released on bail.

(12) Nothing in [subsection (1A) or section 30A] above shall be taken to affect—

(a) paragraphs 16(3) or 18(1) of Schedule 2 to the Immigration Act 1971;

(b) section 34(1) of the Criminal Justice Act 1972; or

(c) any provision of the Terrorism Act 2000.

(13) Nothing in subsection (10) above shall be taken to affect paragraph 18(3) of Schedule 2 to the Immigration Act 1971.

31 Arrest for further offence

Where—

(a) a person—

    (i)   has been arrested for an offence; and

    (ii) is at a police station in consequence of that arrest; and

  (b) it appears to a constable that, if he were released from that arrest, he would be liable to arrest for some other offence, he shall be arrested for that other offence.

32—Search upon arrest

(1) A constable may search an arrested person, in any case where the person to be searched has been arrested at a place other than a police station, if the constable has reasonable grounds for believing that the arrested person may present a danger to himself or others.

(2) Subject to subsections (3) to (5) below, a constable shall also have power in any such case—

  (a) to search the arrested person for anything—

    (i)   which he might use to assist him to escape from lawful custody; or

    (ii) which might be evidence relating to an offence; and

  (b) if the offence for which he has been arrested is an indictable offence, to enter and search any premises in which he was when arrested or immediately before he was arrested for evidence relating to the offence.

(3) The power to search conferred by subsection (2) above is only a power to search to the extent that is reasonably required for the purpose of discovering any such thing or any such evidence.

(4) The powers conferred by this section to search a person are not to be construed as authorising a constable to require a person to remove any of his clothing in public other than an outer coat, jacket or gloves but they do authorise a search of a person's mouth.

(5) A constable may not search a person in the exercise of the power conferred by subsection (2)(a) above unless he has reasonable grounds for believing that the person to be searched may have concealed on him anything for which a search is permitted under that paragraph.

(6) A constable may not search premises in the exercise of the power conferred by subsection (2)(b) above unless he has reasonable grounds for believing that there is evidence for which a search is permitted under that paragraph on the premises.

(7) In so far as the power of search conferred by subsection (2)(b) above relates to premises consisting of two or more separate dwellings, it is limited to a power to search—

  (a) any dwelling in which the arrest took place or in which the person arrested was immediately before his arrest; and

  (b) any parts of the premises which the occupier of any such dwelling uses in common with the occupiers of any other dwellings comprised in the premises.

(8) A constable searching a person in the exercise of the power conferred by subsection (1) above may seize and retain anything he finds, if he has reasonable grounds for believing that the person searched might use it to cause physical injury to himself or to any other person.

(9) A constable searching a person in the exercise of the power conferred by subsection (2)(a) above may seize and retain anything he finds, other than an item subject to legal privilege, if he has reasonable grounds for believing—

   (a) that he might use it to assist him to escape from lawful custody; or

   (b) that it is evidence of an offence or has been obtained in consequence of the commission of an offence.

(10) Nothing in this section shall be taken to affect the power conferred by section 43 of the Terrorism Act 2000.

PART IV
DETENTION

Detention—conditions and duration

34—Limitations on police detention

(1) A person arrested for an offence shall not be kept in police detention except in accordance with the provisions of this Part of this Act.

(2) Subject to subsection (3) below, if at any time a custody officer—

   (a) becomes aware, in relation to any person in police detention, that the grounds for the detention of that person have ceased to apply; and

   (b) is not aware of any other grounds on which the continued detention of that person could be justified under the provisions of this Part of this Act,

it shall be the duty of the custody officer, subject to subsection (4) below, to order his immediate release from custody.

(3) No person in police detention shall be released except on the authority of a custody officer at the police station where his detention was authorised or, if it was authorised at more than one station, a custody officer at the station where it was last authorised.

(4) A person who appears to the custody officer to have been unlawfully at large when he was arrested is not to be released under subsection (2) above.

(5) A person whose release is ordered under subsection (2) above shall be released without bail unless it appears to the custody officer—

   (a) that there is need for further investigation of any matter in connection with which he was detained at any time during the period of his detention; or

(b) that, in respect of any such matter, proceedings may be taken against him or he may be reprimanded or warned under section 65 of the Crime and Disorder Act 1998

and, if it so appears, he shall be released on bail.

(6) For the purposes of this Part of this Act a person arrested under section 6D of the Road Traffic Act 1988 or section 30(2) of the Transport and Works Act 1992 (c. 42) is arrested for an offence.

(7) For the purposes of this Part a person who—
(a) attends a police station to answer to bail granted under section 30A,
(b) returns to a police station to answer to bail granted under this Part, or
(c) is arrested under section 30D or 46A,

is to be treated as arrested for an offence and that offence is the offence in connection with which he was granted bail.

(8) Subsection (7) does not apply in relation to a person who is granted bail subject to the duty mentioned in section 47(3)(b) and who either–
(a) attends a police station to answer to such bail, or
(b) is arrested under section 46A for failing to do so,

(provision as to the treatment of such persons for the purposes of this Part being made by section 46ZA).

35—Designated police stations

(1) The chief officer of police for each police area shall designate the police stations in his area which, subject to sections 30(3) and (5), 30A(5) and 30D(2), are to be the stations in that area to be used for the purpose of detaining arrested persons.

(2) A chief officer's duty under subsection (1) above is to designate police stations appearing to him to provide enough accommodation for that purpose.

(2A) The Chief Constable of the British Transport Police Force may designate police stations which (in addition to those designated under subsection (1) above) may be used for the purpose of detaining arrested persons.

(3) Without prejudice to section 12 of the Interpretation Act 1978 (continuity of duties) a chief officer—
(a) may designate a station which was not previously designated; and
(b) may direct that a designation of a station previously made shall cease to operate.

(4) In this Act "designated police station" means a police station for the time being designated under this section.

36—Custody officers at police stations

(1) One or more custody officers shall be appointed for each designated police station.

(2) A custody officer for a police station designated under section 35(1) above shall be appointed—

(a) by the chief officer of police for the area in which the designated police station is situated; or

(b) by such other police officer as the chief officer of police for that area may direct.

(2A) A custody officer for a police station designated under section 35(2A) above shall be appointed—

(a) by the Chief Constable of the British Transport Police Force; or

(b) by such other member of that Force as that Chief Constable may direct.

(3) No officer may be appointed a custody officer unless he is of at least the rank of sergeant.

(4) An officer of any rank may perform the functions of a custody officer at a designated police station if a custody officer is not readily available to perform them.

(5) Subject to the following provisions of this section and to section 39(2) below, none of the functions of a custody officer in relation to a person shall be performed by an officer who at the time when the function falls to be performed is involved in the investigation of an offence for which that person is in police detention at that time.

(6) Nothing in subsection (5) above is to be taken to prevent a custody officer—

(a) performing any function assigned to custody officers—

(i) by this Act; or

(ii) by a code of practice issued under this Act;

(b) carrying out the duty imposed on custody officers by section 39 below;

(c) doing anything in connection with the identification of a suspect; or

(d) doing anything under sections 7 and 8 of the Road Traffic Act 1988.

(7) Where an arrested person is taken to a police station which is not a designated police station, the functions in relation to him which at a designated police station would be the functions of a custody officer shall be performed—

(a) by an officer who is not involved in the investigation of an offence for which he is in police detention, if such an officer is readily available; and

(b) if no such officer is readily available, by the officer who took him to the station or any other officer.

(7A)   Subject to subsection (7B), subsection (7) applies where a person attends a police station which is not a designated station to answer to bail granted under section 30A as it applies where a person is taken to such a station.

(7B)   Where subsection (7) applies because of subsection (7A), the reference in subsection (7)(b) to the officer who took him to the station is to be read as a reference to the officer who granted him bail.

(8)   References to a custody officer in the following provisions of this Act include references to an officer other than a custody officer who is performing the functions of a custody officer by virtue of subsection (4) or (7) above.

(9)   Where by virtue of subsection (7) above an officer of a force maintained by a police authority who took an arrested person to a police station is to perform the functions of a custody officer in relation to him, the officer shall inform an officer who—

(a)   is attached to a designated police station; and

(b)   is of at least the rank of inspector,

that he is to do so.

(10)   The duty imposed by subsection (9) above shall be performed as soon as it is practicable to perform it.

37—Duties of custody officer before charge

(1)   Where—

(a)   a person is arrested for an offence—

(i)   without a warrant; or

(ii)   under a warrant not endorsed for bail,

the custody officer at each police station where he is detained after his arrest shall determine whether he has before him sufficient evidence to charge that person with the offence for which he was arrested and may detain him at the police station for such period as is necessary to enable him to do so.

(2)   If the custody officer determines that he does not have such evidence before him, the person arrested shall be released either on bail or without bail, unless the custody officer has reasonable grounds for believing that his detention without being charged is necessary to secure or preserve evidence relating to an offence for which he is under arrest or to obtain such evidence by questioning him.

(3)   If the custody officer has reasonable grounds for so believing, he may authorise the person arrested to be kept in police detention.

(4)   Where a custody officer authorises a person who has not been charged to be kept in police detention, he shall, as soon as is practicable, make a written record of the grounds for the detention.

(5) Subject to subsection (6) below, the written record shall be made in the presence of the person arrested who shall at that time be informed by the custody officer of the grounds for his detention.

(6) Subsection (5) above shall not apply where the person arrested is, at the time when the written record is made—

(a) incapable of understanding what is said to him;

(b) violent or likely to become violent; or

(c) in urgent need of medical attention.

(7) Subject to section 41(7) below, if the custody officer determines that he has before him sufficient evidence to charge the person arrested with the offence for which he was arrested, the person arrested—

(a) shall be–

    (i) released without charge and on bail, or

    (ii) kept in police detention,

for the purpose of enabling the Director of Public Prosecutions to make a decision under section 37B below,

(b) shall be released without charge and on bail but not for that purpose,

(c) shall be released without charge and without bail, or

(d) shall be charged.

(7A) The decision as to how a person is to be dealt with under subsection (7) above shall be that of the custody officer.

(7B) Where a person is dealt with under subsection (7)(a) above, it shall be the duty of the custody officer to inform him that he is being released, or (as the case may be) detained, to enable the Director of Public Prosecutions to make a decision under section 37B below.

(8) Where—

(a) a person is released under subsection (7)(b) or (c) above; and

(b) at the time of his release a decision whether he should be prosecuted for the offence for which he was arrested has not been taken,

it shall be the duty of the custody officer so to inform him.

(8A) Subsection (8B) applies if the offence for which the person is arrested is one in relation to which a sample could be taken under section 63B below and the custody officer–

(a) is required in pursuance of subsection (2) above to release the person arrested and decides to release him on bail, or

(b) decides in pursuance of subsection (7)(a) or (b) above to release the person without charge and on bail.

(8B) The detention of the person may be continued to enable a sample to be taken under section 63B, but this subsection does not permit a person to be detained for a period of more than 24 hours after the relevant time.

(9) If the person arrested is not in a fit state to be dealt with under subsection (7) above, he may be kept in police detention until he is.

(10)   The duty imposed on the custody officer under subsection (1) above shall be carried out by him as soon as practicable after the person arrested arrives at the police station or, in the case of a person arrested at the police station, as soon as practicable after the arrest.

(15)   In this Part of this Act—

"arrested juvenile" means a person arrested with or without a warrant who appears to be under the age of 17;

"endorsed for bail" means endorsed with a direction for bail in accordance with section 117(2) of the Magistrates' Courts Act 1980.

38—Duties of custody officer after charge

(1) Where a person arrested for an offence otherwise than under a warrant endorsed for bail is charged with an offence, the custody officer shall, subject to section 25 of the Criminal Justice and Public Order Act 1994, order his release from police detention, either on bail or without bail, unless—

(a) if the person arrested is not an arrested juvenile—

(i) his name or address cannot be ascertained or the custody officer has reasonable grounds for doubting whether a name or address furnished by him as his name or address is his real name or address;

(ii) the custody officer has reasonable grounds for believing that the person arrested will fail to appear in court to answer to bail;

(iii) in the case of a person arrested for an imprisonable offence, the custody officer has reasonable grounds for believing that the detention of the person arrested is necessary to prevent him from committing an offence;

(iiia)   in a case where a sample may be taken from the person under section 63B below, the custody officer has reasonable grounds for believing that the detention of the person is necessary to enable the sample to be taken from him;

(iv) in the case of a person arrested for an offence which is not an imprisonable offence, the custody officer has reasonable grounds for believing that the detention of the person arrested is necessary to prevent him from causing physical injury to any other person or from causing loss of or damage to property;

(v) the custody officer has reasonable grounds for believing that the detention of the person arrested is necessary to prevent him from interfering with the administration of justice or with the investigation of offences or of a particular offence; or

(vi) the custody officer has reasonable grounds for believing that the detention of the person arrested is necessary for his own protection;

(b) if he is an arrested juvenile—

(i) any of the requirements of paragraph (a) above is satisfied [(but, in the case of paragraph (a)(iiia) above, only if the arrested juvenile has attained the minimum age); or

(ii) the custody officer has reasonable grounds for believing that he ought to be detained in his own interests.

(2) If the release of a person arrested is not required by subsection (1) above, the custody officer may authorise him to be kept in police detention but may not authorise a person to be kept in police detention by virtue of subsection (1)(a)(iiia) after the end of the period of six hours beginning when he was charged with the offence.

(2A) The custody officer, in taking the decisions required by subsection (1)(a) and (b) above (except (a)(i) and (vi) and (b)(ii)), shall have regard to the same considerations as those which a court is required to have regard to in taking the corresponding decisions under paragraph 2(1) of Part I of Schedule 1 to the Bail Act 1976 (disregarding paragraph 2(2) of that Part).

(3) Where a custody officer authorises a person who has been charged to be kept in police detention, he shall, as soon as practicable, make a written record of the grounds for the detention.

(4) Subject to subsection (5) below, the written record shall be made in the presence of the person charged who shall at that time be informed by the custody officer of the grounds for his detention.

(5) Subsection (4) above shall not apply where the person charged is, at the time when the written record is made—

(a) incapable of understanding what is said to him;

(b) violent or likely to become violent; or

(c) in urgent need of medical attention.

(6) Where a custody officer authorises an arrested juvenile to be kept in police detention under subsection (1) above, the custody officer shall, unless he certifies—

(a) that, by reason of such circumstances as are specified in the certificate, it is impracticable for him to do so; or

(b) in the case of an arrested juvenile who has attained the age of 12 years, that no secure accommodation is available and that keeping him in other local authority accommodation would not be adequate to protect the public from serious harm from him,

secure that the arrested juvenile is moved to local authority accommodation.

(6A) In this section—

'local authority accommodation' means accommodation provided by or on behalf of a local authority (within the meaning of the Children Act 1989);

"minimum age" means the age specified in [section 63B(3)(b) below;

'secure accommodation' means accommodation provided for the purpose of restricting liberty;

"sexual offence" means an offence specified in Part 2 of Schedule 15 to the Criminal Justice Act 2003;

"violent offence" means murder or an offence specified in Part 1 of that Schedule;

and any reference, in relation to an arrested juvenile charged with a violent or sexual offence, to protecting the public from serious harm from him shall be construed as a reference to protecting members of the public from death or serious personal injury, whether physical or psychological, occasioned by further such offences committed by him.

(6B)   Where an arrested juvenile is moved to local authority accommodation under subsection (6) above, it shall be lawful for any person acting on behalf of the authority to detain him.

(7)   A certificate made under subsection (6) above in respect of an arrested juvenile shall be produced to the court before which he is first brought thereafter.

(7A)   In this section "imprisonable offence" has the same meaning as in Schedule 1 to the Bail Act 1976.

(8)   In this Part of this Act "local authority" has the same meaning as in the Children and Young Persons Act 1969.

39—Responsibilities in relation to persons detained

(1)   Subject to subsections (2) and (4) below, it shall be the duty of the custody officer at a police station to ensure—
  (a)   that all persons in police detention at that station are treated in accordance with this Act and any code of practice issued under it and relating to the treatment of persons in police detention; and
  (b)   that all matters relating to such persons which are required by this Act or by such codes of practice to be recorded are recorded in the custody records relating to such persons.

(2)   If the custody officer, in accordance with any code of practice issued under this Act, transfers or permits the transfer of a person in police detention—
  (a)   to the custody of a police officer investigating an offence for which that person is in police detention; or
  (b)   to the custody of an officer who has charge of that person outside the police station,

the custody officer shall cease in relation to that person to be subject to the duty imposed on him by subsection (1)(a) above; and it shall be the duty of the officer to whom the transfer is made to ensure that he is treated in accordance with the provisions of this Act and of any such codes of practice as are mentioned in subsection (1) above.

(3) If the person detained is subsequently returned to the custody of the custody officer, it shall be the duty of the officer investigating the offence to report to the custody officer as to the manner in which this section and the codes of practice have been complied with while that person was in his custody.

(4) If an arrested juvenile is transferred to the care of a local authority in pursuance of arrangements made under section 38(6) above, the custody officer shall cease in relation to that person to be subject to the duty imposed on him by subsection (1) above.

(6) Where—
   (a) an officer of higher rank than the custody officer gives directions relating to a person in police detention; and
   (b) the directions are at variance—
      (i) with any decision made or action taken by the custody officer in the performance of a duty imposed on him under this Part of this Act; or
      (ii) with any decision or action which would but for the directions have been made or taken by him in the performance of such a duty,

the custody officer shall refer the matter at once to an officer of the rank of superintendent or above who is responsible for the police station for which the custody officer is acting as custody officer.

40—Review of police detention

(1) Reviews of the detention of each person in police detention in connection with the investigation of an offence shall be carried out periodically in accordance with the following provisions of this section—
   (a) in the case of a person who has been arrested and charged, by the custody officer; and
   (b) in the case of a person who has been arrested but not charged, by an officer of at least the rank of inspector who has not been directly involved in the investigation.

(2) The officer to whom it falls to carry out a review is referred to in this section as a "review officer".

(3) Subject to subsection (4) below—
   (a) the first review shall be not later than six hours after the detention was first authorised;
   (b) the second review shall be not later than nine hours after the first;

    (c) subsequent reviews shall be at intervals of not more than nine hours.

(4) A review may be postponed—

    (a) if, having regard to all the circumstances prevailing at the latest time for it specified in subsection (3) above, it is not practicable to carry out the review at that time;

    (b) without prejudice to the generality of paragraph (a) above—

        (i) if at that time the person in detention is being questioned by a police officer and the review officer is satisfied that an interruption of the questioning for the purpose of carrying out the review would prejudice the investigation in connection with which he is being questioned; or

        (ii) if at that time no review officer is readily available.

(5) If a review is postponed under subsection (4) above it shall be carried out as soon as practicable after the latest time specified for it in subsection (3) above.

(6) If a review is carried out after postponement under subsection (4) above, the fact that it was so carried out shall not affect any requirement of this section as to the time at which any subsequent review is to be carried out.

(7) The review officer shall record the reasons for any postponement of a review in the custody record.

(8) Subject to subsection (9) below, where the person whose detention is under review has not been charged before the time of the review, section 37(1) to (6) above shall have effect in relation to him, but with the modifications specified in subsection (8A).

(8A) The modifications are—

    (a) the substitution of references to the person whose detention is under review for references to the person arrested;

    (b) the substitution of references to the review officer for references to the custody officer; and

    (c) in subsection (6), the insertion of the following paragraph after paragraph (a)—

    '(aa) asleep;'.

(9) Where a person has been kept in police detention by virtue of section 37(9) or 37D(5) above, section 37(1) to (6) shall not have effect in relation to him but it shall be the duty of the review officer to determine whether he is yet in a fit state.

(10) Where the person whose detention is under review has been charged before the time of the review, section 38(1) to (6B) above shall have effect in relation to him, but with the modifications specified in subsection (10A).

(10A)   The modifications are—
- (a)   the substitution of a reference to the person whose detention is under review for any reference to the person arrested or to the person charged; and
- (b)   in subsection (5), the insertion of the following paragraph after paragraph (a)—

'(aa)   asleep;'.

(11)   Where—
- (a)   an officer of higher rank than the review officer gives directions relating to a person in police detention; and
- (b)   the directions are at variance—
  - (i)   with any decision made or action taken by the review officer in the performance of a duty imposed on him under this Part of this Act; or
  - (ii)   with any decision or action which would but for the directions have been made or taken by him in the performance of such a duty.

the review officer shall refer the matter at once to an officer of the rank of superintendent or above who is responsible for the police station for which the review officer is acting as review officer in connection with the detention.

(12)   Before determining whether to authorise a person's continued detention the review officer shall give—
- (a)   that person (unless he is asleep); or
- (b)   any solicitor representing him who is available at the time of the review,

an opportunity to make representations to him about the detention.

(13)   Subject to subsection (14) below, the person whose detention is under review or his solicitor may make representations under subsection (12) above either orally or in writing.

(14)   The review officer may refuse to hear oral representations from the person whose detention is under review if he considers that he is unfit to make such representations by reason of his condition or behaviour.

41—Limits on period of detention without charge

(1)   Subject to the following provisions of this section and to sections 42 and 43 below, a person shall not be kept in police detention for more than 24 hours without being charged.

(2)   The time from which the period of detention of a person is to be calculated (in this Act referred to as "the relevant time")—
- (a)   in the case of a person to whom this paragraph applies, shall be—

      (i)   the time at which that person arrives at the relevant police station; or

      (ii) the time 24 hours after the time of that person's arrest,

whichever is the earlier;

(b) in the case of a person arrested outside England and Wales, shall be—

      (i)   the time at which that person arrives at the first police station to which he is taken in the police area in England or Wales in which the offence for which he was arrested is being investigated; or

      (ii) the time 24 hours after the time of that person's entry into England and Wales,

whichever is the earlier;

(c) in the case of a person who—

      (i)   attends voluntarily at a police station; or

      (ii) accompanies a constable to a police station without having been arrested,

and is arrested at the police station, the time of his arrest;

(ca) in the case of a person who attends a police station to answer to bail granted under section 30A, the time when he arrives at the police station;

(d) in any other case, except where subsection (5) below applies, shall be the time at which the person arrested arrives at the first police station to which he is taken after his arrest.

(3) Subsection (2)(a) above applies to a person if—

(a) his arrest is sought in one police area in England and Wales;

(b) he is arrested in another police area; and

(c) he is not questioned in the area in which he is arrested in order to obtain evidence in relation to an offence for which he is arrested;

and in sub-paragraph (i) of that paragraph "the relevant police station" means the first police station to which he is taken in the police area in which his arrest was sought.

(4) Subsection (2) above shall have effect in relation to a person arrested under section 31 above as if every reference in it to his arrest or his being arrested were a reference to his arrest or his being arrested for the offence for which he was originally arrested.

(5) If—

(a) a person is in police detention in a police area in England and Wales ("the first area"); and

(b) his arrest for an offence is sought in some other police area in England and Wales ("the second area"); and

(c)   he is taken to the second area for the purposes of investigating that offence, without being questioned in the first area in order to obtain evidence in relation to it,

the relevant time shall be—

(i)   the time 24 hours after he leaves the place where he is detained in the first area; or

(ii)   the time at which he arrives at the first police station to which he is taken in the second area,

whichever is the earlier.

(6)   When a person who is in police detention is removed to hospital because he is in need of medical treatment, any time during which he is being questioned in hospital or on the way there or back by a police officer for the purpose of obtaining evidence relating to an offence shall be included in any period which falls to be calculated for the purposes of this Part of this Act, but any other time while he is in hospital or on his way there or back shall not be so included.

(7)   Subject to subsection (8) below, a person who at the expiry of 24 hours after the relevant time is in police detention and has not been charged shall be released at that time either on bail or without bail.

(8)   Subsection (7) above does not apply to a person whose detention for more than 24 hours after the relevant time has been authorised or is otherwise permitted in accordance with section 42 or 43 below.

(9)   A person released under subsection (7) above shall not be re-arrested without a warrant for the offence for which he was previously arrested unless new evidence justifying a further arrest has come to light since his release; but this subsection does not prevent an arrest under section 46A below.

42—Authorisation of continued detention

(1)   Where a police officer of the rank of superintendent or above who is responsible for the police station at which a person is detained has reasonable grounds for believing that—

(a)   the detention of that person without charge is necessary to secure or preserve evidence relating to an offence for which he is under arrest or to obtain such evidence by questioning him;

(b)   an offence for which he is under arrest is an indictable offence; and

(c)   the investigation is being conducted diligently and expeditiously.

he may authorise the keeping of that person in police detention for a period expiring at or before 36 hours after the relevant time.

(2)   Where an officer such as is mentioned in subsection (1) above has authorised the keeping of a person in police detention for a period expiring less than 36 hours after the relevant time, such an officer may authorise the keeping of that person in police detention for a further

period expiring not more than 36 hours after that time if the conditions specified in subsection (1) above are still satisfied when he gives the authorisation.

(3) If it is proposed to transfer a person in police detention to another police area, the officer determining whether or not to authorise keeping him in detention under subsection (1) above shall have regard to the distance and the time the journey would take.

(4) No authorisation under subsection (1) above shall be given in respect of any person—

    (a)   more than 24 hours after the relevant time; or

    (b)   before the second review of his detention under section 40 above has been carried out.

(5) Where an officer authorises the keeping of a person in police detention under subsection (1) above, it shall be his duty—

    (a)   to inform that person of the grounds for his continued detention; and

    (b)   to record the grounds in that person's custody record.

(6) Before determining whether to authorise the keeping of a person in detention under subsection (1) or (2) above, an officer shall give—

    (a)   that person; or

    (b)   any solicitor representing him who is available at the time when it falls to the officer to determine whether to give the authorisation,

an opportunity to make representations to him about the detention.

(7) Subject to subsection (8) below, the person in detention or his solicitor may make representations under subsection (6) above either orally or in writing.

(8) The officer to whom it falls to determine whether to give the authorisation may refuse to hear oral representations from the person in detention if he considers that he is unfit to make such representations by reason of his condition or behaviour.

(9) Where—

    (a)   an officer authorises the keeping of a person in detention under subsection (1) above; and

    (b)   at the time of the authorisation he has not yet exercised a right conferred on him by section 56 or 58 below,

the officer—

    (i)   shall inform him of that right;

    (ii)   shall decide whether he should be permitted to exercise it;

    (iii) shall record the decision in his custody record; and

    (iv) if the decision is to refuse to permit the exercise of the right, shall also record the grounds for the decision in that record.

(10)   Where an officer has authorised the keeping of a person who has not been charged in detention under subsection (1) or (2) above, he shall be released from detention, either on bail or without bail, not later than 36 hours after the relevant time, unless—

(a)   he has been charged with an offence; or

(b)   his continued detention is authorised or otherwise permitted in accordance with section 43 below.

(11)   A person released under subsection (10) above shall not be re-arrested without a warrant for the offence for which he was previously arrested unless new evidence justifying a further arrest has come to light since his release; but this subsection does not prevent an arrest under section 46A below.

43—Warrants of further detention

(1)   Where, on an application on oath made by a constable and supported by an information, a magistrates' court is satisfied that there are reasonable grounds for believing that the further detention of the person to whom the application relates is justified, it may issue a warrant of further detention authorising the keeping of that person in police detention.

(2)   A court may not hear an application for a warrant of further detention unless the person to whom the application relates—

(a)   has been furnished with a copy of the information; and

(b)   has been brought before the court for the hearing.

(3)   The person to whom the application relates shall be entitled to be legally represented at the hearing and, if he is not so represented but wishes to be so represented—

(a)   the court shall adjourn the hearing to enable him to obtain representation; and

(b)   he may be kept in police detention during the adjournment.

(4)   A person's further detention is only justified for the purposes of this section or section 44 below if—

(a)   his detention without charge is necessary to secure or preserve evidence relating to an offence for which he is under arrest or to obtain such evidence by questioning him;

(b)   an offence for which he is under arrest is an indictable offence; and

(c)   the investigation is being conducted diligently and expeditiously.

(5)   Subject to subsection (7) below, an application for a warrant of further detention may be made—

(a)   at any time before the expiry of 36 hours after the relevant time; or

(b)   in a case where—

(i)   it is not practicable for the magistrates' court to which the application will be made to sit at the expiry of 36 hours after the relevant time; but

(ii) the court will sit during the 6 hours following the end of that
period,

at any time before the expiry of the said 6 hours.

(6) In a case to which subsection (5)(b) above applies—

(a) the person to whom the application relates may be kept in police
detention until the application is heard; and

(b) the custody officer shall make a note in that person's custody
record—

(i) of the fact that he was kept in police detention for more than 36
hours after the relevant time; and

(ii) of the reason why he was so kept.

(7) If—

(a) an application for a warrant of further detention is made after the
expiry of 36 hours after the relevant time; and

(b) it appears to the magistrates' court that it would have been
reasonable for the police to make it before the expiry of that period,

the court shall dismiss the application.

(8) Where on an application such as is mentioned in subsection (1) above a
magistrates' court is not satisfied that there are reasonable grounds for
believing that the further detention of the person to whom the
application relates is justified, it shall be its duty—

(a) to refuse the application; or

(b) to adjourn the hearing of it until a time not later than 36 hours after
the relevant time.

(9) The person to whom the application relates may be kept in police
detention during the adjournment.

(10)   A warrant of further detention shall—

(a) state the time at which it is issued;

(b) authorise the keeping in police detention of the person to whom it
relates for the period stated in it.

(11)   Subject to subsection (12) below, the period stated in a warrant of
further detention shall be such period as the magistrates' court thinks fit,
having regard to the evidence before it.

(12)   The period shall not be longer than 36 hours.

(13)   If it is proposed to transfer a person in police detention to a police area
other than that in which he is detained when the application for a
warrant of further detention is made, the court hearing the application
shall have regard to the distance and the time the journey would take.

(14)   Any information submitted in support of an application under this
section shall state—

(a) the nature of the offence for which the person to whom the
application relates has been arrested;

(b) the general nature of the evidence on which that person was arrested;

(c) what inquiries relating to the offence have been made by the police and what further inquiries are proposed by them;

(d) the reasons for believing the continued detention of that person to be necessary for the purposes of such further inquiries.

(15) Where an application under this section is refused, the person to whom the application relates shall forthwith be charged or, subject to subsection (16) below, released, either on bail or without bail.

(16) A person need not be released under subsection (15) above—
(a) before the expiry of 24 hours after the relevant time; or

(b) before the expiry of any longer period for which his continued detention is or has been authorised under section 42 above.

(17) Where an application under this section is refused, no further application shall be made under this section in respect of the person to whom the refusal relates, unless supported by evidence which has come to light since the refusal.

(18) Where a warrant of further detention is issued, the person to whom it relates shall be released from police detention, either on bail or without bail, upon or before the expiry of the warrant unless he is charged.

(19) A person released under subsection (18) above shall not be re-arrested without a warrant for the offence for which he was previously arrested unless new evidence justifying a further arrest has come to light since his release; but this subsection does not prevent an arrest under section 46A below.

44—Extension of warrants of further detention

(1) On an application on oath made by a constable and supported by an information a magistrates' court may extend a warrant of further detention issued under section 43 above if it is satisfied that there are reasonable grounds for believing that the further detention of the person to whom the application relates is justified.

(2) Subject to subsection (3) below, the period for which a warrant of further detention may be extended shall be such period as the court thinks fit, having regard to the evidence before it.

(3) The period shall not—
(a) be longer than 36 hours; or

(b) end later than 96 hours after the relevant time.

(4) Where a warrant of further detention has been extended under subsection (1) above, or further extended under this subsection, for a period ending before 96 hours after the relevant time, on an application such as is mentioned in that subsection a magistrates' court may further extend the warrant if it is satisfied as there mentioned; and

subsections (2) and (3) above apply to such further extensions as they apply to extensions under subsection (1) above.

(5) A warrant of further detention shall, if extended or further extended under this section, be endorsed with a note of the period of the extension.

(6) Subsections (2), (3) and (14) of section 43 above shall apply to an application made under this section as they apply to an application made under that section.

(7) Where an application under this section is refused, the person to whom the application relates shall forthwith be charged or, subject to subsection (8) below, released, either on bail or without bail.

(8) A person need not be released under subsection (7) above before the expiry of any period for which a warrant of further detention issued in relation to him has been extended or further extended on an earlier application made under this section.

45—Detention before charge—supplementary

(1) In sections 43 and 44 of this Act "magistrates' court" means a court consisting of two or more justices of the peace sitting otherwise than in open court.

(2) Any reference in this Part of this Act to a period of time or a time of day is to be treated as approximate only.

46—Detention after charge

(1) Where a person—
(a) is charged with an offence; and
(b) after being charged—
(i) is kept in police detention; or
(ii) is detained by a local authority in pursuance of arrangements made under section 38(6) above,

he shall be brought before a magistrates' court in accordance with the provisions of this section.

(2) If he is to be brought before a magistrates' court in the local justice area in which the police station at which he was charged is situated, he shall be brought before such a court as soon as is practicable and in any event not later than the first sitting after he is charged with the offence.

(3) If no magistrates' court in that area is due to sit either on the day on which he is charged or on the next day, the custody officer for the police station at which he was charged shall inform the designated officer for the area that there is a person in the area to whom subsection (2) above applies.

(4) If the person charged is to be brought before a magistrates' court in a local justice area other than that in which the police station at which he

was charged is situated, he shall be removed to that area as soon as is practicable and brought before such a court as soon as is practicable after his arrival in the area and in any event not later than the first sitting of a magistrates' court in that area after his arrival in the area.

(5) If no magistrates' court for that area is due to sit either on the day on which he arrives in the area or on the next day—

(a) he shall be taken to a police station in the area; and

(b) the custody officer at that station shall inform the designated officer in that area that there is a person in the area to whom subsection (4) applies.

(6) Subject to subsection (8) below, where the designated officer for a local justice area has been informed—

(a) under subsection (3) above that there is a person in the area to whom subsection (2) above applies; or

(b) under subsection (5) above that there is a person in the area to whom subsection (4) above applies,

the designated officer shall arrange for a magistrates' court to sit not later than the day next following the relevant day.

(7) In this section "the relevant day"—

(a) in relation to a person who is to be brought before a magistrates' court in the local justice area in which the police station at which he was charged is situated, means the day on which he was charged; and

(b) in relation to a person who is to be brought before a magistrates' court in any other local justice area, means the day on which he arrives in the area.

(8) Where the day next following the relevant day is Christmas Day, Good Friday or a Sunday, the duty of the designated officer under subsection (6) above is a duty to arrange for a magistrates' court to sit not later than the first day after the relevant day which is not one of those days.

(9) Nothing in this section requires a person who is in hospital to be brought before a court if he is not well enough.

46A—Power of arrest for failure to answer to police bail

(1) A constable may arrest without a warrant any person who, having been released on bail under this Part of this Act subject to a duty to attend at a police station, fails to attend at that police station at the time appointed for him to do so.

(1ZA) The reference in subsection (1) to a person who fails to attend at a police station at the time appointed for him to do so includes a reference to a person who—

(a) attends at a police station to answer to bail granted subject to the duty mentioned in section 47(3)(b), but

(b) leaves the police station at any time before the beginning of proceedings in relation to a live link direction under section 57C of the Crime and Disorder Act 1998 in relation to him, without informing a constable that he does not intend to give his consent to the direction.

(1A) A person who has been released on bail under section 37, 37C(2)(b) or 37CA(2)(b) above may be arrested without warrant by a constable if the constable has reasonable grounds for suspecting that the person has broken any of the conditions of bail.

(2) A person who is arrested under this section shall be taken to the police station appointed as the place at which he is to surrender to custody as soon as practicable after the arrest.

(3) For the purposes of—
(a) section 30 above (subject to the obligation in subsection (2) above), and
(b) section 31 above,
an arrest under this section shall be treated as an arrest for an offence.

47—Bail after arrest

(1) Subject to the following provisions of this section, a release on bail of a person under this Part of this Act shall be a release on bail granted in accordance with sections 3, 3A, 5 and 5A of the Bail Act 1976 as they apply to bail granted by a constable.

(1A) The normal powers to impose conditions of bail shall be available to him where a custody officer releases a person on bail under section 37 above or section 38(1) above (including that subsection as applied by section 40(10) above) but not in any other cases.

In this subsection, "the normal powers to impose conditions of bail" has the meaning given in section 3(6) of the Bail Act 1976.

(1B) No application may be made under section 5B of the Bail Act 1976 if a person is released on bail under 37, 37C(2)(b), or 37CA(2)(b) above.

(1C) Subsections (1D) to (1F) below apply where a person released on bail under section 37, 37C(2)(b) or 37CA(2)(b) above is on bail subject to conditions.

(1D) The person shall not be entitled to make an application under section 43B of the Magistrates' Courts Act 1980.

(1E) A magistrates' court may, on an application by or on behalf of the person, vary the conditions of bail; and in this subsection "vary" has the same meaning as in the Bail Act 1976.

(1F) Where a magistrates' court varies the conditions of bail under subsection (1E) above, that bail shall not lapse but shall continue subject to the conditions as so varied.

(2) Nothing in the Bail Act 1976 shall prevent the re-arrest without warrant of a person released on bail subject to a duty to attend at a police station if new evidence justifying a further arrest has come to light since his release.

(3) Subject to [subsections (3A) and (4)] below, in this Part of this Act references to "bail" are references to bail subject to a duty—

(a) to appear before a magistrates' court at such time and such place as the custody officer may appoint;

(b) to attend at such police station as the custody officer may appoint at such time as he may appoint for the purposes of–

(i) proceedings in relation to a live link direction under section 57C of the Crime and Disorder Act 1998 (use of live link direction at preliminary hearings where accused is at police station); and

(ii) any preliminary hearing in relation to which such a direction is given; or

(c) to attend at such police station as the custody officer may appoint at such time as he may appoint for purposes other than those mentioned in paragraph (b).

(3A) Where a custody officer grants bail to a person subject to a duty to appear before a magistrates' court, he shall appoint for the appearance—

(a) a date which is not later than the first sitting of the court after the person is charged with the offence; or

(b) where he is informed by the designated officer for the relevant local justice area that the appearance cannot be accommodated until a later date, that later date.

(4) Where a custody officer has granted bail to a person subject to a duty to appear at a police station, the custody officer may give notice in writing to that person that his attendance at the police station is not required.

(6) Where a person who has been granted bail under this Part and either has attended at the police station in accordance with the grant of bail or has been arrested under section 46A above is detained at a police station, any time during which he was in police detention prior to being granted bail shall be included as part of any period which falls to be calculated under this Part of this Act.

(7) Where a person who was released on bail under this Part subject to a duty to attend at a police station is re-arrested, the provisions of this Part of this Act shall apply to him as they apply to a person arrested for the first time; but this subsection does not apply to a person who is arrested under section 46A above or has attended a police station in accordance with the grant of bail (and who accordingly is deemed by section 34(7) above to have been arrested for an offence) or to a person to whom section 46ZA(4) or (5) applies.

PART V
QUESTIONING AND TREATMENT OF PERSONS BY POLICE

53—Abolition of certain powers of constables to search persons

(1) Subject to subsection (2) below, there shall cease to have effect any Act (including a local Act) passed before this Act in so far as it authorises—

(a) any search by a constable of a person in police detention at a police station; or

(b) an intimate search of a person by a constable;

and any rule of common law which authorises a search such as is mentioned in paragraph (a) or (b) above is abolished.

54—Searches of detained persons

(1) The custody officer at a police station shall ascertain [. . .] everything which a person has with him when he is—

(a) brought to the station after being arrested elsewhere or after being committed to custody by an order or sentence of a court; or

(b) arrested at the station or detained there, as a person falling within section 34(7), under section 37 above or as a person to whom section 46ZA(4) or (5) applies.

(2) The custody officer may record or cause to be recorded all or any of the things which he ascertains under subsection (1).

(2A)　In the case of an arrested person, any such record may be made as part of his custody record.

(3) Subject to subsection (4) below, a custody officer may seize and retain any such thing or cause any such thing to be seized and retained.

(4) Clothes and personal effects may only be seized if the custody officer—

(a) believes that the person from whom they are seized may use them—

(i) to cause physical injury to himself or any other person;

(ii) to damage property;

(iii) to interfere with evidence; or

(iv) to assist him to escape; or

(b) has reasonable grounds for believing that they may be evidence relating to an offence.

(5) Where anything is seized, the person from whom it is seized shall be told the reason for the seizure unless he is—

(a) violent or likely to become violent; or

(b) incapable of understanding what is said to him.

(6) Subject to subsection (7) below, a person may be searched if the custody officer considers it necessary to enable him to carry out his duty under

subsection (1) above and to the extent that the custody officer considers necessary for that purpose.

(6A) A person who is in custody at a police station or is in police detention otherwise than at a police station may at any time be searched in order to ascertain whether he has with him anything which he could use for any of the purposes specified in subsection (4)(a) above.

(6B) Subject to subsection (6C) below, a constable may seize and retain, or cause to be seized and retained, anything found on such a search.

(6C) A constable may only seize clothes and personal effects in the circumstances specified in subsection (4) above.

(7) An intimate search may not be conducted under this section.

(8) A search under this section shall be carried out by a constable.

(9) The constable carrying out a search shall be of the same sex as the person searched.

54A   Searches and examination to ascertain identity

(1) If an officer of at least the rank of inspector authorises it, a person who is detained in a police station may be searched or examined, or both—

    (a) for the purpose of ascertaining whether he has any mark that would tend to identify him as a person involved in the commission of an offence; or

    (b) for the purpose of facilitating the ascertainment of his identity.

(2) An officer may only give an authorisation under subsection (1) for the purpose mentioned in paragraph (a) of that subsection if—

    (a) the appropriate consent to a search or examination that would reveal whether the mark in question exists has been withheld; or

    (b) it is not practicable to obtain such consent.

(3) An officer may only give an authorisation under subsection (1) in a case in which subsection (2) does not apply if—

    (a) the person in question has refused to identify himself; or

    (b) the officer has reasonable grounds for suspecting that that person is not who he claims to be.

(4) An officer may give an authorisation under subsection (1) orally or in writing but, if he gives it orally, he shall confirm it in writing as soon as is practicable.

(5) Any identifying mark found on a search or examination under this section may be photographed—

    (a) with the appropriate consent; or

    (b) if the appropriate consent is withheld or it is not practicable to obtain it, without it.

(6) Where a search or examination may be carried out under this section, or a photograph may be taken under this section, the only persons entitled

to carry out the search or examination, or to take the photograph, are constables.

(7) A person may not under this section carry out a search or examination of a person of the opposite sex or take a photograph of any part of the body of a person of the opposite sex.

(8) An intimate search may not be carried out under this section.

(9) A photograph taken under this section—

(a) may be used by, or disclosed to, any person for any purpose related to the prevention or detection of crime, the investigation of an offence or the conduct of a prosecution; and

(b) after being so used or disclosed, may be retained but may not be used or disclosed except for a purpose so related.

(10) In subsection (9)—

(a) the reference to crime includes a reference to any conduct which—

(i) constitutes one or more criminal offences (whether under the law of a part of the United Kingdom or of a country or territory outside the United Kingdom); or

(ii) is, or corresponds to, any conduct which, if it all took place in any one part of the United Kingdom, would constitute one or more criminal offences;

and

(b) the references to an investigation and to a prosecution include references, respectively, to any investigation outside the United Kingdom of any crime or suspected crime and to a prosecution brought in respect of any crime in a country or territory outside the United Kingdom.

(11) In this section—

(a) references to ascertaining a person's identity include references to showing that he is not a particular person; and

(b) references to taking a photograph include references to using any process by means of which a visual image may be produced, and references to photographing a person shall be construed accordingly.

(12) In this section 'mark' includes features and injuries; and a mark is an identifying mark for the purposes of this section if its existence in any person's case facilitates the ascertainment of his identity or his identification as a person involved in the commission of an offence.

(13) Nothing in this section applies to a person arrested under an extradition arrest power.

55—Intimate searches

(1) Subject to the following provisions of this section, if an officer of at least the rank of inspector has reasonable grounds for believing—

(a) that a person who has been arrested and is in police detention may have concealed on him anything which—

    (i) he could use to cause physical injury to himself or others; and

    (ii) he might so use while he is in police detention or in the custody of a court; or

(b) that such a person—

    (i) may have a Class A drug concealed on him; and

    (ii) was in possession of it with the appropriate criminal intent before his arrest,

he may authorise an intimate search of that person.

(2) An officer may not authorise an intimate search of a person for anything unless he has reasonable grounds for believing that it cannot be found without his being intimately searched.

(3) An officer may give an authorisation under subsection (1) above orally or in writing but, if he gives it orally, he shall confirm it in writing as soon as is practicable.

(3A) A drug offence search shall not be carried out unless the appropriate consent has been given in writing.

(3B) Where it is proposed that a drug offence search be carried out, an appropriate officer shall inform the person who is to be subject to it–
(a) of the giving of the authorisation for it; and

(b) of the grounds for giving the authorisation.

(4) An intimate search which is only a drug offence search shall be by way of examination by a suitably qualified person.

(5) Except as provided by subsection (4) above, an intimate search shall be by way of examination by a suitably qualified person unless an officer of at least the rank of inspector considers that this is not practicable.

(6) An intimate search which is not carried out as mentioned in subsection (5) above shall be carried out by a constable.

(7) A constable may not carry out an intimate search of a person of the opposite sex.

(8) No intimate search may be carried out except—
(a) at a police station;

(b) at a hospital;

(c) at a registered medical practitioner's surgery; or

(d) at some other place used for medical purposes.

(9) An intimate search which is only a drug offence search may not be carried out at a police station.

(10) If an intimate search of a person is carried out, the custody record relating to him shall state—

(a) which parts of his body were searched; and

(b) why they were searched.

(10A) If the intimate search is a drug offence search, the custody record relating to that person shall also state–

(a) the authorisation by virtue of which the search was carried out;

(b) the grounds for giving the authorisation; and

(c) the fact that the appropriate consent was given.

(11) The information required to be recorded by subsections (10) and (10A) above shall be recorded as soon as practicable after the completion of the search.

(12) The custody officer at a police station may seize and retain anything which is found on an intimate search of a person, or cause any such thing to be seized and retained—

(a) if he believes that the person from whom it is seized may use it—

(i)   to cause physical injury to himself or any other person;

(ii) to damage property;

(iii) to interfere with evidence; or

(iv) to assist him to escape; or

(b) if he has reasonable grounds for believing that it may be evidence relating to an offence.

(13) Where anything is seized under this section, the person from whom it is seized shall be told the reason for the seizure unless he is—

(a) violent or likely to become violent; or

(b) incapable of understanding what is said to him.

(13A) Where the appropriate consent to a drug offence search of any person was refused without good cause, in any proceedings against that person for an offence–

(a) the court, in determining whether there is a case to answer;

(b) a judge, in deciding whether to grant an application made by the accused under paragraph 2 of Schedule 3 to the Crime and Disorder Act 1998 (applications for dismissal); and

(c) the court or jury, in determining whether that person is guilty of the offence charged,

may draw such inferences from the refusal as appear proper.

(14) Every annual report—

(a) under section 22 of the Police Act 1996; or

(b) made by the Commissioner of Police of the Metropolis,

shall contain information about searches under this section which have been carried out in the area to which the report relates during the period to which it relates.

(15)   The information about such searches shall include—

    (a)   the total number of searches;

    (b)   the number of searches conducted by way of examination by a suitably qualified person;

    (c)   the number of searches not so conducted but conducted in the presence of such a person; and

    (d)   the result of the searches carried out.

(16)   The information shall also include, as separate items—

    (a)   the total number of drug offence searches; and

    (b)   the result of those searches.

(17)   In this section—

"the appropriate criminal intent" means an intent to commit an offence under—

    (a)   section 5(3) of the Misuse of Drugs Act 1971 (possession of controlled drug with intent to supply to another); or

    (b)   section 68(2) of the Customs and Excise Management Act 1979 (exportation etc. with intent to evade a prohibition or restriction);

"appropriate officer" means–

    (a)   a constable,

    (b)   a person who is designated as a detention officer in pursuance of section 38 of the Police Reform Act 2002 if his designation applies paragraph 33D of Schedule 4 to that Act, or

    (c)   a person who is designated as a staff custody officer in pursuance of section 38 of that Act if his designation applies paragraph 35C of Schedule 4 to that Act;

"Class A drug" has the meaning assigned to it by section 2(1)(b) of the Misuse of Drugs Act 1971;

"drug offence search" means an intimate search for a Class A drug which an officer has authorised by virtue of subsection (1)(b) above; and

"suitably qualified person" means —

    (a)   a registered medical practitioner; or

    (b)   a registered nurse.

55A   X-rays and ultrasound scans

(1)   If an officer of at least the rank of inspector has reasonable grounds for believing that a person who has been arrested for an offence and is in police detention–

    (a)   may have swallowed a Class A drug, and

    (b)   was in possession of it with the appropriate criminal intent before his arrest, the officer may authorise that an x-ray is taken of the person or an ultrasound scan is carried out on the person (or both).

(2) An x-ray must not be taken of a person and an ultrasound scan must not be carried out on him unless the appropriate consent has been given in writing.

(3) If it is proposed that an x-ray is taken or an ultrasound scan is carried out, an appropriate officer must inform the person who is to be subject to it–

(a) of the giving of the authorisation for it, and

(b) of the grounds for giving the authorisation.

(4) An x-ray may be taken or an ultrasound scan carried out only by a suitably qualified person and only at–

(a) a hospital,

(b) a registered medical practitioner's surgery, or

(c) some other place used for medical purposes.

(5) The custody record of the person must also state–

(a) the authorisation by virtue of which the x-ray was taken or the ultrasound scan was carried out,

(b) the grounds for giving the authorisation, and

(c) the fact that the appropriate consent was given.

(6) The information required to be recorded by subsection (5) must be recorded as soon as practicable after the x-ray has been taken or ultrasound scan carried out (as the case may be).

(7) Every annual report–

(a) under section 22 of the Police Act 1996, or

(b) made by the Commissioner of Police of the Metropolis,

must contain information about x-rays which have been taken and ultrasound scans which have been carried out under this section in the area to which the report relates during the period to which it relates.

(8) The information about such x-rays and ultrasound scans must be presented separately and must include–

(a) the total number of x-rays;

(b) the total number of ultrasound scans;

(c) the results of the x-rays;

(d) the results of the ultrasound scans.

(9) If the appropriate consent to an x-ray or ultrasound scan of any person is refused without good cause, in any proceedings against that person for an offence–

(a) the court, in determining whether there is a case to answer,

(b) a judge, in deciding whether to grant an application made by the accused under paragraph 2 of Schedule 3 to the Crime and Disorder Act 1998 (applications for dismissal), and

(c) the court or jury, in determining whether that person is guilty of the offence charged,

may draw such inferences from the refusal as appear proper.

(10) In this section "the appropriate criminal intent", "appropriate officer", "Class A drug" and "suitably qualified person" have the same meanings as in section 55 above.

56—Right to have someone informed when arrested

(1) Where a person has been arrested and is being held in custody in a police station or other premises, he shall be entitled, if he so requests, to have one friend or relative or other person who is known to him or who is likely to take an interest in his welfare told, as soon as is practicable except to the extent that delay is permitted by this section, that he has been arrested and is being detained there.

(2) Delay is only permitted—
(a) in the case of a person who is in police detention for an indictable offence; and
(b) if an officer of at least the rank of inspector authorises it.

(3) In any case the person in custody must be permitted to exercise the right conferred by subsection (1) above within 36 hours from the relevant time, as defined in section 41(2) above.

(4) An officer may give an authorisation under subsection (2) above orally or in writing but, if he gives it orally, he shall confirm it in writing as soon as is practicable.

(5) Subject to sub-section (5A) below an officer may only authorise delay where he has reasonable grounds for believing that telling the named person of the arrest—
(a) will lead to interference with or harm to evidence connected with an indictable offence or interference with or physical injury to other persons; or
(b) will lead to the alerting of other persons suspected of having committed such an offence but not yet arrested for it; or
(c) will hinder the recovery of any property obtained as a result of such an offence.

(5A) An officer may also authorise delay where he has reasonable grounds for believing that—
(a) the person detained for the indictable offence has benefited from his criminal conduct, and
(b) the recovery of the value of the property constituting the benefit will be hindered by telling the named person of the arrest.

(5B) For the purposes of subsection (5A) above the question whether a person has benefited from his criminal conduct is to be decided in accordance with Part 2 of the Proceeds of Crime Act 2002.

(6) If a delay is authorised—
  (a) the detained person shall be told the reason for it; and
  (b) the reason shall be noted on his custody record.

(7) The duties imposed by subsection (6) above shall be performed as soon as is practicable.

(8) The rights conferred by this section on a person detained at a police station or other premises are exercisable whenever he is transferred from one place to another; and this section applies to each subsequent occasion on which they are exercisable as it applies to the first such occasion.

(9) There may be no further delay in permitting the exercise of the right conferred by subsection (1) above once the reason for authorising delay ceases to subsist.

(10) Nothing in this section applies to a person arrested or detained under the terrorism provisions.

58—Access to legal advice

(1) A person arrested and held in custody in a police station or other premises shall be entitled, if he so requests, to consult a solicitor privately at any time.

(2) Subject to subsection (3) below, a request under subsection (1) above and the time at which it was made shall be recorded in the custody record.

(3) Such a request need not be recorded in the custody record of a person who makes it at a time while he is at a court after being charged with an offence.

(4) If a person makes such a request, he must be permitted to consult a solicitor as soon as is practicable except to the extent that delay is permitted by this section.

(5) In any case he must be permitted to consult a solicitor within 36 hours from the relevant time, as defined in section 41(2) above.

(6) Delay in compliance with a request is only permitted—
  (a) in the case of a person who is in police detention for an indictable offence; and
  (b) if an officer of at least the rank of superintendent authorises it.

(7) An officer may give an authorisation under subsection (6) above orally or in writing but, if he gives it orally, he shall confirm it in writing as soon as is practicable.

(8) Subject to sub-section (8A) below an officer may only authorise delay where he has reasonable grounds for believing that the exercise of the right conferred by subsection (1) above at the time when the person detained desires to exercise it—

    (a) will lead to interference with or harm to evidence connected with an indictable offence or interference with or physical injury to other persons; or

    (b) will lead to the alerting of other persons suspected of having committed such an offence but not yet arrested for it; or

    (c) will hinder the recovery of any property obtained as a result of such an offence.

(8A) An officer may also authorise delay where he has reasonable grounds for believing that—

    (a) the person detained for the indictable offence has benefited from his criminal conduct, and

    (b) the recovery of the value of the property constituting the benefit will be hindered by the exercise of the right conferred by subsection (1) above.

(8B) For the purposes of subsection (8A) above the question whether a person has benefited from his criminal conduct is to be decided in accordance with Part 2 of the Proceeds of Crime Act 2002.

(9) If delay is authorised—

    (a) the detained person shall be told the reason for it; and

    (b) the reason shall be noted on his custody record.

(10) The duties imposed by subsection (9) above shall be performed as soon as is practicable.

(11) There may be no further delay in permitting the exercise of the right conferred by subsection (1) above once the reason for authorising delay ceases to subsist.

(12) Nothing in this section applies to a person arrested or detained under the terrorism provisions.

60—Tape-recording of interviews

(1) It shall be the duty of the Secretary of State—

    (a) to issue a code of practice in connection with the tape-recording of interviews of persons suspected of the commission of criminal offences which are held by police officers at police stations; and

    (b) to make an order requiring the tape-recording of interviews of persons suspected of the commission of criminal offences, or of such descriptions of criminal offences as may be specified in the order, which are so held, in accordance with the code as it has effect for the time being.

(2) An order under subsection (1) above shall be made by statutory instrument and shall be subject to annulment in pursuance of a resolution of either House of Parliament.

60A   Visual recording of interviews

(1)   The Secretary of State shall have power–
- (a)   to issue a code of practice for the visual recording of interviews held by police officers at police stations; and
- (b)   to make an order requiring the visual recording of interviews so held, and requiring the visual recording to be in accordance with the code for the time being in force under this section.

(2)   A requirement imposed by an order under this section may be imposed in relation to such cases or police stations in such areas, or both, as may be specified or described in the order.

(3)   An order under subsection (1) above shall be made by statutory instrument and shall be subject to annulment in pursuance of a resolution of either House of Parliament.

(4)   In this section–
- (a)   references to any interview are references to an interview of a person suspected of a criminal offence; and
- (b)   references to a visual recording include references to a visual recording in which an audio recording is comprised.

61—Finger-printing

(1)   Except as provided by this section no person's fingerprints may be taken without the appropriate consent.

(2)   Consent to the taking of a person's fingerprints must be in writing if it is given at a time when he is at a police station.

(3)   The fingerprints of a person detained at a police station may be taken without the appropriate consent if—
- (a)   he is detained in consequence of his arrest for a recordable offence; and
- (b)   he has not had his fingerprints taken in the course of the investigation of the offence by the police.

(3A)   [Where a person mentioned in paragraph (a) of subsection (3) or (4) has already had his fingerprints taken in the course of the investigation of the offence by the police, that fact shall be disregarded for the purposes of that subsection if–
- (a)   the fingerprints taken on the previous occasion do not constitute a complete set of his fingerprints; or
- (b)   some or all of the fingerprints taken on the previous occasion are not of sufficient quality to allow satisfactory analysis, comparison or matching (whether in the case in question or generally).

(4)   The fingerprints of a person detained at a police station may be taken without the appropriate consent if—
- (a)   he has been charged with a recordable offence or informed that he will be reported for such an offence; and

(b)   he has not had his fingerprints taken in the course of the investigation of the offence by the police.

(4A)   The fingerprints of a person who has answered to bail at a court or police station may be taken without the appropriate consent at the court or station if–

(a)   the court, or

(b)   an officer of at least the rank of inspector,

authorises them to be taken.

(4B)   A court or officer may only give an authorisation under subsection (4A) if–

(a)   the person who has answered to bail has answered to it for a person whose fingerprints were taken on a previous occasion and there are reasonable grounds for believing that he is not the same person; or

(b)   the person who has answered to bail claims to be a different person from a person whose fingerprints were taken on a previous occasion.

(5)   An officer may give an authorisation under [subsection (4A)] above orally or in writing but, if he gives it orally, he shall confirm it in writing as soon as is practicable.

(6)   Any person's fingerprints may be taken without the appropriate consent if —

(a)   he has been convicted of a recordable offence;

(b)   he has been given a caution in respect of a recordable offence which, at the time of the caution, he has admitted; or

(c)   he has been warned or reprimanded under section 65 of the Crime and Disorder Act 1998 (c. 37) for a recordable offence.

(7)   In a case where by virtue of subsection (3), (4) or (6) above a person's fingerprints are taken without the appropriate consent—

(a)   he shall be told the reason before his fingerprints are taken; and

(b)   the reason shall be recorded as soon as is practicable after the fingerprints are taken.

(7A)   If a person's fingerprints are taken at a police station, whether with or without the appropriate consent—

(a)   before the fingerprints are taken, an officer shall inform him that they may be the subject of a speculative search; and

(b)   the fact that the person has been informed of this possibility shall be recorded as soon as is practicable after the fingerprints have been taken.

(8)   If he is detained at a police station when the fingerprints are taken, the reason for taking them and, in the case falling within subsection (7A) above, the fact referred to in paragraph (b) of that subsection shall be recorded on his custody record.

(8B)   The power to take the fingerprints of a person detained at a police station without the appropriate consent shall be exercisable by any constable.

(9)   Nothing in this section—

(a)   affects any power conferred by paragraph 18(2) of Schedule 2 to the Immigration Act 1971; or

(b)   applies to a person arrested or detained under the terrorism provisions.

(10)   Nothing in this section applies to a person arrested under an extradition arrest power.

61A   Impressions of footwear

(1)   Except as provided by this section, no impression of a person's footwear may be taken without the appropriate consent.

(2)   Consent to the taking of an impression of a person's footwear must be in writing if it is given at a time when he is at a police station.

(3)   Where a person is detained at a police station, an impression of his footwear may be taken without the appropriate consent if—

(a)   he is detained in consequence of his arrest for a recordable offence, or has been charged with a recordable offence, or informed that he will be reported for a recordable offence; and

(b)   he has not had an impression taken of his footwear in the course of the investigation of the offence by the police.

(4)   Where a person mentioned in paragraph (a) of subsection (3) above has already had an impression taken of his footwear in the course of the investigation of the offence by the police, that fact shall be disregarded for the purposes of that subsection if the impression of his footwear taken previously is—

(a)   incomplete; or

(b)   is not of sufficient quality to allow satisfactory analysis, comparison or matching (whether in the case in question or generally).

(5)   If an impression of a person's footwear is taken at a police station, whether with or without the appropriate consent—

(a)   before it is taken, an officer shall inform him that it may be the subject of a speculative search; and

(b)   the fact that the person has been informed of this possibility shall be recorded as soon as is practicable after the impression has been taken, and if he is detained at a police station, the record shall be made on his custody record.

(6)   In a case where, by virtue of subsection (3) above, an impression of a person's footwear is taken without the appropriate consent—

(a)   he shall be told the reason before it is taken; and

(b)   the reason shall be recorded on his custody record as soon as is practicable after the impression is taken.

(7) The power to take an impression of the footwear of a person detained at a police station without the appropriate consent shall be exercisable by any constable.

(8) Nothing in this section applies to any person—

(a)   arrested or detained under the terrorism provisions;

(b)   arrested under an extradition arrest power.

62—Intimate samples

(1) Subject to section 63B below an intimate sample may be taken from a person in police detention only—

(a)   if a police officer of at least the rank of inspector authorises it to be taken; and

(b)   if the appropriate consent is given.

(1A)   An intimate sample may be taken from a person who is not in police detention but from whom, in the course of the investigation of an offence, two or more non-intimate samples suitable for the same means of analysis have been taken which have proved insufficient—

(a)   if a police officer of at least the rank of inspector authorises it to be taken; and

(b)   if the appropriate consent is given.

(2) An officer may only give an authorisation under subsection (1) or (1A) above if he has reasonable grounds—

(a)   for suspecting the involvement of the person from whom the sample is to be taken in a recordable offence; and

(b)   for believing that the sample will tend to confirm or disprove his involvement.

(3) An officer may give an authorisation under subsection (1) or (1A) above orally or in writing but, if he gives it orally, he shall confirm it in writing as soon as is practicable.

(4) The appropriate consent must be given in writing.

(5) Where—

(a)   an authorisation has been given; and

(b)   it is proposed that an intimate sample shall be taken in pursuance of the authorisation,

an officer shall inform the person from whom the sample is to be taken—

(i)   of the giving of the authorisation; and

(ii) of the grounds for giving it.

(6) The duty imposed by subsection (5)(ii) above includes a duty to state the nature of the offence in which it is suspected that the person from whom the sample is to be taken has been involved.

(7) If an intimate sample is taken from a person—

  (a) the authorisation by virtue of which it was taken;

  (b) the grounds for giving the authorisation; and

  (c) the fact that the appropriate consent was given,

shall be recorded as soon as is practicable after the sample is taken.

(7A) If an intimate sample is taken from a person at a police station—

  (a) before the sample is taken, an officer shall inform him that it may be the subject of a speculative search; and

  (b) the fact that the person has been informed of this possibility shall be recorded as soon as practicable after the sample has been taken.

(8) If an intimate sample is taken from a person detained at a police station, the matters required to be recorded by subsection (7) or (7A) above shall be recorded in his custody record.

(9) In the case of an intimate sample which is a dental impression, the sample may be taken from a person only by a registered dentist.

(9A) In the case of any other form of intimate sample, except in the case of a sample of urine, the sample may be taken from a person only by—

  (a) a registered medical practitioner; or

  (b) a registered health care professional.

(10) Where the appropriate consent to the taking of an intimate sample from a person was refused without good cause, in any proceedings against that person for an offence—

  (a) the court, in determining—

    (i) whether to commit that person for trial; or

    (ii) whether there is a case to answer; and

  (aa) a judge, in deciding whether to grant an application made by the accused under [paragraph 2 of Schedule 3 to the Crime and Disorder Act 1998 (applications for dismissal); and

  (b) the court or jury, in determining whether that person is guilty of the offence charged,

may draw such inferences from the refusal as appear proper.

(11) Nothing in this section applies to the taking of a specimen for the purposes of any of the provisions of sections 4 to 11 of the Road Traffic Act 1988 or of sections 26 to 38 of the Transport and Works Act 1992.

(12) Nothing in this section applies to a person arrested or detained under the terrorism provisions; and subsection (1A) shall not apply where the non-intimate samples mentioned in that subsection were taken under paragraph 10 of Schedule 8 to the Terrorism Act 2000.

63—Other samples

(1) Except as provided by this section, a non-intimate sample may not be taken from a person without the appropriate consent.

(2) Consent to the taking of a non-intimate sample must be given in writing.

(2A)   A non-intimate sample may be taken from a person without the appropriate consent if two conditions are satisfied.

(2B)   The first is that the person is in police detention in consequence of his arrest for a recordable offence.

(2C)   The second is that—

    (a) he has not had a non-intimate sample of the same type and from the same part of the body taken in the course of the investigation of the offence by the police, or

    (b) he has had such a sample taken but it proved insufficient.

(3) A non-intimate sample may be taken from a person without the appropriate consent if—

    (a) he is being held in custody by the police on the authority of a court; and

    (b) an officer of at least the rank of inspector authorises it to be taken without the appropriate consent.

(3A)   A non-intimate sample may be taken from a person (whether or not he is in police detention or held in custody by the police on the authority of a court) without the appropriate consent if—

    (a) he has been charged with a recordable offence or informed that he will be reported for such an offence; and

    (b) either he has not had a non-intimate sample taken from him in the course of the investigation of the offence by the police or he had a non-intimate sample taken from him but either it was not suitable for the same means of analysis or, though so suitable, the sample proved insufficient.

(3B)   A non-intimate sample may be taken from a person without the appropriate consent if he has been convicted of a recordable offence.

(3C)   A non-intimate sample may also be taken from a person without the appropriate consent if he is a person to whom section 2 of the Criminal Evidence (Amendment) Act 1997 applies (persons detained following acquittal on grounds of insanity or finding of unfitness to plead).

(4) An officer may only give an authorisation under subsection (3) above if he has reasonable grounds—

    (a) for suspecting the involvement of the person from whom the sample is to be taken in a recordable offence; and

    (b) for believing that the sample will tend to confirm or disprove his involvement.

(5) An officer may give an authorisation under subsection (3) above orally or in writing but, if he gives it orally, he shall confirm it in writing as soon as is practicable.

(5A) An officer shall not give an authorisation under subsection (3) above for the taking from any person of a non-intimate sample consisting of a skin impression if–

(a) a skin impression of the same part of the body has already been taken from that person in the course of the investigation of the offence; and

(b) the impression previously taken is not one that has proved insufficient.

(6) Where—

(a) an authorisation has been given; and

(b) it is proposed that a non-intimate sample shall be taken in pursuance of the authorisation,

an officer shall inform the person from whom the sample is to be taken—

(i) of the giving of the authorisation; and

(ii) of the grounds for giving it.

(7) The duty imposed by subsection (6)(ii) above includes a duty to state the nature of the offence in which it is suspected that the person from whom the sample is to be taken has been involved.

(8) If a non-intimate sample is taken from a person by virtue of subsection (3) above—

(a) the authorisation by virtue of which it was taken; and

(b) the grounds for giving the authorisation,

shall be recorded as soon as is practicable after the sample is taken.

(8A) In a case where by virtue of subsection (2A), (3A), (3B) or (3C) above a sample is taken from a person without the appropriate consent—

(a) he shall be told the reason before the sample is taken; and

(b) the reason shall be recorded as soon as practicable after the sample is taken.

(8B) If a non-intimate sample is taken from a person at a police station, whether with or without the appropriate consent—

(a) before the sample is taken, an officer shall inform him that it may be the subject of a speculative search; and

(b) the fact that the person has been informed of this possibility shall be recorded as soon as practicable after the sample has been taken.

(9) If a non-intimate sample is taken from a person detained at a police station, the matters required to be recorded by subsection (8) or (8A) or (8B) above shall be recorded in his custody record.

(9ZA) The power to take a non-intimate sample from a person without the appropriate consent shall be exercisable by any constable.

(9A) Subsection (3B) above shall not apply to any person convicted before 10th April 1995 unless he is a person to whom section 1 of the Criminal

Evidence (Amendment) Act 1997 applies (persons imprisoned or detained by virtue of pre-existing conviction for sexual offence etc.).

(10)   Nothing in this section applies to a person arrested or detained under the terrorism provisions.

(11)   Nothing in this section applies to a person arrested under an extradition arrest power.

63B—Testing for presence of Class A drugs

(1) A sample of urine or a non-intimate sample may be taken from a person in police detention for the purpose of ascertaining whether he has any specified Class A drug in his body if—
(a)   either the arrest condition or the charge condition is met;
(b)   both the age condition and the request condition are met; and
(c)   the notification condition is met in relation to the arrest condition, the charge condition or the age condition (as the case may be).

(1A)   The arrest condition is that the person concerned has been arrested for an offence but has not been charged with that offence and either–
(a)   the offence is a trigger offence; or
(b)   a police officer of at least the rank of inspector has reasonable grounds for suspecting that the misuse by that person of a specified Class A drug caused or contributed to the offence and has authorised the sample to be taken.

(2) [The charge condition is either —
(a)   that the person concerned has been charged with a trigger offence; or
(b)   that the person concerned has been charged with an offence and a police officer of at least the rank of inspector, who has reasonable grounds for suspecting that the misuse by that person of any specified Class A drug caused or contributed to the offence, has authorised the sample to be taken.

(3) The age condition is–
(a)   if the arrest condition is met, that the person concerned has attained the age of 18;
(b)   if the charge condition is met, that he has attained the age of 14.

(4) The request condition is that a police officer has requested the person concerned to give the sample.

(4A)   The notification condition is that–
(a)   the relevant chief officer has been notified by the Secretary of State that appropriate arrangements have been made for the police area as a whole, or for the particular police station, in which the person is in police detention, and
(b)   the notice has not been withdrawn.

(4B)   For the purposes of subsection (4A) above, appropriate arrangements are arrangements for the taking of samples under this section from whichever of the following is specified in the notification–

(a)   persons in respect of whom the arrest condition is met;

(b)   persons in respect of whom the charge condition is met;

(c)   persons who have not attained the age of 18.

(5)   Before requesting the person concerned to give a sample, an officer must—

(a)   warn him that if, when so requested, he fails without good cause to do so he may be liable to prosecution, and

(b)   in a case within subsection (1A)(b) or (2)(b) above, inform him of the giving of the authorisation and of the grounds in question.

(5A)   In the case of a person who has not attained the age of 17—

(a)   the making of the request under subsection (4) above;

(b)   the giving of the warning and (where applicable) the information under subsection (5) above; and

(c)   the taking of the sample,

may not take place except in the presence of an appropriate adult.

(5B)   If a sample is taken under this section from a person in respect of whom the arrest condition is met no other sample may be taken from him under this section during the same continuous period of detention but–

(a)   if the charge condition is also met in respect of him at any time during that period, the sample must be treated as a sample taken by virtue of the fact that the charge condition is met;

(b)   the fact that the sample is to be so treated must be recorded in the person's custody record.

(5C)   Despite subsection (1)(a) above, a sample may be taken from a person under this section if–

(a)   he was arrested for an offence (the first offence),

(b)   the arrest condition is met but the charge condition is not met,

(c)   before a sample is taken by virtue of subsection (1) above he would (but for his arrest as mentioned in paragraph (d) below) be required to be released from police detention,

(d)   he continues to be in police detention by virtue of his having been arrested for an offence not falling within subsection (1A) above, and

(e)   the sample is taken before the end of the period of 24 hours starting with the time when his detention by virtue of his arrest for the first offence began.

(5D)   A sample must not be taken from a person under this section if he is detained in a police station unless he has been brought before the custody officer.

(6) A sample may be taken under this section only by a person prescribed by regulations made by the Secretary of State by statutory instrument.

No regulations shall be made under this subsection unless a draft has been laid before, and approved by resolution of, each House of Parliament.

(6A) The Secretary of State may by order made by statutory instrument amend–

(a) paragraph (a) of subsection (3) above, by substituting for the age for the time being specified a different age specified in the order, or different ages so specified for different police areas so specified;

(b) paragraph (b) of that subsection, by substituting for the age for the time being specified a different age specified in the order.

(6B) A statutory instrument containing an order under subsection (6A) above shall not be made unless a draft of the instrument has been laid before, and approved by a resolution of, each House of Parliament.

(7) Information obtained from a sample taken under this section may be disclosed—

(a) for the purpose of informing any decision about granting bail in criminal proceedings (within the meaning of the Bail Act 1976) to the person concerned;

(aa) for the purpose of informing any decision about the giving of a conditional caution under Part 3 of the Criminal Justice Act 2003 to the person concerned;

(b) where the person concerned is in police detention or is remanded in or committed to custody by an order of a court or has been granted such bail, for the purpose of informing any decision about his supervision;

(c) where the person concerned is convicted of an offence, for the purpose of informing any decision about the appropriate sentence to be passed by a court and any decision about his supervision or release;

(ca) for the purpose of an assessment which the person concerned is required to attend by virtue of section 9(2) or 10(2) of the Drugs Act 2005;

(cb) for the purpose of proceedings against the person concerned for an offence under section 12(3) or 14(3) of that Act;

(d) for the purpose of ensuring that appropriate advice and treatment is made available to the person concerned.

(8) A person who fails without good cause to give any sample which may be taken from him under this section shall be guilty of an offence.

(10) In this section—

"appropriate adult", in relation to a person who has not attained the age of 17, means—

(a) his parent or guardian or, if he is in the care of a local authority or voluntary organisation, a person representing that authority or organisation; or

(b) a social worker of a local authority; or

(c) if no person falling within paragraph (a) or (b) is available, any responsible person aged 18 or over who is not a police officer or a person employed by the police;

"relevant chief officer" means—

(a) in relation to a police area, the chief officer of police of the police force for that police area; or

(b) in relation to a police station, the chief officer of police of the police force for the police area in which the police station is situated.

64—Destruction of fingerprints and samples

(1A) Where–

(a) fingerprints, impressions of footwear or samples are taken from a person in connection with the investigation of an offence, and

(b) subsection (3) below does not require them to be destroyed,

the fingerprints, impressions of footwear or samples may be retained after they have fulfilled the purposes for which they were taken but shall not be used by any person except for purposes related to the prevention or detection of crime, the investigation of an offence, the conduct of a prosecution or the identification of a deceased person or of the person from whom a body part came.

(1B) In subsection (1A) above–

(a) the reference to using a fingerprint or an impression of footwear includes a reference to allowing any check to be made against it under section 63A(1) or (1C) above and to disclosing it to any person;

(b) the reference to using a sample includes a reference to allowing any check to be made under section 63A(1) or (1C) above against it or against information derived from it and to disclosing it or any such information to any person;

(c) the reference to crime includes a reference to any conduct which–

(i) constitutes one or more criminal offences (whether under the law of a part of the United Kingdom or of a country or territory outside the United Kingdom); or

(ii) is, or corresponds to, any conduct which, if it all took place in any one part of the United Kingdom, would constitute one or more criminal offences;

and

(d) the references to an investigation and to a prosecution include references, respectively, to any investigation outside the United Kingdom of any crime or suspected crime and to a prosecution brought in respect of any crime in a country or territory outside the United Kingdom.

(3) If—

(a) fingerprints, impressions of footwear or samples are taken from a person in connection with the investigation of an offence; and

(b) that person is not suspected of having committed the offence,

they must, except as provided in the following provisions of this section below, be destroyed as soon as they have fulfilled the purpose for which they were taken.

(3AA) Samples, fingerprints and impressions of footwear are not required to be destroyed under subsection (3) above if–

(a) they were taken for the purposes of the investigation of an offence of which a person has been convicted; and

(b) a sample, fingerprint, (or as the case may be) an impression of footwear was also taken from the convicted person for the purposes of that investigation.

(3AB) Subject to subsection (3AC) below, where a person is entitled under subsection (3) above to the destruction of any fingerprint, impression of footwear or sample taken from him (or would be but for subsection (3AA) above), neither the fingerprint, nor the impression of footwear, nor the sample, nor any information derived from the sample, shall be used–

(a) in evidence against the person who is or would be entitled to the destruction of that fingerprint, impression of footwear or sample; or

(b) for the purposes of the investigation of any offence;

and subsection (1B) above applies for the purposes of this subsection as it applies for the purposes of subsection (1A) above.

(3AC) Where a person from whom a fingerprint, impression of footwear or sample has been taken consents in writing to its retention–

(a) that sample need not be destroyed under subsection (3) above;

(b) subsection (3AB) above shall not restrict the use that may be made of the fingerprint, impression of footwear or sample or, in the case of a sample, of any information derived from it; and

(c) that consent shall be treated as comprising a consent for the purposes of section 63A(1C) above;

and a consent given for the purpose of this subsection shall not be capable of being withdrawn.

(3AD) For the purposes of subsection (3AC) above it shall be immaterial whether the consent is given at, before or after the time when the entitlement to the destruction of the fingerprint, impression of footwear or sample arises.

(5) If fingerprints or impressions of footwear are destroyed—

   (a) any copies of the fingerprints or impressions of footwear shall also be destroyed; and

   (b) any chief officer of police controlling access to computer data relating to the fingerprints or impressions of footwear shall make access to the data impossible, as soon as it is practicable to do so.

(6) A person who asks to be allowed to witness the destruction of his fingerprints or impressions of footwear or copies of them shall have a right to witness it.

(6A) If—

   (a) subsection (5)(b) above falls to be complied with; and

   (b) the person to whose fingerprints or impressions of footwear the data relate asks for a certificate that it has been complied with,

   such a certificate shall be issued to him, not later than the end of the period of three months beginning with the day on which he asks for it, by the responsible chief officer of police or a person authorised by him or on his behalf for the purposes of this section.

(6B) In this section—

   "the responsible chief officer of police" means the chief officer of police in whose police area the computer data were put on to the computer.

(7) Nothing in this section—

   (a) affects any power conferred by paragraph 18(2) of Schedule 2 to the Immigration Act 1971 or section 20 of the Immigration and Asylum Act 1999 (c. 33) (disclosure of police information to the Secretary of State for use for immigration purposes); or

   (b) applies to a person arrested or detained under the terrorism provisions.

64A   Photographing of suspects etc

(1) A person who is detained at a police station may be photographed—

   (a) with the appropriate consent; or

   (b) if the appropriate consent is withheld or it is not practicable to obtain it, without it.

(1A) A person falling within subsection (1B) below may, on the occasion of the relevant event referred to in subsection (1B), be photographed elsewhere than at a police station—

   (a) with the appropriate consent; or

   (b) if the appropriate consent is withheld or it is not practicable to obtain it, without it.

(1B) A person falls within this subsection if he has been—

   (a) arrested by a constable for an offence;

(b)   taken into custody by a constable after being arrested for an offence by a person other than a constable;

(c)   made subject to a requirement to wait with a community support officer under paragraph 2(3) or (3B) of Schedule 4 to the Police Reform Act 2002 ("the 2002 Act");

(ca) given a direction by a constable under section 27 of the Violent Crime Reduction Act 2006;

(d)   given a penalty notice by a constable in uniform under Chapter 1 of Part 1 of the Criminal Justice and Police Act 2001, a penalty notice by a constable under section 444A of the Education Act 1996, or a fixed penalty notice by a constable in uniform under section 54 of the Road Traffic Offenders Act 1988;

(e)   given a notice in relation to a relevant fixed penalty offence (within the meaning of paragraph 1 of Schedule 4 to the 2002 Act) by a community support officer by virtue of a designation applying that paragraph to him;

(f)   given a notice in relation to a relevant fixed penalty offence (within the meaning of paragraph 1 of Schedule 5 to the 2002 Act) by an accredited person by virtue of accreditation specifying that that paragraph applies to him; or

(g)   given a notice in relation to a relevant fixed penalty offence (within the meaning of Schedule 5A to the 2002 Act) by an accredited inspector by virtue of accreditation specifying that paragraph 1 of Schedule 5A to the 2002 Act applies to him.

(2) A person proposing to take a photograph of any person under this section—

(a)   may, for the purpose of doing so, require the removal of any item or substance worn on or over the whole or any part of the head or face of the person to be photographed; and

(b)   if the requirement is not complied with, may remove the item or substance himself.

(3) Where a photograph may be taken under this section, the only persons entitled to take the photograph are constables.

(4) A photograph taken under this section—

(a)   may be used by, or disclosed to, any person for any purpose related to the prevention or detection of crime, the investigation of an offence or the conduct of a prosecution or to the enforcement of a sentence; and

(b)   after being so used or disclosed, may be retained but may not be used or disclosed except for a purpose so related.

(5) In subsection (4)—

(a)   the reference to crime includes a reference to any conduct which—

(i) constitutes one or more criminal offences (whether under the law of a part of the United Kingdom or of a country or territory outside the United Kingdom); or

(ii) is, or corresponds to, any conduct which, if it all took place in any one part of the United Kingdom, would constitute one or more criminal offences;

and

(b) the references to an investigation and to a prosecution include references, respectively, to any investigation outside the United Kingdom of any crime or suspected crime and to a prosecution brought in respect of any crime in a country or territory outside the United Kingdom; and

(c) "sentence" includes any order made by a court in England and Wales when dealing with an offender in respect of his offence.

(6) References in this section to taking a photograph include references to using any process by means of which a visual image may be produced; and references to photographing a person shall be construed accordingly.

(6A) In this section, a "photograph" includes a moving image, and corresponding expressions shall be construed accordingly.

(7) Nothing in this section applies to a person arrested under an extradition arrest power.

65 Part V—supplementary

(1) In this Part of this Act—

"analysis", in relation to a skin impression, includes comparison and matching; "appropriate consent" means —

(a) in relation to a person who has attained the age of 17 years, the consent of that person;

(b) in relation to a person who has not attained that age but has attained the age of 14 years, the consent of that person and his parent or guardian; and

(c) in relation to a person who has not attained the age of 14 years, the consent of his parent or guardian;

"extradition arrest power" means any of the following—

(a) a Part 1 warrant (within the meaning given by the Extradition Act 2003) in respect of which a certificate under section 2 of that Act has been issued;

(b) section 5 of that Act;

(c) a warrant issued under section 71 of that Act;

(d) a provisional warrant (within the meaning given by that Act);

"fingerprints", in relation to any person, means a record (in any form and produced by any method) of the skin pattern and other physical characteristics or features of–

(a) any of that person's fingers; or

(b) either of his palms;

"intimate sample" means—

(a) a sample of blood, semen or any other tissue fluid, urine or pubic hair;

(b) a dental impression;

(c) a swab taken from any part of a person's genitals (including pubic hair) or from a person's body orifice other than the mouth;

"intimate search" means a search which consists of the physical examination of a person's body orifices other than the mouth;

"non-intimate sample" means—

(a) a sample of hair other than pubic hair;

(b) a sample taken from a nail on from under a nail;

(c) a swab taken from any part of a person's body other than a part from which a swab taken would be an intimate sample;

(d) saliva;

(e) a skin impression;

"registered dentist" has the same meaning as in the Dentists Act 1984;

"skin impression", in relation to any person, means any record (other than a fingerprint) which is a record (in any form and produced by any method) of the skin pattern and other physical characteristics or features of the whole or any part of his foot or of any other part of his body;

"registered health care professional" means a person (other than a medical practitioner) who is—

(a) a registered nurse; or

(b) a registered member of a health care profession which is designated for the purposes of this paragraph by an order made by the Secretary of State;

"speculative search", in relation to a person's fingerprints or samples, means such a check against other fingerprints or samples or against information derived from other samples as is referred to in section 63A(1) above;

"sufficient" and "insufficient", in relation to a sample, means (subject to subsection (2) below) sufficient or insufficient (in point of quantity or quality) for the purpose of enabling information to be produced by the means of analysis used or to be used in relation to the sample.

"the terrorism provisions" means section 41 of the Terrorism Act 2000, and any provision of Schedule 7 to that Act conferring a power of detention; and

"terrorism" has the meaning given in section 1 of that Act.

(1A)   A health care profession is any profession mentioned in section 60(2) of the Health Act 1999 (c. 8) other than the profession of practising medicine and the profession of nursing.

(1B)   An order under subsection (1) shall be made by statutory instrument and shall be subject to annulment in pursuance of a resolution of either House of Parliament.

(2)   References in this Part of this Act to a sample's proving insufficient include references to where, as a consequence of–
   (a)   the loss, destruction or contamination of the whole or any part of the sample,
   (b)   any damage to the whole or a part of the sample, or
   (c)   the use of the whole or a part of the sample for an analysis which produced no results or which produced results some or all of which must be regarded, in the circumstances, as unreliable,

the sample has become unavailable or insufficient for the purpose of enabling information, or information of a particular description, to be obtained by means of analysis of the sample.

PART VI
CODES OF PRACTICE—GENERAL

66   Codes of practice

(1)   The Secretary of State shall issue codes of practice in connection with—
   (a)   the exercise by police officers of statutory powers—
      (i)   to search a person without first arresting him;
      (ii)   to search a vehicle without making an arrest;

      or

      (iii) to arrest a person;
   (b)   the detention, treatment, questioning and identification of persons by police officers;
   (c)   searches of premises by police officers; and
   (d)   the seizure of property found by police officers on persons or premises.

(2)   Codes shall (in particular) include provision in connection with the exercise by police officers of powers under section 63B above.

67—Codes of practice—supplementary

(1) In this section, "code" means a code of practice under section 60, 60A or 66.

(2) The Secretary of State may at any time revise the whole or any part of a code.

(3) A code may be made, or revised, so as to—
   (a) apply only in relation to one or more specified areas,
   (b) have effect only for a specified period,
   (c) apply only in relation to specified offences or descriptions of offender.

(4) Before issuing a code, or any revision of a code, the Secretary of State must consult—
   (a) the Association of Police Authorities,
   (b) the Association of Chief Police Officers of England, Wales and Northern Ireland,
   (c) the General Council of the Bar,
   (d) the Law Society of England and Wales,
   (e) the Institute of Legal Executives, and
   (f) such other persons as he thinks fit.

(5) A code, or a revision of a code, does not come into operation until the Secretary of State by order so provides.

(6) The power conferred by subsection (5) is exercisable by statutory instrument.

(7) An order bringing a code into operation may not be made unless a draft of the order has been laid before Parliament and approved by a resolution of each House.

(7A) An order bringing a revision of a code into operation must be laid before Parliament if the order has been made without a draft having been so laid and approved by a resolution of each House.

(7B) When an order or draft of an order is laid, the code or revision of a code to which it relates must also be laid.

(7C) No order or draft of an order may be laid until the consultation required by subsection (4) has taken place.

(7D) An order bringing a code, or a revision of a code, into operation may include transitional or saving provisions.

(9) Persons other than police officers who are charged with the duty of investigating offences or charging offenders shall in the discharge of that duty have regard to any relevant provision of a code.

(9A) Persons on whom powers are conferred by—
   (a) any designation under section 38 or 39 of the Police Reform Act 2002 (c. 30) (police powers for police authority employees), or

(b)   any accreditation under section 41 of that Act (accreditation under community safety accreditation schemes),

shall have regard to any relevant provision of a code in the exercise or performance of the powers and duties conferred or imposed on them by that designation or accreditation.

(10)   A failure on the part—

(a)   of a police officer to comply with any provision of a code;

(b)   of any person other than a police officer who is charged with the duty of investigating offences or charging offenders to have regard to any relevant provision of a code in the discharge of that duty, or

(c)   of a person designated under section 38 or 39 or accredited under section 41 of the Police Reform Act 2002 (c. 30) to have regard to any relevant provision of a code in the exercise or performance of the powers and duties conferred or imposed on him by that designation or accreditation.

shall not of itself render him liable to any criminal or civil proceedings.

(11)   In all criminal and civil proceedings any code shall be admissible in evidence; and if any provision of a code appears to the court or tribunal conducting the proceedings to be relevant to any question arising in the proceedings it shall be taken into account in determining that question.

(12)   In this section "criminal proceedings" includes—

(a)   proceedings in the United Kingdom or elsewhere before a court-martial constituted under the Army Act 1955, the Air Force Act 1955 or the Naval Discipline Act 1957;

(b)   proceedings before the Courts-Martial Appeal Court;

and

(c)   proceedings before a Standing Civilian Court.

PART VII
DOCUMENTARY EVIDENCE IN CRIMINAL PROCEEDINGS

71   Microfilm copies

In any proceedings the contents of a document may (whether or not the document is still in existence) be proved by the production of an enlargement of a microfilm copy of that document or of the material part of it, authenticated in such manner as the court may approve. Where the proceedings concerned are proceedings before a magistrates' court inquiring into an offence as examining justices this section shall have effect with the omission of the words "authenticated in such manner as the court may approve."

72—Part VII—supplementary

(1) In this Part of this Act—

'copy', in relation to a document, means anything onto which information recorded in the document has been copied, by whatever means and whether directly or indirectly and 'statement' means any representation of fact, however made; and

"proceedings" means criminal proceedings, including—

(a) proceedings in the United Kingdom or elsewhere before a court martial constituted under the Army Act 1955, the Air Force Act 1955 or the Naval Discipline Act 1957;

(b) proceedings in the United Kingdom or elsewhere before the Courts-Martial Appeal Court—

    (i) on an appeal from a court-martial so constituted; or

    (ii) on a reference under section 34 of the Courts-Martial (Appeals) Act 1968; and

(c) proceedings before a Standing Civilian Court.

(2) Nothing in this Part of this Act shall prejudice any power of a court to exclude evidence (whether by preventing questions from being put or otherwise) at its discretion.

PART VIII
EVIDENCE IN CRIMINAL PROCEEDINGS—GENERAL

Convictions and acquittals

73—Proof of convictions and acquittals

(1) Where in any proceedings the fact that a person has in the United Kingdom been convicted or acquitted of an offence otherwise than by a Service court is admissible in evidence, it may be proved by producing a certificate of conviction or, as the case may be, of acquittal relating to that offence, and proving that the person named in the certificate as having been convicted or acquitted of the offence is the person whose conviction or acquittal of the offence is to be proved.

(2) For the purposes of this section a certificate of conviction or of acquittal—

(a) shall, as regards a conviction or acquittal on indictment, consist of a certificate, signed by the proper officer of the court where the conviction or acquittal took place, giving the substance and effect (omitting the formal parts) of the indictment and of the conviction or acquittal; and

(b) shall, as regards a conviction or acquittal on a summary trial, consist of a copy of the conviction or of the dismissal of the information, signed by the of the court where the conviction or acquittal took place or by the [proper officer] of the court, if any, to which a memorandum of the conviction or acquittal was sent;

and a document purporting to be a duly signed certificate of conviction or acquittal under this section shall be taken to be such a certificate unless the contrary is proved.

(3) In subsection (2) above "proper officer" means—

(a) in relation to a magistrates' court in England and Wales, the [designated officer] for the court; and

(b) in relation to any other court, the clerk of the court, his deputy or any other person having custody of the court record.

(4) The method of proving a conviction or acquittal authorised by this section shall be in addition to and not to the exclusion of any other authorised manner of proving a conviction or acquittal.

74—Conviction as evidence of commission of offence

(1) In any proceedings the fact that a person other than the accused has been convicted of an offence by or before any court in the United Kingdom or by a Service court outside the United Kingdom shall be admissible in evidence for the purpose of proving that that person committed that offence, where evidence of his having done so is admissible, whether or not any other evidence of his having committed that offence is given.

(2) In any proceedings in which by virtue of this section a person other than the accused is proved to have been convicted of an offence by or before any court in the United Kingdom or by a Service court outside the United Kingdom, he shall be taken to have committed that offence unless the contrary is proved.

(3) In any proceedings where evidence is admissible of the fact that the accused has committed an offence, if the accused is proved to have been convicted of the offence—

(a) by or before any court in the United Kingdom; or

(b) by a Service court outside the United Kingdom,

he shall be taken to have committed that offence unless the contrary is proved.

(4) Nothing in this section shall prejudice—

(a) the admissibility in evidence of any conviction which would be admissible apart from this section; or

(b) the operation of any enactment whereby a conviction or a finding of fact in any proceedings is for the purposes of any other proceedings made conclusive evidence of any fact.

75—Provisions supplementary to section 74

(1) Where evidence that a person has been convicted of an offence is admissible by virtue of section 74 above, then without prejudice to the reception of any other admissible evidence for the purpose of identifying the facts on which the conviction was based—

   (a) the contents of any document which is admissible as evidence of the conviction; and

   (b) the contents of the information, complaint, indictment or charge-sheet on which the person in question was convicted,

shall be admissible in evidence for that purpose.

(2) Where in any proceedings the contents of any document are admissible in evidence by virtue of subsection (1) above, a copy of that document, or of the material part of it, purporting to be certified or otherwise authenticated by or on behalf of the court or authority having custody of that document shall be admissible in evidence and shall be taken to be a true copy of that document or part unless the contrary is shown.

(3) Nothing in any of the following—

   (a) [section 14 of the Powers of Criminal Courts (Sentencing) Act 2000] (under which a conviction leading to probation or discharge is to be disregarded except as mentioned in that section);

   (b) [section 247 of the Criminal Procedure (Scotland) Act 1995] (which makes similar provision in respect of convictions on indictment in Scotland); and

   (c) section 8 of the Probation Act (Northern Ireland) 1950 (which corresponds to section 13 of the Powers of Criminal Courts Act 1973) or any legislation which is in force in Northern Ireland for the time being and corresponds to that section,

shall affect the operation of section 74 above; and for the purposes of that section any order made by a court of summary jurisdiction in Scotland under section 228 or section 246(3) of the said Act of 1995 shall be treated as a conviction.

(4) Nothing in section 74 above shall be construed as rendering admissible in any proceedings evidence of any conviction other than a subsisting one.

PART VIII
EVIDENCE IN CRIMINAL PROCEEDINGS—GENERAL

Confessions

76—Confessions

(1) In any proceedings a confession made by an accused person may be given in evidence against him in so far as it is relevant to any matter in issue in

the proceedings and is not excluded by the court in pursuance of this section.

(2) If, in any proceedings where the prosecution proposes to give in evidence a confession made by an accused person, it is represented to the court that the confession was or may have been obtained—

   (a) by oppression of the person who made it; or

   (b) in consequence of anything said or done which was likely, in the circumstances existing at the time, to render unreliable any confession which might be made by him in consequence thereof.

the court shall not allow the confession to be given in evidence against him except in so far as the prosecution proves to the court beyond reasonable doubt that the confession (notwithstanding that it may be true) was not obtained as aforesaid.

(3) In any proceedings where the prosecution proposes to give in evidence a confession made by an accused person, the court may of its own motion require the prosecution, as a condition of allowing it to do so, to prove that the confession was not obtained as mentioned in subsection (2) above.

(4) The fact that a confession is wholly or partly excluded in pursuance of this section shall not affect the admissibility in evidence—

   (a) of any facts discovered as a result of the confession; or

   (b) where the confession is relevant as showing that the accused speaks, writes or expresses himself in a particular way, of so much of the confession as is necessary to show that he does so.

(5) Evidence that a fact to which this subsection applies was discovered as a result of a statement made by an accused person shall not be admissible unless evidence of how it was discovered is given by him or on his behalf.

(6) Subsection (5) above applies—

   (a) to any fact discovered as a result of a confession which is wholly excluded in pursuance of this section; and

   (b) to any fact discovered as a result of a confession which is partly so excluded, if the fact is discovered as a result of the excluded part of the confession.

(7) Nothing in Part VII of this Act shall prejudice the admissibility of a confession made by an accused person.

(8) In this section "oppression" includes torture, inhuman or degrading treatment, and the use or threat of violence (whether or not amounting to torture).

(9) Where the proceedings mentioned in subsection (1) above are proceedings before a magistrates' court inquiring into an offence as examining justices this section shall have effect with the omission of—

   (a) in subsection (1) the words "and is not excluded by the court in pursuance of this section", and

   (b) subsections (2) to (6) and (8).

76A   Confessions may be given in evidence for co-accused

(1) In any proceedings a confession made by an accused person may be given in evidence for another person charged in the same proceedings (a co-accused) in so far as it is relevant to any matter in issue in the proceedings and is not excluded by the court in pursuance of this section.

(2) If, in any proceedings where a co-accused proposes to give in evidence a confession made by an accused person, it is represented to the court that the confession was or may have been obtained—

(a) by oppression of the person who made it; or

(b) in consequence of anything said or done which was likely, in the circumstances existing at the time, to render unreliable any confession which might be made by him in consequence thereof,

the court shall not allow the confession to be given in evidence for the co-accused except in so far as it is proved to the court on the balance of probabilities that the confession (notwithstanding that it may be true) was not so obtained.

(3) Before allowing a confession made by an accused person to be given in evidence for a co-accused in any proceedings, the court may of its own motion require the fact that the confession was not obtained as mentioned in subsection (2) above to be proved in the proceedings on the balance of probabilities.

(4) The fact that a confession is wholly or partly excluded in pursuance of this section shall not affect the admissibility in evidence—

(a) of any facts discovered as a result of the confession; or

(b) where the confession is relevant as showing that the accused speaks, writes or expresses himself in a particular way, of so much of the confession as is necessary to show that he does so.

(5) Evidence that a fact to which this subsection applies was discovered as a result of a statement made by an accused person shall not be admissible unless evidence of how it was discovered is given by him or on his behalf.

(6) Subsection (5) above applies—

(a) to any fact discovered as a result of a confession which is wholly excluded in pursuance of this section; and

(b) to any fact discovered as a result of a confession which is partly so excluded, if the fact is discovered as a result of the excluded part of the confession.

(7) In this section "oppression" includes torture, inhuman or degrading treatment, and the use or threat of violence (whether or not amounting to torture).

77—Confessions by mentally handicapped persons

(1) Without prejudice to the general duty of the court at a trial on indictment with a jury to direct the jury on any matter on which it appears to the court appropriate to do so, where at such a trial—

    (a) the case against the accused depends wholly or substantially on a confession by him; and

    (b) the court is satisfied—

        (i) that he is mentally handicapped; and

        (ii) that the confession was not made in the presence of an independent person,

the court shall warn the jury that there is special need for caution before convicting the accused in reliance on the confession, and shall explain that the need arises because of the circumstances mentioned in paragraphs (a) and (b) above.

(2) In any case where at the summary trial of a person for an offence it appears to the court that a warning under subsection (1) above would be required if the trial were on indictment with a jury, the court shall treat the case as one in which there is a special need for caution before convicting the accused on his confession.

(2A) In any case where at the trial on indictment without a jury of a person for an offence it appears to the court that a warning under subsection (1) above would be required if the trial were with a jury, the court shall treat the case as one in which there is a special need for caution before convicting the accused on his confession.

(3) In this section—

"independent person" does not include a police officer or a person employed for, or engaged on, police purposes;

"mentally handicapped", in relation to a person, means that he is in a state of arrested or incomplete development of mind which includes significant impairment of intelligence and social functioning; and

"police purposes" has the meaning assigned to it by section 101(2) of the Police Act 1996.

78—Exclusion of unfair evidence

(1) In any proceedings the court may refuse to allow evidence on which the prosecution proposes to rely to be given if it appears to the court that, having regard to all the circumstances, including the circumstances in which the evidence was obtained, the admission of the evidence would have such an adverse effect on the fairness of the proceedings that the court ought not to admit it.

(2) Nothing in this section shall prejudice any rule of law requiring a court to exclude evidence.

(3) This section shall not apply in the case of proceedings before a magistrates' court inquiring into an offences as examining justices.

80—Competence and compellability of accused's spouse or civil partner

(2) In any proceedings the [spouse or civil partner] of a person charged in the proceedings shall, subject to subsection (4) below, be compellable to give evidence on behalf of that person.

(2A) In any proceedings the spouse or civil partner of a person charged in the proceedings shall, subject to subsection (4) below, be compellable—

(a) to give evidence on behalf of any other person charged in the proceedings but only in respect of any specified offence with which that other person is charged; or

(b) to give evidence for the prosecution but only in respect of any specified offence with which any person is charged in the proceedings.

(3) In relation to the spouse or civil partner of a person charged in any proceedings, an offence is a specified offence for the purposes of subsection (2A) above if—

(a) it involves an assault on, or injury or a threat of injury to, the spouse or civil partner or a person who was at the material time under the age of 16;

(b) it is a sexual offence alleged to have been committed in respect of a person who was at the material time under that age; or

(c) it consists of attempting or conspiring to commit, or of aiding, abetting, counselling, procuring or inciting the commission of, an offence falling within paragraph (a) or (b) above.

(4) No person who is charged in any proceedings shall be compellable by virtue of subsection (2) or (2A) above to give evidence in the proceedings.

(4A) References in this section to a person charged in any proceedings do not include a person who is not, or is no longer, liable to be convicted of any offence in the proceedings (whether as a result of pleading guilty or for any other reason).

(5) In any proceedings a person who has been but is no longer married to the accused shall be compellable to give evidence as if that person and the accused had never been married.

(5A) In any proceedings a person who has been but is no longer the civil partner of the accused shall be compellable to give evidence as if that person and the accused had never been civil partners.

(6) Where in any proceedings the age of any person at any time is material for the purposes of subsection (3) above, his age at the material time shall for the purposes of that provision be deemed to be or to have been that which appears to the court to be or to have been his age at that time.

(7) In subsection (3)(b) above "sexual-offence" means an offence under the Protection of Children Act 1978 or Part 1 of the Sexual Offences Act 2003.

(9) Section 1(d) of the Criminal Evidence Act 1898 (communications between husband and wife) and section 43(1) of the Matrimonial Causes Act 1965 (evidence as to marital intercourse) shall cease to have effect.

80A   Rule where accused's spouse or civil partner not compellable

The failure of the spouse or civil partner of a person charged in any proceedings to give evidence in the proceedings shall not be made the subject of any comment by the prosecution.

81—Advance notice of expert evidence in Crown Court

(1) Criminal Procedure Rules may make provision for—
   (a) requiring any party to proceedings before the court to disclose to the other party or parties any expert evidence which he proposes to adduce in the proceedings; and
   (b) prohibiting a party who fails to comply in respect of any evidence with any requirement imposed by virtue of paragraph (a) above from adducing that evidence without the leave of the court.

(2) Criminal Procedure Rules made by virtue of this section may specify the kinds of expert evidence to which they apply and may exempt facts or matters of any description specified in the rules.

PART VIII
SUPPLEMENTARY

82—Part VIII—interpretation

(1) In this Part of this Act—

"confession", includes any statement wholly or partly adverse to the person who made it, whether made to a person in authority or not and whether made in words or otherwise;

"court-martial" means a court-martial constituted under the Army Act 955, the Air Force Act 1955 or the Naval Discipline Act 1957;

"proceedings" means criminal proceedings, including—
   (a) proceedings in the United Kingdom or elsewhere before a court-martial constituted under the Army Act 1955, the Air Force Act 1955 or the Naval Discipline Act 1957;
   (b) proceedings in the United Kingdom or elsewhere before the Courts-Martial Appeal Court—

    (i)   on an appeal from a court-martial so constituted; or

    (ii) on a reference under section 34 of the Courts-Martial (Appeals) Act 1968; and

(c) proceedings before a Standing Civilian Court;

and

"Service court" means a court-martial or a Standing Civilian Court.

(2) In this Part of this Act references to conviction before a Service court are references to a finding of guilty which is, or falls to be treated as, the finding of the court; and "convicted" shall be construed accordingly.

(3) Nothing in this Part of this Act shall prejudice any power of a court to exclude evidence (whether by preventing questions from being put or otherwise) at its discretion.

XI   MISCELLANEOUS AND SUPPLEMENTARY

117   Power of constable to use reasonable force

Where any provision of this Act—

(a) confers a power on a constable; and

(b) does not provide that the power may only be exercised with the consent of some person, other than a police officer,

the officer may use reasonable force, if necessary, in the exercise of the power.

SCHEDULE 1
SPECIAL PROCEDURE

Making of orders by circuit judge

1. If on an application made by a constable a circuit judge is satisfied that one or other of the sets of access conditions is fulfilled, he may make an order under paragraph 4 below.

2. The first set of access conditions is fulfilled if—

(a) there are reasonable grounds for believing—

    (i)   that an indictable offence has been committed;

    (ii) that there is material which consists of special procedure material or includes special procedure material and does not also include excluded material on premises specified in the application, or on premises occupied or controlled by a person specified in the application (including all such premises on which there are reasonable grounds for believing that there is such material as it is reasonably practicable so to specify);

> (iii) that the material is likely to be of substantial value (whether by itself or together with other material) to the investigation in connection with which the application is made; and
>
> (iv) that the material is likely to be relevant evidence;
>
> (b) other methods of obtaining the material—
>
> (i) have been tried without success; or
>
> (ii) have not been tried because it appeared that they were bound to fail; and
>
> (c) it is in the public interest, having regard—
>
> (i) to the benefit likely to accrue to the investigation if the material is obtained; and
>
> (ii) to the circumstances under which the person in possession of the material holds it,
>
> that the material should be produced or that access to it should be given.

3   The second set of access conditions is fulfilled if—

> (a) there are reasonable grounds for believing that there is material which consists of or includes excluded material or special procedure material on premises specified in the application, or on premises occupied or controlled by a person specified in the application (including all such premises on which there are reasonable grounds for believing that there is such material as it is reasonably practicable so to specify);
>
> (b) but for section 9(2) above a search of such premises for that material could have been authorised by the issue of a warrant to a constable under an enactment other than this Schedule; and
>
> (c) the issue of such a warrant would have been appropriate.

ROAD TRAFFIC REGULATION ACT 1984
(c. 27)

PART VI
SPEED LIMITS

89—Speeding offences generally

(1) A person who drives a motor vehicle on a road at a speed exceeding a limit imposed by or under any enactment to which this section applies shall be guilty of an offence.

(2) A person prosecuted for such an offence shall not be liable to be convicted solely on the evidence of one witness to the effect that, in the opinion of the witness, the person prosecuted was driving the vehicle at a speed exceeding a specified limit.

(3) The enactments to which this section applies are—
    (a) any enactment contained in this Act except section 17(2);
    (b) section 2 of the Parks Regulation (Amendment) Act 1926; and
    (c) any enactment not contained in this Act, but passed after 1st September 1960, whether before or after the passing of this Act.

(4) If a person who employs other persons to drive motor vehicles on roads publishes or issues any time-table or schedule, or gives any directions, under which any journey, or any stage or part of any journey, is to be completed within some specified time, and it is not practicable in the circumstances of the case for that journey (or that stage or part of it) to be completed in the specified time without the commission of such an offence as is mentioned in subsection (1) above, the publication or issue of the time-table or schedule, or the giving of the directions, may be produced as prima facie evidence that the employer procured or (as the case may be) incited the persons employed by him to drive the vehicles to commit such an offence.

CRIMINAL JUSTICE ACT 1988
(c. 33)

PART III
OTHER PROVISIONS ABOUT EVIDENCE IN CRIMINAL PROCEEDINGS

30—Expert reports

(1) An expert report shall be admissible as evidence in criminal proceedings, whether or not the person making it attends to give oral evidence in those proceedings.

(2) If it is proposed that the person making the report shall not give oral evidence, the report shall only be admissible with the leave of the court.

(3) For the purpose of determining whether to give leave the court shall have regard—

    (a) to the contents of the report;

    (b) to the reasons why it is proposed that the person making the report shall not give oral evidence;

    (c) to any risk, having regard in particular to whether it is likely to be possible to controvert statements in the report if the person making it does not attend to give oral evidence in the proceedings, that its admission or exclusion will result in unfairness to the accused or, if there is more than one, to any of them; and

    (d) to any other circumstances that appear to the court to be relevant.

(4) An expert report, when admitted, shall be evidence of any fact or opinion of which the person making it could have given oral evidence.

(4A) Where the proceedings mentioned in subsection (1) above are proceedings before a magistrates' court inquiring into an offence as examining justices this section shall have effect with the omission of—

    (a) in subsection (1) the words "whether or not the person making it attends to give oral evidence in those proceedings", and

    (b) subsections (2) to (4).

(5) In this section "expert report" means a written report by a person dealing wholly or mainly with matters on which he is (or would if living be) qualified to give expert evidence.

32—Evidence through television links

(1) A person other than the accused may give evidence through a live television link in proceedings to which subsection (1A) below applies if—

   (a)   the witness is outside the United Kingdom;

but evidence may not be so given without the leave of the court.

(1A)   This subsection applies—

   (a)   to trials on indictment, appeals to the criminal division of the Court of Appeal and hearings of references under section 9 of the Criminal Appeal Act 1995; and

   (b)   to proceedings in youth courts, appeals to the Crown Court arising out of such proceedings and hearings of references under section 11 of the Criminal Appeal Act 1995 so arising.

(3) A statement made on oath by a witness outside the United Kingdom and given in evidence through a link by virtue of this section shall be treated for the purposes of section 1 of the Perjury Act 1911 as having been made in the proceedings in which it is given in evidence.

(4) Without prejudice to the generality of any enactment conferring power to make Criminal Procedure Rules, such rules may make such provision as appears to the Criminal Procedure Rule Committee to be necessary or expedient for the purposes of this section.

34—Abolition of requirement of corroboration for unsworn evidence of children

(2) Any requirement whereby at a trial on indictment it is obligatory for the court to give the jury a warning about convicting the accused on the uncorroborated evidence of a child is abrogated.

(3) Unsworn evidence admitted by virtue of [section 56 of the Youth Justice and Criminal Evidence Act 1999] may corroborate evidence (sworn or unsworn) given by any other person.

ROAD TRAFFIC OFFENDERS ACT 1988
(c. 53)

PART I
TRIAL

15—Use of specimens in proceedings for an offence under section 4 or 5 of the Road Traffic Act

(1) This section and section 16 of this Act apply in respect of proceedings for an offence under section 3A, 4 or 5 of the Road Traffic Act 1988 (driving offences connected with drink or drugs); and expressions used in this section and section 16 of this Act have the same meaning as in sections 3A to 10 of that Act.

(2) Evidence of the proportion of alcohol or any drug in a specimen of breath, blood or urine provided by or taken from the accused shall, in all cases (including cases where the specimen was not provided or taken in connection with the alleged offence), be taken into account and, subject to subsection (3) below, it shall be assumed that the proportion of alcohol in the accused's breath, blood or urine at the time of the alleged offence was not less than in the specimen.

(3) That assumption shall not be made if the accused proves—
   (a) that he consumed alcohol before he provided the specimen or had it taken from him and—
      (i)   in relation to an offence under section 3A, after the time of the alleged offence, and
      (ii) otherwise, after he had ceased to drive, attempt to drive or be in charge of a vehicle on a road or other public place, and
   (b) that had he not done so the proportion of alcohol in his breath, blood or urine would not have exceeded the prescribed limit and, if it is alleged that he was unfit to drive through drink, would not have been such as to impair his ability to drive properly.
      (i)   A specimen of blood shall be disregarded unless—
   (a) it was taken from the accused with his consent and either—
      (i)   in a police station by a medical practitioner; or a registered health care professional; or
      (ii) elsewhere by a medical practitioner;

   or

   (b) it was taken from the accused by a medical practitioner under section 7A of the Road Traffic Act 1988 and the accused subsequently gave his permission for a laboratory test of the specimen.

(5) Where, at the time a specimen of blood or urine was provided by the accused, he asked to be provided with such a specimen, evidence of the proportion of alcohol or any drug found in the specimen is not admissible on behalf of the prosecution unless—

(a) the specimen in which the alcohol or drug was found is one of two parts into which the specimen provided by the accused was divided at the time it was provided, and

(b) the other part was supplied to the accused.

(5A) Where a specimen of blood was taken from the accused under section 7A of the Road Traffic Act 1988, evidence of the proportion of alcohol or any drug found in the specimen is not admissible on behalf of the prosecution unless—

(a) the specimen in which the alcohol or drug was found is one of two parts into which the specimen taken from the accused was divided at the time it was taken; and

(b) any request to be supplied with the other part which was made by the accused at the time when he gave his permission for a laboratory test of the specimen was complied with.

CHILDREN ACT 1989
(c. 41)

PART XII
MISCELLANEOUS AND GENERAL

Jurisdiction and procedure etc

96—Evidence given by, or with respect to, children

(1) Subsection (2) applies where a child who is called as a witness in any civil proceedings does not, in the opinion of the court, understand the nature of an oath.

(2) The child's evidence may be heard by the court if, in its opinion—

    (a) he understands that it is his duty to speak the truth; and

    (b) he has sufficient understanding to justify his evidence being heard.

(3) The Lord Chancellor may, with the concurrence of the Lord Chief Justice, by order make provision for the admissibility of evidence which would otherwise be inadmissible under any rule of law relating to hearsay.

(4) An order under subsection (3) may only be made with respect to—

    (a) civil proceedings in general or such civil proceedings, or class of civil proceedings, as may be prescribed; and

    (b) evidence in connection with the upbringing, maintenance or welfare of a child.

(5) An order under subsection (3)—

    (a) may, in particular, provide for the admissibility of statements which are made orally or in a prescribed form or which are recorded by any prescribed method of recording;

    (b) may make different provision for different purposes and in relation to different descriptions of court; and

    (c) may make such amendments and repeals in any enactment relating to evidence (other than in this Act) as the Lord Chancellor considers necessary or expedient in consequence of the provision made by the order.

(6) Subsection (5)(b) is without prejudice to section 104(4).

(7) In this section—

"civil proceedings" means civil proceeding, before any tribunal, in relation to which the strict rules of evidence apply, whether as a matter of law or by agreement of the parties, and references to "the court" shall be construed accordingly;

"prescribed" means prescribed by an order under subsection (3).

98—Self-incrimination

(1) In any proceedings in which a court is hearing an application for an order under Part IV or V, no person shall be excused from—

    (a) giving evidence on any matter; or

    (b) answering any question put to him in the course of his giving evidence,

on the ground that doing so might incriminate him or his spouse or civil partner of an offence.

(2) A statement or admission made in such proceedings shall not be admissible in evidence against the person making it or his spouse or civil partner in proceedings for an offence other than perjury.

CRIMINAL JUSTICE AND PUBLIC ORDER ACT 1994

(c. 33)

PART III
COURSE OF JUSTICE: EVIDENCE, PROCEDURE, ETC

Corroboration

32—Abolition of corroboration rules

(1) Any requirement whereby at a trial on indictment it is obligatory for the court to give the jury a warning about convicting the accused on the uncorroborated evidence of a person merely because that person is—

   (a) an alleged accomplice of the accused, or

   (b) where the offence charged is a sexual offence, the person in respect of whom it is alleged to have been committed,

   is hereby abrogated.

(2) In section 34(2) of the Criminal Justice Act 1988 (abolition of requirement of corroboration warning in respect of evidence of a child) the words from "in relation to" to the end shall be omitted.

(3) Any requirement that—

   (a) is applicable at the summary trial of a person for an offence, and

   (b) corresponds to the requirement mentioned in subsection (1) above or that mentioned in section 34(2) of the Criminal Justice Act 1988,

   is hereby abrogated.

(4) Nothing in this section applies in relation to—

   (a) any trial, or

   (b) any proceedings before a magistrates' court as examining justices,

   which began before the commencement of this section.

34—Effect of accused's failure to mention facts when questioned or charged

(1) Where, in any proceedings against a person for an offence, evidence is given that the accused—

   (a) at any time before he was charged with the offence, on being questioned under caution by a constable trying to discover whether or by whom the offence had been committed, failed to mention any fact relied on in his defence in those proceedings; or

   (b) on being charged with the offence or officially informed that he might be prosecuted for it, failed to mention any such fact, being a fact which in the circumstances existing at the time the accused could reasonably have been expected to mention when so questioned, charged or informed, as the case may be, subsection (2) below applies.

(2)   Where this subsection applies—

    (a)   a magistrates' court inquiring into the offence as examining justices;

    (b)   a judge, in deciding whether to grant an application made by the accused under paragraph 2 of Schedule 3 to the Crime and Disorder Act 1998;

    (c)   the court, in determining whether there is a case to answer; and

    (d)   the court or jury, in determining whether the accused is guilty of the offence charged,

may draw such inferences from the failure as appear proper.

(2A)   Where the accused was at an authorised place of detention at the time of the failure, subsections (1) and (2) above do not apply if he had not been allowed an opportunity to consult a solicitor prior to being questioned, charged or informed as mentioned in subsection (1) above.

(3)   Subject to any directions by the court, evidence tending to establish the failure may be given before or after evidence tending to establish the fact which the accused is alleged to have failed to mention.

(4)   This section applies in relation to questioning by persons (other than constables) charged with the duty of investigating offences or charging offenders as it applies in relation to questioning by constables; and in subsection (1) above "officially informed" means informed by a constable or any such person.

(5)   This section does not—

    (a)   prejudice the admissibility in evidence of the silence or other reaction of the accused in the face of anything said in his presence relating to the conduct in respect of which he is charged, in so far as evidence thereof would be admissible apart from this section; or

    (b)   preclude the drawing of any inference from any such silence or other reaction of the accused which could properly be drawn apart from this section.

(6)   This section does not apply in relation to a failure to mention a fact if the failure occurred before the commencement of this section.

35—Effect of accused's silence at trial

(1)   At the trial of any person for an offence, subsections (2) and (3) below apply unless—

    (a)   the accused's guilt is not in issue; or

    (b)   it appears to the court that the physical or mental condition of the accused makes it undesirable for him to give evidence;

but subsection (2) below does not apply if, at the conclusion of the evidence for the prosecution, his legal representative informs the court that the accused will give evidence or, where he is unrepresented, the court ascertains from him that he will give evidence.

(2) Where this subsection applies, the court shall, at the conclusion of the evidence for the prosecution, satisfy itself (in the case of proceedings on indictment with a jury, in the presence of the jury) that the accused is aware that the stage has been reached at which evidence can be given for the defence and that he can, if he wishes, give evidence and that, if he chooses not to give evidence, or having been sworn, without good cause refuses to answer any question, it will be permissible for the court or jury to draw such inferences as appear proper from his failure to give evidence or his refusal, without good cause, to answer any question.

(3) Where this subsection applies, the court or jury, in determining whether the accused is guilty of the offence charged, may draw such inferences as appear proper from the failure of the accused to give evidence or his refusal, without good cause, to answer any question.

(4) This section does not render the accused compellable to give evidence on his own behalf, and he shall accordingly not be guilty of contempt of court by reason of a failure to do so.

(5) For the purposes of this section a person who, having been sworn, refuses to answer any question shall be taken to do so without good cause unless—

   (a) he is entitled to refuse to answer the question by virtue of any enactment, whenever passed or made, or on the ground of privilege; or

   (b) the court in the exercise of its general discretion excuses him from answering it.

(7) This section applies—

   (a) in relation to proceedings on indictment for an offence, only if the person charged with the offence is arraigned on or after the commencement of this section;

   (b) in relation to proceedings in a magistrates' court, only if the time when the court begins to receive evidence in the proceedings falls after the commencement of this section.

36—Effect of accused's failure or refusal to account for objects, substances or marks

(1) Where—

   (a) a person is arrested by a constable, and there is—

      (i) on his person; or

      (ii) in or on his clothing or footwear; or

(iii) otherwise in his possession; or

(iv) in any place in which he is at the time of his arrest,

any object, substance or mark, or there is any mark on any such object; and

(b) that or another constable investigating the case reasonably believes that the presence of the object, substance or mark may be attributable to the participation of the person arrested in the commission of an offence specified by the constable; and

(c) the constable informs the person arrested that he so believes, and requests him to account for the presence of the object, substance or mark; and

(d) the person fails or refuses to do so,

then if, in any proceedings against the person for the offence so specified, evidence of those matters is given, subsection (2) below applies.

(2) Where this subsection applies—

(a) a magistrates' court inquiring into the offence as examining justices;

(b) a judge, in deciding whether to grant an application made by the accused under paragraph 2 of Schedule 3 to the Crime and Disorder Act 1998;

(c) the court, in determining whether there is a case to answer; and

(d) the court or jury, in determining whether the accused is guilty of the offence charged,

may draw such inferences from the failure or refusal as appear proper.

(3) Subsections (1) and (2) above apply to the condition of clothing or footwear as they apply to a substance or mark thereon.

(4) Subsections (1) and (2) above do not apply unless the accused was told in ordinary language by the constable when making the request mentioned in subsection (1)(c) above what the effect of this section would be if he failed or refused to comply with the request.

(4A) Where the accused was at an authorised place of detention at the time of the failure or refusal, subsections (1) and (2) above do not apply if he had not been allowed an opportunity to consult a solicitor prior to the request being made.

(5) This section applies in relation to officers of customs and excise as it applies in relation to constables.

(6) This section does not preclude the drawing of any inference from a failure or refusal of the accused to account for the presence of an object, substance or mark or from the condition of clothing or footwear which could properly be drawn apart from this section.

(7) This section does not apply in relation to a failure or refusal which occurred before the commencement of this section.

37—Effect of accused's failure or refusal to account for presence at a particular place

(1) Where—

   (a) a person arrested by a constable was found by him at a place at or about the time the offence for which he was arrested is alleged to have been committed; and

   (b) that or another constable investigating the offence reasonably believes that the presence of the person at that place and at that time may be attributable to his participation in the commission of the offence; and

   (c) the constable informs the person that he so believes, and requests him to account for that presence; and

   (d) the person fails or refuses to do so,

then if, in any proceedings against the person for the offence, evidence of those matters is given, subsection (2) below applies.

(2) Where this subsection applies—

   (a) a magistrates' court inquiring into the offence as examining justices;

   (b) a judge, in deciding whether to grant an application made by the accused under paragraph 2 of Schedule 3 to the Crime and Disorder Act 1998;

   (c) the court, in determining whether there is a case to answer; and

   (d) the court or jury, in determining whether the accused is guilty of the offence charged,

may draw such inferences from the failure or refusal as appear proper.

(3) Subsections (1) and (2) do not apply unless the accused was told in ordinary language by the constable when making the request mentioned in subsection (1)(c) above what the effect of this section would be if he failed or refused to comply with the request.

(3A) Where the accused was at an authorised place of detention at the time of the failure or refusal, subsections (1) and (2) do not apply if he had not been allowed an opportunity to consult a solicitor prior to the request being made.

(4) This section applies in relation to officers of customs and excise as it applies in relation to constables.

(5) This section does not preclude the drawing of any inference from a failure or refusal of the accused to account for his presence at a place which could properly be drawn apart from this section.

(6) This section does not apply in relation to a failure or refusal which occurred before the commencement of this section.

38—Interpretation and savings for sections 34, 35, 36 and 37

(1) In sections 34, 35, 36 and 37 of this Act—

"legal representative" means an authorised advocate or authorised litigator, as defined by section 119(1) of the Courts and Legal Services Act 1990; and

"place" includes any building or part of a building, any vehicle, vessel, aircraft or hovercraft and any other place whatsoever.

(2) In sections 34(2), 35(3), 36(2) and 37(2), references to an offence charged include references to any other offence of which the accused could lawfully be convicted on that charge.

(2A) In each of sections 34(2A), 36(4A) and 37(3A)"authorised place of detention" means—

(a) a police station; or

(b) any other place prescribed for the purposes of that provision by order made by the Secretary of State;

and the power to make an order under this subsection shall be exercisable by statutory instrument which shall be subject to annulment in pursuance of a resolution of either House of Parliament.

(3) A person shall not have the proceedings against him transferred to the Crown Court for trial, have a case to answer or be convicted of an offence solely on an inference drawn from such a failure or refusal as is mentioned in section 34(2), 35(3), 36(2) or 37(2).

(4) A judge shall not refuse to grant such an application as is mentioned in section 34(2)(b), 36(2)(b) and 37(2)(b) solely on an inference drawn from such a failure as is mentioned in section 34(2), 36(2) or 37(2).

(5) Nothing in sections 34, 35, 36 or 37 prejudices the operation of a provision of any enactment which provides (in whatever words) that any answer or evidence given by a person in specified circumstances shall not be admissible in evidence against him or some other person in any proceedings or class of proceedings (however described, and whether civil or criminal).

In this subsection, the reference to giving evidence is a reference to giving evidence in any manner, whether by furnishing information, making discovery, producing documents or otherwise.

(6) Nothing in section 34, 35, 36 or 37 prejudices any power of a court, in any proceedings, to exclude evidence (whether by preventing questions being put or otherwise) at its discretion.

CIVIL EVIDENCE ACT 1995
(c. 38)

Admissibility of hearsay evidence

1—Admissibility of hearsay evidence

(1) In civil proceedings evidence shall not be excluded on the ground that it is hearsay.

(2) In this Act—

    (a) "hearsay" means a statement made otherwise than by a person while giving oral evidence in the proceedings which is tendered as evidence of the matters stated; and

    (b) references to hearsay include hearsay of whatever degree.

(3) Nothing in this Act affects the admissibility of evidence admissible apart from this section.

(4) The provisions of sections 2 to 6 (safeguards and supplementary provisions relating to hearsay evidence) do not apply in relation to hearsay evidence admissible apart from this section, notwithstanding that it may also be admissible by virtue of this section.

2—Notice of proposal to adduce hearsay evidence

(1) A party proposing to adduce hearsay evidence in civil proceedings shall, subject to the following provisions of this section, give to the other party or parties to the proceedings—

    (a) such notice (if any) of the fact, and

    (b) on request, such particulars of or relating to the evidence,

as is reasonable and practicable in the circumstances for the purpose of enabling him or them to deal with any matters arising from its being hearsay.

(2) Provision may be made by rules of court—

    (a) specifying classes of proceedings or evidence in relation to which subsection (1) does not apply, and

    (b) as to the manner in which (including the time within which) the duties imposed by that subsection are to be complied with in the cases where it does apply.

(3) Subsection (1) may also be excluded by agreement of the parties; and compliance with the duty to give notice may in any case be waived by the person to whom notice is required to be given.

(4) A failure to comply with subsection (1), or with rules under subsection (2)(b), does not affect the admissibility of the evidence but may be taken into account by the court—

   (a) in considering the exercise of its powers with respect to the course of proceedings and costs, and

   (b) as a matter adversely affecting the weight to be given to the evidence in accordance with section 4.

3   **Power to call witness of cross-examination on hearsay statement**

Rules of court may provide that where a party to civil proceedings adduces hearsay evidence of a statement made by a person and does not call that person as a witness, any other party to the proceedings may, with the leave of the court, call that person as a witness and cross-examine him on the statement as if he had been called by the first-mentioned party and as if the hearsay statement were his evidence in chief.

4—Considerations relevant to weighing of hearsay evidence

(1) In estimating the weight (if any) to be given to hearsay evidence in civil proceedings the court shall have regard to any circumstances from which any inference can reasonably be drawn as to the reliability or otherwise of the evidence.

(2) Regard may be had, in particular, to the following—

   (a) whether it would have been reasonable and practicable for the party by whom the evidence was adduced to have produced the maker of the original statement as a witness;

   (b) whether the original statement was made contemporaneously with the occurrence or existence of the matters stated;

   (c) whether the evidence involves multiple hearsay;

   (d) whether any person involved had any motive to conceal or misrepresent matters;

   (e) whether the original statement was an edited account, or was made in collaboration with another or for a particular purpose;

   (f) whether the circumstances in which the evidence is adduced as hearsay are such as to suggest an attempt to prevent proper evaluation of its weight.

5—Competence and credibility

(1) Hearsay evidence shall not be admitted in civil proceedings if or to the extent that it is shown to consist of, or to be proved by means of, a statement made by a person who at the time he made the statement was not competent as a witness.

For this purpose "not competent as a witness" means suffering from such mental or physical infirmity, or lack of understanding, as would render a person incompetent as a witness in civil proceedings; but a child shall be treated as competent as a witness if he satisfies the requirements of section 96(2)(a) and (b) of the Children Act 1989 (conditions for reception of unsworn evidence of child).

(2) Where in civil proceedings hearsay evidence is adduced and the maker of the original statement, or of any statement relied upon to prove another statement, is not called as a witness—

(a) evidence which if he had been so called would be admissible for the purpose of attacking or supporting his credibility as a witness is admissible for that purpose in the proceedings; and

(b) evidence tending to prove that, whether before or after he made the statement, he made any other statement inconsistent with it is admissible for the purpose of showing that he had contradicted himself.

Provided that evidence may not be given of any matter of which, if he had been called as a witness and had denied that matter in cross-examination, evidence could not have been adduced by the cross-examining party.

6—Previous statements of witness

(1) Subject as follows, the provisions of this Act as to hearsay evidence in civil proceedings apply equally (but with any necessary modifications) in relation to a previous statement made by a person called as a witness in the proceedings.

(2) A party who has called or intends to call a person as a witness in civil proceedings may not in those proceedings adduce evidence of a previous statement made by that person, except—

(a) with the leave of the court, or

(b) for the purpose of rebutting a suggestion that his evidence has been fabricated.

This shall not be construed as preventing a witness statement (that is, a written statement of oral evidence which a party to the proceedings intends to lead) from being adopted by a witness in giving evidence or treated as his evidence.

(3) Where in the case of civil proceedings section 3, 4 or 5 of the Criminal Procedure Act 1865 applies, which make provision as to—

(a) how far a witness may be discredited by the party producing him,

(b) the proof of contradictory statements made by a witness, and

(c) cross-examination as to previous statements in writing,

this Act does not authorise the adducing of evidence of a previous inconsistent or contradictory statement otherwise than in accordance with those sections.

This is without prejudice to any provision made by rules of court under section 3 above (power to call witness for cross-examination on hearsay statement).

(4) Nothing in this Act affects any of the rules of law as to the circumstances in which, where a person called as a witness in civil proceedings is cross-examined on a document used by him to refresh his memory, that document may be made evidence in the proceedings.

(5) Nothing in this section shall be construed as preventing a statement of any description referred to above from being admissible by virtue of section 1 as evidence of the matters stated.

7—Evidence formerly admissible at common law

(1) The common law rule effectively preserved by section 9(1) and (2)(a) of the Civil Evidence Act 1968 (admissibility of admissions adverse to a party) is superseded by the provisions of this Act.

(2) The common law rules effectively preserved by section 9(1) and (2)(b) to (d) of the Civil Evidence Act 1968, that is, any rule of law whereby in civil proceedings—

(a) published works dealing with matters of a public nature (for example, histories, scientific works, dictionaries and maps) are admissible as evidence of facts of a public nature stated in them,

(b) public documents (for example, public registers, and returns made under public authority with respect to matters of public interest) are admissible as evidence of facts stated in them, or

(c) records (for example, the records of certain courts, treaties, Crown grants, pardons and commissions) are admissible as evidence of facts stated in them,

shall continue to have effect.

(3) The common law rules effectively preserved by section 9(3) and (4) of the Civil Evidence Act 1968, that is, any rule of law whereby in civil proceedings—

(a) evidence of a person's reputation is admissible for the purpose of proving his good or bad character, or

(b) evidence of reputation or family tradition is admissible—

(i) for the purpose of proving or disproving pedigree or the existence of a marriage, or

(ii) for the purpose of proving or disproving the existence of any public or general right or of identifying any person or thing, shall continue to have effect in so far as they authorise the court to treat such evidence as proving or disproving that matter.

Where any such rule applies, reputation or family tradition shall be treated for the purposes of this Act as a fact and not as a statement or multiplicity of statements about the matter in question.

(4) The words in which a rule of law mentioned in this section is described are intended only to identify the rule and shall not be construed as altering it in any way.

Other Matters

8—Proof of statements contained in documents

(1) Where a statement contained in a document is admissible as evidence in civil proceedings, it may be proved—
   (a) by the production of that document, or
   (b) whether or not that document is still in existence, by the production of a copy of that document or of the material part of it,

authenticated in such manner as the court may approve.

(2) It is immaterial for this purpose how many removes there are between a copy and the original.

9—Proof of records of business or public authority

(1) A document which is shown to form part of the records of a business or public authority may be received in evidence in civil proceedings without further proof.

(2) A document shall be taken to form part of the records of a business or public authority if there is produced to the court a certificate to that effect signed by an officer of the business or authority to which the records belong.

For this purpose—
   (a) a document purporting to be a certificate signed by an officer of a business or public authority shall be deemed to have been duly given by such an officer and signed by him; and
   (b) a certificate shall be treated as signed by a person if it purports to bear a facsimile of his signature.

(3) The absence of an entry in the records of a business or public authority may be proved in civil proceedings by affidavit of an officer of the business or authority to which the records belong.

(4) In this section—

"records" means records in whatever form;

"business" includes any activity regularly carried on over a period of time, whether for profit or not, by any body (whether corporate or not) or by an individual;

"officer" includes any person occupying a responsible position in relation to the relevant activities of the business or public authority or in relation to its records; and

"public authority" includes any public or statutory undertaking, any government department and any person holding office under Her Majesty.

(5) The court may, having regard to the circumstances of the case, direct that all or any of the above provisions of this section do not apply in relation to a particular document or record, or description of documents or records.

General

11 Meaning of "civil proceedings"

In this Act "civil proceedings" means civil proceedings, before any tribunal, in relation to which the strict rules of evidence apply, whether as a matter of law or by agreement of the parties. References to "the court" and "rules of court" shall be construed accordingly.

13 Interpretation

In this Act—

"civil proceedings" has the meaning given by section 11 and "court" and "rules of court" shall be construed in accordance with that section;

"document" means anything in which information of any description is recorded, and

"copy", in relation to a document, means anything onto which information recorded in the document has been copied, by whatever means and whether directly or indirectly;

"hearsay" shall be construed in accordance with section 1(2);

"oral evidence" includes evidence which, by reason of a defect of speech or hearing, a person called as a witness gives in writing or by signs;

"the original statement", in relation to hearsay evidence, means the underlying statement (if any) by—

(a) in the case of evidence of fact, a person having personal knowledge of that fact, or

(b) in the case of evidence of opinion, the person whose opinion it is; and

"statement" means any representation of fact or opinion, however made.

14—Savings

(1) Nothing in this Act affects the exclusion of evidence on grounds other than that it is hearsay.

This applies whether the evidence falls to be excluded in pursuance of any enactment or rule of law, for failure to comply with rules of court or an order of the court, or otherwise.

(2) Nothing in this Act affects the proof of documents by means other than those specified in section 8 or 9.

(3) Nothing in this Act affects the operation of the following enactments—

    (a) section 2 of the Documentary Evidence Act 1868 (mode of proving certain official documents);

    (b) section 2 of the Documentary Evidence Act 1882 (documents printed under the superintendence of Stationery Office);

    (c) section 1 of the Evidence (Colonial Statutes) Act 1907 (proof of statues of certain legislatures);

    (d) section 1 of the Evidence (Foreign, Dominion and Colonial Documents) Act 1933 (proof and effect of registers and official certificates of certain countries);

    (e) section 5 of the Oaths and Evidence (Overseas Authorities and Countries) Act 1963 (provision in respect of public registers of other countries).

CRIMINAL PROCEDURE AND INVESTIGATIONS ACT 1996
(c. 25)

PART I
DISCLOSURE

The main provisions

3—Initial duty of prosecutor to disclose

(1) The prosecutor must—

    (a) disclose to the accused any prosecution material which has not previously been disclosed to the accused and which [might reasonably be considered capable of undermining the case for the prosecution against the accused or of assisting the case for the accused, or

    (b) give to the accused a written statement that there is no material of a description mentioned in paragraph (a)

(2) For the purposes of this section prosecution material is material—

    (a) which is in the prosecutor's possession, and came into his possession in connection with the case for the prosecution against the accused, or

    (b) which, in pursuance of a code operative under Part II, he has inspected in connection with the case for the prosecution against the accused.

(3) Where material consists of information which has been recorded in any form the prosecutor discloses it for the purposes of this section—

    (a) by securing that a copy is made of it and that the copy is given to the accused, or

    (b) if in the prosecutor's opinion that is not practicable or not desirable, by allowing the accused to inspect it at a reasonable time and a reasonable place or by taking steps to secure that he is allowed to do so;

and a copy may be in such form as the prosecutor thinks fit and need not be in the same form as that in which the information has already been recorded.

(4) Where material consists of information which has not been recorded the prosecutor discloses it for the purposes of this section by securing that it is recorded in such form as he thinks fit and—

    (a) by securing that a copy is made of it and that the copy is given to the accused, or

(b) if in the prosecutor's opinion that is not practicable or not desirable, by allowing the accused to inspect it at a reasonable time and a reasonable place or by taking steps to secure that he is allowed to do so.

(5) Where material does not consist of information the prosecutor discloses it for the purposes of this section by allowing the accused to inspect it at a reasonable time and a reasonable place or by taking steps to secure that he is allowed to do so.

(6) Material must not be disclosed under this section to the extent that the court, on an application by the prosecutor, concludes it is not in the public interest to disclose it and orders accordingly.

(7) Material must not be disclosed under this section to the extent that [it is material the disclosure of which is prohibited by section 17 of the Regulation of Investigatory Powers Act 2000.

(8) The prosecutor must act under this section during the period which, by virtue of section 12, is the relevant period for this section.

5—Compulsory disclosure by accused

(1) Subject to subsections (2) to (4), this section applies where—
    (a) this Part applies by virtue of section 1(2), and

    (b) the prosecutor complies with section 3 or purports to comply with it.

(2) Where this Part applies by virtue of section 1(2)(b), this section does not apply unless—
    (a) a copy of the notice of transfer, and

    (b) copies of the documents containing the evidence.

have been given to the accused under regulations made under section 5(9) of the Criminal Justice Act 1987.

(3) Where this Part applies by virtue of section 1(2)(c), this section does not apply unless—
    (a) a copy of the notice of transfer, and

    (b) copies of the documents containing the evidence.

have been given to the accused under regulations made under paragraph 4 of Schedule 6 to the Criminal Justice Act 1991.

(3A) Where this Part applies by virtue of section 1(2)(cc), this section does not apply unless—
    (a) copies of the documents containing the evidence have been served on the accused under regulations made under paragraph 1 of Schedule 3 to the Crime and Disorder Act 1998; and

    (b) a copy of the notice under subsection (1) of section 51D of that Act has been served on him under that subsection.

(4) Where this Part applies by virtue of section 1(2)(e), this section does not apply unless the prosecutor has served on the accused a copy of the

indictment and a copy of the set of documents containing the evidence which is the basis of the charge.

(5) Where this section applies, the accused must give a defence statement to the court and the prosecutor.

(5A) Where there are other accused in the proceedings and the court so orders, the accused must also give a defence statement to each other accused specified by the court.

(5B) The court may make an order under subsection (5A) either of its own motion or on the application of any party.

(5C) A defence statement that has to be given to the court and the prosecutor (under subsection (5)) must be given during the period which, by virtue of section 12, is the relevant period for this section.

(5D) A defence statement that has to be given to a co-accused (under sub-section (5A)) must be given within such period as the court may specify.

6—Voluntary disclosure by accused

(1) This section applies where—
   (a) this Part applies by virtue of section 1(1), and
   (b) the prosecutor complies with section 3 or purports to comply with it.

(2) The accused—
   (a) may give a defence statement to the prosecutor, and
   (b) if he does so, must also give such a statement to the court.

(4) If the accused gives a defence statement under this section he must give it during the period which, by virtue of section 12 is the relevant period for this section.

6A Contents of defence statement

(1) For the purposes of this Part a defence statement is a written statement—
   (a) setting out the nature of the accused's defence, including any particular defences on which he intends to rely,
   (b) indicating the matters of fact on which he takes issue with the prosecution,
   (c) setting out, in the case of each such matter, why he takes issue with the prosecution,
   (ca) setting out particulars of the matters of fact on which he intends to rely for the purposes of his defence, and
   (d) indicating any point of law (including any point as to the admissibility of evidence or an abuse of process) which he wishes to take, and any authority on which he intends to rely for that purpose.

(2) A defence statement that discloses an alibi must give particulars of it, including—

    (a)   the name, address and date of birth of any witness the accused believes is able to give evidence in support of the alibi, or as many of those details as are known to the accused when the statement is given;

    (b)   any information in the accused's possession which might be of material assistance in identifying or finding any such witness in whose case any of the details mentioned in paragraph (a) are not known to the accused when the statement is given.

(3) For the purposes of this section evidence in support of an alibi is evidence tending to show that by reason of the presence of the accused at a particular place or in a particular area at a particular time he was not, or was unlikely to have been, at the place where the offence is alleged to have been committed at the time of its alleged commission.

(4) The Secretary of State may by regulations make provision as to the details of the matters that, by virtue of subsection (1), are to be included in defence statements.

Words added by Criminal Justice and Immigration Act 2008 c. 4 Pt 4 s.60(1) (November 3, 2008: insertion has effect subject to savings and transitional provisions specified in SI 2008/2712 art.3)

6E   Disclosure by accused: further provisions

(1) Where an accused's solicitor purports to give on behalf of the accused—

    (a)   a defence statement under section 5, 6 or 6B, or

    (b)   a statement of the kind mentioned in section 6B(4),

the statement shall, unless the contrary is proved, be deemed to be given with the authority of the accused.

(2) If it appears to the judge at a pre-trial hearing that an accused has failed to comply fully with section 5, 6B or 6C, so that there is a possibility of comment being made or inferences drawn under section 11(5), he shall warn the accused accordingly.

(3) In subsection (2) "pre-trial hearing" has the same meaning as in Part 4 (see section 39).

(4) The judge in a trial before a judge and jury—

    (a)   may direct that the jury be given a copy of any defence statement, and

    (b)   if he does so, may direct that it be edited so as not to include references to matters evidence of which would be inadmissible.

(5) A direction under subsection (4)—

    (a)   may be made either of the judge's own motion or on the application of any party;

    (b)   may be made only if the judge is of the opinion that seeing a copy of the defence statement would help the jury to understand the case or to resolve any issue in the case.

(6) The reference in subsection (4) to a defence statement is a reference—
  (a) where the accused has given only an initial defence statement (that is, a defence statement given under section 5 or 6), to that statement;
  (b) where he has given both an initial defence statement and an updated defence statement (that is, a defence statement given under section 6B), to the updated defence statement;
  (c) where he has given both an initial defence statement and a statement of the kind mentioned in section 6B(4), to the initial defence statement.

7A Continuing duty of prosecutor to disclose

(1) This section applies at all times—
  (a) after the prosecutor has complied with section 3 or purported to comply with it, and
  (b) before the accused is acquitted or convicted or the prosecutor decides not to proceed with the case concerned.

(2) The prosecutor must keep under review the question whether at any given time (and, in particular, following the giving of a defence statement) there is prosecution material which—
  (a) might reasonably be considered capable of undermining the case for the prosecution against the accused or of assisting the case for the accused, and
  (b) has not been disclosed to the accused.

(3) If at any time there is any such material as is mentioned in subsection (2) the prosecutor must disclose it to the accused as soon as is reasonably practicable (or within the period mentioned in subsection (5)(a), where that applies).

(4) In applying subsection (2) by reference to any given time the state of affairs at that time (including the case for the prosecution as it stands at that time) must be taken into account.

(5) Where the accused gives a defence statement under section 5, 6 or 6B—
  (a) if as a result of that statement the prosecutor is required by this section to make any disclosure, or further disclosure, he must do so during the period which, by virtue of section 12, is the relevant period for this section;
  (b) if the prosecutor considers that he is not so required, he must during that period give to the accused a written statement to that effect.

(6) For the purposes of this section prosecution material is material—
  (a) which is in the prosecutor's possession and came into his possession in connection with the case for the prosecution against the accused, or
  (b) which, in pursuance of a code operative under Part 2, he has inspected in connection with the case for the prosecution against the accused.

(7) Subsections (3) to (5) of section 3 (method by which prosecutor discloses) apply for the purposes of this section as they apply for the purposes of that.

(8) Material must not be disclosed under this section to the extent that the court, on an application by the prosecutor, concludes it is not in the public interest to disclose it and orders accordingly.

(9) Material must not be disclosed under this section to the extent that it is material the disclosure of which is prohibited by section 17 of the Regulation of Investigatory Powers Act 2000 (c. 23).

8—Application by accused for disclosure

(1) This section applies where the accused has given a defence statement under section 5, 6 or 6B and the prosecutor has complied with section 7A(5) or has purported to comply with it or has failed to comply with it.

(2) If the accused has at any time reasonable cause to believe that there is prosecution material which is required by section 7A to be disclosed to him and has not been, he may apply to the court for an order requiring the prosecutor to disclose it to him.

(3) For the purposes of this section prosecution material is material—
  (a) which is in the prosecutor's possession and came into his possession in connection with the case for the prosecution against the accused.
  (b) which, in pursuance of a code operative under Part II, he has inspected in connection with the case for the prosecution against the accused, or
  (c) which falls within subsection (4).

(4) Material falls within this subsection if in pursuance of a code operative under Part II the prosecutor must, if he asks for the material, be given a copy of it or be allowed to inspect it in connection with the case for the prosecution against the accused.

(5) Material must not be disclosed under this section to the extent that the court, on an application by the prosecutor, concludes it is not in the public interest to disclose it and orders accordingly.

(6) Material must not be disclosed under this section to the extent that it is material the disclosure of which is prohibited by section 17 of the Regulation of Investigatory Powers Act 2000.

11 Faults in disclosure by accused

(1) This section applies in the three cases set out in subsections (2), (3) and (4).

(2) The first case is where section 5 applies and the accused—
  (a) fails to give an initial defence statement,

(b)   gives an initial defence statement but does so after the end of the period which, by virtue of section 12, is the relevant period for section 5,

(c)   is required by section 6B to give either an updated defence statement or a statement of the kind mentioned in subsection (4) of that section but fails to do so,

(d)   gives an updated defence statement or a statement of the kind mentioned in section 6B(4) but does so after the end of the period which, by virtue of section 12, is the relevant period for section 6B,

(e)   sets out inconsistent defences in his defence statement, or

(f)   at his trial—

    (i)   puts forward a defence which was not mentioned in his defence statement or is different from any defence set out in that statement,

    (ii)   relies on a matter (or any particular of any matter of fact) which, in breach of the requirements imposed by or under section 6A, was not mentioned in his defence statement,

    (iii)   adduces evidence in support of an alibi without having given particulars of the alibi in his defence statement, or

    (iv)   calls a witness to give evidence in support of an alibi without having complied with section 6A(2)(a) or (b) as regards the witness in his defence statement.

(3)   The second case is where section 6 applies, the accused gives an initial defence statement, and the accused—

(a)   gives the initial defence statement after the end of the period which, by virtue of section 12, is the relevant period for section 6, or

(b)   does any of the things mentioned in paragraphs (c) to (f) of subsection (2).

(5)   Where this section applies—

(a)   the court or any other party may make such comment as appears appropriate;

(b)   the court or jury may draw such inferences as appear proper in deciding whether the accused is guilty of the offence concerned.

(6)   Where—

(a)   this section applies by virtue of subsection (2)(f)(ii) (including that provision as it applies by virtue of subsection (3)(b)), and

(b)   the matter which was not mentioned is a point of law (including any point as to the admissibility of evidence or an abuse of process) or an authority,

comment by another party under subsection (5)(a) may be made only with the leave of the court.

(8)   Where the accused puts forward a defence which is different from any

defence set out in his defence statement, in doing anything under subsection (5) or in deciding whether to do anything under it the court shall have regard—

(a) to the extent of the differences in the defences, and

(b) to whether there is any justification for it.

(9) Where the accused calls a witness whom he has failed to include, or to identify adequately, in a witness notice, in doing anything under subsection (5) or in deciding whether to do anything under it the court shall have regard to whether there is any justification for the failure.

(10)   A person shall not be convicted of an offence solely on an inference drawn under subsection (5).

(12)   In this section—

(a) "initial defence statement" means a defence statement given under section 5 or 6;

(b) "updated defence statement" means a defence statement given under section 6B;

(c) a reference simply to an accused's "defence statement" is a reference—

(i)   where he has given only an initial defence statement, to that statement;

(ii) where he has given both an initial and an updated defence statement, to the updated defence statement;

(iii) where he has given both an initial defence statement and a statement of the kind mentioned in section 6B(4), to the initial defence statement;

(d) a reference to evidence in support of an alibi shall be construed in accordance with section 6A(3);

(e) "witness notice" means a notice given under section 6C.

Words inserted by Criminal Justice and Immigration Act 2008 c. 4 Pt 4 s.60(2) (November 3, 2008: insertion has effect subject to savings and transitional provisions specified in SI 2008/2712 art.3)

Human Rights Act 1998

(c. 42)

Introduction

2—Interpretation of Convention rights

(1) A court or tribunal determining a question which has arisen in connection with a Convention right must take into account any—

(a) judgment, decision, declaration or advisory opinion of the European Court of Human Rights,

(b) opinion of the Commission given in a report adopted under Article 31 of the Convention,

(c) decision of the Commission in connection with Article 26 or 27(2) of the Convention, or

(d) decision of the Committee of Ministers taken under Article 46 of the Convention,

whenever made or given, so far as, in the opinion of the court or tribunal, it is relevant to the proceedings in which that question has arisen.

(2) Evidence of any judgment, decision, declaration or opinion of which account may have to be taken under this section is to be given in proceedings before any court or tribunal in such manner as may be provided by rules.

(3) In this section "rules" means rules of court or, in the case of proceedings before a tribunal, rules made for the purposes of this section—

(a) by [the Lord Chancellor or the Secretary of State, in relation to any proceedings outside Scotland;

(b) by the Secretary of State, in relation to proceedings in Scotland; or

(c) by a Northern Ireland department, in relation to proceedings before a tribunal in Northern Ireland—

(i) which deals with transferred matters; and

(ii) for which no rules made under paragraph (a) are in force.

3—Interpretation of legislation

(1) So far as it is possible to do so, primary legislation and subordinate legislation must be read and given effect in a way which is compatible with the Convention rights.

(2) This section—

(a)   applies to primary legislation and subordinate legislation whenever enacted;

(b)   does not affect the validity, continuing operation or enforcement of any incompatible primary legislation; and

(c)   does not affect the validity, continuing operation or enforcement of any incompatible subordinate legislation if (disregarding any possibility of revocation) primary legislation prevents removal of the incompatibility.

4—Declaration of incompatibility

(1) Subsection (2) applies in any proceedings in which a court determines whether a provision of primary legislation is compatible with a Convention right.

(2) If the court is satisfied that the provision is incompatible with a Convention right, it may make a declaration of that incompatibility.

(3) Subsection (4) applies in any proceedings in which a court determines whether a provision of subordinate legislation, made in the exercise of a power conferred by primary legislation, is compatible with a Convention right.

(4) If the court is satisfied—

(a)   that the provision is incompatible with a Convention right, and

(b)   that (disregarding any possibility of revocation) the primary legislation concerned prevents removal of the incompatibility,

it may make a declaration of that incompatibility.

(5) In this section "court" means —

(a)   the House of Lords;

(b)   the Judicial Committee of the Privy Council;

(c)   the Courts-Martial Appeal Court;

(d)   in Scotland, the High Court of Justiciary sitting otherwise than as a trial court or the Court of Session;

(e)   in England and Wales or Northern Ireland, the High Court or the Court of Appeal;

(f)   the Court of Protection, in any matter being dealt with by the President of the Family Division, the Vice-Chancellor or a puisne judge of the High Court.

(6) A declaration under this section ("a declaration of incompatibility")—

(a)   does not affect the validity, continuing operation or enforcement of the provision in respect of which it is given; and

(b)   is not binding on the parties to the proceedings in which it is made.

6—Acts of public authorities

(1) It is unlawful for a public authority to act in a way which is incompatible with a Convention right.

(2) Subsection (1) does not apply to an act if—

(a) as the result of one or more provisions of primary legislation, the authority could not have acted differently; or

(b) in the case of one or more provisions of, or made under, primary legislation which cannot be read or given effect in a way which is compatible with the Convention rights, the authority was acting so as to give effect to or enforce those provisions.

(3) In this section "public authority" includes—

(a) a court or tribunal, and

(b) any person certain of whose functions are functions of a public nature,

but does not include either House of Parliament or a person exercising functions in connection with proceedings in Parliament.

(4) In subsection (3) "Parliament" does not include the House of Lords in its judicial capacity.

(5) In relation to a particular act, a person is not a public authority by virtue only of subsection (3)(b) if the nature of the act is private.

(6) "An act" includes a failure to act but does not include a failure to—

(a) introduce in, or lay before, Parliament a proposal for legislation; or

(b) make any primary legislation or remedial order.

Youth Justice and Criminal Evidence Act 1999
(c. 23)

PART II
GIVING OF EVIDENCE OR INFORMATION FOR PURPOSES OF CRIMINAL PROCEEDINGS

CHAPTER I
SPECIAL MEASURES DIRECTIONS IN CASE OF VULNERABLE AND INTIMIDATED WITNESSES

Preliminary

16—Witnesses eligible for assistance on grounds of age or incapacity

(1) For the purposes of this Chapter a witness in criminal proceedings (other than the accused) is eligible for assistance by virtue of this section—
  (a) if under the age of 17 at the time of the hearing; or
  (b) if the court considers that the quality of evidence given by the witness is likely to be diminished by reason of any circumstances falling within subsection (2).

(2) The circumstances falling within this subsection are—
  (a) that the witness—
    (i) suffers from mental disorder within the meaning of the Mental Health Act 1983, or
    (ii) otherwise has a significant impairment of intelligence and social functioning;

(b)   that the witness has a physical disability or is suffering from a physical disorder.

(3)   In subsection (1)(a) "the time of the hearing", in relation to a witness, means the time when it falls to the court to make a determination for the purposes of section 19(2) in relation to the witness.

(4)   In determining whether a witness falls within subsection (1)(b) the court must consider any views expressed by the witness.

(5)   In this Chapter references to the quality of a witness's evidence are to its quality in terms of completeness, coherence and accuracy; and for this purpose "coherence" refers to a witness's ability in giving evidence to give answers which address the questions put to the witness and can be understood both individually and collectively.

17—Witnesses eligible for assistance on grounds of fear or distress about testifying

(1)   For the purposes of this Chapter a witness in criminal proceedings (other than the accused) is eligible for assistance by virtue of this subsection if the court is satisfied that the quality of evidence given by the witness is likely to be diminished by reason of fear or distress on the part of the witness in connection with testifying in the proceedings.

(2)   In determining whether a witness falls within subsection (1) the court must take into account, in particular—

(a)   the nature and alleged circumstances of the offence to which the proceedings relate;

(b)   the age of the witness;

(c)   such of the following matters as appear to the court to be relevant, namely—

(i)   the social and cultural background and ethnic origins of the witness,

(ii)   the domestic and employment circumstances of the witness, and

(iii)   any religious beliefs or political opinions of the witness;

(d)   any behaviour towards the witness on the part of—

(i)   the accused,

(ii)   members of the family or associates of the accused, or

(iii)   any other person who is likely to be an accused or a witness in the proceedings.

(3)   In determining that question the court must in addition consider any views expressed by the witness.

(4)   Where the complainant in respect of a sexual offence is a witness in proceedings relating to that offence (or to that offence and any other offences), the witness is eligible for assistance in relation to those proceedings by virtue of this subsection unless the witness has informed

the court of the witness' wish not to be so eligible by virtue of this subsection.

18—Special measures available to eligible witnesses

(1) For the purposes of this Chapter—

   (a) the provision which may be made by a special measures direction by virtue of each of sections 23 to 30 is a special measure available in relation to a witness eligible for assistance by virtue of section 16; and

   (b) the provision which may be made by such a direction by virtue of each of sections 23 to 28 is a special measure available in relation to a witness eligible for assistance by virtue of section 17;

but this subsection has effect subject to subsection (2).

(2) Where (apart from this subsection) a special measure would, in accordance with subsection (1)(a) or (b), be available in relation to a witness in any proceedings, it shall not be taken by a court to be available in relation to the witness unless—

   (a) the court has been notified by the Secretary of State that relevant arrangements may be made available in the area in which it appears to the court that the proceedings will take place, and

   (b) the notice has not been withdrawn.

(3) In subsection (2) "relevant arrangements" means arrangements for implementing the measure in question which cover the witness and the proceedings in question.

(4) The withdrawal of a notice under that subsection relating to a special measure shall not affect the availability of that measure in relation to a witness if a special measures direction providing for that measure to apply to the witness's evidence has been made by the court before the notice is withdrawn.

(5) The Secretary of State may by order make such amendments of this Chapter as he considers appropriate for altering the special measures which, in accordance with subsection (1)(a) or (b), are available in relation to a witness eligible for assistance by virtue of section 16 or (as the case may be) section 17, whether—

   (a) by modifying the provisions relating to any measure for the time being available in relation to such a witness,

   (b) by the addition—

      (i) (with or without modifications) of any measure which is for the time being available in relation to a witness eligible for assistance by virtue of the other of those sections, or

      (ii) of any new measure, or

   (c) by the removal of any measure.

19—Special measures direction relating to eligible witness

(1) This section applies where in any criminal proceedings—

   (a) a party to the proceedings makes an application for the court to give a direction under this section in relation to a witness in the proceedings other than the accused, or

   (b) the court of its own motion raises the issue whether such a direction should be given.

(2) Where the court determines that the witness is eligible for assistance by virtue of section 16 or 17, the court must then—

   (a) determine whether any of the special measures available in relation to the witness (or any combination of them) would, in its opinion, be likely to improve the quality of evidence given by the witness; and

   (b) if so—

      (i) determine which of those measures (or combination of them) would, in its opinion, be likely to maximise so far as practicable the quality of such evidence; and

      (ii) give a direction under this section providing for the measure or measures so determined to apply to evidence given by the witness.

(3) In determining for the purposes of this Chapter whether any special measure or measures would or would not be likely to improve, or to maximise so far as practicable, the quality of evidence given by the witness, the court must consider all the circumstances of the case, including in particular—

   (a) any views expressed by the witness; and

   (b) whether the measure or measures might tend to inhibit such evidence being effectively tested by a party to the proceedings.

(4) A special measures direction must specify particulars of the provision made by the direction in respect of each special measure which is to apply to the witness's evidence.

(5) In this Chapter "special measures direction" means a direction under this section.

(6) Nothing in this Chapter is to be regarded as affecting any power of a court to make an order or give leave of any description (in the exercise of its inherent jurisdiction or otherwise)—

   (a) in relation to a witness who is not an eligible witness, or

   (b) in relation to an eligible witness where (as, for example, in a case where a foreign language interpreter is to be provided) the order is made or the leave is given otherwise than by reason of the fact that the witness is an eligible witness.

20—Further provisions about directions: general

(1) Subject to subsection (2) and section 21(8), a special measures direction has binding effect from the time it is made until the proceedings for the purposes of which it is made are either—

(a)   determined (by acquittal, conviction or otherwise), or

(b)   abandoned,

in relation to the accused or (if there is more than one) in relation to each of the accused.

(2) The court may discharge or vary (or further vary) a special measures direction if it appears to the court to be in the interests of justice to do so, and may do so either—

(a)   on an application made by a party to the proceedings, if there has been a material change of circumstances since the relevant time, or

(b)   of its own motion.

(3) In subsection (2) "the relevant time" means —

(a)   the time when the direction was given, or

(b)   if a previous application has been made under that subsection, the time when the application (or last application) was made.

(4) Nothing in section 24(2) and (3), 27(4) to (7) or 28(4) to (6) is to be regarded as affecting the power of the court to vary or discharge a special measures direction under subsection (2).

(5) The court must state in open court its reasons for—

(a)   giving or varying,

(b)   refusing an application for, or for the variation or discharge of, or

(c)   discharging,

a special measures direction and, if it is a magistrates' court, must cause them to be entered in the register of its proceedings.

(6) Criminal Procedure Rules may make provision—

(a)   for uncontested applications to be determined by the court without a hearing;

(b)   for preventing the renewal of an unsuccessful application for a special measures direction except where there has been a material change of circumstances;

(c)   for expert evidence to be given in connection with an application for, or for varying or discharging, such a direction;

(d)   for the manner in which confidential or sensitive information is to be treated in connection with such an application and in particular as to its being disclosed to, or withheld from, a party to the proceedings.

21—Special provisions relating to child witnesses

(1) For the purposes of this section—

(a)   a witness in criminal proceedings is a "child witness" if he is an eligible witness by reason of section 16(1)(a) (whether or not he is an eligible witness by reason of any other provision of section 16 or 17);

(b)   a child witness is "in need of special protection" if the offence (or any of the offences) to which the proceedings relate is—

     (i)   an offence falling within section 35(3)(a) (sexual offences etc.), or

     (ii)   an offence falling within section 35(3)(b), (c) or (d) (kidnapping, assaults etc.); and

(c)   a "relevant recording", in relation to a child witness, is a video recording of an interview of the witness made with a view to its admission as evidence in chief of the witness.

(2)   Where the court, in making a determination for the purposes of section 19(2), determines that a witness in criminal proceedings is a child witness, the court must—

(a)   first have regard to subsections (3) to (7) below; and

(b)   then have regard to section 19(2);

and for the purposes of section 19(2), as it then applies to the witness, any special measures required to be applied in relation to him by virtue of this section shall be treated as if they were measures determined by the court, pursuant to section 19(2)(a) and (b)(i), to be ones that (whether on their own or with any other special measures) would be likely to maximise, so far as practicable, the quality of his evidence.

(3)   The primary rule in the case of a child witness is that the court must give a special measures direction in relation to the witness which complies with the following requirements—

(a)   it must provide for any relevant recording to be admitted under section 27 (video recorded evidence in chief); and

(b)   it must provide for any evidence given by the witness in the proceedings which is not given by means of a video recording (whether in chief or otherwise) to be given by means of a live link in accordance with section 24.

(4)   The primary rule is subject to the following limitations—

(a)   the requirement contained in subsection (3)(a) or (b) has effect subject to the availability (within the meaning of section 18(2)) of the special measure in question in relation to the witness;

(b)   the requirement contained in subsection (3)(a) also has effect subject to section 27(2); and

(c)   the rule does not apply to the extent that the court is satisfied that compliance with it would not be likely to maximise the quality of the witness's evidence so far as practicable (whether because the application to that evidence of one or more other special measures available in relation to the witness would have that result or for any other reason).

(5) However, subsection (4)(c) does not apply in relation to a child witness in need of special protection.

(6) Where a child witness is in need of special protection by virtue of subsection (1)(b)(i), any special measures direction given by the court which complies with the requirement contained in subsection (3)(a) must in addition provide for the special measure available under section 28 (video recorded cross-examination or re-examination) to apply in relation to—

(a) any cross-examination of the witness otherwise than by the accused in person, and

(b) any subsequent re-examination.

(7) The requirement contained in subsection (6) has effect subject to the following limitations—

(a) it has effect subject to the availability (within the meaning of section 18(2)) of that special measure in relation to the witness; and

(b) it does not apply if the witness has informed the court that he does not want that special measure to apply in relation to him.

(8) Where a special measures direction is given in relation to a child witness who is an eligible witness by reason only of section 16(1)(a), then—

(a) subject to subsection (9) below, and

(b) except where the witness has already begun to give evidence in the proceedings,

the direction shall cease to have effect at the time when the witness attains the age of 17.

(9) Where a special measures direction is given in relation to a child witness who is an eligible witness by reason only of section 16(1)(a) and—

(a) the direction provides—

(i) for any relevant recording to be admitted under section 27 as evidence in chief of the witness, or

(ii) for the special measure available under section 28 to apply in relation to the witness, and

(b) if it provides for that special measure to so apply, the witness is still under the age of 17 when the video recording is made for the purposes of section 28,

then, so far as it provides as mentioned in paragraph (a)(i) or (ii) above, the direction shall continue to have effect in accordance with section 20(1) even though the witness subsequently attains that age.

22—Extension of provisions of section 21 to certain witnesses over 17

(1) For the purposes of this section—

    (a) a witness in criminal proceedings (other than the accused) is a "qualifying witness" if he—

        (i) is not an eligible witness at the time of the hearing (as defined by section 16(3)), but

        (ii) was under the age of 17 when a relevant recording was made;

    (b) a qualifying witness is "in need of special protection" if the offence (or any of the offences) to which the proceedings relate is—

        (i) an offence falling within section 35(3)(a) (sexual offences etc.), or

        (ii) an offence falling within section 35(3)(b), (c) or (d) (kidnapping, assaults etc.); and

    (c) a "relevant recording", in relation to a witness, is a video recording of an interview of the witness made with a view to its admission as evidence in chief of the witness.

(2) Subsections (2) to (7) of section 21 shall apply as follows in relation to a qualifying witness—

    (a) subsections (2) to (4), so far as relating to the giving of a direction complying with the requirement contained in subsection (3)(a), shall apply to a qualifying witness in respect of the relevant recording as they apply to a child witness (within the meaning of that section);

    (b) subsection (5), so far as relating to the giving of such a direction, shall apply to a qualifying witness in need of special protection as it applies to a child witness in need of special protection (within the meaning of that section); and

    (c) subsections (6) and (7) shall apply to a qualifying witness in need of special protection by virtue of subsection (1)(b)(i) above as they apply to such a child witness as is mentioned in subsection (6).

23—Screening witness from accused

(1) A special measures direction may provide for the witness, while giving testimony or being sworn in court, to be prevented by means of a screen or other arrangement from seeing the accused.

(2) But the screen or other arrangement must not prevent the witness from being able to see, and to be seen by—

    (a) the judge or justices (or both) and the jury (if there is one);

    (b) legal representatives acting in the proceedings; and

    (c) any interpreter or other person appointed (in pursuance of the direction or otherwise) to assist the witness.

(3) Where two or more legal representatives are acting for a party to the proceedings, subsection (2)(b) is to be regarded as satisfied in relation to those representatives if the witness is able at all material times to see and be seen by at least one of them.

24—Evidence by live link

(1) A special measures direction may provide for the witness to give evidence by means of a live link.

(2) Where a direction provides for the witness to give evidence by means of a live link, the witness may not give evidence in any other way without the permission of the court.

(3) The court may give permission for the purposes of subsection (2) if it appears to the court to be in the interests of justice to do so, and may do so either—

    (a) on an application by a party to the proceedings, if there has been a material change of circumstances since the relevant time, or

    (b) of its own motion.

(4) In subsection (3) "the relevant time" means —

    (a) the time when the direction was given, or

    (b) if a previous application has been made under that subsection, the time when the application (or last application) was made.

(8) In this Chapter "live link" means a live television link or other arrangement whereby a witness, while absent from the courtroom or other place where the proceedings are being held, is able to see and hear a person there and to be seen and heard by the persons specified in section 23(2)(a) to (c).

25—Evidence given in private

(1) A special measures direction may provide for the exclusion from the court, during the giving of the witness's evidence, of persons of any description specified in the direction.

(2) The persons who may be so excluded do not include—

    (a) the accused,

    (b) legal representatives acting in the proceedings, or

    (c) any interpreter or other person appointed (in pursuance of the direction or otherwise) to assist the witness.

(3) A special measures direction providing for representatives of news gathering or reporting organisations to be so excluded shall be expressed not to apply to one named person who—

    (a) is a representative of such an organisation, and

    (b) has been nominated for the purpose by one or more such organisations,

unless it appears to the court that no such nomination has been made.

(4) A special measures direction may only provide for the exclusion of persons under this section where—

    (a) the proceedings relate to a sexual offence; or

(b)   it appears to the court that there are reasonable grounds for
believing that any person other than the accused has sought, or will
seek, to intimidate the witness in connection with testifying in the
proceedings.

(5)   Any proceedings from which persons are excluded under this section
(whether or not those persons include representatives of news gathering
or reporting organisations) shall nevertheless be taken to be held in
public for the purposes of any privilege or exemption from liability
available in respect of fair, accurate and contemporaneous reports of
legal proceedings held in public.

26   Removal of wigs and gowns

A special measures direction may provide for the wearing of wigs or
gowns to be dispensed with during the giving of the witness's evidence.

27—Video recorded evidence in chief

(1)   A special measures direction may provide for a video recording of an
interview of the witness to be admitted as evidence in chief of the witness.

(2)   A special measures direction may, however, not provide for a video
recording, or a part of such a recording, to be admitted under this section
if the court is of the opinion, having regard to all the circumstances of the
case, that in the interests of justice the recording, or that part of it, should
not be so admitted.

(3)   In considering for the purposes of subsection (2) whether any part of a
recording should not be admitted under this section, the court must
consider whether any prejudice to the accused which might result from
that part being so admitted is outweighed by the desirability of showing
the whole, or substantially the whole, of the recorded interview.

(4)   Where a special measures direction provides for a recording to be
admitted under this section, the court may nevertheless subsequently
direct that it is not to be so admitted if—
(a)   it appears to the court that—
(i)   the witness will not be available for cross-examination (whether
conducted in the ordinary way or in accordance with any such
direction), and
(ii)   the parties to the proceedings have not agreed that there is no
need for the witness to be so available; or
(b)   any Criminal Procedure Rules requiring disclosure of the
circumstances in which the recording was made have not been
complied with to the satisfaction of the court.

(5)   Where a recording is admitted under this section—
(a)   the witness must be called by the party tendering it in evidence,
unless—

(i)   a special measures direction provides for the witness's evidence on cross-examination to be given otherwise than by testimony in court, or

(ii)   the parties to the proceedings have agreed as mentioned in subsection (4)(a)(ii); and

(b)   the witness may not give evidence in chief otherwise than by means of the recording—

(i)   as to any matter which, in the opinion of the court, has been dealt with adequately in the witness's recorded testimony, or

(ii)   without the permission of the court, as to any other matter which, in the opinion of the court, is dealt with in that testimony.

(6)   Where in accordance with subsection (2) a special measures direction provides for part only of a recording to be admitted under this section, references in subsections (4) and (5) to the recording or to the witness's recorded testimony are references to the part of the recording or testimony which is to be so admitted.

(7)   The court may give permission for the purposes of subsection (5)(b)(ii) if it appears to the court to be in the interests of justice to do so, and may do so either—

(a)   on an application by a party to the proceedings, if there has been a material change of circumstances since the relevant time, or

(b)   of its own motion.

(8)   In subsection (7) "the relevant time" means —

(a)   the time when the direction was given, or

(b)   if a previous application has been made under that subsection, the time when the application (or last application) was made.

(9)   The court may, in giving permission for the purposes of subsection (5)(b)(ii), direct that the evidence in question is to be given by the witness by means of a live link; and, if the court so directs, subsections (5) to (7) of section 24 shall apply in relation to that evidence as they apply in relation to evidence which is to be given in accordance with a special measures direction.

(10)   A magistrates' court inquiring into an offence as examining justices under section 6 of the Magistrates' Courts Act 1980 may consider any video recording in relation to which it is proposed to apply for a special measures direction providing for it to be admitted at the trial in accordance with this section.

(11)   Nothing in this section affects the admissibility of any video recording which would be admissible apart from this section.

28—Video recorded cross-examination or re-examination

(1) Where a special measures direction provides for a video recording to be admitted under section 27 as evidence in chief of the witness, the direction may also provide—

(a) for any cross-examination of the witness, and any re-examination, to be recorded by means of a video recording; and

(b) for such a recording to be admitted, so far as it relates to any such cross-examination or re-examination, as evidence of the witness under cross-examination or on re-examination, as the case may be.

(2) Such a recording must be made in the presence of such persons as Criminal Procedure Rules or the direction may provide and in the absence of the accused, but in circumstances in which—

(a) the judge or justices (or both) and legal representatives acting in the proceedings are able to see and hear the examination of the witness and to communicate with the persons in whose presence the recording is being made, and

(b) the accused is able to see and hear any such examination and to communicate with any legal representative acting for him.

(3) Where two or more legal representatives are acting for a party to the proceedings, subsection (2)(a) and (b) are to be regarded as satisfied in relation to those representatives if at all material times they are satisfied in relation to at least one of them.

(4) Where a special measures direction provides for a recording to be admitted under this section, the court may nevertheless subsequently direct that it is not to be so admitted if any requirement of subsection (2) or Criminal Procedure Rules or the direction has not been complied with to the satisfaction of the court.

(5) Where in pursuance of subsection (1) a recording has been made of any examination of the witness, the witness may not be subsequently cross-examined or re-examined in respect of any evidence given by the witness in the proceedings (whether in any recording admissible under section 27 or this section or otherwise than in such a recording) unless the court gives a further special measures direction making such provision as is mentioned in subsection (1)(a) and (b) in relation to any subsequent cross-examination, and re-examination, of the witness.

(6) The court may only give such a further direction if it appears to the court—

(a) that the proposed cross-examination is sought by a party to the proceedings as a result of that party having become aware, since the time when the original recording was made in pursuance of subsection (1), of a matter which that party could not with reasonable diligence have ascertained by then, or

(b) that for any other reason it is in the interests of justice to give the further direction.

(7) Nothing in this section shall be read as applying in relation to any cross-examination of the witness by the accused in person (in a case where the accused is to be able to conduct any such cross-examination).

29—Examination of witness through intermediary

(1) A special measures direction may provide for any examination of the witness (however and wherever conducted) to be conducted through an interpreter or other person approved by the court for the purposes of this section ("an intermediary").

(2) The function of an intermediary is to communicate—

(a) to the witness, questions put to the witness, and

(b) to any person asking such questions, the answers given by the witness in reply to them,

and to explain such questions or answers so far as necessary to enable them to be understood by the witness or person in question.

(3) Any examination of the witness in pursuance of subsection (1) must take place in the presence of such persons as Criminal Procedure Rules or the direction may provide, but in circumstances in which—

(a) the judge or justices (or both) and legal representatives acting in the proceedings are able to see and hear the examination of the witness and to communicate with the intermediary, and

(b) (except in the case of a video recorded examination) the jury (if there is one) are able to see and hear the examination of the witness.

(4) Where two or more legal representatives are acting for a party to the proceedings, subsection (3)(a) is to be regarded as satisfied in relation to those representatives if at all material times it is satisfied in relation to at least one of them.

(5) A person may not act as an intermediary in a particular case except after making a declaration, in such form as may be prescribed by Criminal Procedure Rules, that he will faithfully perform his function as intermediary.

(6) Subsection (1) does not apply to an interview of the witness which is recorded by means of a video recording with a view to its admission as evidence in chief of the witness; but a special measures direction may provide for such a recording to be admitted under section 27 if the interview was conducted through an intermediary and—

(a) that person complied with subsection (5) before the interview began, and

(b) the court's approval for the purposes of this section is given before the direction is given.

(7) Section 1 of the Perjury Act 1911 (perjury) shall apply in relation to a person acting as an intermediary as it applies in relation to a person lawfully sworn as an interpreter in a judicial proceeding; and for this

purpose, where a person acts as an intermediary in any proceeding which is not a judicial proceeding for the purposes of that section, that proceeding shall be taken to be part of the judicial proceeding in which the witness's evidence is given.

30 Aids to communication

A special measures direction may provide for the witness, while giving evidence (whether by testimony in court or otherwise), to be provided with such device as the court considers appropriate with a view to enabling questions or answers to be communicated to or by the witness despite any disability or disorder or other impairment which the witness has or suffers from.

31—Status of evidence given under Chapter I

(1) Subsections (2) to (4) apply to a statement made by a witness in criminal proceedings which, in accordance with a special measures direction, is not made by the witness in direct oral testimony in court but forms part of the witness's evidence in those proceedings.

(2) The statement shall be treated as if made by the witness in direct oral testimony in court; and accordingly—
   (a) it is admissible evidence of any fact of which such testimony from the witness would be admissible;
   (b) it is not capable of corroborating any other evidence given by the witness.

(3) Subsection (2) applies to a statement admitted under section 27 or 28 which is not made by the witness on oath even though it would have been required to be made on oath if made by the witness in direct oral testimony in court.

(4) In estimating the weight (if any) to be attached to the statement, the court must have regard to all the circumstances from which an inference can reasonably be drawn (as to the accuracy of the statement or otherwise).

(5) Nothing in this Chapter (apart from subsection (3)) affects the operation of any rule of law relating to evidence in criminal proceedings.

(6) Where any statement made by a person on oath in any proceeding which is not a judicial proceeding for the purposes of section 1 of the Perjury Act 1911 (perjury) is received in evidence in pursuance of a special measures direction, that proceeding shall be taken for the purposes of that section to be part of the judicial proceeding in which the statement is so received in evidence.

(7) Where in any proceeding which is not a judicial proceeding for the purposes of that Act—
   (a) a person wilfully makes a false statement otherwise than on oath which is subsequently received in evidence in pursuance of a special measures direction, and

(b) the statement is made in such circumstances that had it been given on oath in any such judicial proceeding that person would have been guilty of perjury,

he shall be guilty of an offence and liable to any punishment which might be imposed on conviction of an offence under section 57(2) (giving of false unsworn evidence in criminal proceedings).

(8) In this section "statement" includes any representation of fact, whether made in words or otherwise.

32 Warning to jury

Where on a trial on indictment with a jury evidence has been given in accordance with a special measures direction, the judge must give the jury such warning (if any) as the judge considers necessary to ensure that the fact that the direction was given in relation to the witness does not prejudice the accused.

33—Interpretation etc. of Chapter I

(1) In this Chapter—

"eligible witness" means a witness eligible for assistance by virtue of section 16 or 17;

"live link" has the meaning given by section 24(8);

"quality", in relation to the evidence of a witness, shall be construed in accordance with section 16(5);

"special measures direction" means (in accordance with section 19(5)) a direction under section 19.

(2) In this Chapter references to the special measures available in relation to a witness shall be construed in accordance with section 18.

(3) In this Chapter references to a person being able to see or hear, or be seen or heard by, another person are to be read as not applying to the extent that either of them is unable to see or hear by reason of any impairment of eyesight or hearing.

(4) In the case of any proceedings in which there is more than one accused—

(a) any reference to the accused in sections 23 to 28 may be taken by a court, in connection with the giving of a special measures direction, as a reference to all or any of the accused, as the court may determine, and

(b) any such direction may be given on the basis of any such determination.

33A Live link directions

(1) This section applies to any proceedings (whether in a magistrates' court or before the Crown Court) against a person for an offence.

(2)   The court may, on the application of the accused, give a live link
       direction if it is satisfied–
       (a)   that the conditions in subsection (4) or, as the case may be,
              subsection (5) are met in relation to the accused, and
       (b)   that it is in the interests of justice for the accused to give evidence
              through a live link.

(3)   A live link direction is a direction that any oral evidence to be given
       before the court by the accused is to be given through a live link.

(4)   Where the accused is aged under 18 when the application is made, the
       conditions are that–
       (a)   his ability to participate effectively in the proceedings as a witness
              giving oral evidence in court is compromised by his level of
              intellectual ability or social functioning, and
       (b)   use of a live link would enable him to participate more effectively in
              the proceedings as a witness (whether by improving the quality of his
              evidence or otherwise).

(5)   Where the accused has attained the age of 18 at that time, the conditions
       are that–
       (a)   he suffers from a mental disorder (within the meaning of the Mental
              Health Act 1983) or otherwise has a significant impairment of
              intelligence and social function,
       (b)   he is for that reason unable to participate effectively in the
              proceedings as a witness giving oral evidence in court, and
       (c)   use of a live link would enable him to participate more effectively in
              the proceedings as a witness (whether by improving the quality of his
              evidence or otherwise).

(6)   While a live link direction has effect the accused may not give oral
       evidence before the court in the proceedings otherwise than through a
       live link.

(7)   The court may discharge a live link direction at any time before or during
       any hearing to which it applies if it appears to the court to be in the
       interests of justice to do so (but this does not affect the power to give a
       further live link direction in relation to the accused).

       The court may exercise this power of its own motion or on an
       application by a party.

(8)   The court must state in open court its reasons for–
       (a)   giving or discharging a live link direction, or
       (b)   refusing an application for or for the discharge of a live link
              direction,

       and, if it is a magistrates' court, it must cause those reasons to be entered
       in the register of its proceedings.

33B   Section 33A: meaning of "live link"

(1) In section 33A "live link" means an arrangement by which the accused, while absent from the place where the proceedings are being held, is able–
   (a)   to see and hear a person there, and
   (b)   to be seen and heard by the persons mentioned in subsection (2),
   and for this purpose any impairment of eyesight or hearing is to be disregarded.

(2) The persons are–
   (a)   the judge or justices (or both) and the jury (if there is one),
   (b)   where there are two or more accused in the proceedings, each of the other accused,
   (c)   legal representatives acting in the proceedings, and
   (d)   any interpreter or other person appointed by the court to assist the accused.

33C   Saving

Nothing in this Chapter affects–
   (a)   any power of a court to make an order, give directions or give leave of any description in relation to any witness (including an accused), or
   (b)   the operation of any rule of law relating to evidence in criminal proceedings.

CHAPTER II
PROTECTION OF WITNESSES FROM CROSS-EXAMINATION BY ACCUSED IN PERSON

General prohibitions

34   Complainants in proceedings for sexual offences

No person charged with a sexual offence may in any criminal proceedings cross-examine in person a witness who is the complainant, either—
   (a)   in connection with that offence, or
   (b)   in connection with any other offence (of whatever nature) with which that person is charged in the proceedings.

35—Child complainants and other child witnesses

(1) No person charged with an offence to which this section applies may in any criminal proceedings cross-examine in person a protected witness, either—

(a)   in connection with that offence, or

(b)   in connection with any other offence (of whatever nature) with which that person is charged in the proceedings.

(2) For the purposes of subsection (1) a "protected witness" is a witness who—

(a)   either is the complainant or is alleged to have been a witness to the commission of the offence to which this section applies, and

(b)   either is a child or falls to be cross-examined after giving evidence in chief (whether wholly or in part)—

(i)   by means of a video recording made (for the purposes of section 27) at a time when the witness was a child, or

(ii) in any other way at any such time.

(3) The offences to which this section applies are—

(a)   any offence under—

(iva)   any of sections 33 to 36 of the Sexual Offences Act 1956,

(v) the Protection of Children Act 1978, or

(vi) Part 1 of the Sexual Offences Act 2003 or any relevant superseded enactment;

(b)   kidnapping, false imprisonment or an offence under section 1 or 2 of the Child Abduction Act 1984;

(c)   any offence under section 1 of the Children and Young Persons Act 1933;

(d)   any offence (not within any of the preceding paragraphs) which involves an assault on, or injury or a threat of injury to, any person.

(3A)   In subsection (3)(a)(vi) "relevant superseded enactment" means—

(a)   any of sections 1 to 32 of the Sexual Offences Act 1956;

(b)   the Indecency with Children Act 1960;

(c)   the Sexual Offences Act 1967;

(d)   section 54 of the Criminal Law Act 1977.

(4) In this section "child" means—

(a)   where the offence falls within subsection (3)(a), a person under the age of 17; or

(b)   where the offence falls within subsection (3)(b), (c) or (d), a person under the age of 14.

(5) For the purposes of this section "witness" includes a witness who is charged with an offence in the proceedings.

Words added by Criminal Justice and Immigration Act 2008 c. 4 Sch.26(2) para.36(2)(a) (May 1, 2004: substitution has effect from May 1, 2004) 4. Words inserted by Criminal Justice and Immigration Act 2008 c. 4 Sch.26(2) para.36(2)(b) (May 1, 2004: substitution has effect from May 1, 2004); words added by Criminal Justice and Immigration Act 2008 c. 4 Sch.26(2) para.36(3) (May 1, 2004: substitution has effect from May 1, 2004)

36—Direction prohibiting accused from cross-examining particular witness

(1) This section applies where, in a case where neither of sections 34 and 35 operates to prevent an accused in any criminal proceedings from cross-examining a witness in person—

(a) the prosecutor makes an application for the court to give a direction under this section in relation to the witness, or

(b) the court of its own motion raises the issue whether such a direction should be given.

(2) If it appears to the court—

(a) that the quality of evidence given by the witness on cross-examination—

(i) is likely to be diminished if the cross-examination (or further cross-examination) is conducted by the accused in person, and

(ii) would be likely to be improved if a direction were given under this section, and

(b) that it would not be contrary to the interests of justice to give such a direction,

the court may give a direction prohibiting the accused from cross-examining (or further cross-examining) the witness in person.

(3) In determining whether subsection (2)(a) applies in the case of a witness the court must have regard, in particular, to—

(a) any views expressed by the witness as to whether or not the witness is content to be cross-examined by the accused in person;

(b) the nature of the questions likely to be asked, having regard to the issues in the proceedings and the defence case advanced so far (if any);

(c) any behaviour on the part of the accused at any stage of the proceedings, both generally and in relation to the witness;

(d) any relationship (of whatever nature) between the witness and the accused;

(e) whether any person (other than the accused) is or has at any time been charged in the proceedings with a sexual offence or an offence to which section 35 applies, and (if so) whether section 34 or 35 operates or would have operated to prevent that person from cross-examining the witness in person;

(f) any direction under section 19 which the court has given, or proposes to give, in relation to the witness.

(4) For the purposes of this section—

(a) "witness", in relation to an accused, does not include any other person who is charged with an offence in the proceedings; and

(b) any reference to the quality of a witness's evidence shall be construed in accordance with section 16(5).

37—Further provisions about directions under section 36

(1) Subject to subsection (2), a direction has binding effect from the time it is made until the witness to whom it applies is discharged.

In this section "direction" means a direction under section 36.

(2) The court may discharge a direction if it appears to the court to be in the interests of justice to do so, and may do so either—

   (a) on an application made by a party to the proceedings, if there has been a material change of circumstances since the relevant time, or

   (b) of its own motion.

(3) In subsection (2) "the relevant time" means—

   (a) the time when the direction was given, or

   (b) if a previous application has been made under that subsection, the time when the application (or last application) was made.

(4) The court must state in open court its reasons for—

   (a) giving, or

   (b) refusing an application for, or for the discharge of, or

   (c) discharging,

   a direction and, if it is a magistrates' court, must cause them to be entered in the register of its proceedings.

(5) Criminal Procedure Rules may make provision—

   (a) for uncontested applications to be determined by the court without a hearing;

   (b) for preventing the renewal of an unsuccessful application for a direction except where there has been a material change of circumstances;

   (c) for expert evidence to be given in connection with an application for, or for discharging, a direction;

   (d) for the manner in which confidential or sensitive information is to be treated in connection with such an application and in particular as to its being disclosed to, or withheld from, a party to the proceedings.

38—Defence representation for purposes of cross-examination

(1) This section applies where an accused is prevented from cross-examining a witness in person by virtue of section 34, 35 or 36.

(2) Where it appears to the court that this section applies, it must—

   (a) invite the accused to arrange for a legal representative to act for him for the purpose of cross-examining the witness; and

   (b) require the accused to notify the court, by the end of such period as it may specify, whether a legal representative is to act for him for that purpose.

(3) If by the end of the period mentioned in subsection (2)(b) either—

(a)   the accused has notified the court that no legal representative is to act for him for the purpose of cross-examining the witness, or

(b)   no notification has been received by the court and it appears to the court that no legal representative is to so act,

the court must consider whether it is necessary in the interests of justice for the witness to be cross-examined by a legal representative appointed to represent the interests of the accused.

(4) If the court decides that it is necessary in the interests of justice for the witness to be so cross-examined, the court must appoint a qualified legal representative (chosen by the court) to cross-examine the witness in the interests of the accused.

(5) A person so appointed shall not be responsible to the accused.

(6) Criminal Procedure Rules may make provision—

(a)   as to the time when, and the manner in which, subsection (2) is to be complied with;

(b)   in connection with the appointment of a legal representative under subsection (4), and in particular for securing that a person so appointed is provided with evidence or other material relating to the proceedings.

(7) Criminal Procedure Rules made in pursuance of subsection (6)(b) may make provision for the application, with such modifications as are specified in the rules, of any of the provisions of—

(a)   Part I of the Criminal Procedure and Investigations Act 1996 (disclosure of material in connection with criminal proceedings), or

(b)   the Sexual Offences (Protected Material) Act 1997.

(8) For the purposes of this section—

(a)   any reference to cross-examination includes (in a case where a direction is given under section 36 after the accused has begun cross-examining the witness) a reference to further cross-examination; and

(b)   "qualified legal representative" means a legal representative who has a right of audience (within the meaning of the Courts and Legal Services Act 1990) in relation to the proceedings before the court.

39—Warning to jury

(1) Where on a trial on indictment with a jury an accused is prevented from cross-examining a witness in person by virtue of section 34, 35 or 36, the judge must give the jury such warning (if any) as the judge considers necessary to ensure that the accused is not prejudiced—

(a)   by any inferences that might be drawn from the fact that the accused has been prevented from cross-examining the witness in person;

(b)   where the witness has been cross-examined by a legal representative appointed under section 38(4), by the fact that the cross-examination was carried out by such a legal representative and not by a person acting as the accused's own legal representative.

(2) Subsection (8)(a) of section 38 applies for the purposes of this section as it applies for the purposes of section 38.

CHAPTER III
PROTECTION OF COMPLAINANTS IN PROCEEDINGS FOR SEXUAL OFFENCES

41—Restriction on evidence or questions about complainant's sexual history

(1) If at a trial a person is charged with a sexual offence, then, except with the leave of the court—

(a) no evidence may be adduced, and

(b) no question may be asked in cross-examination,

by or on behalf of any accused at the trial, about any sexual behaviour of the complainant.

(2) The court may give leave in relation to any evidence or question only on an application made by or on behalf of an accused, and may not give such leave unless it is satisfied—

(a) that subsection (3) or (5) applies, and

(b) that a refusal of leave might have the result of rendering unsafe a conclusion of the jury or (as the case may be) the court on any relevant issue in the case.

(3) This subsection applies if the evidence or question relates to a relevant issue in the case and either—

(a) that issue is not an issue of consent; or

(b) it is an issue of consent and the sexual behaviour of the complainant to which the evidence or question relates is alleged to have taken place at or about the same time as the event which is the subject matter of the charge against the accused; or

(c) it is an issue of consent and the sexual behaviour of the complainant to which the evidence or question relates is alleged to have been, in any respect, so similar—

(i) to any sexual behaviour of the complainant which (according to evidence adduced or to be adduced by or on behalf of the accused) took place as part of the event which is the subject matter of the charge against the accused, or

(ii) to any other sexual behaviour of the complainant which (according to such evidence) took place at or about the same time as that event,

that the similarity cannot reasonably be explained as a coincidence.

(4) For the purposes of subsection (3) no evidence or question shall be regarded as relating to a relevant issue in the case if it appears to the court to be reasonable to assume that the purpose (or main purpose) for which it would be adduced or asked is to establish or elicit material for impugning the credibility of the complainant as a witness.

(5) This subsection applies if the evidence or question—

    (a) relates to any evidence adduced by the prosecution about any sexual behaviour of the complainant; and

    (b) in the opinion of the court, would go no further than is necessary to enable the evidence adduced by the prosecution to be rebutted or explained by or on behalf of the accused.

(6) For the purposes of subsections (3) and (5) the evidence or question must relate to a specific instance (or specific instances) of alleged sexual behaviour on the part of the complainant (and accordingly nothing in those subsections is capable of applying in relation to the evidence or question to the extent that it does not so relate).

(7) Where this section applies in relation to a trial by virtue of the fact that one or more of a number of persons charged in the proceedings is or are charged with a sexual offence—

    (a) it shall cease to apply in relation to the trial if the prosecutor decides not to proceed with the case against that person or those persons in respect of that charge; but

    (b) it shall not cease to do so in the event of that person or those persons pleading guilty to, or being convicted of, that charge.

(8) Nothing in this section authorises any evidence to be adduced or any question to be asked which cannot be adduced or asked apart from this section.

42—Interpretation and application of section 41

(1) In section 41—

    (a) "relevant issue in the case" means any issue falling to be proved by the prosecution or defence in the trial of the accused;

    (b) "issue of consent" means any issue whether the complainant in fact consented to the conduct constituting the offence with which the accused is charged (and accordingly does not include any issue as to the belief of the accused that the complainant so consented);

    (c) "sexual behaviour" means any sexual behaviour or other sexual experience, whether or not involving any accused or other person, but excluding (except in section 41(3)(c)(i) and (5)(a)) anything alleged to have taken place as part of the event which is the subject matter of the charge against the accused; and

    (d) subject to any order made under subsection (2), "sexual offence" shall be construed in accordance with section 62.

(2) The Secretary of State may by order make such provision as he considers appropriate for adding or removing, for the purposes of section 41, any offence to or from the offences which are sexual offences for the purposes of this Act by virtue of section 62.

(3) Section 41 applies in relation to the following proceedings as it applies to a trial, namely—

(a) proceedings before a magistrates' court inquiring into an offence as examining justices,

(b) the hearing of an application under paragraph 5(1) of Schedule 6 to the Criminal Justice Act 1991 (application to dismiss charge following notice of transfer of case to Crown Court),

(c) the hearing of an application under paragraph 2(1) of Schedule 3 to the Crime and Disorder Act 1998 (application to dismiss charge by person sent for trial under section 51 or 51A of that Act),

(d) any hearing held, between conviction and sentencing, for the purpose of determining matters relevant to the court's decision as to how the accused is to be dealt with, and

(e) the hearing of an appeal,

and references (in section 41 or this section) to a person charged with an offence accordingly include a person convicted of an offence.

43—Procedure on applications under section 41

(1) An application for leave shall be heard in private and in the absence of the complainant.

In this section "leave" means leave under section 41.

(2) Where such an application has been determined, the court must state in open court (but in the absence of the jury, if there is one)—

(a) its reasons for giving, or refusing, leave, and

(b) if it gives leave, the extent to which evidence may be adduced or questions asked in pursuance of the leave,

and, if it is a magistrates' court, must cause those matters to be entered in the register of its proceedings.

(3) Criminal Procedure Rules may make provision—

(a) requiring applications for leave to specify, in relation to each item of evidence or question to which they relate, particulars of the grounds on which it is asserted that leave should be given by virtue of subsection (3) or (5) of section 41;

(b) enabling the court to request a party to the proceedings to provide the court with information which it considers would assist it in determining an application for leave;

(c) for the manner in which confidential or sensitive information is to be treated in connection with such an application, and in particular as to its being disclosed to, or withheld from, parties to the proceedings.

CHAPTER V

COMPETENCE OF WITNESSES AND CAPACITY TO BE SWORN

Competence of witnesses

53—Competence of witnesses to give evidence

(1) At every stage in criminal proceedings all persons are (whatever their age) competent to give evidence.

(2) Subsection (1) has effect subject to subsections (3) and (4).

(3) A person is not competent to give evidence in criminal proceedings if it appears to the court that he is not a person who is able to—

(a) understand questions put to him as a witness, and

(b) give answers to them which can be understood.

(4) A person charged in criminal proceedings is not competent to give evidence in the proceedings for the prosecution (whether he is the only person, or is one of two or more persons, charged in the proceedings).

(5) In subsection (4) the reference to a person charged in criminal proceedings does not include a person who is not, or is no longer, liable to be convicted of any offence in the proceedings (whether as a result of pleading guilty or for any other reason).

54—Determining competence of witnesses

(1) Any question whether a witness in criminal proceedings is competent to give evidence in the proceedings, whether raised—

(a) by a party to the proceedings, or

(b) by the court of its own motion,

shall be determined by the court in accordance with this section.

(2) It is for the party calling the witness to satisfy the court that, on a balance of probabilities, the witness is competent to give evidence in the proceedings.

(3) In determining the question mentioned in subsection (1) the court shall treat the witness as having the benefit of any directions under section 19 which the court has given, or proposes to give, in relation to the witness.

(4) Any proceedings held for the determination of the question shall take place in the absence of the jury (if there is one).

(5) Expert evidence may be received on the question.

(6) Any questioning of the witness (where the court considers that necessary) shall be conducted by the court in the presence of the parties.

55—Determining whether witness to be sworn

(1) Any question whether a witness in criminal proceedings may be sworn for the purpose of giving evidence on oath, whether raised—

(a) by a party to the proceedings, or

(b) by the court of its own motion,

shall be determined by the court in accordance with this section.

(2) The witness may not be sworn for that purpose unless—

(a) he has attained the age of 14, and

(b) he has a sufficient appreciation of the solemnity of the occasion and of the particular responsibility to tell the truth which is involved in taking an oath.

(3) The witness shall, if he is able to give intelligible testimony, be presumed to have a sufficient appreciation of those matters if no evidence tending to show the contrary is adduced (by any party).

(4) If any such evidence is adduced, it is for the party seeking to have the witness sworn to satisfy the court that, on a balance of probabilities, the witness has attained the age of 14 and has a sufficient appreciation of the matters mentioned in subsection (2)(b).

(5) Any proceedings held for the determination of the question mentioned in subsection (1) shall take place in the absence of the jury (if there is one).

(6) Expert evidence may be received on the question.

(7) Any questioning of the witness (where the court considers that necessary) shall be conducted by the court in the presence of the parties.

(8) For the purposes of this section a person is able to give intelligible testimony if he is able to—

(a) understand questions put to him as a witness, and

(b) give answers to them which can be understood.

56—Reception of unsworn evidence

(1) Subsections (2) and (3) apply to a person (of any age) who—

(a) is competent to give evidence in criminal proceedings, but

(b) (by virtue of section 55(2)) is not permitted to be sworn for the purpose of giving evidence on oath in such proceedings.

(2) The evidence in criminal proceedings of a person to whom this subsection applies shall be given unsworn.

(3) A deposition of unsworn evidence given by a person to whom this subsection applies may be taken for the purposes of criminal proceedings as if that evidence had been given on oath.

(4) A court in criminal proceedings shall accordingly receive in evidence any evidence given unsworn in pursuance of subsection (2) or (3).

(5) Where a person ("the witness") who is competent to give evidence in criminal proceedings gives evidence in such proceedings unsworn, no conviction, verdict or finding in those proceedings shall be taken to be unsafe for the purposes of any of sections 2(1), 13(1) and 16(1) of the Criminal Appeal Act 1968 (grounds for allowing appeals) by reason only that it appears to the Court of Appeal that the witness was a person falling within section 55(2) (and should accordingly have given his evidence on oath).

57—Penalty for giving false unsworn evidence

(1) This section applies where a person gives unsworn evidence in criminal proceedings in pursuance of section 56(2) or (3).

(2) If such a person wilfully gives false evidence in such circumstances that, had the evidence been given on oath, he would have been guilty of perjury, he shall be guilty of an offence and liable on summary conviction to—

(a) imprisonment for a term not exceeding 6 months, or

(b) a fine not exceeding £1,000,

or both.

(3) In relation to a person under the age of 14, subsection (2) shall have effect as if for the words following "on summary conviction" there were substituted "to a fine not exceeding £250".

CHAPTER VI
RESTRICTIONS ON USE OF EVIDENCE

Additional restrictions

58—Inferences from silence not permissible where no prior access to legal advice

(1) Sections 34 and 36 to 38 of the Criminal Justice and Public Order Act 1994 (inferences from accused's silence) shall be amended as follows.

(2) In section 34 (effect of accused's failure to mention facts when questioned or charged), after subsection (2) there shall be inserted—

"(2A) Where the accused was at an authorised place of detention at the time of the failure, subsections (1) and (2) above do not apply if he had not been allowed an opportunity to consult a solicitor prior to being questioned, charged or informed as mentioned in subsection (1) above."

(3) In section 36 (effect of accused's failure or refusal to account for objects, substances or marks), after subsection (4) there shall be inserted—

"(4A) Where the accused was at an authorised place of detention at the time of the failure or refusal, subsections (1) and (2) above do not apply if he had not been allowed an opportunity to consult a solicitor prior to the request being made."

(4) In section 37 (effect of accused's failure or refusal to account for presence at a particular place), after subsection (3) there shall be inserted—

"(3A) Where the accused was at an authorised place of detention at the time of the failure or refusal, subsections (1) and (2) do not apply if he had not been allowed an opportunity to consult a solicitor prior to the request being made."

(5) In section 38 (interpretation), after subsection (2) there shall be inserted—

"(2A) In each of sections 34(2A), 36(4A) and 37(3A) "authorised place of detention" means—

(a) a police station; or

(b) any other place prescribed for the purposes of that provision by order made by the Secretary of State;

and the power to make an order under this subsection shall be exercisable by statutory instrument which shall be subject to annulment in pursuance of a resolution of either House of Parliament."

59   Restriction on use of answers etc. obtained under compulsion

Schedule 3, which amends enactments providing for the use of answers and statements given under compulsion so as to restrict in criminal proceedings their use in evidence against the persons giving them, shall have effect.

PART VII
GENERAL

62—Meaning of "sexual offence" and other references to offences

(1) In this Part "sexual offence" means any offence under Part 1 of the Sexual Offences Act 2003 or any relevant superseded offence.

(1A)   In subsection (1) "relevant superseded offence" means—
(a) rape or burglary with intent to rape;
(b) an offence under any of sections 2 to 12 and 14 to 17 of the Sexual Offences Act 1956 (unlawful intercourse, indecent assault, forcible abduction etc.);
(c) an offence under section 128 of the Mental Health Act 1959 (unlawful intercourse with person receiving treatment for mental disorder by member of hospital staff etc.);
(d) an offence under section 1 of the Indecency with Children Act 1960 (indecent conduct towards child under 14);

(e)   an offence under section 54 of the Criminal Law Act 1977 (incitement of child under 16 to commit incest).

(2) In this Part any reference (including a reference having effect by virtue of this subsection) to an offence of any description ("the substantive offence") is to be taken to include a reference to an offence which consists of attempting or conspiring to commit, or of aiding, abetting, counselling, procuring or inciting the commission of, the substantive offence.

Words inserted by Criminal Justice and Immigration Act 2008 c. 4 Sch.26(2) para.37(2) (May 1, 2004: substitution has effect from May 1, 2004); Words added by Criminal Justice and Immigration Act 2008 c. 4 Sch.26(2) para.37(3) (May 1, 2004: substitution has effect from May 1, 2004)

Regulation of Investigatory Powers Act 2000
(c. 23)

PART II
SURVEILLANCE AND COVERT HUMAN INTELLIGENCE SOURCES

Introductory

26—Conduct to which Part II applies

(1) This Part applies to the following conduct–
   (a) directed surveillance;
   (b) intrusive surveillance; and
   (c) the conduct and use of covert human intelligence sources.

(2) Subject to subsection (6), surveillance is directed for the purposes of this Part if it is covert but not intrusive and is undertaken–
   (a) for the purposes of a specific investigation or a specific operation;
   (b) in such a manner as is likely to result in the obtaining of private information about a person (whether or not one specifically identified for the purposes of the investigation or operation); and
   (c) otherwise than by way of an immediate response to events or circumstances the nature of which is such that it would not be reasonably practicable for an authorisation under this Part to be sought for the carrying out of the surveillance.

(3) Subject to subsections (4) to (6), surveillance is intrusive for the purposes of this Part if, and only if, it is covert surveillance that–
   (a) is carried out in relation to anything taking place on any residential premises or in any private vehicle; and
   (b) involves the presence of an individual on the premises or in the vehicle or is carried out by means of a surveillance device.

(4) For the purposes of this Part surveillance is not intrusive to the extent that–
   (a) it is carried out by means only of a surveillance device designed or adapted principally for the purpose of providing information about the location of a vehicle; or
   (b) it is surveillance consisting in any such interception of a communication as falls within section 48(4).

(5) For the purposes of this Part surveillance which–

(a) is carried out by means of a surveillance device in relation to anything taking place on any residential premises or in any private vehicle, but

(b) is carried out without that device being present on the premises or in the vehicle,

is not intrusive unless the device is such that it consistently provides information of the same quality and detail as might be expected to be obtained from a device actually present on the premises or in the vehicle.

(6) For the purposes of this Part surveillance which–

(a) is carried out by means of apparatus designed or adapted for the purpose of detecting the installation or use in any residential or other premises of a television receiver (within the meaning of Part 4 of the Communications Act 2003), and

(b) is carried out from outside those premises exclusively for that purpose,

is neither directed nor intrusive.

(7) In this Part–

(a) references to the conduct of a covert human intelligence source are references to any conduct of such a source which falls within any of paragraphs (a) to (c) of subsection (8), or is incidental to anything falling within any of those paragraphs; and

(b) references to the use of a covert human intelligence source are references to inducing, asking or assisting a person to engage in the conduct of such a source, or to obtain information by means of the conduct of such a source.

(8) For the purposes of this Part a person is a covert human intelligence source if–

(a) he establishes or maintains a personal or other relationship with a person for the covert purpose of facilitating the doing of anything falling within paragraph (b) or (c);

(b) he covertly uses such a relationship to obtain information or to provide access to any information to another person; or

(c) he covertly discloses information obtained by the use of such a relationship, or as a consequence of the existence of such a relationship.

(9) For the purposes of this section–

(a) surveillance is covert if, and only if, it is carried out in a manner that is calculated to ensure that persons who are subject to the surveillance are unaware that it is or may be taking place;

(b) a purpose is covert, in relation to the establishment or maintenance of a personal or other relationship, if and only if the relationship is conducted in a manner that is calculated to ensure that one of the parties to the relationship is unaware of the purpose; and

    (c)   a relationship is used covertly, and information obtained as mentioned in subsection (8)(c) is disclosed covertly, if and only if it is used or, as the case may be, disclosed in a manner that is calculated to ensure that one of the parties to the relationship is unaware of the use or disclosure in question.

(10)   In this section "private information", in relation to a person, includes any information relating to his private or family life.

(11)   References in this section, in relation to a vehicle, to the presence of a surveillance device in the vehicle include references to its being located on or under the vehicle and also include references to its being attached to it.

32—Authorisation of intrusive surveillance

(1)   Subject to the following provisions of this Part, the Secretary of State and each of the senior authorising officers shall have power to grant authorisations for the carrying out of intrusive surveillance.

(2)   Neither the Secretary of State nor any senior authorising officer shall grant an authorisation for the carrying out of intrusive surveillance unless he believes–

    (a)   that the authorisation is necessary on grounds falling within subsection (3); and

    (b)   that the authorised surveillance is proportionate to what is sought to be achieved by carrying it out.

(3)   Subject to the following provisions of this section, an authorisation is necessary on grounds falling within this subsection if it is necessary–

    (a)   in the interests of national security;

    (b)   for the purpose of preventing or detecting serious crime; or

    (c)   in the interests of the economic well-being of the United Kingdom.

(3A)   In the case of an authorisation granted by the chairman of the OFT, the authorisation is necessary on grounds falling within subsection (3) only if it is necessary for the purpose of preventing or detecting an offence under section 188 of the Enterprise Act 2002 (cartel offence).

(4)   The matters to be taken into account in considering whether the requirements of subsection (2) are satisfied in the case of any authorisation shall include whether the information which it is thought necessary to obtain by the authorised conduct could reasonably be obtained by other means.

(5)   The conduct that is authorised by an authorisation for the carrying out of intrusive surveillance is any conduct that–

    (a)   consists in the carrying out of intrusive surveillance of any such description as is specified in the authorisation;

    (b)   is carried out in relation to the residential premises specified or described in the authorisation or in relation to the private vehicle so specified or described; and

(c) is carried out for the purposes of, or in connection with, the investigation or operation so specified or described.

(6) For the purposes of this section the senior authorising officers are–

(a) the chief constable of every police force maintained under section 2 of the Police Act 1996 (police forces in England and Wales outside London);

(b) the Commissioner of Police of the Metropolis and every Assistant Commissioner of Police of the Metropolis;

(c) the Commissioner of Police for the City of London;

(d) the chief constable of every police force maintained under or by virtue of section 1 of the Police (Scotland) Act 1967 (police forces for areas in Scotland);

(e) the Chief Constable of the Royal Ulster Constabulary and the Deputy Chief Constable of the Royal Ulster Constabulary;

(f) the Chief Constable of the Ministry of Defence Police;

(g) the Provost Marshal of the [Royal Navy Police] 4;

(h) the Provost Marshal of the Royal Military Police;

(i) the Provost Marshal of the Royal Air Force Police;

(j) the Chief Constable of the British Transport Police;

(k) the Director General of the Serious Organised Crime Agency and any member of the staff of that Agency who is designated for the purposes of this paragraph by that Director General;

(m) an officer of Revenue and Customs who is a senior official and who is designated for the purposes of this paragraph by the Commissioners for Her Majesty's Revenue and Customs; and

(n) the chairman of the OFT.

35—Notification of authorisations for intrusive surveillance

(1) Where a person grants or cancels a police, SOCA, Revenue and Customs or OFT authorisation for the carrying out of intrusive surveillance, he shall give notice that he has done so to an ordinary Surveillance Commissioner.

(2) A notice given for the purposes of subsection (1)–

(a) must be given in writing as soon as reasonably practicable after the grant or, as the case may be, cancellation of the authorisation to which it relates;

(b) must be given in accordance with any such arrangements made for the purposes of this paragraph by the Chief Surveillance Commissioner as are for the time being in force; and

(c) must specify such matters as the Secretary of State may by order prescribe.

(3) A notice under this section of the grant of an authorisation shall, as the case may be, either–
   (a) state that the approval of a Surveillance Commissioner is required by section 36 before the grant of the authorisation will take effect; or
   (b) state that the case is one of urgency and set out the grounds on which the case is believed to be one of urgency.

(4) Where a notice for the purposes of subsection (1) of the grant of an authorisation has been received by an ordinary Surveillance Commissioner, he shall, as soon as practicable–
   (a) scrutinise the authorisation; and
   (b) in a case where notice has been given in accordance with subsection (3)(a), decide whether or not to approve the authorisation.

(5) Subject to subsection (6), the Secretary of State shall not make an order under subsection (2)(c) unless a draft of the order has been laid before Parliament and approved by a resolution of each House.

(6) Subsection (5) does not apply in the case of the order made on the first occasion on which the Secretary of State exercises his power to make an order under subsection (2)(c).

(7) The order made on that occasion shall cease to have effect at the end of the period of forty days beginning with the day on which it was made unless, before the end of that period, it has been approved by a resolution of each House of Parliament.

(8) For the purposes of subsection (7)–
   (a) the order's ceasing to have effect shall be without prejudice to anything previously done or to the making of a new order; and
   (b) in reckoning the period of forty days no account shall be taken of any period during which Parliament is dissolved or prorogued or during which both Houses are adjourned for more than four days.

(9) Any notice that is required by any provision of this section to be given in writing may be given, instead, by being transmitted by electronic means.

(10) In this section references to a police, SOCA, Revenue and Customs or OFT authorisation are references to an authorisation granted by–
   (a) a person who is a senior authorising officer by reference to a police force or the Serious Organised Crime Agency;
   (b) a person who is a senior authorising officer by virtue of a designation by [the Commissioners for Her Majesty's Revenue and Customs;
   (ba) the chairman of the OFT; or
   (c) a person who for the purposes of section 34 is entitled to act for a person falling within paragraph (a) or for a person falling within paragraph (b) or for a person falling within paragraph (ba).

TERRORISM ACT 2000
(c. 11)

PART VIII
GENERAL

118—Defences

(1) Subsection (2) applies where in accordance with a provision mentioned in subsection (5) it is a defence for a person charged with an offence to prove a particular matter.

(2) If the person adduces evidence which is sufficient to raise an issue with respect to the matter the court or jury shall assume that the defence is satisfied unless the prosecution proves beyond reasonable doubt that it is not.

(3) Subsection (4) applies where in accordance with a provision mentioned in subsection (5) a court–
  (a) may make an assumption in relation to a person charged with an offence unless a particular matter is proved, or
  (b) may accept a fact as sufficient evidence unless a particular matter is proved.

(4) If evidence is adduced which is sufficient to raise an issue with respect to the matter mentioned in subsection (3)(a) or (b) the court shall treat it as proved unless the prosecution disproves it beyond reasonable doubt.

(5) The provisions in respect of which subsections (2) and (4) apply are–
  (a) [sections 12(4), 39(5)(a), 54, 57, 58, 58A, 77 and 103] of this Act, and
  (b) sections 13, 32 and 33 of the Northern Ireland (Emergency Provisions) Act 1996 (possession and information offences) as they have effect by virtue of Schedule 1 to this Act.

Words inserted by Counter-Terrorism Act 2008 c. 28 Pt 7 s.76(3) (February 16, 2009)

CRIME (INTERNATIONAL CO-OPERATION) ACT 2003
(c. 32)

PART 1
MUTUAL ASSISTANCE IN CRIMINAL MATTERS

Assistance in obtaining evidence abroad

7 Requests for assistance in obtaining evidence abroad

(1) If it appears to a judicial authority in the United Kingdom on an application made by a person mentioned in subsection (3)—
    (a) that an offence has been committed or that there are reasonable grounds for suspecting that an offence has been committed, and
    (b) that proceedings in respect of the offence have been instituted or that the offence is being investigated,
the judicial authority may request assistance under this section.

(2) The assistance that may be requested under this section is assistance in obtaining outside the United Kingdom any evidence specified in the request for use in the proceedings or investigation.

(3) The application may be made—
    (a) in relation to England and Wales and Northern Ireland, by a prosecuting authority,
    (b) in relation to Scotland, by the Lord Advocate or a procurator fiscal,
    (c) where proceedings have been instituted, by the person charged in those proceedings.

(4) The judicial authorities are—
    (a) in relation to England and Wales, any judge or justice of the peace,
    (b) in relation to Scotland, any judge of the High Court or sheriff,
    (c) in relation to Northern Ireland, any judge or resident magistrate.

(5) In relation to England and Wales or Northern Ireland, a designated prosecuting authority may itself request assistance under this section if—
    (a) it appears to the authority that an offence has been committed or that there are reasonable grounds for suspecting that an offence has been committed, and
    (b) the authority has instituted proceedings in respect of the offence in question or it is being investigated.

"Designated" means designated by an order made by the Secretary of State.

(6) In relation to Scotland, the Lord Advocate or a procurator fiscal may himself request assistance under this section if it appears to him—

   (a) that an offence has been committed or that there are reasonable grounds for suspecting that an offence has been committed, and

   (b) that proceedings in respect of the offence have been instituted or that the offence is being investigated.

(7) If a request for assistance under this section is made in reliance on Article 2 of the 2001 Protocol (requests for information on banking transactions) in connection with the investigation of an offence, the request must state the grounds on which the person making the request considers the evidence specified in it to be relevant for the purposes of the investigation.

8 Sending requests for assistance

(1) A request for assistance under section 7 may be sent—

   (a) to a court exercising jurisdiction in the place where the evidence is situated, or

   (b) to any authority recognised by the government of the country in question as the appropriate authority for receiving requests of that kind.

(2) Alternatively, if it is a request by a judicial authority or a designated prosecuting authority it may be sent to the Secretary of State (in Scotland, the Lord Advocate) for forwarding to a court or authority mentioned in subsection (1).

(3) In cases of urgency, a request for assistance may be sent to—

   (a) the International Criminal Police Organisation, or

   (b) any body or person competent to receive it under any provisions adopted under the Treaty on European Union,

for forwarding to any court or authority mentioned in subsection (1).

9 Use of evidence obtained

(1) This section applies to evidence obtained pursuant to a request for assistance under section 7.

(2) The evidence may not without the consent of the appropriate overseas authority be used for any purpose other than that specified in the request.

(3) When the evidence is no longer required for that purpose (or for any other purpose for which such consent has been obtained), it must be returned to the appropriate overseas authority, unless that authority indicates that it need not be returned.

(4) In exercising the discretion conferred by Article 5 of the Criminal Justice (Evidence, Etc.) (Northern Ireland) Order 1988 (S.I. 1988/ 1847 (N.I. 17)) (exclusion of evidence otherwise admissible) in relation to a statement contained in the evidence, the court must have regard—

    (a) to whether it was possible to challenge the statement by questioning the person who made it, and

    (b) if proceedings have been instituted, to whether the local law allowed the parties to the proceedings to be legally represented when the evidence was being obtained.

(5) In Scotland, the evidence may be received in evidence without being sworn to by witnesses, so far as that may be done without unfairness to either party.

(6) In this section, the appropriate overseas authority means the authority recognised by the government of the country in question as the appropriate authority for receiving requests of the kind in question.

CRIMINAL JUSTICE ACT 2003
(c. 44)

PART 8
LIVE LINKS

51   Live links in criminal proceedings

(1)   A witness (other than the defendant) may, if the court so directs, give evidence through a live link in the following criminal proceedings.

(2)   They are—
   (a)   a summary trial,
   (b)   an appeal to the Crown Court arising out of such a trial,
   (c)   a trial on indictment,
   (d)   an appeal to the criminal division of the Court of Appeal,
   (e)   the hearing of a reference under section 9 or 11 of the Criminal Appeal Act 1995 (c. 35),
   (f)   a hearing before a magistrates' court or the Crown Court which is held after the defendant has entered a plea of guilty, and
   (g)   a hearing before the Court of Appeal under section 80 of this Act.

(3)   A direction may be given under this section—
   (a)   on an application by a party to the proceedings, or
   (b)   of the court's own motion.

(4)   But a direction may not be given under this section unless—
   (a)   the court is satisfied that it is in the interests of the efficient or effective administration of justice for the person concerned to give evidence in the proceedings through a live link,
   (b)   it has been notified by the Secretary of State that suitable facilities for receiving evidence through a live link are available in the area in

which it appears to the court that the proceedings will take place, and

(c)   that notification has not been withdrawn.

(5) The withdrawal of such a notification is not to affect a direction given under this section before that withdrawal.

(6) In deciding whether to give a direction under this section the court must consider all the circumstances of the case.

(7) Those circumstances include in particular—
   (a)   the availability of the witness,
   (b)   the need for the witness to attend in person,
   (c)   the importance of the witness's evidence to the proceedings,
   (d)   the views of the witness,
   (e)   the suitability of the facilities at the place where the witness would give evidence through a live link,
   (f)   whether a direction might tend to inhibit any party to the proceedings from effectively testing the witness's evidence.

(8) The court must state in open court its reasons for refusing an application for a direction under this section and, if it is a magistrates' court, must cause them to be entered in the register of its proceedings.

52   Effect of, and rescission of, direction

(1) Subsection (2) applies where the court gives a direction under section 51 for a person to give evidence through a live link in particular proceedings.

(2) The person concerned may not give evidence in those proceedings after the direction is given otherwise than through a live link (but this is subject to the following provisions of this section).

(3) The court may rescind a direction under section 51 if it appears to the court to be in the interests of justice to do so.

(4) Where it does so, the person concerned shall cease to be able to give evidence in the proceedings through a live link, but this does not prevent the court from giving a further direction under section 51 in relation to him.

(5) A direction under section 51 may be rescinded under subsection (3)—
   (a)   on an application by a party to the proceedings, or
   (b)   of the court's own motion.

(6) But an application may not be made under subsection (5)(a) unless there has been a material change of circumstances since the direction was given.

(7) The court must state in open court its reasons—
   (a)   for rescinding a direction under section 51, or
   (b)   for refusing an application to rescind such a direction,

and, if it is a magistrates' court, must cause them to be entered in the register of its proceedings.

53 Magistrates' courts permitted to sit at other locations

(1) This section applies where—
   (a) a magistrates' court is minded to give a direction under section 51 for evidence to be given through a live link in proceedings before the court, and
   (b) suitable facilities for receiving such evidence are not available at any petty-sessional court-house in which the court can (apart from subsection (2)) lawfully sit.

(2) The court may sit for the purposes of the whole or any part of the proceedings at any place at which such facilities are available and which has been appointed for the purposes of this section by the justices acting for the petty sessions area for which the court acts.

(3) A place appointed under subsection (2) may be outside the petty sessions area for which it is appointed; but (if so) it shall be deemed to be in that area for the purpose of the jurisdiction of the justices acting for that area.

54 Warning to jury

(1) This section applies where, as a result of a direction under section 51, evidence has been given through a live link in proceedings before the Crown Court.

(2) The judge may give the jury (if there is one) such direction as he thinks necessary to ensure that the jury gives the same weight to the evidence as if it had been given by the witness in the courtroom or other place where the proceedings are held.

55 Rules of court

(1) Rules of court may make such provision as appears to the authority making them to be necessary or expedient for the purposes of this Part.

(2) Rules of court may in particular make provision—
   (a) as to the procedure to be followed in connection with applications under section 51 or 52, and
   (b) as to the arrangements or safeguards to be put in place in connection with the operation of live links.

(3) The provision which may be made by virtue of subsection (2)(a) includes provision—
   (a) for uncontested applications to be determined by the court without a hearing,
   (b) for preventing the renewal of an unsuccessful application under section 51 unless there has been a material change of circumstances,

    (c) for the manner in which confidential or sensitive information is to be treated in connection with an application under section 51 or 52 and in particular as to its being disclosed to, or withheld from, a party to the proceedings.

(4) Nothing in this section is to be taken as affecting the generality of any enactment conferring power to make rules of court.

56 Interpretation of Part 8

(1) In this Part—

"legal representative" means an authorised advocate or authorised litigator (as defined by section 119(1) of the Courts and Legal Services Act 1990 (c. 41)),

"petty-sessional court-house" has the same meaning as in the Magistrates' Courts Act 1980 (c. 43),

"petty sessions area" has the same meaning as in the Justices of the Peace Act 1997 (c. 25),

"rules of court" means Magistrates' Courts Rules, Crown Court Rules or Criminal Appeal Rules,

"witness", in relation to any criminal proceedings, means a person called, or proposed to be called, to give evidence in the proceedings.

(2) In this Part "live link" means a live television link or other arrangement by which a witness, while at a place in the United Kingdom which is outside the building where the proceedings are being held, is able to see and hear a person at the place where the proceedings are being held and to be seen and heard by the following persons.

(3) They are—
    (a) the defendant or defendants,
    (b) the judge or justices (or both) and the jury (if there is one),
    (c) legal representatives acting in the proceedings, and
    (d) any interpreter or other person appointed by the court to assist the witness.

(4) The extent (if any) to which a person is unable to see or hear by reason of any impairment of eyesight or hearing is to be disregarded for the purposes of subsection (2).

(5) Nothing in this Part is to be regarded as affecting any power of a court—
    (a) to make an order, give directions or give leave of any description in relation to any witness (including the defendant or defendants), or
    (b) to exclude evidence at its discretion (whether by preventing questions being put or otherwise).

PART 9
PROSECUTION APPEALS

57 Introduction

(1) In relation to a trial on indictment, the prosecution is to have the rights of appeal for which provision is made by this Part.

(2) But the prosecution is to have no right of appeal under this Part in respect of—
- (a) a ruling that a jury be discharged, or
- (b) a ruling from which an appeal lies to the Court of Appeal by virtue of any other enactment.

(3) An appeal under this Part is to lie to the Court of Appeal.

(4) Such an appeal may be brought only with the leave of the judge or the Court of Appeal.

General right of appeal in respect of rulings

58 General right of appeal in respect of rulings

(1) This section applies where a judge makes a ruling in relation to a trial on indictment at an applicable time and the ruling relates to one or more offences included in the indictment.

(2) The prosecution may appeal in respect of the ruling in accordance with this section.

(3) The ruling is to have no effect whilst the prosecution is able to take any steps under subsection (4).

(4) The prosecution may not appeal in respect of the ruling unless—
- (a) following the making of the ruling, it—
  - (i) informs the court that it intends to appeal, or
  - (ii) requests an adjournment to consider whether to appeal, and
- (b) if such an adjournment is granted, it informs the court following the adjournment that it intends to appeal.

(5) If the prosecution requests an adjournment under subsection (4)(a)(ii), the judge may grant such an adjournment.

(6) Where the ruling relates to two or more offences—
- (a) any one or more of those offences may be the subject of the appeal, and
- (b) if the prosecution informs the court in accordance with subsection (4) that it intends to appeal, it must at the same time inform the court of the offence or offences which are the subject of the appeal.

(7) Where—
- (a) the ruling is a ruling that there is no case to answer, and

(b)   the prosecution, at the same time that it informs the court in accordance with subsection (4) that it intends to appeal, nominates one or more other rulings which have been made by a judge in relation to the trial on indictment at an applicable time and which relate to the offence or offences which are the subject of the appeal,

that other ruling, or those other rulings, are also to be treated as the subject of the appeal.

(8)   The prosecution may not inform the court in accordance with subsection (4) that it intends to appeal, unless, at or before that time, it informs the court that it agrees that, in respect of the offence or each offence which is the subject of the appeal, the defendant in relation to that offence should be acquitted of that offence if either of the conditions mentioned in subsection (9) is fulfilled.

(9)   Those conditions are—

(a)   that leave to appeal to the Court of Appeal is not obtained, and

(b)   that the appeal is abandoned before it is determined by the Court of Appeal.

(10)   If the prosecution informs the court in accordance with subsection (4) that it intends to appeal, the ruling mentioned in subsection (1) is to continue to have no effect in relation to the offence or offences which are the subject of the appeal whilst the appeal is pursued.

(11)   If and to the extent that a ruling has no effect in accordance with this section—

(a)   any consequences of the ruling are also to have no effect,

(b)   the judge may not take any steps in consequence of the ruling, and

(c)   if he does so, any such steps are also to have no effect.

(12)   Where the prosecution has informed the court of its agreement under subsection (8) and either of the conditions mentioned in subsection (9) is fulfilled, the judge or the Court of Appeal must order that the defendant in relation to the offence or each offence concerned be acquitted of that offence.

(13)   In this section "applicable time", in relation to a trial on indictment, means any time (whether before or after the commencement of the trial) before the start of the judge's summing-up to the jury.

59   Expedited and non-expedited appeals

(1)   Where the prosecution informs the court in accordance with section 58(4) that it intends to appeal, the judge must decide whether or not the appeal should be expedited.

(2)   If the judge decides that the appeal should be expedited, he may order an adjournment.

(3)   If the judge decides that the appeal should not be expedited, he may—

(a) order an adjournment, or

(b) discharge the jury (if one has been sworn).

(4) If he decides that the appeal should be expedited, he or the Court of Appeal may subsequently reverse that decision and, if it is reversed, the judge may act as mentioned in subsection (3)(a) or (b).

60 Continuation of proceedings for offences not affected by ruling

(1) This section applies where the prosecution informs the court in accordance with section 58(4) that it intends to appeal.

(2) Proceedings may be continued in respect of any offence which is not the subject of the appeal.

61 Determination of appeal by Court of Appeal

(1) On an appeal under section 58, the Court of Appeal may confirm, reverse or vary any ruling to which the appeal relates.

(2) Subsections (3) to (5) apply where the appeal relates to a single ruling.

(3) Where the Court of Appeal confirms the ruling, it must, in respect of the offence or each offence which is the subject of the appeal, order that the defendant in relation to that offence be acquitted of that offence.

(4) Where the Court of Appeal reverses or varies the ruling, it must, in respect of the offence or each offence which is the subject of the appeal, do any of the following—

(a) order that proceedings for that offence may be resumed in the Crown Court,

(b) order that a fresh trial may take place in the Crown Court for that offence,

(c) order that the defendant in relation to that offence be acquitted of that offence.

(5) But the Court of Appeal may not make an order under subsection (4)(a) or (b) in respect of an offence unless it considers it necessary in the interests of justice to do so.

(6) Subsections (7) and (8) apply where the appeal relates to a ruling that there is no case to answer and one or more other rulings.

(7) Where the Court of Appeal confirms the ruling that there is no case to answer, it must, in respect of the offence or each offence which is the subject of the appeal, order that the defendant in relation to that offence be acquitted of that offence.

(8) Where the Court of Appeal reverses or varies the ruling that there is no case to answer, it must in respect of the offence or each offence which is the subject of the appeal, make any of the orders mentioned in subsection (4)(a) to (c) (but subject to subsection (5)).

Right of appeal in respect of evidentiary rulings

62   Right of appeal in respect of evidentiary rulings

(1) The prosecution may, in accordance with this section and section 63, appeal in respect of—

   (a)   a single qualifying evidentiary ruling, or

   (b)   two or more qualifying evidentiary rulings.

(2) A "qualifying evidentiary ruling" is an evidentiary ruling of a judge in relation to a trial on indictment which is made at any time (whether before or after the commencement of the trial) before the opening of the case for the defence.

(3) The prosecution may not appeal in respect of a single qualifying evidentiary ruling unless the ruling relates to one or more qualifying offences (whether or not it relates to any other offence).

(4) The prosecution may not appeal in respect of two or more qualifying evidentiary rulings unless each ruling relates to one or more qualifying offences (whether or not it relates to any other offence).

(5) If the prosecution intends to appeal under this section, it must before the opening of the case for the defence inform the court—

   (a)   of its intention to do so, and

   (b)   of the ruling or rulings to which the appeal relates.

(6) In respect of the ruling, or each ruling, to which the appeal relates—

   (a)   the qualifying offence, or at least one of the qualifying offences, to which the ruling relates must be the subject of the appeal, and

   (b)   any other offence to which the ruling relates may, but need not, be the subject of the appeal.

(7) The prosecution must, at the same time that it informs the court in accordance with subsection (5), inform the court of the offence or offences which are the subject of the appeal.

(8) For the purposes of this section, the case for the defence opens when, after the conclusion of the prosecution evidence, the earliest of the following events occurs—

   (a)   evidence begins to be adduced by or on behalf of a defendant,

   (b)   it is indicated to the court that no evidence will be adduced by or on behalf of a defendant,

   (c)   a defendant's case is opened, as permitted by section 2 of the Criminal Procedure Act 1865 (c. 18).

(9) In this section—

   "evidentiary ruling" means a ruling which relates to the admissibility or exclusion of any prosecution evidence,

   "qualifying offence" means an offence described in Part 1 of Schedule 4.

(10)   The Secretary of State may by order amend that Part by doing any one or more of the following—

    (a)   adding a description of offence,

    (b)   removing a description of offence for the time being included,

    (c)   modifying a description of offence for the time being included.

(11)   Nothing in this section affects the right of the prosecution to appeal in respect of an evidentiary ruling under section 58.

63   Condition that evidentiary ruling significantly weakens prosecution case

(1)   Leave to appeal may not be given in relation to an appeal under section 62 unless the judge or, as the case may be, the Court of Appeal is satisfied that the relevant condition is fulfilled.

(2)   In relation to an appeal in respect of a single qualifying evidentiary ruling, the relevant condition is that the ruling significantly weakens the prosecution's case in relation to the offence or offences which are the subject of the appeal.

(3)   In relation to an appeal in respect of two or more qualifying evidentiary rulings, the relevant condition is that the rulings taken together significantly weaken the prosecution's case in relation to the offence or offences which are the subject of the appeal.

64   Expedited and non-expedited appeals

(1)   Where the prosecution informs the court in accordance with section 62(5), the judge must decide whether or not the appeal should be expedited.

(2)   If the judge decides that the appeal should be expedited, he may order an adjournment.

(3)   If the judge decides that the appeal should not be expedited, he may—

    (a)   order an adjournment, or

    (b)   discharge the jury (if one has been sworn).

(4)   If he decides that the appeal should be expedited, he or the Court of Appeal may subsequently reverse that decision and, if it is reversed, the judge may act as mentioned in subsection (3)(a) or (b).

65   Continuation of proceedings for offences not affected by ruling

(1)   This section applies where the prosecution informs the court in accordance with section 62(5).

(2)   Proceedings may be continued in respect of any offence which is not the subject of the appeal.

66   Determination of appeal by Court of Appeal

(1)   On an appeal under section 62, the Court of Appeal may confirm, reverse or vary any ruling to which the appeal relates.

(2) In addition, the Court of Appeal must, in respect of the offence or each offence which is the subject of the appeal, do any of the following—

    (a) order that proceedings for that offence be resumed in the Crown Court,

    (b) order that a fresh trial may take place in the Crown Court for that offence,

    (c) order that the defendant in relation to that offence be acquitted of that offence.

(3) But no order may be made under subsection (2)(c) in respect of an offence unless the prosecution has indicated that it does not intend to continue with the prosecution of that offence.

Miscellaneous and supplemental

67 Reversal of rulings

The Court of Appeal may not reverse a ruling on an appeal under this Part unless it is satisfied—

    (a) that the ruling was wrong in law,

    (b) that the ruling involved an error of law or principle, or

    (c) that the ruling was a ruling that it was not reasonable for the judge to have made.

PART 10
RETRIAL FOR SERIOUS OFFENCES

75 Cases that may be retried

(1) This Part applies where a person has been acquitted of a qualifying offence in proceedings—

    (a) on indictment in England and Wales,

    (b) on appeal against a conviction, verdict or finding in proceedings on indictment in England and Wales, or

    (c) on appeal from a decision on such an appeal.

(2) A person acquitted of an offence in proceedings mentioned in subsection (1) is treated for the purposes of that subsection as also acquitted of any qualifying offence of which he could have been convicted in the proceedings because of the first-mentioned offence being charged in the indictment, except an offence—

    (a) of which he has been convicted,

    (b) of which he has been found not guilty by reason of insanity, or

    (c) in respect of which, in proceedings where he has been found to be under a disability (as defined by section 4 of the Criminal Procedure (Insanity) Act 1964 (c. 84)), a finding has been made that he did the act or made the omission charged against him.

(3) References in subsections (1) and (2) to a qualifying offence do not include references to an offence which, at the time of the acquittal, was the subject of an order under section 77(1) or (3).

(4) This Part also applies where a person has been acquitted, in proceedings elsewhere than in the United Kingdom, of an offence under the law of the place where the proceedings were held, if the commission of the offence as alleged would have amounted to or included the commission (in the United Kingdom or elsewhere) of a qualifying offence.

(5) Conduct punishable under the law in force elsewhere than in the United Kingdom is an offence under that law for the purposes of subsection (4), however it is described in that law.

(6) This Part applies whether the acquittal was before or after the passing of this Act.

(7) References in this Part to acquittal are to acquittal in circumstances within subsection (1) or (4).

(8) In this Part "qualifying offence" means an offence listed in Part 1 of Schedule 5.

Application for retrial

76 Application to Court of Appeal

(1) A prosecutor may apply to the Court of Appeal for an order—
   (a) quashing a person's acquittal in proceedings within section 75(1), and
   (b) ordering him to be retried for the qualifying offence.

(2) A prosecutor may apply to the Court of Appeal, in the case of a person acquitted elsewhere than in the United Kingdom, for—
   (a) a determination whether the acquittal is a bar to the person being tried in England and Wales for the qualifying offence, and
   (b) if it is, an order that the acquittal is not to be a bar.

(3) A prosecutor may make an application under subsection (1) or (2) only with the written consent of the Director of Public Prosecutions.

(4) The Director of Public Prosecutions may give his consent only if satisfied that—
   (a) there is evidence as respects which the requirements of section 78 appear to be met,
   (b) it is in the public interest for the application to proceed, and
   (c) any trial pursuant to an order on the application would not be inconsistent with obligations of the United Kingdom under Article 31 or 34 of the Treaty on European Union relating to the principle of *ne bis in idem*.

(5) Not more than one application may be made under subsection (1) or (2) in relation to an acquittal.

77 Determination by Court of Appeal

(1) On an application under section 76(1), the Court of Appeal—
   (a) if satisfied that the requirements of sections 78 and 79 are met, must make the order applied for;
   (b) otherwise, must dismiss the application.

(2) Subsections (3) and (4) apply to an application under section 76(2).

(3) Where the Court of Appeal determines that the acquittal is a bar to the person being tried for the qualifying offence, the court—
   (a) if satisfied that the requirements of sections 78 and 79 are met, must make the order applied for;
   (b) otherwise, must make a declaration to the effect that the acquittal is a bar to the person being tried for the offence.

(4) Where the Court of Appeal determines that the acquittal is not a bar to the person being tried for the qualifying offence, it must make a declaration to that effect.

78 New and compelling evidence

(1) The requirements of this section are met if there is new and compelling evidence against the acquitted person in relation to the qualifying offence.

(2) Evidence is new if it was not adduced in the proceedings in which the person was acquitted (nor, if those were appeal proceedings, in earlier proceedings to which the appeal related).

(3) Evidence is compelling if—
   (a) it is reliable,
   (b) it is substantial, and
   (c) in the context of the outstanding issues, it appears highly probative of the case against the acquitted person.

(4) The outstanding issues are the issues in dispute in the proceedings in which the person was acquitted and, if those were appeal proceedings, any other issues remaining in dispute from earlier proceedings to which the appeal related.

(5) For the purposes of this section, it is irrelevant whether any evidence would have been admissible in earlier proceedings against the acquitted person.

79 Interests of justice

(1) The requirements of this section are met if in all the circumstances it is in the interests of justice for the court to make the order under section 77.

(2) That question is to be determined having regard in particular to—
   (a) whether existing circumstances make a fair trial unlikely;

(b) for the purposes of that question and otherwise, the length of time since the qualifying offence was allegedly committed;

(c) whether it is likely that the new evidence would have been adduced in the earlier proceedings against the acquitted person but for a failure by an officer or by a prosecutor to act with due diligence or expedition;

(d) whether, since those proceedings or, if later, since the commencement of this Part, any officer or prosecutor has failed to act with due diligence or expedition.

(3) In subsection (2) references to an officer or prosecutor include references to a person charged with corresponding duties under the law in force elsewhere than in England and Wales.

(4) Where the earlier prosecution was conducted by a person other than a prosecutor, subsection (2)(c) applies in relation to that person as well as in relation to a prosecutor.

80 Procedure and evidence

(1) A prosecutor who wishes to make an application under section 76(1) or (2) must give notice of the application to the Court of Appeal.

(2) Within two days beginning with the day on which any such notice is given, notice of the application must be served by the prosecutor on the person to whom the application relates, charging him with the offence to which it relates or, if he has been charged with it in accordance with section 87(4), stating that he has been so charged.

(3) Subsection (2) applies whether the person to whom the application relates is in the United Kingdom or elsewhere, but the Court of Appeal may, on application by the prosecutor, extend the time for service under that subsection if it considers it necessary to do so because of that person's absence from the United Kingdom.

(4) The Court of Appeal must consider the application at a hearing.

(5) The person to whom the application relates—
(a) is entitled to be present at the hearing, although he may be in custody, unless he is in custody elsewhere than in England and Wales or Northern Ireland, and

(b) is entitled to be represented at the hearing, whether he is present or not.

(6) For the purposes of the application, the Court of Appeal may, if it thinks it necessary or expedient in the interests of justice—
(a) order the production of any document, exhibit or other thing, the production of which appears to the court to be necessary for the determination of the application, and

(b) order any witness who would be a compellable witness in proceedings pursuant to an order or declaration made on the application to attend for examination and be examined before the court.

(7) The Court of Appeal may at one hearing consider more than one application (whether or not relating to the same person), but only if the offences concerned could be tried on the same indictment.

PART 11
EVIDENCE

CHAPTER 1
EVIDENCE OF BAD CHARACTER

98 "Bad character"

References in this Chapter to evidence of a person's "bad character" are to evidence of, or of a disposition towards, misconduct on his part, other than evidence which—

(a) has to do with the alleged facts of the offence with which the defendant is charged, or

(b) is evidence of misconduct in connection with the investigation or prosecution of that offence.

99 Abolition of common law rules

(1) The common law rules governing the admissibility of evidence of bad character in criminal proceedings are abolished.

(2) Subsection (1) is subject to section 118(1) in so far as it preserves the rule under which in criminal proceedings a person's reputation is admissible for the purposes of proving his bad character.

Persons other than defendants

100   Non-defendant's bad character

(1) In criminal proceedings evidence of the bad character of a person other than the defendant is admissible if and only if—

(a) it is important explanatory evidence,

(b) it has substantial probative value in relation to a matter which—

    (i) is a matter in issue in the proceedings, and

    (ii) is of substantial importance in the context of the case as a whole,

or

(c) all parties to the proceedings agree to the evidence being admissible.

(2) For the purposes of subsection (1)(a) evidence is important explanatory evidence if—

(a) without it, the court or jury would find it impossible or difficult properly to understand other evidence in the case, and

(b) its value for understanding the case as a whole is substantial.

(3) In assessing the probative value of evidence for the purposes of subsection (1)(b) the court must have regard to the following factors (and to any others it considers relevant)—

(a) the nature and number of the events, or other things, to which the evidence relates;

(b) when those events or things are alleged to have happened or existed;

(c) where—

    (i) the evidence is evidence of a person's misconduct, and

    (ii) it is suggested that the evidence has probative value by reason of similarity between that misconduct and other alleged misconduct,

the nature and extent of the similarities and the dissimilarities between each of the alleged instances of misconduct;

(d) where—

    (i) the evidence is evidence of a person's misconduct,

    (ii) it is suggested that that person is also responsible for the misconduct charged, and

    (iii) the identity of the person responsible for the misconduct charged is disputed,

the extent to which the evidence shows or tends to show that the same person was responsible each time.

(4) Except where subsection (1)(c) applies, evidence of the bad character of a person other than the defendant must not be given without leave of the court.

Defendants

101 Defendant's bad character

(1) In criminal proceedings evidence of the defendant's bad character is admissible if, but only if—

(a) all parties to the proceedings agree to the evidence being admissible,

(b) the evidence is adduced by the defendant himself or is given in answer to a question asked by him in cross-examination and intended to elicit it,

(c) it is important explanatory evidence,

(d) it is relevant to an important matter in issue between the defendant and the prosecution,

(e) it has substantial probative value in relation to an important matter in issue between the defendant and a co-defendant,

    (f)   it is evidence to correct a false impression given by the defendant, or

    (g) the defendant has made an attack on another person's character.

(2) Sections 102 to 106 contain provision supplementing subsection (1).

(3) The court must not admit evidence under subsection (1)(d) or (g) if, on an application by the defendant to exclude it, it appears to the court that the admission of the evidence would have such an adverse effect on the fairness of the proceedings that the court ought not to admit it.

(4) On an application to exclude evidence under subsection (3) the court must have regard, in particular, to the length of time between the matters to which that evidence relates and the matters which form the subject of the offence charged.

102   "Important explanatory evidence"

For the purposes of section 101(1)(c) evidence is important explanatory evidence if—

    (a) without it, the court or jury would find it impossible or difficult properly to understand other evidence in the case, and

    (b) its value for understanding the case as a whole is substantial.

103   "Matter in issue between the defendant and the prosecution"

(1) For the purposes of section 101(1)(d) the matters in issue between the defendant and the prosecution include—

    (a) the question whether the defendant has a propensity to commit offences of the kind with which he is charged, except where his having such a propensity makes it no more likely that he is guilty of the offence;

    (b) the question whether the defendant has a propensity to be untruthful, except where it is not suggested that the defendant's case is untruthful in any respect.

(2) Where subsection (1)(a) applies, a defendant's propensity to commit offences of the kind with which he is charged may (without prejudice to any other way of doing so) be established by evidence that he has been convicted of—

    (a) an offence of the same description as the one with which he is charged, or

    (b) an offence of the same category as the one with which he is charged.

(3) Subsection (2) does not apply in the case of a particular defendant if the court is satisfied, by reason of the length of time since the conviction or for any other reason, that it would be unjust for it to apply in his case.

(4) For the purposes of subsection (2)—

(a) two offences are of the same description as each other if the statement of the offence in a written charge or indictment would, in each case, be in the same terms;

(b) two offences are of the same category as each other if they belong to the same category of offences prescribed for the purposes of this section by an order made by the Secretary of State.

(5) A category prescribed by an order under subsection (4)(b) must consist of offences of the same type.

(6) Only prosecution evidence is admissible under section 101(1)(d).

104 "Matter in issue between the defendant and a co-defendant"

(1) Evidence which is relevant to the question whether the defendant has a propensity to be untruthful is admissible on that basis under section 101(1)(e) only if the nature or conduct of his defence is such as to undermine the co-defendant's defence.

(2) Only evidence—
(a) which is to be (or has been) adduced by the co-defendant, or
(b) which a witness is to be invited to give (or has given) in cross-examination by the co-defendant,

is admissible under section 101(1)(e).

105 "Evidence to correct a false impression"

(1) For the purposes of section 101(1)(f)—
(a) the defendant gives a false impression if he is responsible for the making of an express or implied assertion which is apt to give the court or jury a false or misleading impression about the defendant;
(b) evidence to correct such an impression is evidence which has probative value in correcting it.

(2) A defendant is treated as being responsible for the making of an assertion if—
(a) the assertion is made by the defendant in the proceedings (whether or not in evidence given by him),
(b) the assertion was made by the defendant—
(i) on being questioned under caution, before charge, about the offence with which he is charged, or
(ii) on being charged with the offence or officially informed that he might be prosecuted for it,

and evidence of the assertion is given in the proceedings,

(c) the assertion is made by a witness called by the defendant,
(d) the assertion is made by any witness in cross-examination in response to a question asked by the defendant that is intended to elicit it, or is likely to do so, or

(e)   the assertion was made by any person out of court, and the defendant adduces evidence of it in the proceedings.

(3)   A defendant who would otherwise be treated as responsible for the making of an assertion shall not be so treated if, or to the extent that, he withdraws it or disassociates himself from it.

(4)   Where it appears to the court that a defendant, by means of his conduct (other than the giving of evidence) in the proceedings, is seeking to give the court or jury an impression about himself that is false or misleading, the court may if it appears just to do so treat the defendant as being responsible for the making of an assertion which is apt to give that impression.

(5)   In subsection (4) "conduct" includes appearance or dress.

(6)   Evidence is admissible under section 101(1)(f) only if it goes no further than is necessary to correct the false impression.

(7)   Only prosecution evidence is admissible under section 101(1)(f).

106   "Attack on another person's character"

(1)   For the purposes of section 101(1)(g) a defendant makes an attack on another person's character if—
  (a)   he adduces evidence attacking the other person's character,
  (b)   he (or any legal representative appointed under section 38(4) of the Youth Justice and Criminal Evidence Act 1999 (c. 23) to cross-examine a witness in his interests) asks questions in cross-examination that are intended to elicit such evidence, or are likely to do so, or
  (c)   evidence is given of an imputation about the other person made by the defendant—
    (i)   on being questioned under caution, before charge, about the offence with which he is charged, or
    (ii)   on being charged with the offence or officially informed that he might be prosecuted for it.

(2)   In subsection (1) "evidence attacking the other person's character" means evidence to the effect that the other person—
  (a)   has committed an offence (whether a different offence from the one with which the defendant is charged or the same one), or
  (b)   has behaved, or is disposed to behave, in a reprehensible way;
  and "imputation about the other person" means an assertion to that effect.

(3)   Only prosecution evidence is admissible under section 101(1)(g).

107   Stopping the case where evidence contaminated

(1)   If on a defendant's trial before a judge and jury for an offence—

(a) evidence of his bad character has been admitted under any of paragraphs (c) to (g) of section 101(1), and

(b) the court is satisfied at any time after the close of the case for the prosecution that—

 (i) the evidence is contaminated, and

 (ii) the contamination is such that, considering the importance of the evidence to the case against the defendant, his conviction of the offence would be unsafe,

the court must either direct the jury to acquit the defendant of the offence or, if it considers that there ought to be a retrial, discharge the jury.

(2) Where—

(a) a jury is directed under subsection (1) to acquit a defendant of an offence, and

(b) the circumstances are such that, apart from this subsection, the defendant could if acquitted of that offence be found guilty of another offence,

the defendant may not be found guilty of that other offence if the court is satisfied as mentioned in subsection (1)(b) in respect of it.

(3) If—

(a) a jury is required to determine under section 4A(2) of the Criminal Procedure (Insanity) Act 1964 (c. 84) whether a person charged on an indictment with an offence did the act or made the omission charged,

(b) evidence of the person's bad character has been admitted under any of paragraphs (c) to (g) of section 101(1), and

(c) the court is satisfied at any time after the close of the case for the prosecution that—

 (i) the evidence is contaminated, and

 (ii) the contamination is such that, considering the importance of the evidence to the case against the person, a finding that he did the act or made the omission would be unsafe,

the court must either direct the jury to acquit the defendant of the offence or, if it considers that there ought to be a rehearing, discharge the jury.

(4) This section does not prejudice any other power a court may have to direct a jury to acquit a person of an offence or to discharge a jury.

(5) For the purposes of this section a person's evidence is contaminated where—

(a) as a result of an agreement or understanding between the person and one or more others, or

(b) as a result of the person being aware of anything alleged by one or more others whose evidence may be, or has been, given in the proceedings, the evidence is false or misleading in any respect, or is different from what it would otherwise have been.

108   Offences committed by defendant when a child

(1) Section 16(2) and (3) of the Children and Young Persons Act 1963 (c. 37) (offences committed by person under 14 disregarded for purposes of evidence relating to previous convictions) shall cease to have effect.

(2) In proceedings for an offence committed or alleged to have been committed by the defendant when aged 21 or over, evidence of his conviction for an offence when under the age of 14 is not admissible unless—
   (a) both of the offences are triable only on indictment, and
   (b) the court is satisfied that the interests of justice require the evidence to be admissible.

(3) Subsection (2) applies in addition to section 101.

General

109   Assumption of truth in assessment of relevance or probative value

(1) Subject to subsection (2), a reference in this Chapter to the relevance or probative value of evidence is a reference to its relevance or probative value on the assumption that it is true.

(2) In assessing the relevance or probative value of an item of evidence for any purpose of this Chapter, a court need not assume that the evidence is true if it appears, on the basis of any material before the court (including any evidence it decides to hear on the matter), that no court or jury could reasonably find it to be true.

110   Court's duty to give reasons for rulings

(1) Where the court makes a relevant ruling—
   (a) it must state in open court (but in the absence of the jury, if there is one) its reasons for the ruling;
   (b) if it is a magistrates' court, it must cause the ruling and the reasons for it to be entered in the register of the court's proceedings.

(2) In this section "relevant ruling" means—
   (a) a ruling on whether an item of evidence is evidence of a person's bad character;
   (b) a ruling on whether an item of such evidence is admissible under section 100 or 101 (including a ruling on an application under section 101(3));
   (c) a ruling under section 107.

111 Rules of court

(1) Rules of court may make such provision as appears to the appropriate authority to be necessary or expedient for the purposes of this Act; and the appropriate authority is the authority entitled to make the rules.

(2) The rules may, and, where the party in question is the prosecution, must, contain provision requiring a party who—

(a) proposes to adduce evidence of a defendant's bad character, or

(b) proposes to cross-examine a witness with a view to eliciting such evidence,

to serve on the defendant such notice, and such particulars of or relating to the evidence, as may be prescribed.

(3) The rules may provide that the court or the defendant may, in such circumstances as may be prescribed, dispense with a requirement imposed by virtue of subsection (2).

(4) In considering the exercise of its powers with respect to costs, the court may take into account any failure by a party to comply with a requirement imposed by virtue of subsection (2) and not dispensed with by virtue of subsection (3).

(5) The rules may—

(a) limit the application of any provision of the rules to prescribed circumstances;

(b) subject any provision of the rules to prescribed exceptions;

(c) make different provision for different cases or circumstances.

(6) Nothing in this section prejudices the generality of any enactment conferring power to make rules of court; and no particular provision of this section prejudices any general provision of it.

(7) In this section—

"prescribed" means prescribed by rules of court;

"rules of court" means—

(a) Crown Court Rules;

(b) Criminal Appeal Rules;

(c) rules under section 144 of the Magistrates' Courts Act 1980 (c. 43).

112 Interpretation of Chapter 1

(1) In this Chapter—

"bad character" is to be read in accordance with section 98;

"criminal proceedings" means criminal proceedings in relation to which the strict rules of evidence apply;

"defendant", in relation to criminal proceedings, means a person charged with an offence in those proceedings; and "co-defendant", in relation to a defendant, means a person charged with an offence in the same proceedings;

"important matter" means a matter of substantial importance in the context of the case as a whole;

"misconduct" means the commission of an offence or other reprehensible behaviour;

"offence" includes a service offence;

"probative value", and "relevant" (in relation to an item of evidence), are to be read in accordance with section 109;

"prosecution evidence" means evidence which is to be (or has been) adduced by the prosecution, or which a witness is to be invited to give (or has given) in cross-examination by the prosecution;

"service offence" means an offence under the Army Act 1955 (3 & 4 Eliz. 2 c. 18), the Air Force Act 1955 (3 & 4 Eliz. 2 c. 19) or the Naval Discipline Act 1957 (c. 53);

"written charge" has the same meaning as in section 29 and also includes an information.

(2) Where a defendant is charged with two or more offences in the same criminal proceedings, this Chapter (except section 101(3)) has effect as if each offence were charged in separate proceedings; and references to the offence with which the defendant is charged are to be read accordingly.

(3) Nothing in this Chapter affects the exclusion of evidence—

(a) under the rule in section 3 of the Criminal Procedure Act 1865 (c. 18) against a party impeaching the credit of his own witness by general evidence of bad character,

(b) under section 41 of the Youth Justice and Criminal Evidence Act 1999 (c. 23) (restriction on evidence or questions about complainant's sexual history), or

(c) on grounds other than the fact that it is evidence of a person's bad character.

113   Armed forces

Schedule 6 (armed forces) has effect.

CHAPTER 2
HEARSAY EVIDENCE

Hearsay: main provisions

114   Admissibility of hearsay evidence

(1) In criminal proceedings a statement not made in oral evidence in the proceedings is admissible as evidence of any matter stated if, but only if—

(a) any provision of this Chapter or any other statutory provision makes it admissible,

(b) any rule of law preserved by section 118 makes it admissible,

(c) all parties to the proceedings agree to it being admissible, or

(d) the court is satisfied that it is in the interests of justice for it to be admissible.

(2) In deciding whether a statement not made in oral evidence should be admitted under subsection (1)(d), the court must have regard to the following factors (and to any others it considers relevant)—

(a) how much probative value the statement has (assuming it to be true) in relation to a matter in issue in the proceedings, or how valuable it is for the understanding of other evidence in the case;

(b) what other evidence has been, or can be, given on the matter or evidence mentioned in paragraph (a);

(c) how important the matter or evidence mentioned in paragraph (a) is in the context of the case as a whole;

(d) the circumstances in which the statement was made;

(e) how reliable the maker of the statement appears to be;

(f) how reliable the evidence of the making of the statement appears to be;

(g) whether oral evidence of the matter stated can be given and, if not, why it cannot;

(h) the amount of difficulty involved in challenging the statement;

(i) the extent to which that difficulty would be likely to prejudice the party facing it.

(3) Nothing in this Chapter affects the exclusion of evidence of a statement on grounds other than the fact that it is a statement not made in oral evidence in the proceedings.

115   Statements and matters stated

(1) In this Chapter references to a statement or to a matter stated are to be read as follows.

(2) A statement is any representation of fact or opinion made by a person by whatever means; and it includes a representation made in a sketch, photofit or other pictorial form.

(3) A matter stated is one to which this Chapter applies if (and only if) the purpose, or one of the purposes, of the person making the statement appears to the court to have been—

(a) to cause another person to believe the matter, or

(b) to cause another person to act or a machine to operate on the basis that the matter is as stated.

116   Cases where a witness is unavailable

(1)   In criminal proceedings a statement not made in oral evidence in the proceedings is admissible as evidence of any matter stated if—

(a)   oral evidence given in the proceedings by the person who made the statement would be admissible as evidence of that matter,

(b)   the person who made the statement (the relevant person) is identified to the court's satisfaction, and

(c)   any of the five conditions mentioned in subsection (2) is satisfied.

(2)   The conditions are—

(a)   that the relevant person is dead;

(b)   that the relevant person is unfit to be a witness because of his bodily or mental condition;

(c)   that the relevant person is outside the United Kingdom and it is not reasonably practicable to secure his attendance;

(d)   that the relevant person cannot be found although such steps as it is reasonably practicable to take to find him have been taken;

(e)   that through fear the relevant person does not give (or does not continue to give) oral evidence in the proceedings, either at all or in connection with the subject matter of the statement, and the court gives leave for the statement to be given in evidence.

(3)   For the purposes of subsection (2)(e) "fear" is to be widely construed and (for example) includes fear of the death or injury of another person or of financial loss.

(4)   Leave may be given under subsection (2)(e) only if the court considers that the statement ought to be admitted in the interests of justice, having regard—

(a)   to the statement's contents,

(b)   to any risk that its admission or exclusion will result in unfairness to any party to the proceedings (and in particular to how difficult it will be to challenge the statement if the relevant person does not give oral evidence),

(c)   in appropriate cases, to the fact that a direction under section 19 of the Youth Justice and Criminal Evidence Act 1999 (c. 23) (special measures for the giving of evidence by fearful witnesses etc) could be made in relation to the relevant person, and

(d)   to any other relevant circumstances.

(5)   A condition set out in any paragraph of subsection (2) which is in fact satisfied is to be treated as not satisfied if it is shown that the circumstances described in that paragraph are caused—

(a)   by the person in support of whose case it is sought to give the statement in evidence, or

(b)   by a person acting on his behalf,

in order to prevent the relevant person giving oral evidence in the proceedings (whether at all or in connection with the subject matter of the statement).

117 Business and other documents

(1) In criminal proceedings a statement contained in a document is admissible as evidence of any matter stated if—

  (a) oral evidence given in the proceedings would be admissible as evidence of that matter,

  (b) the requirements of subsection (2) are satisfied, and

  (c) the requirements of subsection (5) are satisfied, in a case where subsection (4) requires them to be.

(2) The requirements of this subsection are satisfied if—

  (a) the document or the part containing the statement was created or received by a person in the course of a trade, business, profession or other occupation, or as the holder of a paid or unpaid office,

  (b) the person who supplied the information contained in the statement (the relevant person) had or may reasonably be supposed to have had personal knowledge of the matters dealt with, and

  (c) each person (if any) through whom the information was supplied from the relevant person to the person mentioned in paragraph (a) received the information in the course of a trade, business, profession or other occupation, or as the holder of a paid or unpaid office.

(3) The persons mentioned in paragraphs (a) and (b) of subsection (2) may be the same person.

(4) The additional requirements of subsection (5) must be satisfied if the statement—

  (a) was prepared for the purposes of pending or contemplated criminal proceedings, or for a criminal investigation, but

  (b) was not obtained pursuant to a request under section 7 of the Crime (International Co-operation) Act 2003 (c. 32) or an order under paragraph 6 of Schedule 13 to the Criminal Justice Act 1988 (c. 33) (which relate to overseas evidence).

(5) The requirements of this subsection are satisfied if—

  (a) any of the five conditions mentioned in section 116(2) is satisfied (absence of relevant person etc), or

  (b) the relevant person cannot reasonably be expected to have any recollection of the matters dealt with in the statement (having regard to the length of time since he supplied the information and all other circumstances).

(6) A statement is not admissible under this section if the court makes a direction to that effect under subsection (7).

(7) The court may make a direction under this subsection if satisfied that the statement's reliability as evidence for the purpose for which it is tendered is doubtful in view of—

(a) its contents,

(b) the source of the information contained in it,

(c) the way in which or the circumstances in which the information was supplied or received, or

(d) the way in which or the circumstances in which the document concerned was created or received.

118   Preservation of certain common law categories of admissibility

(1) The following rules of law are preserved.

Public information etc

1   Any rule of law under which in criminal proceedings—

(a) published works dealing with matters of a public nature (such as histories, scientific works, dictionaries and maps) are admissible as evidence of facts of a public nature stated in them,

(b) public documents (such as public registers, and returns made under public authority with respect to matters of public interest) are admissible as evidence of facts stated in them,

(c) records (such as the records of certain courts, treaties, Crown grants, pardons and commissions) are admissible as evidence of facts stated in them, or

(d) evidence relating to a person's age or date or place of birth may be given by a person without personal knowledge of the matter.

Reputation as to character

2   Any rule of law under which in criminal proceedings evidence of a person's reputation is admissible for the purpose of proving his good or bad character

Note

The rule is preserved only so far as it allows the court to treat such evidence as proving the matter concerned.

Reputation or family tradition

3   Any rule of law under which in criminal proceedings evidence of reputation or family tradition is admissible for the purpose of proving or disproving—

(a) pedigree or the existence of a marriage,

(b) the existence of any public or general right, or

(c) the identity of any person or thing.

Note

The rule is preserved only so far as it allows the court to treat such evidence as proving or disproving the matter concerned.

Res gestae

4   Any rule of law under which in criminal proceedings a statement is admissible as evidence of any matter stated if—
   (a) the statement was made by a person so emotionally overpowered by an event that the possibility of concoction or distortion can be disregarded,
   (b) the statement accompanied an act which can be properly evaluated as evidence only if considered in conjunction with the statement, or
   (c) the statement relates to a physical sensation or a mental state (such as intention or emotion).

Confessions etc

5   Any rule of law relating to the admissibility of confessions or mixed statements in criminal proceedings

Admissions by agents etc

6   Any rule of law under which in criminal proceedings—
   (a) an admission made by an agent of a defendant is admissible against the defendant as evidence of any matter stated, or
   (b) a statement made by a person to whom a defendant refers a person for information is admissible against the defendant as evidence of any matter stated.

Common enterprise

7   Any rule of law under which in criminal proceedings a statement made by a party to a common enterprise is admissible against another party to the enterprise as evidence of any matter stated

Expert evidence

8   Any rule of law under which in criminal proceedings an expert witness may draw on the body of expertise relevant to his field
   (2) With the exception of the rules preserved by this section, the common law rules governing the admissibility of hearsay evidence in criminal proceedings are abolished.

119   Inconsistent statements

(1) If in criminal proceedings a person gives oral evidence and—

(a) he admits making a previous inconsistent statement, or

(b) a previous inconsistent statement made by him is proved by virtue of section 3, 4 or 5 of the Criminal Procedure Act 1865 (c. 18),

the statement is admissible as evidence of any matter stated of which oral evidence by him would be admissible.

(2) If in criminal proceedings evidence of an inconsistent statement by any person is given under section 124(2)(c), the statement is admissible as evidence of any matter stated in it of which oral evidence by that person would be admissible.

120   Other previous statements of witnesses

(1) This section applies where a person (the witness) is called to give evidence in criminal proceedings.

(2) If a previous statement by the witness is admitted as evidence to rebut a suggestion that his oral evidence has been fabricated, that statement is admissible as evidence of any matter stated of which oral evidence by the witness would be admissible.

(3) A statement made by the witness in a document—
(a) which is used by him to refresh his memory while giving evidence,

(b) on which he is cross-examined, and

(c) which as a consequence is received in evidence in the proceedings,

is admissible as evidence of any matter stated of which oral evidence by him would be admissible.

(4) A previous statement by the witness is admissible as evidence of any matter stated of which oral evidence by him would be admissible, if—
(a) any of the following three conditions is satisfied, and

(b) while giving evidence the witness indicates that to the best of his belief he made the statement, and that to the best of his belief it states the truth.

(5) The first condition is that the statement identifies or describes a person, object or place.

(6) The second condition is that the statement was made by the witness when the matters stated were fresh in his memory but he does not remember them, and cannot reasonably be expected to remember them, well enough to give oral evidence of them in the proceedings.

(7) The third condition is that—
(a) the witness claims to be a person against whom an offence has been committed,

(b) the offence is one to which the proceedings relate,

(c) the statement consists of a complaint made by the witness (whether to a person in authority or not) about conduct which would, if proved, constitute the offence or part of the offence,

(d)   the complaint was made as soon as could reasonably be expected after the alleged conduct,

(e)   the complaint was not made as a result of a threat or a promise, and

(f)   before the statement is adduced the witness gives oral evidence in connection with its subject matter.

(8)   For the purposes of subsection (7) the fact that the complaint was elicited (for example, by a leading question) is irrelevant unless a threat or a promise was involved.

Supplementary

121   Additional requirement for admissibility of multiple hearsay

(1)   A hearsay statement is not admissible to prove the fact that an earlier hearsay statement was made unless—

(a)   either of the statements is admissible under section 117, 119 or 120,

(b)   all parties to the proceedings so agree, or

(c)   the court is satisfied that the value of the evidence in question, taking into account how reliable the statements appear to be, is so high that the interests of justice require the later statement to be admissible for that purpose.

(2)   In this section "hearsay statement" means a statement, not made in oral evidence, that is relied on as evidence of a matter stated in it.

122   Documents produced as exhibits

(1)   This section applies if on a trial before a judge and jury for an offence—

(a)   a statement made in a document is admitted in evidence under section 119 or 120, and

(b)   the document or a copy of it is produced as an exhibit.

(2)   The exhibit must not accompany the jury when they retire to consider their verdict unless—

(a)   the court considers it appropriate, or

(b)   all the parties to the proceedings agree that it should accompany the jury.

123   Capability to make statement

(1)   Nothing in section 116, 119 or 120 makes a statement admissible as evidence if it was made by a person who did not have the required capability at the time when he made the statement.

(2)   Nothing in section 117 makes a statement admissible as evidence if any person who, in order for the requirements of section 117(2) to be satisfied, must at any time have supplied or received the information concerned or created or received the document or part concerned—

    (a) did not have the required capability at that time, or

    (b) cannot be identified but cannot reasonably be assumed to have had the required capability at that time.

(3) For the purposes of this section a person has the required capability if he is capable of—

    (a) understanding questions put to him about the matters stated, and

    (b) giving answers to such questions which can be understood.

(4) Where by reason of this section there is an issue as to whether a person had the required capability when he made a statement—

    (a) proceedings held for the determination of the issue must take place in the absence of the jury (if there is one);

    (b) in determining the issue the court may receive expert evidence and evidence from any person to whom the statement in question was made;

    (c) the burden of proof on the issue lies on the party seeking to adduce the statement, and the standard of proof is the balance of probabilities.

124 Credibility

(1) This section applies if in criminal proceedings—

    (a) a statement not made in oral evidence in the proceedings is admitted as evidence of a matter stated, and

    (b) the maker of the statement does not give oral evidence in connection with the subject matter of the statement.

(2) In such a case—

    (a) any evidence which (if he had given such evidence) would have been admissible as relevant to his credibility as a witness is so admissible in the proceedings;

    (b) evidence may with the court's leave be given of any matter which (if he had given such evidence) could have been put to him in cross-examination as relevant to his credibility as a witness but of which evidence could not have been adduced by the cross-examining party;

    (c) evidence tending to prove that he made (at whatever time) any other statement inconsistent with the statement admitted as evidence is admissible for the purpose of showing that he contradicted himself.

(3) If as a result of evidence admitted under this section an allegation is made against the maker of a statement, the court may permit a party to lead additional evidence of such description as the court may specify for the purposes of denying or answering the allegation.

(4) In the case of a statement in a document which is admitted as evidence under section 117 each person who, in order for the statement to be admissible, must have supplied or received the information concerned or

created or received the document or part concerned is to be treated as the maker of the statement for the purposes of subsections (1) to (3) above.

125   Stopping the case where evidence is unconvincing

(1) If on a defendant's trial before a judge and jury for an offence the court is satisfied at any time after the close of the case for the prosecution that—

    (a)   the case against the defendant is based wholly or partly on a statement not made in oral evidence in the proceedings, and

    (b)   the evidence provided by the statement is so unconvincing that, considering its importance to the case against the defendant, his conviction of the offence would be unsafe,

the court must either direct the jury to acquit the defendant of the offence or, if it considers that there ought to be a retrial, discharge the jury.

(2) Where—

    (a)   a jury is directed under subsection (1) to acquit a defendant of an offence, and

    (b)   the circumstances are such that, apart from this subsection, the defendant could if acquitted of that offence be found guilty of another offence,

the defendant may not be found guilty of that other offence if the court is satisfied as mentioned in subsection (1) in respect of it.

(3) If—

    (a)   a jury is required to determine under section 4A(2) of the Criminal Procedure (Insanity) Act 1964 (c. 84) whether a person charged on an indictment with an offence did the act or made the omission charged, and

    (b)   the court is satisfied as mentioned in subsection (1) above at any time after the close of the case for the prosecution that—

        (i)   the case against the defendant is based wholly or partly on a statement not made in oral evidence in the proceedings, and

        (ii) the evidence provided by the statement is so unconvincing that, considering its importance to the case against the person, a finding that he did the act or made the omission would be unsafe,

the court must either direct the jury to acquit the defendant of the offence or, if it considers that there ought to be a rehearing, discharge the jury.

(4) This section does not prejudice any other power a court may have to direct a jury to acquit a person of an offence or to discharge a jury.

126   Court's general discretion to exclude evidence

(1) In criminal proceedings the court may refuse to admit a statement as evidence of a matter stated if—

> (a) the statement was made otherwise than in oral evidence in the proceedings, and
>
> (b) the court is satisfied that the case for excluding the statement, taking account of the danger that to admit it would result in undue waste of time, substantially outweighs the case for admitting it, taking account of the value of the evidence.

(2) Nothing in this Chapter prejudices—

    (a) any power of a court to exclude evidence under section 78 of the Police and Criminal Evidence Act 1984 (c. 60) (exclusion of unfair evidence), or

    (b) any other power of a court to exclude evidence at its discretion (whether by preventing questions from being put or otherwise).

Miscellaneous

127   Expert evidence: preparatory work

(1) This section applies if—

    (a) a statement has been prepared for the purposes of criminal proceedings,

    (b) the person who prepared the statement had or may reasonably be supposed to have had personal knowledge of the matters stated,

    (c) notice is given under the appropriate rules that another person (the expert) will in evidence given in the proceedings orally or under section 9 of the Criminal Justice Act 1967 (c. 80) base an opinion or inference on the statement, and

    (d) the notice gives the name of the person who prepared the statement and the nature of the matters stated.

(2) In evidence given in the proceedings the expert may base an opinion or inference on the statement.

(3) If evidence based on the statement is given under subsection (2) the statement is to be treated as evidence of what it states.

(4) This section does not apply if the court, on an application by a party to the proceedings, orders that it is not in the interests of justice that it should apply.

(5) The matters to be considered by the court in deciding whether to make an order under subsection (4) include—

    (a) the expense of calling as a witness the person who prepared the statement;

    (b) whether relevant evidence could be given by that person which could not be given by the expert;

    (c) whether that person can reasonably be expected to remember the matters stated well enough to give oral evidence of them.

(6) Subsections (1) to (5) apply to a statement prepared for the purposes of a criminal investigation as they apply to a statement prepared for the purposes of criminal proceedings, and in such a case references to the proceedings are to criminal proceedings arising from the investigation.

(7) The appropriate rules are rules made—

   (a) under section 81 of the Police and Criminal Evidence Act 1984 (advance notice of expert evidence in Crown Court), or

   (b) under section 144 of the Magistrates' Courts Act 1980 (c. 43) by virtue of section 20(3) of the Criminal Procedure and Investigations Act 1996 (c. 25) (advance notice of expert evidence in magistrates' courts).

128 Confessions

(1) In the Police and Criminal Evidence Act 1984 (c. 60) the following section is inserted after section 76—

"76A Confessions may be given in evidence for co-accused

   (1) In any proceedings a confession made by an accused person may be given in evidence for another person charged in the same proceedings (a co-accused) in so far as it is relevant to any matter in issue in the proceedings and is not excluded by the court in pursuance of this section.

   (2) If, in any proceedings where a co-accused proposes to give in evidence a confession made by an accused person, it is represented to the court that the confession was or may have been obtained—

      (a) by oppression of the person who made it; or

      (b) in consequence of anything said or done which was likely, in the circumstances existing at the time, to render unreliable any confession which might be made by him in consequence thereof,

   the court shall not allow the confession to be given in evidence for the co-accused except in so far as it is proved to the court on the balance of probabilities that the confession (notwithstanding that it may be true) was not so obtained.

   (3) Before allowing a confession made by an accused person to be given in evidence for a co-accused in any proceedings, the court may of its own motion require the fact that the confession was not obtained as mentioned in subsection (2) above to be proved in the proceedings on the balance of probabilities.

   (4) The fact that a confession is wholly or partly excluded in pursuance of this section shall not affect the admissibility in evidence—

      (a) of any facts discovered as a result of the confession; or

      (b) where the confession is relevant as showing that the accused speaks, writes or expresses himself in a particular way, of so much of the confession as is necessary to show that he does so.

(5) Evidence that a fact to which this subsection applies was discovered as a result of a statement made by an accused person shall not be admissible unless evidence of how it was discovered is given by him or on his behalf.

(6) Subsection (5) above applies—

(a) to any fact discovered as a result of a confession which is wholly excluded in pursuance of this section; and

(b) to any fact discovered as a result of a confession which is partly so excluded, if the fact is discovered as a result of the excluded part of the confession.

(7) In this section "oppression" includes torture, inhuman or degrading treatment, and the use or threat of violence (whether or not amounting to torture)."

(2) Subject to subsection (1), nothing in this Chapter makes a confession by a defendant admissible if it would not be admissible under section 76 of the Police and Criminal Evidence Act 1984 (c. 60).

(3) In subsection (2) "confession" has the meaning given by section 82 of that Act.

129   Representations other than by a person

(1) Where a representation of any fact—
(a) is made otherwise than by a person, but

(b) depends for its accuracy on information supplied (directly or indirectly) by a person,

the representation is not admissible in criminal proceedings as evidence of the fact unless it is proved that the information was accurate.

(2) Subsection (1) does not affect the operation of the presumption that a mechanical device has been properly set or calibrated.

130   Depositions

In Schedule 3 to the Crime and Disorder Act 1998 (c. 37), sub-paragraph (4) of paragraph 5 is omitted (power of the court to overrule an objection to a deposition being read as evidence by virtue of that paragraph).

131   Evidence at retrial

For paragraphs 1 and 1A of Schedule 2 to the Criminal Appeal Act 1968 (c. 19) (oral evidence and use of transcripts etc at retrials under that Act) there is substituted—

"Evidence"

1   (1) Evidence given at a retrial must be given orally if it was given orally at the original trial, unless—

    (a) all the parties to the retrial agree otherwise;

    (b) section 116 of the Criminal Justice Act 2003 applies (admissibility of hearsay evidence where a witness is unavailable); or

    (c) the witness is unavailable to give evidence, otherwise than as mentioned in subsection (2) of that section, and section 114(1)(d) of that Act applies (admission of hearsay evidence under residual discretion).

  (2) Paragraph 5 of Schedule 3 to the Crime and Disorder Act 1998 (use of depositions) does not apply at a retrial to a deposition read as evidence at the original trial."

General

132 Rules of court

(1) Rules of court may make such provision as appears to the appropriate authority to be necessary or expedient for the purposes of this Chapter; and the appropriate authority is the authority entitled to make the rules.

(2) The rules may make provision about the procedure to be followed and other conditions to be fulfilled by a party proposing to tender a statement in evidence under any provision of this Chapter.

(3) The rules may require a party proposing to tender the evidence to serve on each party to the proceedings such notice, and such particulars of or relating to the evidence, as may be prescribed.

(4) The rules may provide that the evidence is to be treated as admissible by agreement of the parties if—

    (a) a notice has been served in accordance with provision made under subsection (3), and

    (b) no counter-notice in the prescribed form objecting to the admission of the evidence has been served by a party.

(5) If a party proposing to tender evidence fails to comply with a prescribed requirement applicable to it—

    (a) the evidence is not admissible except with the court's leave;

    (b) where leave is given the court or jury may draw such inferences from the failure as appear proper;

    (c) the failure may be taken into account by the court in considering the exercise of its powers with respect to costs.

(6) In considering whether or how to exercise any of its powers under subsection (5) the court shall have regard to whether there is any justification for the failure to comply with the requirement.

(7) A person shall not be convicted of an offence solely on an inference drawn under subsection (5)(b).

(8) Rules under this section may—

    (a) limit the application of any provision of the rules to prescribed circumstances;

    (b) subject any provision of the rules to prescribed exceptions;

    (c) make different provision for different cases or circumstances.

(9) Nothing in this section prejudices the generality of any enactment conferring power to make rules of court; and no particular provision of this section prejudices any general provision of it.

(10) In this section—

"prescribed" means prescribed by rules of court;

"rules of court" means—

    (a) Crown Court Rules;

    (b) Criminal Appeal Rules;

    (c) rules under section 144 of the Magistrates' Courts Act 1980 (c. 43).

133   Proof of statements in documents

Where a statement in a document is admissible as evidence in criminal proceedings, the statement may be proved by producing either—

    (a) the document, or

    (b) (whether or not the document exists) a copy of the document or of the material part of it,

authenticated in whatever way the court may approve.

134   Interpretation of Chapter 2

(1) In this Chapter—

"copy", in relation to a document, means anything on to which information recorded in the document has been copied, by whatever means and whether directly or indirectly;

"criminal proceedings" means criminal proceedings in relation to which the strict rules of evidence apply;

"defendant", in relation to criminal proceedings, means a person charged with an offence in those proceedings;

"document" means anything in which information of any description is recorded;

"oral evidence" includes evidence which, by reason of any disability, disorder or other impairment, a person called as a witness gives in writing or by signs or by way of any device;

"statutory provision" means any provision contained in, or in an instrument made under, this or any other Act, including any Act passed after this Act.

(2) Section 115 (statements and matters stated) contains other general interpretative provisions.

(3) Where a defendant is charged with two or more offences in the same criminal proceedings, this Chapter has effect as if each offence were charged in separate proceedings.

135   Armed forces

Schedule 7 (hearsay evidence: armed forces) has effect.

136   Repeals etc

In the Criminal Justice Act 1988 (c. 33), the following provisions (which are to some extent superseded by provisions of this Chapter) are repealed—

(a) Part 2 and Schedule 2 (which relate to documentary evidence);

(b) in Schedule 13, paragraphs 2 to 5 (which relate to documentary evidence in service courts etc).

CHAPTER 3
MISCELLANEOUS AND SUPPLEMENTAL

137   Evidence by video recording

(1) This section applies where—

(a) a person is called as a witness in proceedings for an offence triable only on indictment, or for a prescribed offence triable either way,

(b) the person claims to have witnessed (whether visually or in any other way)—

    (i) events alleged by the prosecution to include conduct constituting the offence or part of the offence, or

    (ii) events closely connected with such events,

(c) he has previously given an account of the events in question (whether in response to questions asked or otherwise),

(d) the account was given at a time when those events were fresh in the person's memory (or would have been, assuming the truth of the claim mentioned in paragraph (b)),

(e) a video recording was made of the account,

(f) the court has made a direction that the recording should be admitted as evidence in chief of the witness, and the direction has not been rescinded, and

(g) the recording is played in the proceedings in accordance with the direction.

(2) If, or to the extent that, the witness in his oral evidence in the proceedings

asserts the truth of the statements made by him in the recorded account, they shall be treated as if made by him in that evidence.

(3) A direction under subsection (1)(f)—

    (a)   may not be made in relation to a recorded account given by the defendant;

    (b)   may be made only if it appears to the court that—

        (i)   the witness's recollection of the events in question is likely to have been significantly better when he gave the recorded account than it will be when he gives oral evidence in the proceedings, and

        (ii) it is in the interests of justice for the recording to be admitted, having regard in particular to the matters mentioned in subsection (4).

(4) Those matters are—

    (a)   the interval between the time of the events in question and the time when the recorded account was made;

    (b)   any other factors that might affect the reliability of what the witness said in that account;

    (c)   the quality of the recording;

    (d)   any views of the witness as to whether his evidence in chief should be given orally or by means of the recording.

(5) For the purposes of subsection (2) it does not matter if the statements in the recorded account were not made on oath.

(6) In this section "prescribed" means of a description specified in an order made by the Secretary of State.

138   Video evidence: further provisions

(1) Where a video recording is admitted under section 137, the witness may not give evidence in chief otherwise than by means of the recording as to any matter which, in the opinion of the court, has been dealt with adequately in the recorded account.

(2) The reference in subsection (1)(f) of section 137 to the admission of a recording includes a reference to the admission of part of the recording; and references in that section and this one to the video recording or to the witness's recorded account shall, where appropriate, be read accordingly.

(3) In considering whether any part of a recording should be not admitted under section 137, the court must consider—

    (a)   whether admitting that part would carry a risk of prejudice to the defendant, and

    (b)   if so, whether the interests of justice nevertheless require it to be admitted in view of the desirability of showing the whole, or substantially the whole, of the recorded interview.

(4) A court may not make a direction under section 137(1)(f) in relation to any proceedings unless—

(a) the Secretary of State has notified the court that arrangements can be made, in the area in which it appears to the court that the proceedings will take place, for implementing directions under that section, and

(b) the notice has not been withdrawn.

(5) Nothing in section 137 affects the admissibility of any video recording which would be admissible apart from that section.

139   Use of documents to refresh memory

(1) A person giving oral evidence in criminal proceedings about any matter may, at any stage in the course of doing so, refresh his memory of it from a document made or verified by him at an earlier time if—

(a) he states in his oral evidence that the document records his recollection of the matter at that earlier time, and

(b) his recollection of the matter is likely to have been significantly better at that time than it is at the time of his oral evidence.

(2) Where—

(a) a person giving oral evidence in criminal proceedings about any matter has previously given an oral account, of which a sound recording was made, and he states in that evidence that the account represented his recollection of the matter at that time,

(b) his recollection of the matter is likely to have been significantly better at the time of the previous account than it is at the time of his oral evidence, and

(c) a transcript has been made of the sound recording,

he may, at any stage in the course of giving his evidence, refresh his memory of the matter from that transcript.

140   Interpretation of Chapter 3

In this Chapter—

"criminal proceedings" means criminal proceedings in relation to which the strict rules of evidence apply;

"defendant", in relation to criminal proceedings, means a person charged with an offence in those proceedings;

"document" means anything in which information of any description is recorded, but not including any recording of sounds or moving images;

"oral evidence" includes evidence which, by reason of any disability, disorder or other impairment, a person called as a witness gives in writing or by signs or by way of any device;

"video recording" means any recording, on any medium, from which a moving image may by any means be produced, and includes the accompanying sound-track.

SEXUAL OFFENCES ACT 2003
(c. 42)

PART 1
SEXUAL OFFENCES

75 Evidential presumptions about consent

(1) If in proceedings for an offence to which this section applies it is proved—

    (a) that the defendant did the relevant act,

    (b) that any of the circumstances specified in subsection (2) existed, and

    (c) that the defendant knew that those circumstances existed,

the complainant is to be taken not to have consented to the relevant act unless sufficient evidence is adduced to raise an issue as to whether he consented, and the defendant is to be taken not to have reasonably believed that the complainant consented unless sufficient evidence is adduced to raise an issue as to whether he reasonably believed it.

(2) The circumstances are that—

    (a) any person was, at the time of the relevant act or immediately before it began, using violence against the complainant or causing the complainant to fear that immediate violence would be used against him;

    (b) any person was, at the time of the relevant act or immediately before it began, causing the complainant to fear that violence was being used, or that immediate violence would be used, against another person;

    (c) the complainant was, and the defendant was not, unlawfully detained at the time of the relevant act;

    (d) the complainant was asleep or otherwise unconscious at the time of the relevant act;

    (e) because of the complainant's physical disability, the complainant would not have been able at the time of the relevant act to communicate to the defendant whether the complainant consented;

    (f) any person had administered to or caused to be taken by the complainant, without the complainant's consent, a substance which, having regard to when it was administered or taken, was capable of causing or enabling the complainant to be stupefied or overpowered at the time of the relevant act.

(3) In subsection (2)(a) and (b), the reference to the time immediately before the relevant act began is, in the case of an act which is one of a continuous series of sexual activities, a reference to the time immediately before the first sexual activity began.

76 Conclusive presumptions about consent

(1) If in proceedings for an offence to which this section applies it is proved that the defendant did the relevant act and that any of the circumstances specified in subsection (2) existed, it is to be conclusively presumed—
(a) that the complainant did not consent to the relevant act, and
(b) that the defendant did not believe that the complainant consented to the relevant act.

(2) The circumstances are that—
(a) the defendant intentionally deceived the complainant as to the nature or purpose of the relevant act;
(b) the defendant intentionally induced the complainant to consent to the relevant act by impersonating a person known personally to the complainant.

77 Sections 75 and 76: relevant acts

In relation to an offence to which sections 75 and 76 apply, references in those sections to the relevant act and to the complainant are to be read as follows—

Offence	Relevant Act
An offence under section 1 (rape).	The defendant intentionally penetrating, with his penis, the vagina, anus or mouth of another person ("the complainant").
An offence under section 2 (assault by penetration).	The defendant intentionally penetrating, with a part of his body or anything else, the vagina or anus of another person ("the complainant"), where the penetration is sexual.
An offence under section 3 (sexual assault).	The defendant intentionally touching another person ("the complainant"), where the touching is sexual.
An offence under section 4 (causing a person to engage in sexual activity without consent).	The defendant intentionally causing another person ("the complainant") to engage in an activity, where the activity is sexual.

78 "Sexual"

For the purposes of this Part (except section 71), penetration, touching or any other activity is sexual if a reasonable person would consider that—

(a) whatever its circumstances or any person's purpose in relation to it, it is because of its nature sexual, or

(b) because of its nature it may be sexual and because of its circumstances or the purpose of any person in relation to it (or both) it is sexual.

Civil Partnership Act 2004
(c. 33)

84 Evidence

(1) Any enactment or rule of law relating to the giving of evidence by a spouse applies in relation to a civil partner as it applies in relation to the spouse.

(2) Subsection (1) is subject to any specific amendment made by or under this Act which relates to the giving of evidence by a civil partner.

(3) For the avoidance of doubt, in any such amendment, references to a person's civil partner do not include a former civil partner.

(4) References in subsections (1) and (2) to giving evidence are to giving evidence in any way (whether by supplying information, making discovery, producing documents or otherwise).

(5) Any rule of law–

    (a) which is preserved by section 7(3) of the Civil Evidence Act 1995 (c. 38) or section 118(1) of the Criminal Justice Act 2003 (c. 44), and

    (b) under which in any proceedings evidence of reputation or family tradition is admissible for the purpose of proving or disproving the existence of a marriage,

is to be treated as applying in an equivalent way for the purpose of proving or disproving the existence of a civil partnership.

International Conventions

EUROPEAN CONVENTION FOR THE PROTECTION OF HUMAN RIGHTS AND FUNDAMENTAL FREEDOMS ROME 4.11.1950

Article 2

1. Everyone's right to life shall be protected by law. No one shall be deprived of his life intentionally save in the execution of a sentence of a court following his conviction of a crime for which this penalty is provided by law.

2. Deprivation of life shall not be regarded as inflicted in contravention of this article when it results from the use of force which is no more than absolutely necessary:
   (a) in defence of any person from unlawful violence;
   (b) in order to effect a lawful arrest or to prevent escape of a person lawfully detained;
   (c) in action lawfully taken for the purpose of quelling a riot or insurrection.

Article 3

No one shall be subjected to torture or to inhuman or degrading treatment or punishment.

Article 5

1. Everyone has the right to liberty and security of person.

   No one shall be deprived of his liberty save in the following cases and in accordance with a procedure prescribed by law:
   (a) the lawful detention of a person after conviction by a competent court;
   (b) the lawful arrest or detention of a person for non-compliance with the lawful order of a court or in order to secure the fulfilment of any obligation prescribed by law;
   (c) the lawful arrest or detention of a person effected for the purpose of bringing him before the competent legal authority of reasonable suspicion of having committed and offence or when it is reasonably considered necessary to prevent his committing an offence or fleeing after having done so;

(d) the detention of a minor by lawful order for the purpose of educational supervision or his lawful detention for the purpose of bringing him before the competent legal authority;

(e) the lawful detention of persons for the prevention of the spreading of infectious diseases, of persons of unsound mind, alcoholics or drug addicts, or vagrants;

(f) the lawful arrest or detention of a person to prevent his effecting an unauthorized entry into the country or of a person against whom action is being taken with a view to deportation or extradition.

2. Everyone who is arrested shall be informed promptly, in a language which he understands, of the reasons for his arrest and the charge against him.

3. Everyone arrested or detained in accordance with the provisions of paragraph 1(c) of this article shall be brought promptly before a judge or other officer authorized by law to exercise judicial power and shall be entitled to trial within a reasonable time or to release pending trial. Release may be conditioned by guarantees to appear for trial.

4. Everyone who is deprived of his liberty by arrest or detention shall be entitled to take proceedings by which the lawfulness of his detention shall be decided speedily by a court and his release ordered if the detention is not lawful.

5. Everyone who has been the victim of arrest or detention in contravention of the provisions of this article shall have an enforceable right to compensation.

Article 6

1. In the determination of his civil rights and obligations or of any criminal charge against him, everyone is entitled to a fair and public hearing within a reasonable time by an independent and impartial tribunal established by law. Judgement shall be pronounced publicly by the press and public may be excluded from all or part of the trial in the interest of morals, public order or national security in a democratic society, where the interests of juveniles or the protection of the private life of the parties so require, or the extent strictly necessary in the opinion of the court in special circumstances where publicity would prejudice the interests of justice.

2. Everyone charged with a criminal offence shall be presumed innocent until proved guilty according to law.

3. Everyone charged with a criminal offence has the following minimum rights:
    (a) to be informed promptly, in a language which he understands and in detail, of the nature and cause of the accusation against him;
    (b) to have adequate time and the facilities for the preparation of his defence;

(c) to defend himself in person or through legal assistance of his own choosing or, if he has not sufficient means to pay for legal assistance, to be given it free when the interests of justice so require;

(d) to examine or have examined witnesses against him and to obtain the attendance and examination of witnesses on his behalf under the same conditions as witnesses against him;

(e) to have the free assistance of an interpreter if he cannot understand or speak the language used in court.

Article 8

1. Everyone has the right to respect for his private and family life, his home and his correspondence.

2. There shall be no interference by a public authority with the exercise of this right except such as is in accordance with the law and is necessary in a democratic society in the interests of national security, public safety or the economic well-being of the country, for the prevention of disorder or crime, for the protection of health or morals, or for the protection of the rights and freedoms of others.

Article 10

1. Everyone has the right to freedom of expression. this right shall include freedom to hold opinions and to receive and impart information and ideas without interference by public authority and regardless of frontiers. This article shall not prevent States from requiring the licensing of broadcasting, television or cinema enterprises.

2. The exercise of these freedoms, since it carries with it duties and responsibilities, may be subject to such formalities, conditions, restrictions or penalties as are prescribed by law and are necessary in a democratic society, in the interests of national security, territorial integrity or public safety, for the prevention of disorder or crime, for the protection of health or morals, for the protection of the reputation or the rights of others, for preventing the disclosure of information received in confidence, or for maintaining the authority and impartiality of the judiciary.

Codes and Rules of Court

Police and Criminal Evidence Act 1984 (PACE)

CODE A   CODE OF PRACTICE FOR THE EXERCISE BY POLICE OFFICERS OF STATUTORY POWERS OF STOP AND SEARCH

General

This code of practice must be readily available at all police stations for consultation by police officers, police staff, detained persons and members of the public.

This code governs the exercise by police officers of statutory powers to search a person or a vehicle without first making an arrest.

In addition, it covers requirements on police officers and police staff to record encounters not governed by statutory powers. This code does not apply to:

   (a)   the powers of stop and search under;

   (i)   Aviation Security Act 1982, section 27(2);

   (ii) Police and Criminal Evidence Act 1984, section 6(1) (which relates specifically to powers of constables employed by statutory undertakers on the premises of the statutory undertakers).

   (b)   searches carried out for the purposes of examination under Schedule 7 to the Terrorism Act 2000 and to which the Code of Practice issued under paragraph 6 of Schedule 14 to the Terrorism Act 2000 applies.

1   Principles governing stop and search

1.1   Powers to stop and search must be used fairly, responsibly, with respect for people being searched and without unlawful discrimination.

The Race Relations (Amendment) Act 2000 makes it unlawful for police officers to discriminate on the grounds of race, colour, ethnic origin, nationality or national origins when using their powers.

1.2   The intrusion on the liberty of the person stopped or searched must be brief and detention for the purposes of a search must take place at or near the location of the stop.

1.3   If these fundamental principles are not observed the use of powers to stop and search may be drawn into question. Failure to use the powers in the proper manner reduces their effectiveness. Stop and search can play an important role in the detection and prevention of crime, and using the powers fairly makes them more effective.

1.4   The primary purpose of stop and search powers is to enable officers to allay or confirm suspicions about individuals without exercising their power of arrest. Officers may be required to justify the use or authorisation of such powers, in relation both to individual searches and the overall pattern of their activity in this regard, to their supervisory officers or in court. Any misuse of the powers is likely to be harmful to policing and lead to mistrust of the police. Officers must also be able to explain their actions to the member of the public searched. The misuse of these powers can lead to disciplinary action.

1.5   An officer must not search a person, even with his or her consent, where no power to search is applicable. Even where a person is prepared to submit to a search voluntarily, the person must not be searched unless the necessary legal power exists, and the search must be in accordance with the relevant power and the provisions of this Code. The only exception, where an officer does not require a specific power, applies to searches of persons entering sports grounds or other premises carried out with their consent given as a condition of entry.

2   Explanation of powers to stop and search

2.1   This code applies to powers of stop and search as follows:
   (a)   powers which require reasonable grounds for suspicion, before they may be exercised; that articles unlawfully obtained or possessed are being carried, or under Section 43 of the Terrorism Act 2000 that a person is a terrorist;
   (b)   authorised under section 60 of the Criminal Justice and Public Order Act 1994, based upon a reasonable belief that incidents involving serious violence may take place or that people are carrying dangerous instruments or offensive weapons within any locality in the police area;
   (c)   authorised under section 44(1) and (2) of the Terrorism Act 2000 based upon a consideration that the exercise of one or both powers is expedient for the prevention of acts of terrorism;
   (d)   powers to search a person who has not been arrested in the exercise of a power to search premises (see Code B paragraph 2.4).

Searches requiring reasonable grounds for suspicion

2.2   Reasonable grounds for suspicion depend on the circumstances in each case. There must be an objective basis for that suspicion based on facts, information, and/or intelligence which are relevant to the likelihood of finding an article of a certain kind or, in the case of searches under section 43 of the Terrorism Act 2000, to the likelihood that the person is a terrorist. Reasonable suspicion can never be supported on the basis of personal factors alone without reliable supporting intelligence or information or some specific behaviour by the person concerned. For example, a person's race, age, appearance, or the fact that the person is known to have a previous conviction, cannot be used alone or in combination with each other as the reason for searching that person. Reasonable suspicion cannot be based on generalisations or stereotypical images of certain groups or categories of people as more likely to be involved in criminal activity. A person's religion cannot be considered as reasonable grounds for suspicion and should never be considered as a reason to stop or stop and search an individual.

2.3   Reasonable suspicion can sometimes exist without specific information or intelligence and on the basis of some level of generalisation stemming from the behaviour of a person. For example, if an officer encounters someone on the street at night who is obviously trying to hide something, the officer may (depending on the other surrounding circumstances) base such suspicion on the fact that this kind of behaviour is often linked to stolen or prohibited articles being carried. Similarly, for the purposes of section 43 of the Terrorism Act 2000, suspicion that a person is a terrorist may arise from the person's behaviour at or near a location which has been identified as a potential target for terrorists.

2.4   However, reasonable suspicion should normally be linked to accurate and current intelligence or information, such as information describing an article being carried, a suspected offender, or a person who has been seen carrying a type of article known to have been stolen recently from premises in the area. Searches based on accurate and current intelligence or information are more likely to be effective. Targeting searches in a particular area at specified crime problems increases their effectiveness and minimises inconvenience to law-abiding members of the public. It also helps in justifying the use of searches both to those who are searched and to the public. This does not however prevent stop and search powers being exercised in other locations where such powers may be exercised and reasonable suspicion exists.

2.5   Searches are more likely to be effective, legitimate, and secure public confidence when reasonable suspicion is based on a range of factors. The overall use of these powers is more likely to be effective when up to date and accurate intelligence or information is communicated to officers and they are well-informed about local crime patterns.

2.6   Where there is reliable information or intelligence that members of a group or gang habitually carry knives unlawfully or weapons or controlled drugs, and wear a distinctive item of clothing or other means of identification to indicate their membership of the group or gang, that distinctive item of clothing or other means of identification may provide reasonable grounds to stop and search a person.

2.7   A police officer may have reasonable grounds to suspect that a person is in innocent possession of a stolen or prohibited article or other item for which he or she is empowered to search. In that case the officer may stop and search the person even though there would be no power of arrest.

2.8   Under section 43(1) of the Terrorism Act 2000 a constable may stop and search a person whom the officer reasonably suspects to be a terrorist to discover whether the person is in possession of anything which may constitute evidence that the person is a terrorist. These searches may only be carried out by an officer of the same sex as the person searched.

2.9   An officer who has reasonable grounds for suspicion may detain the person concerned in order to carry out a search. Before carrying out a search the officer may ask questions about the person's behaviour or presence in circumstances which gave rise to the suspicion. As a result of questioning the detained person, the reasonable grounds for suspicion necessary to detain that person may be confirmed or, because of a satisfactory explanation, be eliminated. Questioning may also reveal reasonable grounds to suspect the possession of a different kind of unlawful article from that originally suspected. Reasonable grounds for suspicion however cannot be provided retrospectively by such questioning during a person's detention or by refusal to answer any questions put.

2.10 If, as a result of questioning before a search, or other circumstances which come to the attention of the officer, there cease to be reasonable grounds for suspecting that an article is being carried of a kind for which there is a power to stop and search, no search may take place. In the absence of any other lawful power to detain, the person is free to leave at will and must be so informed.

2.11 There is no power to stop or detain a person in order to find grounds for a search. Police officers have many encounters with members of the public which do not involve detaining people against their will. If reasonable grounds for suspicion emerge during such an encounter, the officer may search the person, even though no grounds existed when the encounter began. If an officer is detaining someone for the purpose of a search, he or she should inform the person as soon as detention begins. Searches authorised under section 60 of the Criminal Justice and Public Order Act 1994.

2.12 Authority for a constable in uniform to stop and search under section 60 of the Criminal Justice and Public Order Act 1994 may be given if the authorising officer reasonably believes:
      (a) that incidents involving serious violence may take place in any locality in the officer's police area, and it is expedient to use these powers to prevent their occurrence, or

(b)   that persons are carrying dangerous instruments or offensive weapons without good reason in any locality in the officer's police area.

2.13   An authorisation under section 60 may only be given by an officer of the rank of inspector or above, in writing, specifying the grounds on which it was given, the locality in which the powers may be exercised and the period of time for which they are in force. The period authorised shall be no longer than appears reasonably necessary to prevent, or seek to prevent incidents of serious violence, or to deal with the problem of carrying dangerous instruments or offensive weapons. It may not exceed 24 hours.

2.14   If an inspector gives an authorisation, he or she must, as soon as practicable, inform an officer of or above the rank of superintendent. This officer may direct that the authorisation shall be extended for a further 24 hours, if violence or the carrying of dangerous instruments or offensive weapons has occurred, or is suspected to have occurred, and the continued use of the powers is considered necessary to prevent or deal with further such activity. That direction must also be given in writing at the time or as soon as practicable afterwards.

Powers to require removal of face coverings

2.15   Section 60AA of the Criminal Justice and Public Order Act 1994 also provides a power to demand the removal of disguises. The officer exercising the power must reasonably believe that someone is wearing an item wholly or mainly for the purpose of concealing identity. There is also a power to seize such items where the officer believes that a person intends to wear them for this purpose. There is no power to stop and search for disguises. An officer may seize any such item which is discovered when exercising a power of search for something else, or which is being carried, and which the officer reasonably believes is intended to be used for concealing anyone's identity. This power can only be used if an authorisation under section 60 or an authorisation under section 60AA is in force.

2.16   Authority for a constable in uniform to require the removal of disguises and to seize them under section 60AA may be given if the authorising officer reasonably believes that activities may take place in any locality in the officer's police area that are likely to involve the commission of offences and it is expedient to use these powers to prevent or control these activities.

2.17   An authorisation under section 60AA may only be given by an officer of the rank of inspector or above, in writing, specifying the grounds on which it was given, the locality in which the powers may be exercised and the period of time for which they are in force. The period authorised shall be no longer than appears reasonably necessary to prevent, or seek to prevent the commission of offences. It may not exceed 24 hours.

2.18 If an inspector gives an authorisation, he or she must, as soon as practicable, inform an officer of or above the rank of superintendent. This officer may direct that the authorisation shall be extended for a further 24 hours, if crimes have been committed, or is suspected to have been committed, and the continued use of the powers is considered necessary to prevent or deal with further such activity. This direction must also be given in writing at the time or as soon as practicable afterwards.

Searches authorised under section 44 of the Terrorism Act 2000

2.19 An officer of the rank of assistant chief constable (or equivalent) or above, may give authority for the following powers of stop and search under section 44 of the Terrorism Act 2000 to be exercised in the whole or part of his or her police area if the officer considers it is expedient for the prevention of acts of terrorism:

(a)   under section 44(1) of the Terrorism Act 2000, to give a constable in uniform power to stop and search any vehicle, its driver, any passenger in the vehicle and anything in or on the vehicle or carried by the driver or any passenger; and

(b)   under section 44(2) of the Terrorism Act 2000, to give a constable in uniform power to stop and search any pedestrian and anything carried by the pedestrian. An authorisation under section 44(1) may be combined with one under section 44(2).

2.20 If an authorisation is given orally at first, it must be confirmed in writing by the officer who gave it as soon as reasonably practicable.

2.21 When giving an authorisation, the officer must specify the geographical area in which the power may be used, and the time and date that the authorisation ends (up to a maximum of 28 days from the time the authorisation was given).

2.22 The officer giving an authorisation under section 44(1) or (2) must cause the Secretary of State to be informed, as soon as reasonably practicable, that such an authorisation has been given. An authorisation which is not confirmed by the Secretary of State within 48 hours of its having been given, shall have effect up until the end of that 48 hour period or the end of the period specified in the authorisation (whichever is the earlier).

2.23 Following notification of the authorisation, the Secretary of State may:

(i)   cancel the authorisation with immediate effect or with effect from such other time as he or she may direct;

(ii)   confirm it but for a shorter period than that specified in the authorisation; or

(iii)   confirm the authorisation as given.

2.24 When an authorisation under section 44 is given, a constable in uniform
      may exercise the powers:

      (a) only for the purpose of searching for articles of a kind which could
           be used in connection with terrorism (see paragraph 2.25);

      (b) whether or not there are any grounds for suspecting the presence of
           such articles.

2.24A When a Community Support Officer on duty and in uniform has
       been conferred powers under Section 44 of the Terrorism Act 2000 by a
       Chief Officer of their force, the exercise of this power must comply with
       the requirements of this Code of Practice, including the recording
       requirements.

2.25 The selection of persons stopped under section 44 of Terrorism Act
      2000 should reflect an objective assessment of the threat posed by the
      various terrorist groups active in Great Britain. The powers must not be
      used to stop and search for reasons unconnected with terrorism.
      Officers must take particular care not to discriminate against members
      of minority ethnic groups in the exercise of these powers. There may be
      circumstances, however, where it is appropriate for officers to take
      account of a person's ethnic origin in selecting persons to be stopped in
      response to a specific terrorist threat (for example, some international
      terrorist groups are associated with particular ethnic identities).

2.26 The powers under sections 43 and 44 of the Terrorism Act 2000 allow a
      constable to search only for articles which could be used for terrorist
      purposes. However, this would not prevent a search being carried out
      under other powers if, in the course of exercising these powers, the
      officer formed reasonable grounds for suspicion. Powers to search in the
      exercise of a power to search premises

2.27 The following powers to search premises also authorise the search of a
      person, not under arrest, who is found on the premises during the
      course of the search:

      (a) section 139B of the Criminal Justice Act 1988 under which a
           constable may enter school premises and search the premises and
           any person on those premises for any bladed or pointed article or
           offensive weapon; and

      (b) under a warrant issued under section s.23(3) of the Misuse of Drugs
           Act 1971 to search premises for drugs or documents but only if the
           warrant specifically authorises the search of persons found on the
           premises.

2.28 Before the power under section 139B of the Criminal Justice Act 1988
      may be exercised, the constable must have reasonable grounds to believe
      that an offence under section 139A of the Criminal Justice Act 1988
      (having a bladed or pointed article or offensive weapon on school
      premises) has been or is being committed. A warrant to search premises
      and persons found therein may be issued under section s.23(3) of the

Misuse of Drugs Act 1971 if there are reasonable grounds to suspect that controlled drugs or certain documents are in the possession of a person on the premises.

2.29 The powers in paragraph 2.27(a) or (b) do not require prior specific grounds to suspect that the person to be searched is in possession of an item for which there is an existing power to search. However, it is still necessary to ensure that the selection and treatment of those searched under these powers is based upon objective factors connected with the search of the premises, and not upon personal prejudice.

3   Conduct of searches

3.1   All stops and searches must be carried out with courtesy, consideration and respect for the person concerned. This has a significant impact on public confidence in the police. Every reasonable effort must be made to minimise the embarrassment that a person being searched may experience.

3.2   The co-operation of the person to be searched must be sought in every case, even if the person initially objects to the search. A forcible search may be made only if it has been established that the person is unwilling to co-operate or resists. Reasonable force may be used as a last resort if necessary to conduct a search or to detain a person or vehicle for the purposes of a search.

3.3   The length of time for which a person or vehicle may be detained must be reasonable and kept to a minimum. Where the exercise of the power requires reasonable suspicion, the thoroughness and extent of a search must depend on what is suspected of being carried, and by whom. If the suspicion relates to a particular article which is seen to be slipped into a person's pocket, then, in the absence of other grounds for suspicion or an opportunity for the article to be moved elsewhere, the search must be confined to that pocket. In the case of a small article which can readily be concealed, such as a drug, and which might be concealed anywhere on the person, a more extensive search may be necessary. In the case of searches mentioned in paragraph 2.1(b), (c), and (d), which do not require reasonable grounds for suspicion, officers may make any reasonable search to look for items for which they are empowered to search.

3.4   The search must be carried out at or near the place where the person or vehicle was first detained.

3.5   There is no power to require a person to remove any clothing in public other than an outer coat, jacket or gloves except under section 45(3) of the Terrorism Act 2000 (which empowers a constable conducting a search under section 44(1) or 44(2) of that Act to require a person to remove headgear and footwear in public) and under section 60AA of the Criminal Justice and Public Order Act 1994 (which empowers a constable to require a person to remove any item worn to conceal identity). [See *Notes 4* and *6*] A search in public of a person's clothing which has not been removed must be restricted to superficial examination of outer garments. This does not, however, prevent an officer from placing his or her hand inside the pockets of the outer clothing, or feeling round the inside of collars, socks and shoes if this is reasonably necessary in the circumstances to look for the object of the search or to remove and examine any item reasonably suspected to be the object of the search. For the same reasons, subject to the restrictions on the removal of headgear, a person's hair may also be searched in public (see paragraphs 3.1 and 3.3).

3.6 Where on reasonable grounds it is considered necessary to conduct a more thorough search (e.g. by requiring a person to take off a T-shirt), this must be done out of public view, for example, in a police van unless paragraph 3.7 applies, or police station if there is one nearby. Any search involving the removal of more than an outer coat, jacket, gloves, headgear or footwear, or any other item concealing identity, may only be made by an officer of the same sex as the person searched and may not be made in the presence of anyone of the opposite sex unless the person being searched specifically requests it.

3.7 Searches involving exposure of intimate parts of the body must not be conducted as a routine extension of a less thorough search, simply because nothing is found in the course of the initial search. Searches involving exposure of intimate parts of the body may be carried out only at a nearby police station or other nearby location which is out of public view (but not a police vehicle). These searches must be conducted in accordance with paragraph 11 of Annex A to Code C except that an intimate search mentioned in paragraph 11(f) of Annex A to Code C may not be authorised or carried out under any stop and search powers. The other provisions of Code C do not apply to the conduct and recording of searches of persons detained at police stations in the exercise of stop and search powers.

3.8 Steps to be taken prior to a search

Before any search of a detained person or attended vehicle takes place the officer must take reasonable steps to give the person to be searched or in charge of the vehicle the following information:

(a) that they are being detained for the purposes of a search

(b) the officer's name (except in the case of enquiries linked to the investigation of terrorism, or otherwise where the officer reasonably believes that giving his or her name might put him or her in danger, in which case a warrant or other identification number shall be given) and the name of the police station to which the officer is attached;

(c) the legal search power which is being exercised; and

(d) a clear explanation of:

    (i) the purpose of the search in terms of the article or articles for which there is a power to search; and

    (ii) in the case of powers requiring reasonable suspicion (see paragraph 2.1(a)), the grounds for that suspicion; or

    (iii) in the case of powers which do not require reasonable suspicion (see paragraph 2.1(b), and (c)), the nature of the power and of any necessary authorisation and the fact that it has been given.

3.9 Officers not in uniform must show their warrant cards. Stops and searches under the powers mentioned in paragraphs 2.1(b), and (c) may be undertaken only by a constable in uniform.

3.10 Before the search takes place the officer must inform the person (or the owner or person in charge of the vehicle that is to be searched) of his or her entitlement to a copy of the record of the search, including his entitlement to a record of the search if an application is made within 12 months, if it is wholly impracticable to make a record at the time. If a record is not made at the time the person should also be told how a copy can be obtained (see section 4). The person should also be given information about police powers to stop and search and the individual's rights in these circumstances.

3.11 If the person to be searched, or in charge of a vehicle to be searched, does not appear to understand what is being said, or there is any doubt about the person's ability to understand English, the officer must take reasonable steps to bring information regarding the person's rights and any relevant provisions of this Code to his or her attention. If the person is deaf or cannot understand English and is accompanied by someone, then the officer must try to establish whether that person can interpret or otherwise help the officer to give the required information.

4 Recording requirements

4.1 An officer who has carried out a search in the exercise of any power to which this Code applies, must make a record of it at the time, unless there are exceptional circumstances which would make this wholly impracticable (e.g. in situations involving public disorder or when the officer's presence is urgently required elsewhere). If a record is not made at the time, the officer must do so as soon as practicable afterwards. There may be situations in which it is not practicable to obtain the information necessary to complete a record, but the officer should make every reasonable effort to do so.

4.2 A copy of a record made at the time must be given immediately to the person who has been searched. The officer must ask for the name, address and date of birth of the person searched, but there is no obligation on a person to provide these details and no power of detention if the person is unwilling to do so.

4.3   The following information must always be included in the record of a search even if the person does not wish to provide any personal details:

(i)   the name of the person searched, or (if it is withheld) a description;

(ii)   a note of the person's self-defined ethnic background;

(iii) when a vehicle is searched, its registration number;

(iv)   the date, time, and place that the person or vehicle was first detained;

(v)   the date, time and place the person or vehicle was searched (if different from (iv));

(vi)   the purpose of the search;

(vii) the grounds for making it, or in the case of those searches mentioned in paragraph 2.1(b) and (c), the nature of the power and of any necessary authorisation and the fact that it has been given;

(viii)   its outcome (e.g. arrest or no further action);

(ix)   a note of any injury or damage to property resulting from it;

(x)   subject to paragraph 3.8(b), the identity of the officer making the search.

4.4   Nothing in paragraph 4.3 (x) or 4.10A requires the names of police officers to be shown on the search record or any other record required to be made under this code in the case of enquiries linked to the investigation of terrorism or otherwise where an officer reasonably believes that recording names might endanger the officers. In such cases the record must show the officers' warrant or other identification number and duty station.

4.5   A record is required for each person and each vehicle searched. However, if a person is in a vehicle and both are searched, and the object and grounds of the search are the same, only one record need be completed. If more than one person in a vehicle is searched, separate records for each search of a person must be made. If only a vehicle is searched, the name of the driver and his or her self-defined ethnic background must be recorded, unless the vehicle is unattended.

4.6   The record of the grounds for making a search must, briefly but informatively, explain the reason for suspecting the person concerned, by reference to the person's behaviour and/or other circumstances.

4.7   Where officers detain an individual with a view to performing a search, but the search is not carried out due to the grounds for suspicion being eliminated as a result of questioning the person detained, a record must still be made in accordance with the procedure outlined in Paragraph 4.12.

4.8   After searching an unattended vehicle, or anything in or on it, an officer must leave a notice in it (or on it, if things on it have been searched without opening it) recording the fact that it has been searched.

4.9   The notice must include the name of the police station to which the officer concerned is attached and state where a copy of the record of the search may be obtained and where any application for compensation should be directed.

4.10 The vehicle must if practicable be left secure.

4.10A   When an officer makes a record of the stop electronically and is unable to produce a copy of the form at the time, the officer must explain how the person can obtain a full copy of the record of the stop or search and give the person a receipt which contains:

- a unique reference number and guidance on how to obtain a full copy of thestop or search;
- the name of the officer who carried out the stop or search (unless paragraph 4.4 applies); and
- the power used to stop and search them.

Recording of encounters not governed by Statutory Powers

4.11 Not used.

4.12 When an officer requests a person in a public place to account for themselves, i.e. their actions, behaviour, presence in an area or possession of anything, a record of the encounter must be completed at the time and a copy given to the person who has been questioned. The record must identify the name of the officer who has made the stop and conducted the encounter. This does not apply under the exceptional circumstances outlined in paragraph 4.1 of this code.

4.13 This requirement does not apply to general conversations such as when giving directions to a place, or when seeking witnesses. It also does not include occasions on which an officer is seeking general information or questioning people to establish background to incidents which have required officers to intervene to keep the peace or resolve a dispute.

4.14 A separate record need not be completed when:

- stopping a person in a vehicle when an HORT/1 form, a Vehicle Defect Rectification Scheme Notice, or aFixed Penalty Notice is issued. It also does not apply when a specimen of breath is required under Section 6 of the Road Traffic Act 1988.
- stopping a person when a Penalty Notice is issued for an offence.

4.15 Officers must inform the person of their entitlement to a copy of a record of the encounter.

4.16 The provisions of paragraph 4.4 of this code apply equally when the encounters described in 4.12 and 4.13 are recorded.

4.17 The following information must be included in the record

(i)   the date, time and place of the encounter;

(ii) if the person is in a vehicle, the registration number;

(iii) the reason why the officer questioned that person;

(iv) a note of the person's self-defined ethnic background;

(v)   the outcome of the encounter.

4.18 There is no power to require the person questioned to provide personal details. If a person refuses to give their self-defined ethnic background, a form must still be completed, which includes a description of the person's ethnic background.

4.19 A record of an encounter must always be made when the criteria set out in 4.12 have been met. If the criteria are not met but the person requests a record, the officer should provide a copy of the form but record on it that the encounter did not meet the criteria. The officer can refuse to issue the form if he or she reasonably believes that the purpose of the request is deliberately aimed at frustrating or delaying legitimate police activity.

4.20 All references to officers in this section include police staff designated as Community

Support Officers under section 38 of the Police Reform Act 2002.

5   Monitoring and supervising the use of stop and search powers

5.1   Supervising officers must monitor the use of stop and search powers and should consider in particular whether there is any evidence that they are being exercised on the basis of stereotyped images or inappropriate generalisations. Supervising officers should satisfy themselves that the practice of officers under their supervision in stopping, searching and recording is fully in accordance with this Code.

5.2   Supervisors must also examine whether the records reveal any trends or patterns which give cause for concern, and if so take appropriate action to address this. Senior officers with area or force-wide responsibilities must also monitor the broader use of stop and search powers and, where necessary, take action at the relevant level.

5.3   Supervision and monitoring must be supported by the compilation of comprehensive statistical records of stops and searches at force, area and local level. Any apparently disproportionate use of the powers by particular officers or groups of officers or in relation to specific sections of the community should be identified and investigated.

5.4   In order to promote public confidence in the use of the powers, forces in consultation with police authorities must make arrangements for the records to be scrutinised by representatives of the community, and to explain the use of the powers at a local level.

POLICE AND CRIMINAL EVIDENCE ACT 1984 (PACE)

CODE B   CODE OF PRACTICE FOR SEARCHES OF PREMISES BY POLICE OFFICERS AND THE SEIZURE OF PROPERTY FOUND BY POLICE OFFICERS ON PERSONS OR PREMISES

1   Introduction

1.1   This Code of Practice deals with police powers to:
- search premises
- seize and retain property found on premises and persons

1.1A   These powers may be used to find:
- property and material relating to a crime
- wanted persons
- children who abscond from local authority accommodation where they have been remanded or committed by a court

1.2   A justice of the peace may issue a search warrant granting powers of entry, search and seizure, e.g. warrants to search for stolen property, drugs, firearms and evidence of serious offences. Police also have powers without a search warrant. The main ones provided by the Police and Criminal Evidence Act 1984 (PACE) include powers to search premises:
- to make an arrest
- after an arrest

1.3   The right to privacy and respect for personal property are key principles of the Human Rights Act 1998. Powers of entry, search and seizure should be fully and clearly justified before use because they may significantly interfere with the occupier's privacy. Officers should consider if the necessary objectives can be met by less intrusive means.

1.4   In all cases, police should:
- exercise their powers courteously and with respect for persons and property
- only use reasonable force when this is considered necessary and proportionate to the circumstances

1.5   If the provisions of PACE and this Code are not observed, evidence obtained from a search may be open to question.

2   General

2.1   This Code must be readily available at all police stations for consultation by:

- police officers
- police staff
- detained persons
- members of the public

2.2   The *Notes for Guidance* included are not provisions of this Code.

2.3   This Code applies to searches of premises:

(a)   by police for the purposes of an investigation into an alleged offence, with the occupier's consent, other than:

- routine scene of crime searches;
- calls to a fire or burglary made by or on behalf of an occupier or searches following the activation of fire or burglar alarms or discovery of insecure premises;
- searches when *paragraph 5.4* applies;
- bomb threat calls;

(b)   under powers conferred on police officers by PACE, sections 17, 18 and 32;

(c)   undertaken in pursuance of search warrants issued to and executed by constables in accordance with PACE, sections 15 and 16.

(d)   subject to *paragraph 2.6*, under any other power given to police to enter premises with or without a search warrant for any purpose connected with the investigation into an alleged or suspected offence. See *Note 2B*. For the purposes of this Code, 'premises' as defined in PACE, section 23, includes any place, vehicle, vessel, aircraft, hovercraft, tent or movable structure and any offshore installation as defined in the Mineral Workings (Offshore Installations) Act 1971, section 1.

2.4   A person who has not been arrested but is searched during a search of premises should be searched in accordance with Code A.

2.5   This Code does not apply to the exercise of a statutory power to enter premises or to inspect goods, equipment or procedures if the exercise of that power is not dependent on the existence of grounds for suspecting that an offence may have been committed and the person exercising the power has no reasonable grounds for such suspicion.

2.6   This Code does not affect any directions of a search warrant or order, lawfully executed in England or Wales that any item or evidence seized under that warrant or order be handed over to a police force, court, tribunal, or other authority outside England or Wales. For example, warrants and orders issued in Scotland or Northern Ireland, and search warrants issued under the Criminal Justice (International Co-operation) Act 1990, section 7.

2.7   When this Code requires the prior authority or agreement of an officer of at least inspector or superintendent rank, that authority may be given by a sergeant or chief inspector authorised to perform the functions of the higher rank under PACE, section 107.

2.8   Written records required under this Code not made in the search record shall, unless otherwise specified, be made:

- in the recording officer's pocket book ('pocket book' includes any official report book issued to police officers) or

- on forms provided for the purpose

2.9   Nothing in this Code requires the identity of officers, or anyone accompanying them during a search of premises, to be recorded or disclosed:

(a)   in the case of enquiries linked to the investigation of terrorism; or

(b)   if officers reasonably believe recording or disclosing their names might put them in danger. In these cases officers should use warrant or other identification numbers and the name of their police station. Police staff should use any identification number provided to them by the police force.

2.10   The 'officer in charge of the search' means the officer assigned specific duties and responsibilities under this Code. Whenever there is a search of premises to which this Code applies one officer must act as the officer in charge of the search.

2.11   In this Code:

(a)   'designated person' means a person other than a police officer, designated under the Police Reform Act 2002, Part 4 who has specified powers and duties of police officers conferred or imposed on them.

(b)   any reference to a police officer includes a designated person acting in the exercise or performance of the powers and duties conferred or imposed on them by their designation.

(c)   a person authorised to accompany police officers or designated persons in the execution of a warrant has the same powers as a constable in the execution of the warrant and the search and seizure of anything related to the warrant. These powers must be exercised in the company and under the supervision of a police officer.

2.12   If a power conferred on a designated person:

(a)   allows reasonable force to be used when exercised by a police officer, a designated person exercising that power has the same entitlement to use force;

(b)   includes power to use force to enter any premises, that power is not exercisable by that designated person except:

(i)   in the company and under the supervision of a police officer; or

(ii) for the purpose of:

- saving life or limb; or

- preventing serious damage to property.

2.13 Designated persons must have regard to any relevant provisions of the Codes of Practice.

3   Search warrants and production orders

(a) Before making an application

3.1   When information appears to justify an application, the officer must take reasonable steps to check the information is accurate, recent and not provided maliciously or irresponsibly. An application may not be made on the basis of information from an anonymous source if corroboration has not been sought.

3.2   The officer shall ascertain as specifically as possible the nature of the articles concerned and their location.

3.3   The officer shall make reasonable enquiries to:

(i)   establish if:

- anything is known about the likely occupier of the premises and the nature of the premises themselves;

- the premises have been searched previously and how recently;

(ii) obtain any other relevant information.

3.4   An application:

(a) to a justice of the peace for a search warrant or to a judge of the High Court, a Circuit judge, a Recorder or a District Judge for a search warrant or production order under PACE, Schedule 1 must be supported by a signed written authority from an officer of inspector rank or above:

Note: If the case is an urgent application to a justice of the peace and an inspector or above is not readily available, the next most senior officer on duty can give the written authority.

(b) to a circuit judge under the Terrorism Act 2000, Schedule 5 for

- a production order;

- search warrant; or

- an order requiring an explanation of material seized or produced under such a warrant or production order must be supported by a signed written authority from an officer of superintendent rank or above.

3.5   Except in a case of urgency, if there is reason to believe a search might have an adverse effect on relations between the police and the

community, the officer in charge shall consult the local police/
community liaison officer:

- before the search; or

- in urgent cases, as soon as practicable after the search

(b) Making an application

3.6   A search warrant application must be supported in writing, specifying:

(a) the enactment under which the application is made;

(b) (i) whether the warrant is to authorise entry and search of:

- one set of premises; or

- if the application is under PACE section 8, or Schedule 1,
  paragraph 12, more than one set of specified premises or
  all premises occupied or controlled by a specified person,
  and

(ii) the premises to be searched;

(c) the object of the search;

(d) the grounds for the application, including, when the purpose of the
proposed search is to find evidence of an alleged offence, an
indication of how the evidence relates to the investigation; (da)
where the application is under PACE section 8, or Schedule 1,
paragraph 12 for a single warrant to enter and search:

(i) more than one set of specified premises, the officer must specify
each set of premises which it is desired to enter and search

(ii) all premises occupied or controlled by a specified person, the
officer must specify;

- as many sets of premises which it is desired to enter and
  search as it is reasonably practicable to specify

- the person who is in occupation or control of those
  premises and any others which it is desired to search

- why it is necessary to search more premises than those
  which can be specified

- why it is not reasonably practicable to specify all the
  premises which it is desired to enter and search

(db) whether an application under PACE section 8 is for a warrant
authorising entry and search on more than one occasion, and if so,
the officer must state the grounds for this and whether the desired
number of entries authorised is unlimited or a specified maximum.

(e) there are no reasonable grounds to believe the material to be
sought, when making application to a:

(i) justice of the peace or a judge of the High Court, a Circuit
judge, a Recorder or a District Judge, consists of or includes
items subject to legal privilege;

(ii) justice of the peace, consists of or includes excluded material or special procedure material; Note: this does not affect the additional powers of seizure in the Criminal Justice and Police Act 2001, Part 2 covered in paragraph 7.7;

(f) if applicable, a request for the warrant to authorise a person or persons to accompany the officer who executes the warrant.

3.7 A search warrant application under PACE, Schedule 1, paragraph 12(a), shall if appropriate indicate why it is believed service of notice of an application for a production order may seriously prejudice the investigation. Applications for search warrants under the Terrorism Act 2000, Schedule 5, paragraph 11 must indicate why a production order would not be appropriate.

3.8 If a search warrant application is refused, a further application may not be made for those premises unless supported by additional grounds.

4   Entry without warrant – particular powers

(a) Making an arrest etc

4.1 The conditions under which an officer may enter and search premises without a warrant are set out in PACE, section 17. It should be noted that this section does not create or confer any powers of arrest.

(b) Search of premises where arrest takes place or the arrested person was immediately before arrest

4.2 When a person has been arrested for an indictable offence, a police officer has power under PACE, section 32 to search the premises where the person was arrested or where the person was immediately before being arrested.

(c) Search of premises occupied or controlled by the arrested person

4.3 The specific powers to search premises occupied or controlled by a person arrested for an indictable offence are set out in PACE, section 18. They may not be exercised, except if section 18(5) applies, unless an officer of inspector rank or above has given written authority. That authority should only be given when the authorising officer is satisfied the necessary grounds exist. If possible the authorising officer should record the authority on the Notice of Powers and Rights and, subject to *paragraph 2.9*, sign the Notice. The record of the grounds for the search and the nature of the evidence sought as required by section 18(7) of the Act should be made in:

- the custody record if there is one, otherwise
- the officer's pocket book, or
- the search record

5   Search with consent

5.1   Subject to *paragraph 5.4*, if it is proposed to search premises with the consent of a person entitled to grant entry the consent must, if practicable, be given in writing on the Notice of Powers and Rights before the search. The officer must make any necessary enquiries to be satisfied the person is in a position to give such consent.

5.2   Before seeking consent the officer in charge of the search shall state the purpose of the proposed search and its extent. This information must be as specific as possible, particularly regarding the articles or persons being sought and the parts of the premises to be searched. The person concerned must be clearly informed they are not obliged to consent and anything seized may be produced in evidence. If at the time the person is not suspected of an offence, the officer shall say this when stating the purpose of the search.

5.3   An officer cannot enter and search or continue to search premises under *paragraph 5.1* if consent is given under duress or withdrawn before the search is completed.

5.4   It is unnecessary to seek consent under *paragraphs 5.1* and *5.2* if this would cause disproportionate inconvenience to the person concerned.

6   Searching premises – general considerations

(a) Time of searches

6.1   Searches made under warrant must be made within three calendar months of the date of the warrant's issue.

6.2   Searches must be made at a reasonable hour unless this might frustrate the purpose of the search.

6.3   When the extent or complexity of a search mean it is likely to take a long time, the officer in charge of the search may consider using the seize and sift powers referred to in *section 7*.

6.3A   A warrant under PACE, section 8 may authorise entry to and search of premises on more than one occasion if, on the application, the justice of the peace is satisfied that it is necessary to authorise multiple entries in order to achieve the purpose for which the warrant is issued. No premises may be entered or searched on any subsequent occasions without the prior written authority of an officer of the rank of inspector who is not involved in the investigation. All other warrants authorise entry on one occasion only.

6.3B   Where a warrant under PACE section 8, or Schedule 1, paragraph 12 authorises entry to and search of all premises occupied or controlled by specified person, no premises which are not specified in the warrant may be entered and searched without the prior written authority of an officer of the rank of inspector who is not involved in the investigation.

(b) Entry other than with consent

6.4   The officer in charge of the search shall first try to communicate with the occupier, or any other person entitled to grant access to the premises, explain the authority under which entry is sought and ask the occupier to allow entry, unless:

   (i)   the search premises are unoccupied;

   (ii)   the occupier and any other person entitled to grant access are absent;

   (iii) there are reasonable grounds for believing that alerting the occupier or any other person entitled to grant access would frustrate the object of the search or endanger officers or other people.

6.5   Unless *sub-paragraph 6.4(iii)* applies, if the premises are occupied the officer, subject to *paragraph 2.9*, shall, before the search begins:

   (i)   identify him or herself, show their warrant card (if not in uniform) and state the purpose of and grounds for the search;

   (ii)   identify and introduce any person accompanying the officer on the search (such persons should carry identification for production on request) and briefly describe that person's role in the process.

6.6   Reasonable and proportionate force may be used if necessary to enter premises if the officer in charge of the search is satisfied the premises are those specified in any warrant, or in exercise of the powers described in *paragraphs 4.1 to 4.3*, and if:

   (i)   the occupier or any other person entitled to grant access has refused entry;

   (ii)   it is impossible to communicate with the occupier or any other person entitled to grant access; or

   (iii) any of the provisions of *paragraph 6.4* apply.

Notice of Powers and Rights

6.7   If an officer conducts a search to which this Code applies the officer shall, unless it is impracticable to do so, provide the occupier with a copy of a Notice in a standard format:

   (i)   specifying if the search is made under warrant, with consent, or in the exercise of the powers described in *paragraphs 4.1 to 4.3*. Note: the notice format shall provide for authority or consent to be indicated, see *paragraphs 4.3 and 5.1*;

   (ii)   summarising the extent of the powers of search and seizure conferred by PACE;

(iii) explaining the rights of the occupier, and the owner of the property seized;

(iv) explaining compensation may be payable in appropriate cases for damages caused entering and searching premises, and giving the address to send a compensation application;

(v) stating this Code is available at any police station.

6.8   If the occupier is:

- present, copies of the Notice and warrant shall, if practicable, be given to them before the search begins, unless the officer in charge of the search reasonably believes this would frustrate the object of the search or endanger officers or other people

- not present, copies of the Notice and warrant shall be left in a prominent place on the premises or appropriate part of the premises and endorsed, subject to *paragraph 2.9* with the name of the officer in charge of the search, the date and time of the search The warrant shall be endorsed to show this has been done.

(d) Conduct of searches

6.   Premises may be searched only to the extent necessary to achieve the object of the search, having regard to the size and nature of whatever is sought.

6.9A   A search may not continue under:

- a warrant's authority once all the things specified in that warrant have been found

- any other power once the object of that search has been achieved

6.9B   No search may continue once the officer in charge of the search is satisfied whatever is being sought is not on the premises. This does not prevent a further search of the same premises if additional grounds come to light supporting a further application for a search warrant or exercise or further exercise of another power. For example, when, as a result of new information, it is believed articles previously not found or additional articles are on the premises.

6.10 Searches must be conducted with due consideration for the property and privacy of the occupier and with no more disturbance than necessary. Reasonable force may be used only when necessary and proportionate because the co-operation of the occupier cannot be obtained or is insufficient for the purpose.

6.11 A friend, neighbour or other person must be allowed to witness the search if the occupier wishes unless the officer in charge of the search has reasonable grounds for believing the presence of the person asked for would seriously hinder the investigation or endanger officers or other people. A search need not be unreasonably delayed for this purpose. A record of the action taken should be made on the premises search record including the grounds for refusing the occupier's request.

6.12 A person is not required to be cautioned prior to being asked questions that are solely necessary for the purpose of furthering the proper and effective conduct of a search, see Code C, *paragraph 10.1(c)*. For example, questions to discover the occupier of specified premises, to find a key to open a locked drawer or cupboard or to otherwise seek co-operation during the search or to determine if a particular item is liable to be seized.

6.12A   If questioning goes beyond what is necessary for the purpose of the exemption in Code C, the exchange is likely to constitute an interview as defined by Code C, *paragraph 11.1A* and would require the associated safeguards included in Code C, *section 10*.

(e) Leaving premises

6.13 If premises have been entered by force, before leaving the officer in charge of the search must make sure they are secure by:

- arranging for the occupier or their agent to be present

- any other appropriate means

(f) Searches under PACE Schedule 1 or the Terrorism Act 2000, Schedule 5

6.14 An officer shall be appointed as the officer in charge of the search, see *paragraph 2.10*, in respect of any search made under a warrant issued under PACE Act 1984, Schedule 1 or the Terrorism Act 2000, Schedule 5. They are responsible for making sure the search is conducted with discretion and in a manner that causes the least possible disruption to any business or other activities carried out on the premises.

6.15 Once the officer in charge of the search is satisfied material may not be taken from the premises without their knowledge, they shall ask for the documents or other records concerned. The officer in charge of the search may also ask to see the index to files held on the premises, and the officers conducting the search may inspect any files which, according to the index, appear to contain the material sought. A more extensive search of the premises may be made only if:

- the person responsible for them refuses to:
  - produce the material sought, or
  - allow access to the index
- it appears the index is:
  - inaccurate, or
  - incomplete
- for any other reason the officer in charge of the search has reasonable grounds for believing such a search is necessary in order to find the material sought

7   Seizure and retention of property

(a) Seizure

7.1   Subject to *paragraph 7.2*, an officer who is searching any person or premises under any statutory power or with the consent of the occupier may seize anything:

(a)   covered by a warrant

(b)   the officer has reasonable grounds for believing is evidence of an offence or has been obtained in consequence of the commission of an offence but only if seizure is necessary to prevent the items being concealed, lost, disposed of, altered, damaged, destroyed or tampered with

(c)   covered by the powers in the Criminal Justice and Police Act 2001, Part 2 allowing an officer to seize property from persons or premises and retain it for sifting or examination elsewhere

7.2   No item may be seized which an officer has reasonable grounds for believing to be subject to legal privilege, as defined in PACE, section 10, other than under the Criminal Justice and Police Act 2001, Part 2.

7.3   Officers must be aware of the provisions in the Criminal Justice and Police Act 2001, section 59, allowing for applications to a judicial authority for the return of property seized and the subsequent duty to secure in section 60, see *paragraph 7.12(iii)*.

7.4   An officer may decide it is not appropriate to seize property because of an explanation from the person holding it but may nevertheless have reasonable grounds for believing it was obtained in consequence of an offence by some person. In these circumstances, the officer should identify the property to the holder, inform the holder of their suspicions and explain the holder may be liable to civil or criminal proceedings if they dispose of, alter or destroy the property.

7.5   An officer may arrange to photograph, image or copy, any document or other article they have the power to seize in accordance with *paragraph 7.1*. This is subject to specific restrictions on the examination, imaging or copying of certain property seized under the Criminal Justice and Police Act 2001, Part 2. An officer must have regard to their statutory obligation to retain an original document or other article only when a photograph or copy is not sufficient.

7.6   If an officer considers information stored in any electronic form and accessible from the premises could be used in evidence, they may require the information to be produced in a form:

•   which can be taken away and in which it is visible and legible; or

•   from which it can readily be produced in a visible and legible form

(b) Criminal Justice and Police Act 2001: Specific procedures for seize and sift powers

7.7   The Criminal Justice and Police Act 2001, Part 2 gives officers limited powers to seize property from premises or persons so they can sift or examine it elsewhere. Officers must be careful they only exercise these powers when it is essential and they do not remove any more material than necessary. The removal of large volumes of material, much of which may not ultimately be retainable, may have serious implications for the owners, particularly when they are involved in business or activities such as journalism or the provision of medical services. Officers must carefully consider if removing copies or images of relevant material or data would be a satisfactory alternative to removing originals. When originals are taken, officers must be prepared to facilitate the provision of copies or images for the owners when reasonably practicable.

7.8   Property seized under the Criminal Justice and Police Act 2001, sections 50 or 51 must be kept securely and separately from any material seized under other powers. An examination under section 53 to determine which elements may be retained must be carried out at the earliest practicable time, having due regard to the desirability of allowing the person from whom the property was seized, or a person with an interest in the property, an opportunity of being present or represented at the examination.

7.8A   All reasonable steps should be taken to accommodate an interested person's request to be present, provided the request is reasonable and subject to the need to prevent harm to, interference with, or unreasonable delay to the investigatory process. If an examination proceeds in the absence of an interested person who asked to attend or their representative, the officer who exercised the relevant seizure power must give that person a written notice of why the examination was carried out in those circumstances. If it is necessary for security reasons or to maintain confidentiality officers may exclude interested persons from decryption or other processes which facilitate the examination but do not form part of it.

7.9   It is the responsibility of the officer in charge of the investigation to make sure property is returned in accordance with sections 53 to 55. Material which there is no power to retain must be:

- separated from the rest of the seized property
- returned as soon as reasonably practicable after examination of all the seized property

7.9A   Delay is only warranted if very clear and compelling reasons exist, e.g. the:

- unavailability of the person to whom the material is to be returned
- need to agree a convenient time to return a large volume of material

7.9B   Legally privileged, excluded or special procedure material which cannot be retained must be returned:

- as soon as reasonably practicable
- without waiting for the whole examination

7.9C   As set out in section 58, material must be returned to the person from whom it was seized, except when it is clear some other person has a better right to it.

7.10   When an officer involved in the investigation has reasonable grounds to believe a person with a relevant interest in property seized under section 50 or 51 intends to make an application under section 59 for the return of any legally privileged, special procedure or excluded material, the officer in charge of the investigation should be informed as soon as practicable and the material seized should be kept secure in accordance with section 61.

7.11   The officer in charge of the investigation is responsible for making sure property is properly secured. Securing involves making sure the property is not examined, copied, imaged or put to any other use except at the request, or with the consent, of the applicant or in accordance with the directions of the appropriate judicial authority. Any request, consent or directions must be recorded in writing and signed by both the initiator and the officer in charge of the investigation.

7.12   When an officer exercises a power of seizure conferred by sections 50 or 51 they shall provide the occupier of the premises or the person from whom the property is being seized with a written notice:

(i)   specifying what has been seized under the powers conferred by that section;

(ii)   specifying the grounds for those powers;

(iii)   setting out the effect of sections 59 to 61 covering the grounds for a person with a relevant interest in seized property to apply to a judicial authority for its return and the duty of officers to secure property in certain circumstances when an application is made;

(iv)   specifying the name and address of the person to whom:

- notice of an application to the appropriate judicial authority in respect of any of the seized property must be given;
- an application may be made to allow attendance at the initial examination of the property.

7.13   If the occupier is not present but there is someone in charge of the premises, the notice shall be given to them. If no suitable person is available, so the notice will easily be found it should either be:

- left in a prominent place on the premises
- attached to the exterior of the premises

(c) Retention

7.14 Subject to *paragraph 7.15*, anything seized in accordance with the above provisions may be retained only for as long as is necessary. It may be retained, among other purposes:

(i) for use as evidence at a trial for an offence;

(ii) to facilitate the use in any investigation or proceedings of anything to which it is inextricably linked;

(iii) for forensic examination or other investigation in connection with an offence;

(iv) in order to establish its lawful owner when there are reasonable grounds for believing it has been stolen or obtained by the commission of an offence.

7.15 Property shall not be retained under *paragraph 7.14(i), (ii)* or *(iii)* if a copy or image would be sufficient.

(d) Rights of owners etc

7.16 If property is retained, the person who had custody or control of it immediately before seizure must, on request, be provided with a list or description of the property within a reasonable time.

7.17 That person or their representative must be allowed supervised access to the property to examine it or have it photographed or copied, or must be provided with a photograph or copy, in either case within a reasonable time of any request and at their own expense, unless the officer in charge of an investigation has reasonable grounds for believing this would:

(i) prejudice the investigation of any offence or criminal proceedings; or

(ii) lead to the commission of an offence by providing access to unlawful material such as pornography; A record of the grounds shall be made when access is denied.

8   Action after searches

8.1 If premises are searched in circumstances where this Code applies, unless the exceptions in *paragraph 2.3(a)* apply, on arrival at a police station the officer in charge of the search shall make or have made a record of the search, to include:

(i) the address of the searched premises;

(ii) the date, time and duration of the search;

(iii) the authority used for the search:

- if the search was made in exercise of a statutory power to search premises without warrant, the power which was used for the search:

- if the search was made under a warrant or with written consent;
  - — a copy of the warrant and the written authority to apply for it, see paragraph 3.4; or
  - — the written consent;

shall be appended to the record or the record shall show the location of the copy warrant or consent.

(iv) subject to *paragraph 2.9*, the names of:
- the officer(s) in charge of the search;
- all other officers and any authorised persons who conducted the search;

(v) the names of any people on the premises if they are known;

(vi) any grounds for refusing the occupier's request to have someone present during the search, see *paragraph 6.11*;

(vii) a list of any articles seized or the location of a list and, if not covered by a warrant, the grounds for their seizure;

(viii) whether force was used, and the reason;

(ix) details of any damage caused during the search, and the circumstances;

(x) if applicable, the reason it was not practicable;
  (a) to give the occupier a copy of the Notice of Powers and Rights, see *paragraph 6.7*;
  (b) before the search to give the occupier a copy of the Notice, see *paragraph 6.8*;

(xi) when the occupier was not present, the place where copies of the Notice of Powers and Rights and search warrant were left on the premises, see *paragraph 6.8*.

8.2 On each occasion when premises are searched under warrant, the warrant authorising the search on that occasion shall be endorsed to show:

(i) if any articles specified in the warrant were found and the address where found;

(ii) if any other articles were seized;

(iii) the date and time it was executed and if present, the name of the occupier or if the occupier is not present the name of the person in charge of the premises:

(iv) subject to paragraph 2.9, the names of the officers who executed it and any authorised persons who accompanied them;

(v) if a copy, together with a copy of the Notice of Powers and Rights was:
- handed to the occupier; or

- endorsed as required by paragraph 6.8; and left on the premises and where.

8.3 Any warrant shall be returned within three calendar months of its issue or sooner on completion of the search(es) authorised by that warrant, if it was issued by a:

- justice of the peace, to the designated officer for the local justice area in which the justice was acting when issuing the warrant; or
- judge, to the appropriate officer of the court concerned,

9 Search registers

9.1 A search register will be maintained at each sub-divisional or equivalent police station. All search records required under *paragraph 8.1* shall be made, copied, or referred to in the register.

Police and Criminal Evidence Act 1984 (PACE)

CODE C CODE OF PRACTICE FOR THE DETENTION, TREATMENT AND QUESTIONING OF PERSONS BY POLICE OFFICERS

1 General

1.1 All persons in custody must be dealt with expeditiously, and released as soon as the need for detention no longer applies.

1.1A A custody officer must perform the functions in this Code as soon as practicable. A custody officer will not be in breach of this Code if delay is justifiable and reasonable steps are taken to prevent unnecessary delay. The custody record shall show when a delay has occurred and the reason.

1.2 This Code of Practice must be readily available at all police stations for consultation by:

- police officers
- police staff
- detained persons
- members of the public.

1.3 The provisions of this Code:

- include the *Annexes*
- do not include the *Notes for Guidance*.

1.4 If an officer has any suspicion, or is told in good faith, that a person of any age may be mentally disordered or otherwise mentally vulnerable, in the absence of clear evidence to dispel that suspicion, the person shall be treated as such for the purposes of this Code.

1.5 If anyone appears to be under 17, they shall be treated as a juvenile for the purposes of this Code in the absence of clear evidence that they are older.

1.6 If a person appears to be blind, seriously visually impaired, deaf, unable to read or speak or has difficulty orally because of a speech impediment, they shall be treated as such for the purposes of this Code in the absence of clear evidence to the contrary.

1.7 'The appropriate adult' means, in the case of a:
(a) juvenile:

(i) the parent, guardian or, if the juvenile is in local authority or voluntary organisation care, or is otherwise being looked after under the Children Act 1989, a person representing that authority or organisation;

(ii) a social worker of a local authority social services department;

(iii) failing these, some other responsible adult aged 18 or over who is not a police officer or employed by the police.

(b) person who is mentally disordered or mentally vulnerable: See *Note 1D*

(i) a relative, guardian or other person responsible for their care or custody;

(ii) someone experienced in dealing with mentally disordered or mentally vulnerable people but who is not a police officer or employed by the police;

(iii) failing these, some other responsible adult aged 18 or over who is not a police officer or employed by the police.

1.8 If this Code requires a person be given certain information, they do not have to be given it if at the time they are incapable of understanding what is said, are violent or may become violent or in urgent need of medical attention, but they must be given it as soon as practicable.

1.9 References to a custody officer include any:-

• police officer; or

• designated staff custody officer acting in the exercise or performance of the powers and duties conferred or imposed on them by their designation, performing the functions of a custody officer.

1.9A When this Code requires the prior authority or agreement of an officer of at least inspector or superintendent rank, that authority may be given by a sergeant or chief inspector authorised to perform the functions of the higher rank under the Police and Criminal Evidence Act 1984 (PACE), section 107.

1.10 Subject to *paragraph 1.12*, this Code applies to people in custody at police stations in England and Wales, whether or not they have been arrested, and to those removed to a police station as a place of safety under the Mental Health Act 1983, sections 135 and 136. *Section 15* applies solely to people in police detention, e.g. those brought to a police station under arrest or arrested at a police station for an offence after going there voluntarily.

1.11 People in police custody include anyone detained under the Terrorism Act 2000, Schedule 8 and section 41, having been taken to a police station after being arrested under the Terrorism Act 2000, section 41. In these cases, reference to an offence in this Code includes the commission, preparation and instigation of acts of terrorism.

1.12 This Code's provisions do not apply to people in custody:

(i) arrested on warrants issued in Scotland by officers under the Criminal Justice and Public Order Act 1994, section 136(2), or arrested or detained without warrant by officers from a police force in Scotland under section 137(2). In these cases, police powers and duties and the person's rights and entitlements whilst at a police station in England or Wales are the same as those in Scotland;

(ii) arrested under the Immigration and Asylum Act 1999, section 142(3) in order to have their fingerprints taken;

(iii) whose detention is authorised by an immigration officer under the Immigration Act 1971;

(iv) who are convicted or remanded prisoners held in police cells on behalf of the Prison Service under the Imprisonment (Temporary Provisions) Act 1980;

(v) detained for examination under the Terrorism Act 2000, Schedule 7 and to whom the Code of Practice issued under that Act, Schedule 14, paragraph 6 applies;

(vi) detained for searches under stop and search powers except as required by Code A. The provisions on conditions of detention and treatment in *sections* 8 and 9 must be considered as the minimum standards of treatment for such detainees.

1.13 In this Code:

(a) 'designated person' means a person other than a police officer, designated under the Police Reform Act 2002, Part 4 who has specified powers and duties of police officers conferred or imposed on them;

(b) reference to a police officer includes a designated person acting in the exercise or performance of the powers and duties conferred or imposed on them by their designation.

1.14 Designated persons are entitled to use reasonable force as follows:-

(a) when exercising a power conferred on them which allows a police officer exercising that power to use reasonable force, a designated person has the same entitlement to use force; and

(b) at other times when carrying out duties conferred or imposed on them that also entitle them to use reasonable force, for example:

• when at a police station carrying out the duty to keep detainees for whom they are responsible under control and to assist any other police officer or designated person to keep any detainee under control and to prevent their escape.

• when securing, or assisting any other police officer or designated person in securing, the detention of a person at a police station.

- when escorting, or assisting any other police officer or designated person in escorting, a detainee within a police station.

- for the purpose of saving life or limb; or

- preventing serious damage to property.

1.15 Nothing in this Code prevents the custody officer, or other officer given custody of the detainee from allowing police staff who are not designated persons to carry out individual procedures or tasks at the police station if the law allows. However, the officer remains responsible for making sure the procedures and tasks are carried out correctly in accordance with the Codes of Practice. Any such person must be:

(a) a person employed by a police authority maintaining a police force and under the control and direction of the Chief Officer of that force;

(b) employed by a person with whom a police authority has a contract for the provision of services relating to persons arrested or otherwise in custody.

1.16 Designated persons and other police staff must have regard to any relevant provisions of the Codes of Practice.

1.17 References to pocket books include any official report book issued to police officers or other police staff.

2   Custody records

2.1A   When a person is brought to a police station:

- under arrest;

- is arrested at the police station having attended there voluntarily; or

- attends a police station to answer bail

they should be brought before the custody officer as soon as practicable after their arrival at the station or, if appropriate, following arrest after attending the police station voluntarily. This applies to designated and non-designated police stations. A person is deemed to be "at a police station" for these purposes if they are within the boundary of any building or enclosed yard which forms part of that police station.

2.1   A separate custody record must be opened as soon as practicable for each person brought to a police station under arrest or arrested at the station having gone there voluntarily or attending a police station in answer to street bail. All information recorded under this Code must be recorded as soon as practicable in the custody record unless otherwise specified. Any audio or video recording made in the custody area is not part of the custody record.

2.2   If any action requires the authority of an officer of a specified rank, subject to *paragraph 2.6A*, their name and rank must be noted in the custody record.

2.3 The custody officer is responsible for the custody record's accuracy and completeness and for making sure the record or copy of the record accompanies a detainee if they are transferred to another police station. The record shall show the:

- time and reason for transfer;
- time a person is released from detention.

2.4 A solicitor or appropriate adult must be permitted to consult a detainee's custody record as soon as practicable after their arrival at the station and at any other time whilst the person is detained. Arrangements for this access must be agreed with the custody officer and may not unreasonably interfere with the custody officer's duties.

2.4A When a detainee leaves police detention or is taken before a court they, their legal representative or appropriate adult shall be given, on request, a copy of the custody record as soon as practicable. This entitlement lasts for 12 months after release.

2.5 The detainee, appropriate adult or legal representative shall be permitted to inspect the original custody record after the detainee has left police detention provided they give reasonable notice of their request. Any such inspection shall be noted in the custody record.

2.6 Subject to *paragraph 2.6A*, all entries in custody records must be timed and signed by the maker. Records entered on computer shall be timed and contain the operator's identification.

2.6A Nothing in this Code requires the identity of officers or other police staff to be recorded or disclosed:
(a) in the case of enquiries linked to the investigation of terrorism; or
(b) if the officer or police staff reasonably believe recording or disclosing their name might put them in danger. In these cases, they shall use their warrant or other identification numbers and the name of their police station.

2.7 The fact and time of any detainee's refusal to sign a custody record, when asked in accordance with this Code, must be recorded.

3 Initial action

(a) Detained persons – normal procedure

3.1 When a person is brought to a police station under arrest or arrested at the station having gone there voluntarily, the custody officer must make sure the person is told clearly about the following continuing rights which may be exercised at any stage during the period in custody:
(i) the right to have someone informed of their arrest as in *section 5*;
(ii) the right to consult privately with a solicitor and that free independent legal advice is available;
(iii) the right to consult these Codes of Practice. See *Note 3D*

3.2   The detainee must also be given:

- a written notice setting out:
  — the above three rights;
  — the arrangements for obtaining legal advice;
  — the right to a copy of the custody record as in *paragraph 2.4A;*
  — the caution in the terms prescribed in *section 10.*
- an additional written notice briefly setting out their entitlements while in custody.

Note: The detainee shall be asked to sign the custody record to acknowledge receipt of these notices. Any refusal must be recorded on the custody record.

3.3   A citizen of an independent Commonwealth country or a national of a foreign country, including the Republic of Ireland, must be informed as soon as practicable about their rights of communication with their High Commission, Embassy or Consulate. See *section 7*

3.4   The custody officer shall:

- record the offence(s) that the detainee has been arrested for and the reason(s) for the arrest on the custody record. See paragraph 10.3.

- note on the custody record any comment the detainee makes in relation to the arresting officer's account but shall not invite comment. If the arresting officer is not physically present when the detainee is brought to a police station, the arresting officer's account must be made available to the custody officer remotely or by a third party on the arresting officer's behalf. If the custody officer authorises a person's detention the detainee must be informed of the grounds as soon as practicable and before they are questioned about any offence;

- note any comment the detainee makes in respect of the decision to detain them but shall not invite comment;

- not put specific questions to the detainee regarding their involvement in any offence, nor in respect of any comments they may make in response to the arresting officer's account or the decision to place them in detention. Such an exchange is likely to constitute an interview as in *paragraph 11.1A* and require the associated safeguards in *section 11.*

See *paragraph 11.13* in respect of unsolicited comments.

3.5   The custody officer shall:

(a)   ask the detainee, whether at this time, they:

(i)   would like legal advice, see *paragraph 6.5;*

(ii)   want someone informed of their detention, see *section 5;*

(b)   ask the detainee to sign the custody record to confirm their decisions in respect of *(a);*

(c)   determine whether the detainee:

  (i)   is, or might be, in need of medical treatment or attention, see *section 9*;

  (ii)   requires:

  - an appropriate adult;
  - help to check documentation;
  - an interpreter;

(d)   record the decision in respect of (*c*).

3.6   When determining these needs the custody officer is responsible for initiating an assessment to consider whether the detainee is likely to present specific risks to custody staff or themselves. Such assessments should always include a check on the Police National Computer, to be carried out as soon as practicable, to identify any risks highlighted in relation to the detainee. Although such assessments are primarily the custody officer's responsibility, it may be necessary for them to consult and involve others, e.g. the arresting officer or an appropriate health care professional, see *paragraph 9.13*. Reasons for delaying the initiation or completion of the assessment must be recorded.

3.7   Chief Officers should ensure that arrangements for proper and effective risk assessments required by *paragraph 3.6* are implemented in respect of all detainees at police stations in their area.

3.8   Risk assessments must follow a structured process which clearly defines the categories of risk to be considered and the results must be incorporated in the detainee's custody record. The custody officer is responsible for making sure those responsible for the detainee's custody are appropriately briefed about the risks. If no specific risks are identified by the assessment, that should be noted in the custody record.

3.9   The custody officer is responsible for implementing the response to any specific risk assessment, e.g.:

  - reducing opportunities for self harm;
  - calling a health care professional;
  - increasing levels of monitoring or observation.

3.10   Risk assessment is an ongoing process and assessments must always be subject to review if circumstances change.

3.11   If video cameras are installed in the custody area, notices shall be prominently displayed showing cameras are in use. Any request to have video cameras switched off shall be refused.

(b)   Detained persons – special groups

3.12   If the detainee appears deaf or there is doubt about their hearing or speaking ability or ability to understand English, and the custody officer cannot establish effective communication, the custody officer must, as soon as practicable, call an interpreter for assistance in the action under *paragraphs 3.1–3.5*. See *section 13*

3.13 If the detainee is a juvenile, the custody officer must, if it is practicable, ascertain the identity of a person responsible for their welfare. That person:

- may be:
  - the parent or guardian;
  - if the juvenile is in local authority or voluntary organisation care, or is otherwise being looked after under the Children Act 1989, a person appointed by that authority or organisation to have responsibility for the juvenile's welfare;
  - any other person who has, for the time being, assumed responsibility for the juvenile's welfare.
- must be informed as soon as practicable that the juvenile has been arrested, why they have been arrested and where they are detained. This right is in addition to the juvenile's right in *section 5* not to be held incommunicado.

3.14 If a juvenile is known to be subject to a court order under which a person or organisation is given any degree of statutory responsibility to supervise or otherwise monitor them, reasonable steps must also be taken to notify that person or organisation (the 'responsible officer'). The responsible officer will normally be a member of a Youth Offending Team, except for a curfew order which involves electronic monitoring when the contractor providing the monitoring will normally be the responsible officer.

3.15 If the detainee is a juvenile, mentally disordered or otherwise mentally vulnerable, the custody officer must, as soon as practicable:

- inform the appropriate adult, who in the case of a juvenile may or may not be a person responsible for their welfare, as in *paragraph 3.13*, of:
  - the grounds for their detention;
  - their whereabouts.
- ask the adult to come to the police station to see the detainee.

3.16 It is imperative that a mentally disordered or otherwise mentally vulnerable person, detained under the Mental Health Act 1983, section 136, be assessed as soon as possible. If that assessment is to take place at the police station, an approved social worker and a registered medical practitioner shall be called to the station as soon as possible in order to interview and examine the detainee. Once the detainee has been interviewed, examined and suitable arrangements made for their treatment or care, they can no longer be detained under section 136. A detainee must be immediately discharged from detention under section 136 if a registered medical practitioner, having examined them, concludes they are not mentally disordered within the meaning of the Act.

3.17 If the appropriate adult is:

- already at the police station, the provisions of *paragraphs 3.1* to *3.5* must be complied with in the appropriate adult's presence;

- not at the station when these provisions are complied with, they must be complied with again in the presence of the appropriate adult when they arrive.

3.18 The detainee shall be advised that:

- the duties of the appropriate adult include giving advice and assistance;

- they can consult privately with the appropriate adult at any time.

3.19 If the detainee, or appropriate adult on the detainee's behalf, asks for a solicitor to be called to give legal advice, the provisions of *section 6* apply.

3.20 If the detainee is blind, seriously visually impaired or unable to read, the custody officer shall make sure their solicitor, relative, appropriate adult or some other person likely to take an interest in them and not involved in the investigation is available to help check any documentation. When this Code requires written consent or signing the person assisting may be asked to sign instead, if the detainee prefers. This paragraph does not require an appropriate adult to be called solely to assist in checking and signing documentation for a person who is not a juvenile, or mentally disordered or otherwise mentally vulnerable (see *paragraph 3.15*).

(c) Persons attending a police station voluntarily

3.21 Anybody attending a police station voluntarily to assist with an investigation may leave at will unless arrested. If it is decided they shall not be allowed to leave, they must be informed at once that they are under arrest and brought before the custody officer, who is responsible for making sure they are notified of their rights in the same way as other detainees. If they are not arrested but are cautioned as in *section 10*, the person who gives the caution must, at the same time, inform them they are not under arrest, they are not obliged to remain at the station but if they remain at the station they may obtain free and independent legal advice if they want. They shall be told the right to legal advice includes the right to speak with a solicitor on the telephone and be asked if they want to do so.

3.22 If a person attending the police station voluntarily asks about their entitlement to legal advice, they shall be given a copy of the notice explaining the arrangements for obtaining legal advice. See *paragraph 3.2*

(d) Documentation

3.23 The grounds for a person's detention shall be recorded, in the person's presence if practicable.

3.24 Action taken under *paragraphs 3.12* to *3.20* shall be recorded.

(e) Persons answering street bail

3.25 When a person is answering street bail, the custody officer should link any documentation held in relation to arrest with the custody record. Any further action shall be recorded on the custody record in accordance with *paragraphs 3.23* and *3.24* above.

4   Detainee's property

(a) Action

4.1   The custody officer is responsible for:
   (a)   ascertaining what property a detainee:
      (i)   has with them when they come to the police station, whether on:
         •   arrest or re-detention on answering to bail;
         •   commitment to prison custody on the order or sentence of a court;
         •   lodgement at the police station with a view to their production in court from prison custody;
         •   transfer from detention at another station or hospital;
         •   detention under the Mental Health Act 1983, section 135 or 136;
         •   remand into police custody on the authority of a court
      (ii)   might have acquired for an unlawful or harmful purpose while in custody;
   (b)   the safekeeping of any property taken from a detainee which remains at the police station. The custody officer may search the detainee or authorise their being searched to the extent they consider necessary, provided a search of intimate parts of the body or involving the removal of more than outer clothing is only made as in *Annex A*. A search may only be carried out by an officer of the same sex as the detainee.

4.2   Detainees may retain clothing and personal effects at their own risk unless the custody officer considers they may use them to cause harm to themselves or others, interfere with evidence, damage property, effect an escape or they are needed as evidence. In this event the custody officer may withhold such articles as they consider necessary and must tell the detainee why.

4.3   Personal effects are those items a detainee may lawfully need, use or refer to while in detention but do not include cash and other items of value.

(b) Documentation

4.4   It is a matter for the custody officer to determine whether a record should be made of the property a detained person has with him or had · taken from him on arrest. Any record made is not required to be kept as part of the custody record but the custody record should be noted as to where such a record exists. Whenever a record is made the detainee shall be allowed to check and sign the record of property as correct. Any refusal to sign shall be recorded.

4.5   If a detainee is not allowed to keep any article of clothing or personal effects, the reason must be recorded.

5   Right not to be held incommunicado

(a) Action

5.1   Any person arrested and held in custody at a police station or other premises may, on request, have one person known to them or likely to take an interest in their welfare informed at public expense of their whereabouts as soon as practicable. If the person cannot be contacted the detainee may choose up to two alternatives. If they cannot be contacted, the person in charge of detention or the investigation has discretion to allow further attempts until the information has been conveyed.

5.2   The exercise of the above right in respect of each person nominated may be delayed only in accordance with *Annex B*.

5.3   The above right may be exercised each time a detainee is taken to another police station.

5.4   The detainee may receive visits at the custody officer's discretion. See *Note 5B*

5.5   If a friend, relative or person with an interest in the detainee's welfare enquires about their whereabouts, this information shall be given if the suspect agrees and *Annex B* does not apply.

5.6   The detainee shall be given writing materials, on request, and allowed to telephone one person for a reasonable time. Either or both these privileges may be denied or delayed if an officer of inspector rank or above considers sending a letter or making a telephone call may result in any of the consequences in:

(a)   *Annex B paragraphs 1* and *2* and the person is detained in connection with an indictable offence; or

(b)   *Annex B paragraphs 8* and *9* and the person is detained under the Terrorism Act 2000, Schedule 7 or section 41. Nothing in this

paragraph permits the restriction or denial of the rights in
paragraphs 5.1 and *6.1*.

5.7   Before any letter or message is sent, or telephone call made, the detainee
shall be informed that what they say in any letter, call or message (other
than in a communication to a solicitor) may be read or listened to and
may be given in evidence. A telephone call may be terminated if it is
being abused. The costs can be at public expense at the custody officer's
discretion.

5.7A Any delay or denial of the rights in this section should be
proportionate and should last no longer than necessary.

(b) Documentation

5.8   A record must be kept of any:
   (a)   request made under this section and the action taken;
   (b)   letters, messages or telephone calls made or received or visit
         received;
   (c)   refusal by the detainee to have information about them given to an
         outside enquirer. The detainee must be asked to countersign the
         record accordingly and any refusal recorded.

6   Right to legal advice

(a) Action

6.1   Unless *Annex B* applies, all detainees must be informed that they may at
any time consult and communicate privately with a solicitor, whether in
person, in writing or by telephone, and that free independent legal
advice is available from the duty solicitor.

6.2   Not Used

6.3   A poster advertising the right to legal advice must be prominently
displayed in the charging area of every police station.

6.4   No police officer should, at any time, do or say anything with the
intention of dissuading a detainee from obtaining legal advice.

6.5   The exercise of the right of access to legal advice may be delayed only as
in *Annex B*. Whenever legal advice is requested, and unless *Annex B*
applies, the custody officer must act without delay to secure the
provision of such advice. If, on being informed or reminded of this
right, the detainee declines to speak to a solicitor in person, the officer
should point out that the right includes the right to speak with a
solicitor on the telephone. If the detainee continues to waive this
right the officer should ask them why and any reasons should be
recorded on the custody record or the interview record as appropriate.
Reminders of the right to legal advice must be given as in *paragraphs
3.5, 11.2, 15.4, 16.4, 2B of Annex A, 3 of Annex K* and *16.5* and

Code D, *paragraphs 3.17(ii)* and *6.3*. Once it is clear a detainee does not want to speak to a solicitor in person or by telephone they should cease to be asked their reasons.

6.5A   In the case of a juvenile, an appropriate adult should consider whether legal advice from a solicitor is required. If the juvenile indicates that they do not want legal advice, the appropriate adult has the right to ask for a solicitor to attend if this would be in the best interests of the person. However, the detained person cannot be forced to see the solicitor if he is adamant that he does not wish to do so.

6.6   A detainee who wants legal advice may not be interviewed or continue to be interviewed until they have received such advice unless:

(a)   *Annex B* applies, when the restriction on drawing adverse inferences from silence in *Annex C* will apply because the detainee is not allowed an opportunity to consult a solicitor; or

(b)   an officer of superintendent rank or above has reasonable grounds for believing that:

(i)   the consequent delay might:

- lead to interference with, or harm to, evidence connected with an offence;
- lead to interference with, or physical harm to, other people;
- lead to serious loss of, or damage to, property;
- lead to alerting other people suspected of having committed an offence but not yet arrested for it;
- hinder the recovery of property obtained in consequence of the commission of an offence.

(ii)   when a solicitor, including a duty solicitor, has been contacted and has agreed to attend, awaiting their arrival would cause unreasonable delay to the process of investigation. Note: In these cases the restriction on drawing adverse inferences from silence in *Annex C* will apply because the detainee is not allowed an opportunity to consult a solicitor;

(c)   the solicitor the detainee has nominated or selected from a list:

(i)   cannot be contacted;

(ii)   has previously indicated they do not wish to be contacted; or

(iii)   having been contacted, has declined to attend; and the detainee has been advised of the Duty Solicitor Scheme but has declined to ask for the duty solicitor. In these circumstances the interview may be started or continued without further delay provided an officer of inspector rank or above has agreed to the interview proceeding.

Note: The restriction on drawing adverse inferences from silence in *Annex C* will not apply because the detainee is allowed an opportunity to consult the duty solicitor;

  (d) the detainee changes their mind, about wanting legal advice. In these circumstances the interview may be started or continued without delay provided that:

  (i) the detainee agrees to do so, in writing or on the interview record made in accordance with Code E or F; and

  (ii) an officer of inspector rank or above has inquired about the detainee's reasons for their change of mind and gives authority for the interview to proceed. Confirmation of the detainee's agreement, their change of mind, the reasons for it if given and, subject to *paragraph 2.6A*, the name of the authorising officer shall be recorded in the written interview record or the interview record made in accordance with Code E or F.

Note: In these circumstances the restriction on drawing adverse inferences from silence in *Annex C* will not apply because the detainee is allowed an opportunity to consult a solicitor if they wish.

6.7 If *paragraph 6.6(b)(i)* applies, once sufficient information has been obtained to avert the risk, questioning must cease until the detainee has received legal advice unless *paragraph 6.6(a), (b)(ii), (c)* or *(d)* applies.

6.8 A detainee who has been permitted to consult a solicitor shall be entitled on request to have the solicitor present when they are interviewed unless one of the exceptions in *paragraph 6.6* applies.

6.9 The solicitor may only be required to leave the interview if their conduct is such that the interviewer is unable properly to put questions to the suspect.

6.10 If the interviewer considers a solicitor is acting in such a way, they will stop the interview and consult an officer not below superintendent rank, if one is readily available, and otherwise an officer not below inspector rank not connected with the investigation. After speaking to the solicitor, the officer consulted will decide if the interview should continue in the presence of that solicitor. If they decide it should not, the suspect will be given the opportunity to consult another solicitor before the interview continues and that solicitor given an opportunity to be present at the interview.

6.11 The removal of a solicitor from an interview is a serious step and, if it occurs, the officer of superintendent rank or above who took the decision will consider if the incident should be reported to the Law Society. If the decision to remove the solicitor has been taken by an officer below superintendent rank, the facts must be reported to an officer of superintendent rank or above who will similarly consider whether a report to the Law Society would be appropriate. When the solicitor concerned is a duty solicitor, the report should be both to the Law Society and to the Legal Services Commission.

6.12 'Solicitor' in this Code means:

- a solicitor who holds a current practising certificate
- an accredited or probationary representative included on the register of representatives maintained by the Legal Services Commission.

6.12A   An accredited or probationary representative sent to provide advice by, and on behalf of, a solicitor shall be admitted to the police station for this purpose unless an officer of inspector rank or above considers such a visit will hinder the investigation and directs otherwise. Hindering the investigation does not include giving proper legal advice to a detainee. Once admitted to the police station, *paragraphs 6.6 to 6.10* apply.

6.13 In exercising their discretion under *paragraph 6.12A*, the officer should take into account in particular:

- whether:
  — the identity and status of an accredited or probationary representative have been satisfactorily established;
  — they are of suitable character to provide legal advice, e.g. a person with a criminal record is unlikely to be suitable unless the conviction was for a minor offence and not recent.
- any other matters in any written letter of authorisation provided by the solicitor on whose behalf the person is attending the police station.

6.14 If the inspector refuses access to an accredited or probationary representative or a decision is taken that such a person should not be permitted to remain at an interview, the inspector must notify the solicitor on whose behalf the representative was acting and give them an opportunity to make alternative arrangements. The detainee must be informed and the custody record noted.

6.15 If a solicitor arrives at the station to see a particular person, that person must, unless *Annex B* applies, be so informed whether or not they are being interviewed and asked if they would like to see the solicitor. This applies even if the detainee has declined legal advice or, having requested it, subsequently agreed to be interviewed without receiving advice. The solicitor's attendance and the detainee's decision must be noted in the custody record.

(b) Documentation

6.16 Any request for legal advice and the action taken shall be recorded.

6.17 A record shall be made in the interview record if a detainee asks for legal advice and an interview is begun either in the absence of a solicitor or their representative, or they have been required to leave a interview.

7 Citizens of independent Commonwealth countries or foreign nationals

(a) Action

7.1 Any citizen of an independent Commonwealth country or a national of a foreign country, including the Republic of Ireland, may communicate at any time with the appropriate High Commission, Embassy or Consulate. The detainee must be informed as soon as practicable of:

- this right;
- their right, upon request, to have their High Commission, Embassy or Consulate told of their whereabouts and the grounds for their detention. Such a request should be acted upon as soon as practicable.

7.2 If a detainee is a citizen of a country with which a bilateral consular convention or agreement is in force requiring notification of arrest, the appropriate High Commission, Embassy or Consulate shall be informed as soon as practicable, subject to *paragraph 7.4*. The countries to which this applies as at 1st April 2003 are listed in *Annex F*.

7.3 Consular officers may visit one of their nationals in police detention to talk to them and, if required, to arrange for legal advice. Such visits shall take place out of the hearing of a police officer.

7.4 Notwithstanding the provisions of consular conventions, if the detainee is a political refugee whether for reasons of race, nationality, political opinion or religion, or is seeking political asylum, consular officers shall not be informed of the arrest of one of their nationals or given access or information about them except at the detainee's express request.

(b) Documentation

7.5 A record shall be made when a detainee is informed of their rights under this section and of any communications with a High Commission, Embassy or Consulate.

8 Conditions of detention

(a) Action

8.1 So far as it is practicable, not more than one detainee should be detained in each cell.

8.2 Cells in use must be adequately heated, cleaned and ventilated. They must be adequately lit, subject to such dimming as is compatible with safety and security to allow people detained overnight to sleep. No additional restraints shall be used within a locked cell unless absolutely necessary and then only restraint equipment, approved for use in that force by the Chief Officer, which is reasonable and necessary in the circumstances having regard to the detainee's demeanour and with a view to ensuring their safety and the safety of others. If a detainee is deaf, mentally disordered or otherwise mentally vulnerable, particular care must be taken when deciding whether to use any form of approved restraints.

8.3 Blankets, mattresses, pillows and other bedding supplied shall be of a reasonable standard and in a clean and sanitary condition.

8.4 Access to toilet and washing facilities must be provided.

8.5 If it is necessary to remove a detainee's clothes for the purposes of investigation, for hygiene, health reasons or cleaning, replacement clothing of a reasonable standard of comfort and cleanliness shall be provided. A detainee may not be interviewed unless adequate clothing has been offered.

8.6 At least two light meals and one main meal should be offered in any 24 hour period. Drinks should be provided at meal times and upon reasonable request between meals. Whenever necessary, advice shall be sought from the appropriate health care professional on medical and dietary matters. As far as practicable, meals provided shall offer a varied diet and meet any specific dietary needs or religious beliefs the detainee may have. The detainee may, at the custody officer's discretion, have meals supplied by their family or friends at their expense.

8.7 Brief outdoor exercise shall be offered daily if practicable.

8.8 A juvenile shall not be placed in a police cell unless no other secure accommodation is available and the custody officer considers it is not practicable to supervise them if they are not placed in a cell or that a cell provides more comfortable accommodation than other secure accommodation in the station. A juvenile may not be placed in a cell with a detained adult.

(b) Documentation

8.9 A record must be kept of replacement clothing and meals offered.

8.10 If a juvenile is placed in a cell, the reason must be recorded.

8.11 The use of any restraints on a detainee whilst in a cell, the reasons for it and, if appropriate, the arrangements for enhanced supervision of the detainee whilst so restrained, shall be recorded. See *paragraph 3.9*

9   Care and treatment of detained persons

(a) General

9.1 Nothing in this section prevents the police from calling the police surgeon or, if appropriate, some other health care professional, to examine a detainee for the purposes of obtaining evidence relating to any offence in which the detainee is suspected of being involved.

9.2   If a complaint is made by, or on behalf of, a detainee about their treatment since their arrest, or it comes to notice that a detainee may have been treated improperly, a report must be made as soon as practicable to an officer of inspector rank or above not connected with the investigation. If the matter concerns a possible assault or the possibility of the unnecessary or unreasonable use of force, an appropriate health care professional must also be called as soon as practicable.

9.3   Detainees should be visited at least every hour. If no reasonably foreseeable risk was identified in a risk assessment, see *paragraphs 3.6–3.10*, there is no need to wake a sleeping detainee. Those suspected of being intoxicated through drink or drugs or having swallowed drugs, or whose level of consciousness causes concern must, subject to any clinical directions given by the appropriate health care professional, see *paragraph 9.13*:

- be visited and roused at least every half hour
- have their condition assessed as in *Annex H*
- and clinical treatment arranged if appropriate

9.4   When arrangements are made to secure clinical attention for a detainee, the custody officer must make sure all relevant information which might assist in the treatment of the detainee's condition is made available to the responsible health care professional. This applies whether or not the health care professional asks for such information. Any officer or police staff with relevant information must inform the custody officer as soon as practicable.

(b) Clinical treatment and attention

9.5   The custody officer must make sure a detainee receives appropriate clinical attention as soon as reasonably practicable if the person:
(a)   appears to be suffering from physical illness; or
(b)   is injured; or
(c)   appears to be suffering from a mental disorder;
(d)   appears to need clinical attention.

9.5A   This applies even if the detainee makes no request for clinical attention and whether or not they have already received clinical attention elsewhere. If the need for attention appears urgent, e.g. when indicated as in *Annex H*, the nearest available health care professional or an ambulance must be called immediately.

9.5B   The custody officer must also consider the need for clinical attention in relation to those suffering the effects of alcohol or drugs.

9.6   *Paragraph 9.5 is not meant to prevent or delay the transfer to a hospital if necessary of a person detained under the Mental Health Act 1983, section 136. When an assessment under that Act takes place at a police station, see paragraph 3.16, the custody officer must consider whether* an appropriate health care professional should be called to conduct an initial clinical check on the detainee. This applies particularly when there is likely to be any significant delay in the arrival of a suitably qualified medical practitioner.

9.7   If it appears to the custody officer, or they are told, that a person brought to a station under arrest may be suffering from an infectious disease or condition, the custody officer must take reasonable steps to safeguard the health of the detainee and others at the station. In deciding what action to take, advice must be sought from an appropriate health care professional. The custody officer has discretion to isolate the person and their property until clinical directions have been obtained.

9.8   If a detainee requests a clinical examination, an appropriate health care professional must be called as soon as practicable to assess the detainee's clinical needs. If a safe and appropriate care plan cannot be provided, the police surgeon's advice must be sought. The detainee may also be examined by a medical practitioner of their choice at their expense.

9.9   If a detainee is required to take or apply any medication in compliance with clinical directions prescribed before their detention, the custody officer must consult the appropriate health care professional before the use of the medication. Subject to the restrictions in *paragraph 9.10*, the custody officer is responsible for the safekeeping of any medication and for making sure the detainee is given the opportunity to take or apply prescribed or approved medication. Any such consultation and its outcome shall be noted in the custody record.

9.10   No police officer may administer or supervise the self-administration of medically prescribed controlled drugs of the types and forms listed in the Misuse of Drugs Regulations 2001, Schedule 2 or 3. A detainee may only self-administer such drugs under the personal supervision of the registered medical practitioner authorising their use. Drugs listed in Schedule 4 or 5 may be distributed by the custody officer for self-administration if they have consulted the registered medical practitioner authorising their use, this may be done by telephone, and both parties are satisfied self-administration will not expose the detainee, police officers or anyone else to the risk of harm or injury.

9.11   When appropriate health care professionals administer drugs or other medications, or supervise their self-administration, it must be within current medicines legislation and the scope of practice as determined by their relevant professional body.

9.12   If a detainee has in their possession, or claims to need, medication relating to a heart condition, diabetes, epilepsy or a condition of comparable potential seriousness then, even though *paragraph 9.5* may not apply, the advice of the appropriate health care professional must be obtained.

9.13 Whenever the appropriate health care professional is called in accordance with this section to examine or treat a detainee, the custody officer shall ask for their opinion about:

- any risks or problems which police need to take into account when making decisions about the detainee's continued detention;
- when to carry out an interview if applicable; and
- the need for safeguards.

9.14 When clinical directions are given by the appropriate health care professional, whether orally or in writing, and the custody officer has any doubts or is in any way uncertain about any aspect of the directions, the custody officer shall ask for clarification. It is particularly important that directions concerning the frequency of visits are clear, precise and capable of being implemented.

(c) Documentation

9.15 A record must be made in the custody record of:
   (a) the arrangements made for an examination by an appropriate health care professional under *paragraph 9.2* and of any complaint reported under that paragraph together with any relevant remarks by the custody officer;
   (b) any arrangements made in accordance with *paragraph 9.5*;
   (c) any request for a clinical examination under *paragraph 9.8* and any arrangements made in response;
   (d) the injury, ailment, condition or other reason which made it necessary to make the arrangements in *(a)* to *(c)*;
   (e) any clinical directions and advice, including any further clarifications, given to police by a health care professional concerning the care and treatment of the detainee in connection with any of the arrangements made in *(a)* to *(c)*;
   (f) if applicable, the responses received when attempting to rouse a person using the procedure in *Annex H*.

9.16 If a health care professional does not record their clinical findings in the custody record, the record must show where they are recorded. However, information which is necessary to custody staff to ensure the effective ongoing care and well being of the detainee must be recorded openly in the custody record, see *paragraph 3.8* and *Annex G, paragraph 7*.

9.17 Subject to the requirements of *Section 4*, the custody record shall include:
- a record of all medication a detainee has in their possession on arrival at the police station;
- a note of any such medication they claim to need but do not have with them.

10 Cautions

(a) When a caution must be given

10.1 A person whom there are grounds to suspect of an offence, see *Note 10A*, must be cautioned before any questions about an offence, or further questions if the answers provide the grounds for suspicion, are put to them if either the suspect's answers or silence, (i.e. failure or refusal to answer or answer satisfactorily) may be given in evidence to a court in a prosecution. A person need not be cautioned if questions are for other necessary purposes, e.g.:
   (a) solely to establish their identity or ownership of any vehicle;
   (b) to obtain information in accordance with any relevant statutory requirement, see *paragraph 10.9*;
   (c) in furtherance of the proper and effective conduct of a search, e.g. to determine the need to search in the exercise of powers of stop and search or to seek co- operation while carrying out a search;
   (d) to seek verification of a written record as in *paragraph 11.13*;
   (e) when examining a person in accordance with the Terrorism Act 2000, Schedule 7 and the Code of Practice for Examining Officers issued under that Act, Schedule 14, paragraph 6.

10.2 Whenever a person not under arrest is initially cautioned, or reminded they are under caution, that person must at the same time be told they are not under arrest and are free to leave if they want to.

10.3 A person who is arrested, or further arrested, must be informed at the time, or as soon as practicable thereafter, that they are under arrest and the grounds for their arrest, see *paragraph 3.4*, and *Code G, paragraphs 2.2 and 4.3*.

10.4 As per *Code G, section 3*, a person who is arrested, or further arrested, must also be cautioned unless:
   (a) it is impracticable to do so by reason of their condition or behaviour at the time;
   (b) they have already been cautioned immediately prior to arrest as in *paragraph 10.1*.

(b) Terms of the cautions

10.5 The caution which must be given on:
   (a) arrest;
   (b) all other occasions before a person is charged or informed they may be prosecuted, see *section 16*, should, unless the restriction on drawing adverse inferences from silence applies, see *Annex C*, be in the following terms:

"You do not have to say anything. But it may harm your defence if you do not mention when questioned something which you later rely on in Court. Anything you do say may be given in evidence."

10.6 *Annex C, paragraph 2* sets out the alternative terms of the caution to be used when the restriction on drawing adverse inferences from silence applies.

10.7 Minor deviations from the words of any caution given in accordance with this Code do not constitute a breach of this Code, provided the sense of the relevant caution is preserved.

10.8 After any break in questioning under caution, the person being questioned must be made aware they remain under caution. If there is any doubt the relevant caution should be given again in full when the interview resumes.

10.9 When, despite being cautioned, a person fails to co-operate or to answer particular questions which may affect their immediate treatment, the person should be informed of any relevant consequences and that those consequences are not affected by the caution. Examples are when a person's refusal to provide:

- their name and address when charged may make them liable to detention;
- particulars and information in accordance with a statutory requirement, e.g. under the Road Traffic Act 1988, may amount to an offence or may make the person liable to a further arrest.

(c) Special warnings under the Criminal Justice and Public Order Act 1994, sections 36 and 37

10.10 When a suspect interviewed at a police station or authorised place of detention after arrest fails or refuses to answer certain questions, or to answer satisfactorily, after due warning, a court or jury may draw such inferences as appear proper under the Criminal Justice and Public Order Act 1994, sections 36 and 37. Such inferences may only be drawn when:

(a) the restriction on drawing adverse inferences from silence, see *Annex C*, does not apply; and

(b) the suspect is arrested by a constable and fails or refuses to account for any objects, marks or substances, or marks on such objects found:

- on their person;
- in or on their clothing or footwear;
- otherwise in their possession; or
- in the place they were arrested;

(c) the arrested suspect was found by a constable at a place at or about the time the offence for which that officer has arrested them is alleged to have been committed, and the suspect fails or refuses to account for their presence there. When the restriction on drawing adverse inferences from silence applies, the suspect may still be asked to account for any of the matters in (*b*) or (*c*) but the special warning described in *paragraph 10.11* will not apply and must not be given.

10.11   For an inference to be drawn when a suspect fails or refuses to answer a question about one of these matters or to answer it satisfactorily, the suspect must first be told in ordinary language:
(a)   what offence is being investigated;

(b)   what fact they are being asked to account for;

(c)   this fact may be due to them taking part in the commission of the offence;

(d)   a court may draw a proper inference if they fail or refuse to account for this fact;

(e)   a record is being made of the interview and it may be given in evidence if they are brought to trial.

(d) Juveniles and persons who are mentally disordered or otherwise mentally vulnerable

10.12   If a juvenile or a person who is mentally disordered or otherwise mentally vulnerable is cautioned in the absence of the appropriate adult, the caution must be repeated in the adult's presence.

(e) Documentation

10.13   A record shall be made when a caution is given under this section, either in the interviewer's pocket book or in the interview record.

11   Interviews – general

(a) Action

11.1A   An interview is the questioning of a person regarding their involvement or suspected involvement in a criminal offence or offences which, under *paragraph 10.1*, must be carried out under caution. Whenever a person is interviewed they must be informed of the nature of the offence, or further offence. Procedures under the Road Traffic Act 1988, section 7 or the Transport and Works Act 1992, section 31 do not constitute interviewing for the purpose of this Code.

11.1   Following a decision to arrest a suspect, they must not be interviewed about the relevant offence except at a police station or other authorised place of detention, unless the consequent delay would be likely to:
(a)   lead to:
   • interference with, or harm to, evidence connected with an offence;

- interference with, or physical harm to, other people; or
- serious loss of, or damage to, property;

(b) lead to alerting other people suspected of committing an offence but not yet arrested for it; or

(c) hinder the recovery of property obtained in consequence of the commission of an offence. Interviewing in any of these circumstances shall cease once the relevant risk has been averted or the necessary questions have been put in order to attempt to avert that risk.

11.2 Immediately prior to the commencement or re-commencement of any interview at a police station or other authorised place of detention, the interviewer should remind the suspect of their entitlement to free legal advice and that the interview can be delayed for legal advice to be obtained, unless one of the exceptions in *paragraph 6.6* applies. It is the interviewer's responsibility to make sure all reminders are recorded in the interview record.

11.3 Not Used

11.4 At the beginning of an interview the interviewer, after cautioning the suspect, see *section 10*, shall put to them any significant statement or silence which occurred in the presence and hearing of a police officer or other police staff before the start of the interview and which have not been put to the suspect in the course of a previous interview. The interviewer shall ask the suspect whether they confirm or deny that earlier statement or silence and if they want to add anything.

11.4A A significant statement is one which appears capable of being used in evidence against the suspect, in particular a direct admission of guilt. A significant silence is a failure or refusal to answer a question or answer satisfactorily when under caution, which might, allowing for the restriction on drawing adverse inferences from silence, see *Annex C*, give rise to an inference under the Criminal Justice and Public Order Act 1994, Part III.

11.5 No interviewer may try to obtain answers or elicit a statement by the use of oppression. Except as in *paragraph 10.9*, no interviewer shall indicate, except to answer a direct question, what action will be taken by the police if the person being questioned answers questions, makes a statement or refuses to do either. If the person asks directly what action will be taken if they answer questions, make a statement or refuse to do either, the interviewer may inform them what action the police propose to take provided that action is itself proper and warranted.

11.6 The interview or further interview of a person about an offence with which that person has not been charged or for which they have not been informed they may be prosecuted, must cease when:

(a) the officer in charge of the investigation is satisfied all the questions they consider relevant to obtaining accurate and reliable information about the offence have been put to the suspect, this includes allowing the suspect an opportunity to give an innocent explanation and asking questions to test if the explanation is accurate and reliable, e.g. to clear up ambiguities or clarify what the suspect said;

(b) the officer in charge of the investigation has taken account of any other available evidence; and

(c) the officer in charge of the investigation, or in the case of a detained suspect, the custody officer, see paragraph 16.1, reasonably believes there is sufficient evidence to provide a realistic prospect of conviction for that offence. This paragraph does not prevent officers in revenue cases or acting under the confiscation provisions of the Criminal Justice Act 1988 or the Drug Trafficking Act 1994 from inviting suspects to complete a formal question and answer record after the interview is concluded.

(b) Interview records

11.7 (a) An accurate record must be made of each interview, whether or not the interview takes place at a police station

(b) The record must state the place of interview, the time it begins and ends, any interview breaks and, subject to *paragraph 2.6A*, the names of all those present; and must be made on the forms provided for this purpose or in the interviewer's pocket book or in accordance with the Codes of Practice E or F;

(c) Any written record must be made and completed during the interview, unless this would not be practicable or would interfere with the conduct of the interview, and must constitute either a verbatim record of what has been said or, failing this, an account of the interview which adequately and accurately summarises it.

11.8 If a written record is not made during the interview it must be made as soon as practicable after its completion.

11.9 Written interview records must be timed and signed by the maker.

11.10 If a written record is not completed during the interview the reason must be recorded in the interview record.

11.11 Unless it is impracticable, the person interviewed shall be given the opportunity to read the interview record and to sign it as correct or to indicate how they consider it inaccurate. If the person interviewed cannot read or refuses to read the record or sign it, the senior interviewer present shall read it to them and ask whether they would like to sign it as correct or make their mark or to indicate how they consider it inaccurate. The interviewer shall certify on the interview record itself what has occurred.

11.12 If the appropriate adult or the person's solicitor is present during the interview, they should also be given an opportunity to read and sign the interview record or any written statement taken down during the interview.

11.13 A written record shall be made of any comments made by a suspect, including unsolicited comments, which are outside the context of an interview but which might be relevant to the offence. Any such record must be timed and signed by the maker. When practicable the suspect shall be given the opportunity to read that record and to sign it as correct or to indicate how they consider it inaccurate.

11.14 Any refusal by a person to sign an interview record when asked in accordance with this Code must itself be recorded.

(c) Juveniles and mentally disordered or otherwise mentally vulnerable people

11.15 A juvenile or person who is mentally disordered or otherwise mentally vulnerable must not be interviewed regarding their involvement or suspected involvement in a criminal offence or offences, or asked to provide or sign a written statement under caution or record of interview, in the absence of the appropriate adult unless *paragraphs 11.1, 11.18 to 11.20* apply.

11.16 Juveniles may only be interviewed at their place of education in exceptional circumstances and only when the principal or their nominee agrees. Every effort should be made to notify the parent(s) or other person responsible for the juvenile's welfare and the appropriate adult, if this is a different person, that the police want to interview the juvenile and reasonable time should be allowed to enable the appropriate adult to be present at the interview. If awaiting the appropriate adult would cause unreasonable delay, and unless the juvenile is suspected of an offence against the educational establishment, the principal or their nominee can act as the appropriate adult for the purposes of the interview.

11.17 If an appropriate adult is present at an interview, they shall be informed:

- they are not expected to act simply as an observer; and
- the purpose of their presence is to:
  - advise the person being interviewed;
  - observe whether the interview is being conducted properly and fairly;
  - facilitate communication with the person being interviewed.

(d) Vulnerable suspects – urgent interviews at police stations

11.18 The following persons may not be interviewed unless an officer of superintendent rank or above considers delay will lead to the consequences in *paragraph 11.1(a)* to *(c)*, and is satisfied the interview would not significantly harm the person's physical or mental state:

(a)   a juvenile or person who is mentally disordered or otherwise mentally vulnerable if at the time of the interview the appropriate adult is not present;

(b)   anyone other than in (*a*) who at the time of the interview appears unable to:

- appreciate the significance of questions and their answers; or

- understand what is happening because of the effects of drink, drugs or any illness, ailment or condition;

(c)   a person who has difficulty understanding English or has a hearing disability, if at the time of the interview an interpreter is not present.

11.19   These interviews may not continue once sufficient information has been obtained to avert the consequences in *paragraph 11.1(a)* to *(c)*.

11.20   A record shall be made of the grounds for any decision to interview a person under *paragraph 11.18*.

12   Interviews in police stations

(a) Action

12.1 If a police officer wants to interview or conduct enquiries which require the presence of a detainee, the custody officer is responsible for deciding whether to deliver the detainee into the officer's custody.

12.2 Except as below, in any period of 24 hours a detainee must be allowed a continuous period of at least 8 hours for rest, free from questioning, travel or any interruption in connection with the investigation concerned. This period should normally be at night or other appropriate time which takes account of when the detainee last slept or rested. If a detainee is arrested at a police station after going there voluntarily, the period of 24 hours runs from the time of their arrest and not the time of arrival at the police station. The period may not be interrupted or delayed, except:

(a)   when there are reasonable grounds for believing not delaying or interrupting the period would:

(i)   involve a risk of harm to people or serious loss of, or damage to, property;

(ii) delay unnecessarily the person's release from custody;

(iii) otherwise prejudice the outcome of the investigation;

(b)   at the request of the detainee, their appropriate adult or legal representative;

(c)   when a delay or interruption is necessary in order to:

    (i) comply with the legal obligations and duties arising under *section 15*;

   (ii) to take action required under *section 9* or in accordance with medical advice. If the period is interrupted in accordance with *(a)*, a fresh period must be allowed. Interruptions under *(b)* and *(c)*, do not require a fresh period to be allowed.

12.3 Before a detainee is interviewed the custody officer, in consultation with the officer in charge of the investigation and appropriate health care professionals as necessary, shall assess whether the detainee is fit enough to be interviewed. This means determining and considering the risks to the detainee's physical and mental state if the interview took place and determining what safeguards are needed to allow the interview to take place. The custody officer shall not allow a detainee to be interviewed if the custody officer considers it would cause significant harm to the detainee's physical or mental state. Vulnerable suspects listed at *paragraph 11.18* shall be treated as always being at some risk during an interview and these persons may not be interviewed except in accordance with *paragraphs 11.18* to *11.20*.

12.4 As far as practicable interviews shall take place in interview rooms which are adequately heated, lit and ventilated.

12.5 A suspect whose detention without charge has been authorised under PACE, because the detention is necessary for an interview to obtain evidence of the offence for which they have been arrested, may choose not to answer questions but police do not require the suspect's consent or agreement to interview them for this purpose. If a suspect takes steps to prevent themselves being questioned or further questioned, e.g. by refusing to leave their cell to go to a suitable interview room or by trying to leave the interview room, they shall be advised their consent or agreement to interview is not required. The suspect shall be cautioned as in *section 10*, and informed if they fail or refuse to co-operate, the interview may take place in the cell and that their failure or refusal to co-operate may be given in evidence. The suspect shall then be invited to co-operate and go into the interview room.

12.6 People being questioned or making statements shall not be required to stand.

12.7 Before the interview commences each interviewer shall, subject to *paragraph 2.6A*, identify themselves and any other persons present to the interviewee.

12.8 Breaks from interviewing should be made at recognised meal times or at other times that take account of when an interviewee last had a meal. Short refreshment breaks shall be provided at approximately two hour intervals, subject to the interviewer's discretion to delay a break if there are reasonable grounds for believing it would:

    (i) involve a:

- risk of harm to people;
- serious loss of, or damage to, property;

(ii) unnecessarily delay the detainee's release;

(iii) otherwise prejudice the outcome of the investigation.

12.9 If during the interview a complaint is made by or on behalf of the interviewee concerning the provisions of this Code, the interviewer should:

(i) record it in the interview record;

(ii) inform the custody officer, who is then responsible for dealing with it as in *section 9*.

(b) Documentation

12.10 A record must be made of the:

- time a detainee is not in the custody of the custody officer, and why
- reason for any refusal to deliver the detainee out of that custody

12.11 A record shall be made of:

(a) the reasons it was not practicable to use an interview room; and

(b) any action taken as in *paragraph 12.5*.

The record shall be made on the custody record or in the interview record for action taken whilst an interview record is being kept, with a brief reference to this effect in the custody record.

12.12 Any decision to delay a break in an interview must be recorded, with reasons, in the interview record.

12.13 All written statements made at police stations under caution shall be written on forms provided for the purpose.

12.14 All written statements made under caution shall be taken in accordance with *Annex D*. Before a person makes a written statement under caution at a police station they shall be reminded about the right to legal advice.

13 Interpreters

(a) General

13.1 Chief officers are responsible for making sure appropriate arrangements are in place for provision of suitably qualified interpreters for people who:

- are deaf;
- do not understand English.

Whenever possible, interpreters should be drawn from the National Register of Public Service Interpreters (NRPSI) or the Council for the Advancement of Communication with Deaf People (CADCP) Directory of British Sign Language/English Interpreters.

(b) Foreign languages

13.2 Unless *paragraphs 11.1, 11.18* to *11.20* apply, a person must not be interviewed in the absence of a person capable of interpreting if:
(a) they have difficulty understanding English;

(b) the interviewer cannot speak the person's own language;

(c) the person wants an interpreter present.

13.3 The interviewer shall make sure the interpreter makes a note of the interview at the time in the person's language for use in the event of the interpreter being called to give evidence, and certifies its accuracy. The interviewer should allow sufficient time for the interpreter to note each question and answer after each is put, given and interpreted. The person should be allowed to read the record or have it read to them and sign it as correct or indicate the respects in which they consider it inaccurate. If the interview is audibly recorded or visually recorded, the arrangements in Code E or F apply.

13.4 In the case of a person making a statement to a police officer or other police staff other than in English:
(a) the interpreter shall record the statement in the language it is made;

(b) the person shall be invited to sign it;

(c) an official English translation shall be made in due course.

(d) Deaf people and people with speech difficulties

13.5 If a person appears to be deaf or there is doubt about their hearing or speaking ability, they must not be interviewed in the absence of an interpreter unless they agree in writing to being interviewed without one or *paragraphs 11.1, 11.18* to *11.20* apply.

13.6 An interpreter should also be called if a juvenile is interviewed and the parent or guardian present as the appropriate adult appears to be deaf or there is doubt about their hearing or speaking ability, unless they agree in writing to the interview proceeding without one or *paragraphs 11.1, 11.18* to *11.20* apply.

13.7 The interviewer shall make sure the interpreter is allowed to read the interview record and certify its accuracy in the event of the interpreter being called to give evidence. If the interview is audibly recorded or visually recorded, the arrangements in Code E or F apply.

(d) Additional rules for detained persons

13.8 All reasonable attempts should be made to make the detainee understand that interpreters will be provided at public expense.

13.9 If *paragraph 6.1* applies and the detainee cannot communicate with the solicitor because of language, hearing or speech difficulties, an interpreter must be called. The interpreter may not be a police officer or any other police staff when interpretation is needed for the purposes of obtaining legal advice. In all other cases a police officer or other police staff may only interpret if the detainee and the appropriate adult, if applicable, give their agreement in writing or if the interview is audibly recorded or visually recorded as in Code E or F.

13.10   When the custody officer cannot establish effective communication with a person charged with an offence who appears deaf or there is doubt about their ability to hear, speak or to understand English, arrangements must be made as soon as practicable for an interpreter to explain the offence and any other information given by the custody officer.

(e) Documentation

13.11   Action taken to call an interpreter under this section and any agreement to be interviewed in the absence of an interpreter must be recorded.

14   Questioning – special restrictions

14.1   If a person is arrested by one police force on behalf of another and the lawful period of detention in respect of that offence has not yet commenced in accordance with PACE, section 41 no questions may be put to them about the offence while they are in transit between the forces except to clarify any voluntary statement they make.

14.2   If a person is in police detention at a hospital they may not be questioned without the agreement of a responsible doctor.

15   Reviews and extensions of detention

(a) Persons detained under PACE

15.1   The review officer is responsible under PACE, section 40 for periodically determining if a person's detention, before or after charge, continues to be necessary. This requirement continues throughout the detention period and except as in *paragraph 15.10*, the review officer must be present at the police station holding the detainee.

15.2   Under PACE, section 42, an officer of superintendent rank or above who is responsible for the station holding the detainee may give authority any time after the second review to extend the maximum period the person may be detained without charge by up to 12 hours. Further detention without charge may be authorised only by a magistrates' court in accordance with PACE, sections 43 and 44.

15.2A   Section 42(1) of PACE as amended extends the maximum period of detention for indictable offences from 24 hours to 36 hours. Detaining a juvenile or mentally vulnerable person for longer than 24 hours will be dependent on the circumstances of the case and with regard to the person's:

(a) special vulnerability;

(b) the legal obligation to provide an opportunity for representations to be made prior to a decision about extending detention;

(c) the need to consult and consider the views of any appropriate adult; and

(d) any alternatives to police custody.

15.3 Before deciding whether to authorise continued detention the officer responsible under *paragraphs 15.1* or *15.2* shall give an opportunity to make representations about the detention to:

(a) the detainee, unless in the case of a review as in *paragraph 15.1*, the detainee is asleep;

(b) the detainee's solicitor if available at the time; and

(c) the appropriate adult if available at the time.

15.3A   Other people having an interest in the detainee's welfare may also make representations at the authorising officer's discretion.

15.3B   Subject to *paragraph 15.10*, the representations may be made orally in person or by telephone or in writing. The authorising officer may, however, refuse to hear oral representations from the detainee if the officer considers them unfit to make representations because of their condition or behaviour.

15.3C   The decision on whether the review takes place in person or by telephone or by video conferencing (see Note 15G) is a matter for the review officer. In determining the form the review may take, the review officer must always take full account of the needs of the person in custody. The benefits of carrying out a review in person should always be considered, based on the individual circumstances of each case with specific additional consideration if the person is:

(a) a juvenile (and the age of the juvenile); or

(b) mentally vulnerable; or

(c) has been subject to medical attention for other than routine minor ailments; or

(d) there are presentational or community issues around the person's detention.

15.4 Before conducting a review or determining whether to extend the maximum period of detention without charge, the officer responsible must make sure the detainee is reminded of their entitlement to free legal advice, see *paragraph 6.5*, unless in the case of a review the person is asleep.

15.5 If, after considering any representations, the officer decides to keep the detainee in detention or extend the maximum period they may be detained without charge, any comment made by the detainee shall be recorded. If applicable, the officer responsible under *paragraph 15.1* or *15.2* shall be informed of the comment as soon as practicable. See also *paragraphs 11.4* and *11.13*

15.6 No officer shall put specific questions to the detainee:

- regarding their involvement in any offence; or
- in respect of any comments they may make:
  — when given the opportunity to make representations; or
  — in response to a decision to keep them in detention or extend the maximum period of detention. Such an exchange could constitute an interview as in *paragraph 11.1A* and would be subject to the associated safeguards in *section 11* and, in respect of a person who has been charged, *paragraph 16.5*. See also *paragraph 11.13*

15.7 A detainee who is asleep at a review, see *paragraph 15.1*, and whose continued detention is authorised must be informed about the decision and reason as soon as practicable after waking.

(b) Persons detained under the Terrorism Act 2000

15.8 In terrorism cases:
  (a) the powers and duties of the review officer are in the Terrorism Act 2000, Schedule 8, Part II;
  (b) a police officer of at least superintendent rank may apply to a judicial authority for a warrant of further detention under the Terrorism Act 2000, Schedule 8, Part III.

(c) Telephone review of detention

15.9 PACE, section 40A provides that the officer responsible under section 40 for reviewing the detention of a person who has not been charged, need not attend the police station holding the detainee and may carry out the review by telephone.

15.9A   PACE, section 45A(2) provides that the officer responsible under section 40 for reviewing the detention of a person who has not been charged, need not attend the police station holding the detainee and may carry out the review by video conferencing facilities.

15.9B   A telephone review is not permitted where facilities for review by video conferencing exist and it is practicable to use them.

15.9C   The review officer can decide at any stage that a telephone review or review by video conferencing should be terminated and that the review will be conducted in person. The reasons for doing so should be noted in the custody record.

15.10   When a telephone review is carried out, an officer at the station holding the detainee shall be required by the review officer to fulfil that officer's obligations under PACE section 40 or this Code by:

(a)   making any record connected with the review in the detainee's custody record;

(b)   if applicable, making a record in (a) in the presence of the detainee; and

(c)   giving the detainee information about the review.

15.11   When a telephone review is carried out, the requirement in *paragraph 15.3* will be satisfied:

(a)   if facilities exist for the immediate transmission of written representations to the review officer, e.g. fax or email message, by giving the detainee an opportunity to make representations:

(i)   orally by telephone; or

(ii)   in writing using those facilities; and

(b)   in all other cases, by giving the detainee an opportunity to make their representations orally by telephone.

(d) Documentation

15.12   It is the officer's responsibility to make sure all reminders given under *paragraph 15.4* are noted in the custody record.

15.13   The grounds for, and extent of, any delay in conducting a review shall be recorded.

15.14   When a telephone review is carried out, a record shall be made of:

(a)   the reason the review officer did not attend the station holding the detainee;

(b)   the place the review officer was;

(c)   the method representations, oral or written, were made to the review officer, see *paragraph 15.11*.

15.15   Any written representations shall be retained.

15.16   A record shall be made as soon as practicable about the outcome of each review or determination whether to extend the maximum detention period without charge or an application for a warrant of further detention or its extension. If *paragraph 15.7* applies, a record shall also be made of when the person was informed and by whom. If an authorisation is given under PACE, section 42, the record shall state the number of hours and minutes by which the detention period is extended or further extended. If a warrant for further detention, or extension, is granted under section 43 or 44, the record shall state the detention period authorised by the warrant and the date and time it was granted.

16   Charging detained persons

(a) Action

16.1   When the officer in charge of the investigation reasonably believes there is sufficient evidence to provide a realistic prospect of conviction for the offence *(see paragraph 11.6)*, they shall without delay, and subject to the following qualification, inform the custody officer who will be responsible for considering whether the detainee should be charged. When a person is detained in respect of more than one offence it is permissible to delay informing the custody officer until the above conditions are satisfied in respect of all the offences, but *see paragraph 11.6*. If the detainee is a juvenile, mentally disordered or otherwise mentally vulnerable, any resulting action shall be taken in the presence of the appropriate adult if they are present at the time.

16.1A   Where guidance issued by the Director of Public Prosecutions under section 37A is in force the custody officer must comply with that Guidance in deciding how to act in dealing with the detainee.

16.1B   Where in compliance with the DPP's Guidance the custody officer decides that the case should be immediately referred to the CPS to make the charging decision, consultation should take place with a Crown Prosecutor as soon as is reasonably practicable. Where the Crown Prosecutor is unable to make the charging decision on the information available at that time, the detainee may be released without charge and on bail (with conditions if necessary) under section 37(7)(a). In such circumstances, the detainee should be informed that they are being released to enable the Director of Public Prosecutions to make a decision under section 37B.

16.2   When a detainee is charged with or informed they may be prosecuted for an offence, they shall, unless the restriction on drawing adverse inferences from silence applies, see *Annex C*, be cautioned as follows:

'You do not have to say anything. But it may harm your defence if you do not mention now something which you later rely on in court. Anything you do say may be given in evidence.' Annex C, paragraph 2 sets out the alternative terms of the caution to be used when the restriction on drawing adverse inferences from silence applies.

16.3   When a detainee is charged they shall be given a written notice showing particulars of the offence and, subject to *paragraph 2.6A*, the officer's name and the case reference number. As far as possible the particulars of the charge shall be stated in simple terms, but they shall also show the precise offence in law with which the detainee is charged. The notice shall begin: *'You are charged with the offence(s) shown below.'* Followed by the caution. If the detainee is a juvenile, mentally disordered or otherwise mentally vulnerable, the notice should be given to the appropriate adult.

16.4 If, after a detainee has been charged with or informed they may be prosecuted for an offence, an officer wants to tell them about any written statement or interview with another person relating to such an offence, the detainee shall either be handed a true copy of the written statement or the content of the interview record brought to their attention. Nothing shall be done to invite any reply or comment except to:

(a) caution the detainee, '*You do not have to say anything, but anything you do say may be given in evidence.*'; and

(b) remind the detainee about their right to legal advice.

16.4A If the detainee:

- cannot read, the document may be read to them

- is a juvenile, mentally disordered or otherwise mentally vulnerable, the appropriate adult shall also be given a copy, or the interview record shall be brought to their attention

16.5 A detainee may not be interviewed about an offence after they have been charged with, or informed they may be prosecuted for it, unless the interview is necessary:

- to prevent or minimise harm or loss to some other person, or the public

- to clear up an ambiguity in a previous answer or statement

- in the interests of justice for the detainee to have put to them, and have an opportunity to comment on, information concerning the offence which has come to light since they were charged or informed they might be prosecuted. Before any such interview, the interviewer shall:

    (a) caution the detainee, '*You do not have to say anything, but anything you do say may be given in evidence.*';

    (b) remind the detainee about their right to legal advice.

16.6 The provisions of *paragraphs 16.2 to 16.5* must be complied with in the appropriate adult's presence if they are already at the police station. If they are not at the police station then these provisions must be complied with again in their presence when they arrive unless the detainee has been released.

16.7 When a juvenile is charged with an offence and the custody officer authorises their continued detention after charge, the custody officer must try to make arrangements for the juvenile to be taken into the care of a local authority to be detained pending appearance in court unless the custody officer certifies it is impracticable to do so or, in the case of a juvenile of at least 12 years old, no secure accommodation is available and there is a risk to the public of serious harm from that juvenile, in accordance with PACE, section 38(6).

(b) Documentation

16.8 A record shall be made of anything a detainee says when charged.

16.9 Any questions put in an interview after charge and answers given relating to the offence shall be recorded in full during the interview on forms for that purpose and the record signed by the detainee or, if they refuse, by the interviewer and any third parties present. If the questions are audibly recorded or visually recorded the arrangements in Code E or F apply.

16.10   If it is not practicable to make arrangements for a juvenile's transfer into local authority care as in *paragraph 16.7*, the custody officer must record the reasons and complete a certificate to be produced before the court with the juvenile.

17   Testing persons for the presence of specified Class A drugs

(a) Action

17.1 This section of Code C applies only in selected police stations in police areas where the provisions for drug testing under section 63B of PACE (as amended by section 5 of the Criminal Justice Act 2003 and section 7 of the Drugs Act 2005) are in force and in respect of which the Secretary of State has given a notification to the relevant chief officer of police that arrangements for the taking of samples have been made. Such a notification will cover either a police area as a whole or particular stations within a police area. The notification indicates whether the testing applies to those arrested or charged or under the age of 18 as the case may be and testing can only take place in respect of the persons so indicated in the notification. Testing cannot be carried out unless the relevant notification has been given and has not been withdrawn.

17.2 A sample of urine or a non-intimate sample may be taken from a person in police detention for the purpose of ascertaining whether he has any specified Class A drug in his body only where they have been brought before the custody officer and:
   (a)   either the arrest condition, see paragraph 17.3, or the charge condition, see *paragraph 17.4* is met;
   (b)   the age condition see *paragraph 17.5*, is met;
   (c)   the notification condition is met in relation to the arrest condition, the charge condition, or the age condition, as the case may be. (Testing on charge and/or arrest must be specifically provided for in the notification for the power to apply. In addition, the fact that testing of under 18s is authorised must be expressly provided for in the notification before the power to test such persons applies.). See *paragraph 17.1*; and
   (d)   a police officer has requested the person concerned to give the sample (the request condition).

17.3 The arrest condition is met where the detainee:
    (a) has been arrested for a trigger offence, but not charged with that offence; or
    (b) has been arrested for any other offence but not charged with that offence and a police officer of inspector rank or above, who has reasonable grounds for suspecting that their misuse of any specified Class A drug caused or contributed to the offence, has authorised the sample to be taken.

17.4 The charge condition is met where the detainee:
    (a) has been charged with a trigger offence, or
    (b) has been charged with any other offence and a police officer of inspector rank or above, who has reasonable grounds for suspecting that the detainee's misuse of any specified Class A drug caused or contributed to the offence, has authorised the sample to be taken.

17.5 The age condition is met where:
    (a) in the case of a detainee who has been arrested but not charged as in *paragraph 17.3*, they are aged 18 or over;
    (b) in the case of a detainee who has been charged as in *paragraph 17.4*, they are aged 14 or over.

17.6 Before requesting a sample from the person concerned, an officer must:
    (a) inform them that the purpose of taking the sample is for drug testing under PACE. This is to ascertain whether they have a specified Class A drug present in their body;
    (b) warn them that if, when so requested, they fail without good cause to provide a sample they may be liable to prosecution;
    (c) where the taking of the sample has been authorised by an inspector or above in accordance with *paragraph 17.3(b)* or *17.4(b)* above, inform them that the authorisation has been given and the grounds for giving it;
    (d) remind them of the following rights, which may be exercised at any stage during the period in custody:
        (i) the right to have someone informed of their arrest [see *section 5*];
        (ii) the right to consult privately with a solicitor and that free independent legal advice is available [see section 6]; and
        (iii) the right to consult these Codes of Practice [see section 3].

17.7 In the case of a person who has not attained the age of 17 —
    (a) the making of the request for a sample under *paragraph 17.2(d)* above;
    (b) the giving of the warning and the information under *paragraph 17.6* above; and

(c) the taking of the sample, may not take place except in the presence of an appropriate adult.

17.8 Authorisation by an officer of the rank of inspector or above within *paragraph 17.3(b)* or *17.4(b)* may be given orally or in writing but, if it is given orally, it must be confirmed in writing as soon as practicable.

17.9 If a sample is taken from a detainee who has been arrested for an offence but not charged with that offence as in *paragraph 17.3*, no further sample may be taken during the same continuous period of detention. If during that same period the charge condition is also met in respect of that detainee, the sample which has been taken shall be treated as being taken by virtue of the charge condition, see *paragraph 17.4*, being met.

17.10 A detainee from whom a sample may be taken may be detained for up to six hours from the time of charge if the custody officer reasonably believes the detention is necessary to enable a sample to be taken. Where the arrest condition is met, a detainee whom the custody officer has decided to release on bail without charge may continue to be detained, but not beyond 24 hours from the relevant time (as defined in section 41(2) of PACE), to enable a sample to be taken.

17.11 A detainee in respect of whom the arrest condition is met, but not the charge condition, see *paragraphs 17.3* and *17.4*, and whose release would be required before a sample can be taken had they not continued to be detained as a result of being arrested for a further offence which does not satisfy the arrest condition, may have a sample taken at any time within 24 hours after the arrest for the offence that satisfies the arrest condition.

(b) Documentation

17.12 The following must be recorded in the custody record:
(a) if a sample is taken following authorisation by an officer of the rank of inspector or above, the authorisation and the grounds for suspicion;
(b) the giving of a warning of the consequences of failure to provide a sample;
(c) the time at which the sample was given; and
(d) the time of charge or, where the arrest condition is being relied upon, the time of arrest and, where applicable, the fact that a sample taken after arrest but before charge is to be treated as being taken by virtue of the charge condition, where that is met in the same period of continuous detention. See *paragraph 17.9*

(c) General

17.13 A sample may only be taken by a prescribed person.

17.14   Force may not be used to take any sample for the purpose of drug testing.

17.15   The terms "Class A drug" and "misuse" have the same meanings as in the Misuse of Drugs Act 1971. "Specified" (in relation to a Class A drug) and "trigger offence" have the same meanings as in Part III of the Criminal Justice and Court Services Act 2000.

17.16   Any sample taken:

(a)   may not be used for any purpose other than to ascertain whether the person concerned has a specified Class A drug present in his body; and

(b)   must be retained until the person concerned has made their first appearance before the court.

(d) Assessment of misuse of drugs

17.17   Under the provisions of Part 3 of the Drugs Act 2005, where a detainee has tested positive for a specified Class A drug under section 63B of PACE a police officer may, at any time before the person's release from the police station, impose a requirement for them to attend an initial assessment of their drug misuse by a suitably qualified person and to remain for its duration. The requirement may only be imposed on a person if:

(a)   they have reached the age of 18

(b)   notification has been given by the Secretary of State to the relevant chief officer of police that arrangements for conducting initial assessments have been made for those from whom samples for testing have been taken at the police station where the detainee is in custody.

17.18   When imposing a requirement to attend an initial assessment the police officer must:

(a)   inform the person of the time and place at which the initial assessment is to take place;

(b)   explain that this information will be confirmed in writing; and

(c)   warn the person that he may be liable to prosecution if he fails without good cause to attend the initial assessment and remain for it's duration

17.19   Where a police officer has imposed a requirement to attend an initial assessment in accordance with *paragraph 17.17*, he must, before the person is released from detention, give the person notice in writing which:

(a)   confirms that he is required to attend and remain for the duration of an initial assessment; and

(b)   confirms the information and repeats the warning referred to in *paragraph 17.18*.

17.20   The following must be recorded in the custody record:

(a) that the requirement to attend an initial assessment has been imposed; and

(b) the information, explanation, warning and notice given in accordance with *paragraphs 17.17* and *17.19*.

17.21   Where a notice is given in accordance with *paragraph 17.19*, a police officer can give the person a further notice in writing which informs the person of any change to the time or place at which the initial assessment is to take place and which repeats the warning referred to in *paragraph 17.18(c)*. 17.22 Part 3 of the Drugs Act 2005 also requires police officers to have regard to anyguidance issued by the Secretary of State in respect of the assessment provisions.

POLICE AND CRIMINAL EVIDENCE ACT 1984 (PACE)

CODE D   CODE OF PRACTICE FOR THE IDENTIFICATION OF PERSONS BY POLICE OFFICERS

1   Introduction

1.1   This Code of Practice concerns the principal methods used by police to identify people in connection with the investigation of offences and the keeping of accurate and reliable criminal records.

1.2   Identification by witnesses arises, e.g., if the offender is seen committing the crime and a witness is given an opportunity to identify the suspect in a video identification, identification parade or similar procedure. The procedures are designed to:

- test the witness' ability to identify the person they saw on a previous occasion
- provide safeguards against mistaken identification.

While this Code concentrates on visual identification procedures, it does not preclude the police making use of aural identification procedures such as a "voice identification parade", where they judge that appropriate.

1.3   Identification by fingerprints applies when a person's fingerprints are taken to:

- compare with fingerprints found at the scene of a crime
- check and prove convictions
- help to ascertain a person's identity.

1.3A   Identification using footwear impressions applies when a person's footwear impressions are taken to compare with impressions found at the scene of a crime.

1.4   Identification by body samples and impressions includes taking samples such as blood or hair to generate a DNA profile for comparison with material obtained from the scene of a crime, or a victim.

1.5   Taking photographs of arrested people applies to recording and checking identity and locating and tracing persons who:

- are wanted for offences
- fail to answer their bail.

1.6   Another method of identification involves searching and examining detained suspects to find, e.g., marks such as tattoos or scars which may help establish their identity or whether they have been involved in committing an offence.

1.7   The provisions of the Police and Criminal Evidence Act 1984 (PACE) and this Code are designed to make sure fingerprints, samples, impressions and photographs are taken, used and retained, and identification procedures carried out, only when justified and necessary for preventing, detecting or investigating crime. If these provisions are not observed, the application of the relevant procedures in particular cases may be open to question.

2   General

2.1   This Code must be readily available at all police stations for consultation by:

- police officers and police staff
- detained persons
- members of the public

2.2   The provisions of this Code:

- include the *Annexes*
- do not include the *Notes for guidance*.

2.3   Code C, paragraph 1.4, regarding a person who may be mentally disordered or otherwise mentally vulnerable and the *Notes for guidance* applicable to those provisions apply to this Code.

2.4   Code C, paragraph 1.5, regarding a person who appears to be under the age of 17 applies to this Code.

2.5   Code C, paragraph 1.6, regarding a person who appears blind, seriously visually impaired, deaf, unable to read or speak or has difficulty orally because of a speech impediment applies to this Code.

2.6   In this Code:

- 'appropriate adult' means the same as in Code C, paragraph 1.7,
- 'solicitor' means the same as in Code C, paragraph 6.12 and the *Notes for guidance* applicable to those provisions apply to this Code.

2.7   References to custody officers include those performing the functions of custody officer, see *paragraph 1.9* of Code C.

2.8   When a record of any action requiring the authority of an officer of a specified rank is made under this Code, subject to *paragraph 2.18*, the officer's name and rank must be recorded.

2.9   When this Code requires the prior authority or agreement of an officer of at least inspector or superintendent rank, that authority may be given by a sergeant or chief inspector who has been authorised to perform the functions of the higher rank under PACE, section 107.

2.10 Subject to *paragraph 2.18*, all records must be timed and signed by the maker.

2.11 Records must be made in the custody record, unless otherwise specified. References to 'pocket book' include any official report book issued to police officers or police staff.

2.12 If any procedure in this Code requires a person's consent, the consent of a:

- mentally disordered or otherwise mentally vulnerable person is only valid if given in the presence of the appropriate adult

- juvenile, is only valid if their parent's or guardian's consent is also obtained unless the juvenile is under 14, when their parent's or guardian's consent is sufficient in its own right. If the only obstacle to an identification procedure in *section 3* is that a juvenile's parent or guardian refuses consent or reasonable efforts to obtain it have failed, the identification officer may apply the provisions of *paragraph 3.21*.

2.13 If a person is blind, seriously visually impaired or unable to read, the custody officer or identification officer shall make sure their solicitor, relative, appropriate adult or some other person likely to take an interest in them and not involved in the investigation is available to help check any documentation. When this Code requires written consent or signing, the person assisting may be asked to sign instead, if the detainee prefers. This paragraph does not require an appropriate adult to be called solely to assist in checking and signing documentation for a person who is not a juvenile, or mentally disordered or otherwise mentally vulnerable (see Code C *paragraph 3.15*).

2.14 If any procedure in this Code requires information to be given to or sought from a suspect, it must be given or sought in the appropriate adult's presence if the suspect is mentally disordered, otherwise mentally vulnerable or a juvenile. If the appropriate adult is not present when the information is first given or sought, the procedure must be repeated in the presence of the appropriate adult when they arrive. If the suspect appears deaf or there is doubt about their hearing or speaking ability or ability to understand English, and effective communication cannot be established, the information must be given or sought through an interpreter.

2.15 Any procedure in this Code involving the participation of a suspect who is mentally disordered, otherwise mentally vulnerable or a juvenile must take place in the presence of the appropriate adult. See *Code C paragraph 1.4*.

2.15A Any procedure in this Code involving the participation of a witness who is or appears to be mentally disordered, otherwise mentally vulnerable or a juvenile should take place in the presence of a pre-trial support person. However, the support-person must not be allowed to prompt any identification of a suspect by a witness.

2.16 References to:

- 'taking a photograph', include the use of any process to produce a single, still or moving, visual image
- 'photographing a person', should be construed accordingly
- 'photographs', 'films', 'negatives' and 'copies' include relevant visual images recorded, stored, or reproduced through any medium
- 'destruction' includes the deletion of computer data relating to such images or making access to that data impossible.

2.17 Except as described, nothing in this Code affects the powers and procedures:

(i) for requiring and taking samples of breath, blood and urine in relation to driving offences, etc, when under the influence of drink, drugs or excess alcohol under the:

- Road Traffic Act 1988, sections 4 to 11
- Road Traffic Offenders Act 1988, sections 15 and 16
- Transport and Works Act 1992, sections 26 to 38;

(ii) under the Immigration Act 1971, Schedule 2, paragraph 18, for taking photographs and fingerprints from persons detained under that Act, Schedule 2, paragraph 16 (Administrative Controls as to Control on Entry etc.); for taking fingerprints in accordance with the Immigration and Asylum Act 1999; sections 141 and 142(3), or other methods for collecting information about a person's external physical characteristics provided for by regulations made under that Act, section 144;

(iii) under the Terrorism Act 2000, Schedule 8, for taking photographs, fingerprints, skin impressions, body samples or impressions from people:

- arrested under that Act, section 41,
- detained for the purposes of examination under that Act, Schedule 7, and to whom the Code of Practice issued under that Act, Schedule 14, paragraph 6, applies ('the terrorism provisions');

(iv) for taking photographs, fingerprints, skin impressions, body samples or impressions from people who have been:

- arrested on warrants issued in Scotland, by officers exercising powers under the Criminal Justice and Public Order Act 1994, section 136(2)
- arrested or detained without warrant by officers from a police force in Scotland exercising their powers of arrest or detention under the Criminal Justice and Public Order Act 1994, section 137(2), (Cross Border powers of arrest etc.).

Note: In these cases, police powers and duties and the person's rights and entitlements whilst at a police station in England and Wales are the same as if the person had been arrested in Scotland by a Scottish police officer.

2.18 Nothing in this Code requires the identity of officers or police staff to be recorded or disclosed:

(a) in the case of enquiries linked to the investigation of terrorism;

(b) if the officers or police staff reasonably believe recording or disclosing their names might put them in danger. In these cases, they shall use warrant or other identification numbers and the name of their police station.

2.19 In this Code:

(a) 'designated person' means a person other than a police officer, designated under the Police Reform Act 2002, Part 4, who has specified powers and duties of police officers conferred or imposed on them;

(b) any reference to a police officer includes a designated person acting in the exercise or performance of the powers and duties conferred or imposed on them by their designation.

2.20 If a power conferred on a designated person:

(a) allows reasonable force to be used when exercised by a police officer, a designated person exercising that power has the same entitlement to use force;

(b) includes power to use force to enter any premises, that power is not exercisable by that designated person except:

(i) in the company, and under the supervision, of a police officer; or

(ii) for the purpose of:

• saving life or limb; or

• preventing serious damage to property.

2.21 Nothing in this Code prevents the custody officer, or other officer given custody of the detainee, from allowing police staff who are not designated persons to carry out individual procedures or tasks at the police station if the law allows. However, the officer remains responsible for making sure the procedures and tasks are carried out correctly in accordance with the Codes of Practice. Any such person must be:

(a) a person employed by a police authority maintaining a police force and under the control and direction of the Chief Officer of that force;

(b) employed by a person with whom a police authority has a contract for the provision of services relating to persons arrested or otherwise in custody.

2.22 Designated persons and other police staff must have regard to any relevant provisions of the Codes of Practice.

3   Identification by witnesses

3.1   A record shall be made of the suspect's description as first given by a potential witness. This record must:

(a)   be made and kept in a form which enables details of that description to be accurately produced from it, in a visible and legible form, which can be given to the suspect or the suspect's solicitor in accordance with this Code; and

(b)   unless otherwise specified, be made before the witness takes part in any identification procedures under *paragraphs 3.5 to 3.10, 3.21* or *3.23*. A copy of the record shall where practicable, be given to the suspect or their solicitor before any procedures under *paragraphs 3.5 to 3.10, 3.21* or *3.23* are carried out.

(a) Cases when the suspect's identity is not known

3.2   In cases when the suspect's identity is not known, a witness may be taken to a particular neighbourhood or place to see whether they can identify the person they saw. Although the number, age, sex, race, general description and style of clothing of other people present at the location and the way in which any identification is made cannot be controlled, the principles applicable to the formal procedures under *paragraphs 3.5 to 3.10* shall be followed as far as practicable. For example:

(a)   where it is practicable to do so, a record should be made of the witness' description of the suspect, as in paragraph 3.1(a), before asking the witness to make an identification;

(b)   care must be taken not to direct the witness' attention to any individual unless, taking into account all the circumstances, this cannot be avoided. However, this does not prevent a witness being asked to look carefully at the people around at the time or to look towards a group or in a particular direction, if this appears necessary to make sure that the witness does not overlook a possible suspect simply because the witness is looking in the opposite direction and also to enable the witness to make comparisons between any suspect and others who are in the area.

(c)   where there is more than one witness, every effort should be made to keep them separate and witnesses should be taken to see whether they can identify a person independently;

(d)   once there is sufficient information to justify the arrest of a particular individual for suspected involvement in the offence, e.g., after a witness makes a positive identification, the provisions set out from paragraph 3.4 onwards shall apply for any other witnesses in relation to that individual. Subject to *paragraphs 3.12* and *3.13*, it is not necessary for the witness who makes such a positive identification to take part in a further procedure;

(e)   the officer or police staff accompanying the witness must record, in their pocket book, the action taken as soon as, and in as much detail, as possible. The record should include: the date, time and place of the relevant occasion the witness claims to have previously seen the suspect; where any identification was made; how it was made and the conditions at the time (e.g., the distance the witness was from the suspect, the weather and light); if the witness's attention was drawn to the suspect; the reason for this; and anything said by the witness or the suspect about the identification or the conduct of the procedure.

3.3   A witness must not be shown photographs, computerised or artist's composite likenesses or similar likenesses or pictures (including 'E-fit' images) if the identity of the suspect is known to the police and the suspect is available to take part in a video identification, an identification parade or a group identification. If the suspect's identity is not known, the showing of such images to a witness to obtain identification evidence must be done in accordance with *Annex E*.

(b) Cases when the suspect is known and available

3.4   If the suspect's identity is known to the police and they are available, the identification procedures set out in paragraphs 3.5 to 3.10 may be used. References in this section to a suspect being 'known' mean there is sufficient information known to the police to justify the arrest of a particular person for suspected involvement in the offence. A suspect being 'available' means they are immediately available or will be within a reasonably short time and willing to take an effective part in at least one of the following which it is practicable to arrange:

- video identification;
- identification parade; or
- group identification.

Video identification

3.5   Change to: 'A 'video identification' is when the witness is shown moving images of a known suspect, together with similar images of others who resemble the suspect. Moving images must be used unless:

- the suspect is known but not available (see *paragraph 3.21* of this Code); or
- in accordance with *paragraph 2A of Annex A* of this Code, the identification officer does not consider that replication of a physical feature can be achieved or that it is not possible to conceal the location of the feature on the image of the suspect. The identification officer may then decide to make use of video identification but using still images.

3.6   Video identifications must be carried out in accordance with *Annex A*.

Identification parade

3.7 An 'identification parade' is when the witness sees the suspect in a line of others who resemble the suspect.

3.8 Identification parades must be carried out in accordance with *Annex B*.

Group identification

3.9 A 'group identification' is when the witness sees the suspect in an informal group of people.

3.10 Group identifications must be carried out in accordance with *Annex C*.

Arranging identification procedures

3.11 Except for the provisions in *paragraph 3.19*, the arrangements for, and conduct of, the identification procedures in paragraphs 3.5 to 3.10 and circumstances in which an identification procedure must be held shall be the responsibility of an officer not below inspector rank who is not involved with the investigation, 'the identification officer'. Unless otherwise specified, the identification officer may allow another officer or police staff, see *paragraph 2.21*, to make arrangements for, and conduct, any of these identification procedures. In delegating these procedures, the identification officer must be able to supervise effectively and either intervene or be contacted for advice. No officer or any other person involved with the investigation of the case against the suspect, beyond the extent required by these procedures, may take any part in these procedures or act as the identification officer. This does not prevent the identification officer from consulting the officer in charge of the investigation to determine which procedure to use. When an identification procedure is required, in the interest of fairness to suspects and witnesses, it must be held as soon as practicable.

Circumstances in which an identification procedure must be held

3.12 Whenever:

(i) a witness has identified a suspect or purported to have identified them prior to any identification procedure set out in paragraphs 3.5 to 3.10 having been held;

or

(ii) there is a witness available, who expresses an ability to identify the suspect, or where there is a reasonable chance of the witness being able to do so, and they have not been given an opportunity to identify the suspect in any of the procedures set out in paragraphs 3.5 to 3.10, and the suspect disputes being the person the witness claims to have seen, an identification procedure shall be held unless it is not practicable or it would serve no useful purpose in proving or disproving whether the suspect was involved in committing the offence. For example, when it is not disputed that the suspect is already well known to the witness who claims to have seen them commit the crime.

3.13 Such a procedure may also be held if the officer in charge of the investigation considers it would be useful.

Selecting an identification procedure

3.14 If, because of paragraph 3.12, an identification procedure is to be held, the suspect shall initially be offered a video identification unless:

   a) a video identification is not practicable; or

   b) an identification parade is both practicable and more suitable than a video identification; or

   c) paragraph 3.16 applies.

   The identification officer and the officer in charge of the investigation shall consult each other to determine which option is to be offered. An identification parade may not be practicable because of factors relating to the witnesses, such as their number, state of health, availability and travelling requirements. A video identification would normally be more suitable if it could be arranged and completed sooner than an identification parade.

3.15 A suspect who refuses the identification procedure first offered shall be asked to state their reason for refusing and may get advice from their solicitor and/or if present, their appropriate adult. The suspect, solicitor and/or appropriate adult shall be allowed to make representations about why another procedure should be used. A record should be made of the reasons for refusal and any representations made. After considering any reasons given, and representations made, the identification officer shall, if appropriate, arrange for the suspect to be offered an alternative which the officer considers suitable and practicable. If the officer decides it is not suitable and practicable to offer an alternative identification procedure, the reasons for that decision shall be recorded.

3.16 A group identification may initially be offered if the officer in charge of the investigation considers it is more suitable than a video identification or an identification parade and the identification officer considers it practicable to arrange.

Notice to suspect

3.17 Unless *paragraph 3.20* applies, before a video identification, an identification parade or group identification is arranged, the following shall be explained to the suspect:

   (i) the purposes of the video identification, identification parade or group identification;

(ii) their entitlement to free legal advice; see Code C, paragraph 6.5;

(iii) the procedures for holding it, including their right to have a solicitor or friend present;

(iv) that they do not have to consent to or co-operate in a video identification, identification parade or group identification;

(v) that if they do not consent to, and co-operate in, a video identification, identification parade or group identification, their refusal may be given in evidence in any subsequent trial and police may proceed covertly without their consent or make other arrangements to test whether a witness can identify them, see *paragraph 3.21*;

(vi) whether, for the purposes of the video identification procedure, images of them have previously been obtained, see *paragraph 3.20*, and if so, that they may co-operate in providing further, suitable images to be used instead;

(vii) if appropriate, the special arrangements for juveniles;

(viii) if appropriate, the special arrangements for mentally disordered or otherwise mentally vulnerable people;

(ix) that if they significantly alter their appearance between being offered an identification procedure and any attempt to hold an identification procedure, this may be given in evidence if the case comes to trial, and the identification officer may then consider other forms of identification, see *paragraph 3.21*;

(x) that a moving image or photograph may be taken of them when they attend for any identification procedure;

(xi) whether, before their identity became known, the witness was shown photographs, a computerised or artist's composite likeness or similar likeness or image by the police;

(xii) that if they change their appearance before an identification parade, it may not be practicable to arrange one on the day or subsequently and, because of the appearance change, the identification officer may consider alternative methods of identification;

(xiii) that they or their solicitor will be provided with details of the description of the suspect as first given by any witnesses who are to attend the video identification, identification parade, group identification or confrontation, see *paragraph 3.1*.

3.18 This information must also be recorded in a written notice handed to the suspect. The suspect must be given a reasonable opportunity to read the notice, after which, they should be asked to sign a second copy to indicate if they are willing to co-operate with the making of a video or take part in the identification parade or group identification. The signed copy shall be retained by the identification officer.

3.19 The duties of the identification officer under *paragraphs 3.17* and *3.18* may be performed by the custody officer or other officer not involved in the investigation if:

(a) it is proposed to release the suspect in order that an identification procedure can be arranged and carried out and an inspector is not available to act as the identification officer, see *paragraph 3.11*, before the suspect leaves the station; or

(b) it is proposed to keep the suspect in police detention whilst the procedure isarranged and carried out and waiting for an inspector to act as the identification officer, see *paragraph 3.11*, would cause unreasonable delay to the investigation. The officer concerned shall inform the identification officer of the action taken and give them the signed copy of the notice.

3.20 If the identification officer and officer in charge of the investigation suspect, on reasonable grounds that if the suspect was given the information and notice as in *paragraphs 3.17* and *3.18*, they would then take steps to avoid being seen by a witness in any identification procedure, the identification officer may arrange for images of the suspect suitable for use in a video identification procedure to be obtained before giving the information and notice. If suspect's images are obtained in these circumstances, the suspect may, for the purposes of a video identification procedure, co-operate in providing new images which if suitable, would be used instead, see *paragraph 3.17(vi)*.

(c) Cases when the suspect is known but not available

3.21 When a known suspect is not available or has ceased to be available, see *paragraph 3.4*, the identification officer may make arrangements for a video identification (see Annex A). If necessary, the identification officer may follow the video identification procedures but using still images. Any suitable moving or still images may be used and these may be obtained covertly if necessary. Alternatively, the identification officer may make arrangements for a group identification. See *Note 3D*. These provisions may also be applied to juveniles where the consent of their parent or guardian is either refused or reasonable efforts to obtain that consent have failed (see *paragraph 2.12*).

3.22 Any covert activity should be strictly limited to that necessary to test the ability of the witness to identify the suspect.

3.23 The identification officer may arrange for the suspect to be confronted by the witness if none of the options referred to in paragraphs 3.5 to 3.10 or 3.21 are practicable. A "confrontation" is when the suspect is directly confronted by the witness. A confrontation does not require the suspect's consent. Confrontations must be carried out in accordance with Annex D.

3.24 Requirements for information to be given to, or sought from, a suspect or for the suspect to be given an opportunity to view images before they are shown to a witness, do not apply if the suspect's lack of co-operation prevents the necessary action.

(d) Documentation

3.25 A record shall be made of the video identification, identification parade, group identification or confrontation on forms provided for the purpose.

3.26 If the identification officer considers it is not practicable to hold a video identification or identification parade requested by the suspect, the reasons shall be recorded and explained to the suspect.

3.27 A record shall be made of a person's failure or refusal to co-operate in a video identification, identification parade or group identification and, if applicable, of the grounds for obtaining images in accordance with *paragraph 3.20.*

(e) Showing films and photographs of incidents and information released to the media

3.28 Nothing in this Code inhibits showing films or photographs to the public through the national or local media, or to police officers for the purposes of recognition and tracing suspects. However, when such material is shown to potential witnesses, including police officers, to obtain identification evidence, it shall be shown on an individual basis to avoid any possibility of collusion, and, as far as possible, the showing shall follow the principles for video identification if the suspect is known, see *Annex A*, or identification by photographs if the suspect is not known, see *Annex E.*

3.29 When a broadcast or publication is made, see *paragraph 3.28*, a copy of the relevant material released to the media for the purposes of recognising or tracing the suspect, shall be kept. The suspect or their solicitor shall be allowed to view such material before any procedures under *paragraphs 3.5 to 3.10, 3.21 or 3.23* are carried out, provided it is practicable and would not unreasonably delay the investigation. Each witness involved in the procedure shall be asked, after they have taken part, whether they have seen any broadcast or published films or photographs relating to the offence or any description of the suspect and their replies shall be recorded. This paragraph does not affect any separate requirement under the Criminal Procedure and Investigations Act 1996 to retain material in connection with criminal investigations.

(f) Destruction and retention of photographs taken or used in identification procedures

3.30 PACE, section 64A, see *paragraph 5.12*, provides powers to take photographs of suspects and allows these photographs to be used or disclosed only for purposes related to the prevention or detection of crime, the investigation of offences or the conduct of prosecutions by, or on behalf of, police or other law enforcement and prosecuting authorities inside and outside the United Kingdom or the enforcement of a sentence. After being so used or disclosed, they may be retained but can only be used or disclosed for the same purposes.

3.31 Subject to *paragraph 3.33*, the photographs (and all negatives and copies), of suspects not taken in accordance with the provisions in *paragraph 5.12* which are taken for the purposes of, or in connection with, the identification procedures in *paragraphs 3.5 to 3.10, 3.21* or *3.23* must be destroyed unless the suspect:

(a) is charged with, or informed they may be prosecuted for, a recordable offence;

(b) is prosecuted for a recordable offence;

(c) is cautioned for a recordable offence or given a warning or reprimand in accordance with the Crime and Disorder Act 1998 for a recordable offence; or

(d) gives informed consent, in writing, for the photograph or images to be retained for purposes described in *paragraph 3.30*.

3.32 When *paragraph 3.31* requires the destruction of any photograph, the person must be given an opportunity to witness the destruction or to have a certificate confirming the destruction if they request one within five days of being informed that the destruction is required.

3.33 Nothing in *paragraph 3.31* affects any separate requirement under the Criminal Procedure and Investigations Act 1996 to retain material in connection with criminal investigations.

4 Identification by fingerprints and footwear impressions

(A) Taking fingerprints in connection with a criminal investigation

(a) General

4.1 References to 'fingerprints' means any record, produced by any method, of the skin pattern and other physical characteristics or features of a person's:

(i) fingers; or

(ii) palms.

(b) Action

4.2 A person's fingerprints may be taken in connection with the investigation of an offence only with their consent or if *paragraph 4.3* applies. If the person is at a police station consent must be in writing.

4.3 PACE, section 61, provides powers to take fingerprints without consent from any person over the age of ten years:

(a) under section 61(3), from a person detained at a police station in consequence of being arrested for a recordable offence, if they have not had their fingerprints taken in the course of the investigation of the offence unless those previously taken fingerprints are not a complete set or some or all of those fingerprints are not of sufficient quality to allow satisfactory analysis, comparison or matching.

(b) under section 61(4), from a person detained at a police station who has been charged with a recordable offence, see Note 4A, or informed they will be reported for such an offence if they have not had their fingerprints taken in the course of the investigation of the offence unless those previously taken fingerprints are not a complete set or some or all of those fingerprints are not of sufficient quality to allow satisfactory analysis, comparison or matching.

(c) under section 61(4A), from a person who has been bailed to appear at a court or police station if the person:

    (i) has answered to bail for a person whose fingerprints were taken previously and there are reasonable grounds for believing they are not the same person; or

    (ii) who has answered to bail claims to be a different person from a person whose fingerprints were previously taken; and in either case, the court or an officer of inspector rank or above, authorises the fingerprints to be taken at the court or police station;

(d) under section 61(6), from a person who has been:

    (i) convicted of a recordable offence;

    (ii) given a caution in respect of a recordable offence which, at the time of the caution, the person admitted; or

    (iii) warned or reprimanded under the Crime and Disorder Act 1998, section 65, for a recordable offence.

4.4   PACE, section 27, provides power to:

(a) require the person as in *paragraph 4.3(d)* to attend a police station to have their fingerprints taken if the:

    (i) person has not been in police detention for the offence and has not had their fingerprints taken in the course of the investigation of that offence;

or

    (ii) fingerprints that were taken from the person in the course of the investigation of that offence, do not constitute a complete set or some, or all, of the fingerprints are not of sufficient quality to allow satisfactory analysis, comparison or matching; and

(b) arrest, without warrant, a person who fails to comply with the requirement.

Note: The requirement must be made within one month of the date the person is convicted, cautioned, warned or reprimanded and the person must be given a period of at least 7 days within which to attend. This 7 day period need not fall during the month allowed for making the requirement.

4.5   A person's fingerprints may be taken, as above, electronically.

4.6   Reasonable force may be used, if necessary, to take a person's fingerprints without their consent under the powers as in *paragraphs 4.3* and *4.4.*

4.7   Before any fingerprints are taken with, or without, consent as above, the person must be informed:

(a)   of the reason their fingerprints are to be taken;

(b)   of the grounds on which the relevant authority has been given if the power mentioned in *paragraph 4.3 (c) applies;*

(c)   that their fingerprints may be retained and may be subject of a speculative search against other fingerprints, see *Note 4B*, unless destruction of the fingerprints is required in accordance with *Annex F, Part (a)*; and

(d)   that if their fingerprints are required to be destroyed, they may witness their destruction as provided for in *Annex F, Part (a)*.

(c) Documentation

4.8   A record must be made as soon as possible, of the reason for taking a person's fingerprints without consent. If force is used, a record shall be made of the circumstances and those present.

4.9   A record shall be made when a person has been informed under the terms of *paragraph 4.7(c)*, of the possibility that their fingerprints may be subject of a speculative search.

(B) Taking fingerprints in connection with immigration enquiries

Action

4.10 A person's fingerprints may be taken for the purposes of Immigration Service enquiries in accordance with powers and procedures other than under PACE and for which the Immigration Service (not the police) are responsible, only with the person's consent in writing or if *paragraph 4.11* applies.

4.11 Powers to take fingerprints for these purposes without consent are given to police and immigration officers under the:

(a)   Immigration Act 1971, Schedule 2, paragraph 18(2), when it is reasonably necessary for the purposes of identifying a person detained under the Immigration Act 1971, Schedule 2, paragraph 16 (Detention of person liable to examination or removal);

(b) Immigration and Asylum Act 1999, section 141(7)(a), from a person who fails to produce, on arrival, a valid passport with a photograph or some other document satisfactorily establishing their identity and nationality if an immigration officer does not consider the person has a reasonable excuse for the failure;

(c) Immigration and Asylum Act 1999, section 141(7)(b), from a person who has been refused entry to the UK but has been temporarily admitted if an immigration officer reasonably suspects the person might break a condition imposed on them relating to residence or reporting to a police or immigration officer, and their decision is confirmed by a chief immigration officer;

(d) Immigration and Asylum Act 1999, section 141(7)(c), when directions are given to remove a person:

- as an illegal entrant,
- liable to removal under the Immigration and Asylum Act 1999, section 10,
- who is the subject of a deportation order from the UK;

(e) Immigration and Asylum Act 1999, section 141(7)(d), from a person arrested under UK immigration laws under the Immigration Act 1971, Schedule 2, paragraph 17;

(f) Immigration and Asylum Act 1999, section 141(7)(e), from a person who has made a claim:

- for asylum
- under Article 3 of the European Convention on Human Rights; or

(g) Immigration and Asylum Act 1999, section 141(7)(f), from a person who is a dependant of someone who falls into (b) to (f) above.

4.12 The Immigration and Asylum Act 1999, section 142(3), gives a police and immigration officer power to arrest, without warrant, a person who fails to comply with a requirement imposed by the Secretary of State to attend a specified place for fingerprinting.

4.13 Before any fingerprints are taken, with or without consent, the person must be informed:

(a) of the reason their fingerprints are to be taken;

(b) the fingerprints, and all copies of them, will be destroyed.

4.14 Reasonable force may be used, if necessary, to take a person's fingerprints without their consent under powers as in *paragraph 4.11*.

4.15 *Paragraphs 4.1* and *4.8* apply.

(c) Taking footwear impressions in connection with a criminal investigation

(a) Action

4.16 Impressions of a person's footwear may be taken in connection with the investigation of an offence only with their consent or if *paragraph 4.17* applies. If the person is at a police station consent must be in writing.

4.17 PACE, section 61A, provides power for a police officer to take footwear impressions without consent from any person over the age of ten years who is detained at a police station:
  (a) in consequence of being arrested for a recordable offence; or if the detainee has been charged with a recordable offence, or informed they will be reported for such an offence; and
  (b) the detainee has not had an impression of their footwear taken in the course of the investigation of the offence unless the previously taken impression is not complete or is not of sufficient quality to allow satisfactory analysis, comparison or matching (whether in the case in question or generally).

4.18 Reasonable force may be used, if necessary, to take a footwear impression from a detainee without consent under the power in *paragraph 4.17*.

4.19 Before any footwear impression is taken with, or without, consent as above, the person must be informed:
  (a) of the reason the impression is to be taken;
  (b) that the impression may be retained and may be subject of a speculative search against other impressions unless destruction of the impression is required and
  (c) that if their footwear impressions are required to be destroyed, they may witness their destruction.

(b) Documentation

4.20 A record must be made as soon as possible, of the reason for taking a person's footwear impressions without consent. If force is used, a record shall be made of the circumstances and those present.

4.21 A record shall be made when a person has been informed under the terms of *paragraph 4.19(b)*, of the possibility that their footwear impressions may be subject of a speculative search.

5   Examinations to establish identity and the taking of photographs

(A) Detainees at police stations

(a) Searching or examination of detainees at police stations 5.1PACE, section 54A (1), allows a detainee at a police station to be searched or examined or both, to establish:

  (a) whether they have any marks, features or injuries that would tend to identify them as a person involved in the commission of an offence and to photograph any identifying marks, see *paragraph 5.5*; or

(b) their identity. A person detained at a police station to be searched under a stop and search power, see Code A, is not a detainee for the purposes of these powers.

5.2   A search and/or examination to find marks under section 54A (1) (a) may be carried out without the detainee's consent, see *paragraph 2.12*, only if authorised by an officer of at least inspector rank when consent has been withheld or it is not practicable to obtain consent.

5.3   A search or examination to establish a suspect's identity under section 54A (1) (b) may be carried out without the detainee's consent, see *paragraph 2.12*, only if authorised by an officer of at least inspector rank when the detainee has refused to identify themselves or the authorising officer has reasonable grounds for suspecting the person is not who they claim to be.

5.4   Any marks that assist in establishing the detainee's identity, or their identification as a person involved in the commission of an offence, are identifying marks. Such marks may be photographed with the detainee's consent, see *paragraph 2.12*; or without their consent if it is withheld or it is not practicable to obtain it.

5.5   A detainee may only be searched, examined and photographed under section 54A, by a police officer of the same sex.

5.6   Any photographs of identifying marks, taken under section 54A, may be used or disclosed only for purposes related to the prevention or detection of crime, the investigation of offences or the conduct of prosecutions by, or on behalf of, police or other law enforcement and prosecuting authorities inside, and outside, the UK. After being so used or disclosed, the photograph may be retained but must not be used or disclosed except for these purposes.

5.7   The powers, as in *paragraph 5.1*, do not affect any separate requirement under the Criminal Procedure and Investigations Act 1996 to retain material in connection with criminal investigations.

5.8   Authority for the search and/or examination for the purposes of *paragraphs 5.2 and 5.3* may be given orally or in writing. If given orally, the authorising officer must confirm it in writing as soon as practicable. A separate authority is required for each purpose which applies.

5.9   If it is established a person is unwilling to co-operate sufficiently to enable a search and/or examination to take place or a suitable photograph to be taken, an officer may use reasonable force to:
(a)   search and/or examine a detainee without their consent; and

(b)   photograph any identifying marks without their consent.

5.10 The thoroughness and extent of any search or examination carried out in accordance with the powers in section 54A must be no more than the officer considers necessary to achieve the required purpose. Any search or examination which involves the removal of more than the person's outer clothing shall be conducted in accordance with Code C, Annex A, paragraph 11.

5.11 An intimate search may not be carried out under the powers in section 54A.

(b) Photographing detainees at police stations and other persons elsewhere than at a police station

5.12 Under PACE, section 64A, an officer may photograph:
    (a) any person whilst they are detained at a police station; and
    (b) any person who is elsewhere than at a police station and who has been:-
        (i) arrested by a constable for an offence;
        (ii) taken into custody by a constable after being arrested for an offence by a person other than a constable;
        (iii) made subject to a requirement to wait with a community support officer under *paragraph 2(3) or (3B)* of Schedule 4 to the Police Reform Act 2002;
        (iv) given a penalty notice by a constable in uniform under Chapter 1 of Part 1 of the Criminal Justice and Police Act 2001, a penalty notice by a constable under section 444A of the Education Act 1996, or a fixed penalty notice by a constable in uniform under section 54 of the Road Traffic Offenders Act 1988;
        (v) given a notice in relation to a relevant fixed penalty offence (within the meaning of paragraph 1 of Schedule 4 to the Police Reform Act 2002) by a community support officer by virtue of a designation applying that paragraph to him; or
        (vi) given a notice in relation to a relevant fixed penalty offence (within the meaning of paragraph 1 of Schedule 5 to the Police Reform Act 2002) by an accredited person by virtue of accreditation specifying that that paragraph applies to him.

5.12A Photographs taken under PACE, section 64A:
    (a) may be taken with the person's consent, or without their consent if consent is withheld or it is not practicable to obtain their consent; and
    (b) may be used or disclosed only for purposes related to the prevention or detection of crime, the investigation of offences or the conduct of prosecutions by, or on behalf of, police or other law enforcement and prosecuting authorities inside and outside the United Kingdom or the enforcement of any sentence or order made by a court when dealing with an offence. After being so used or

disclosed, they may be retained but can only be used or disclosed for the same purposes.

5.13 The officer proposing to take a detainee's photograph may, for this purpose, require the person to remove any item or substance worn on, or over, all, or any part of, their head or face. If they do not comply with such a requirement, the officer may remove the item or substance.

5.14 If it is established the detainee is unwilling to co-operate sufficiently to enable a suitable photograph to be taken and it is not reasonably practicable to take the photograph covertly, an officer may use reasonable force.

(a) to take their photograph without their consent; and

(b) for the purpose of taking the photograph, remove any item or substance worn on, or over, all, or any part of, the person's head or face which they have failed to remove when asked.

5.15 For the purposes of this Code, a photograph may be obtained without the person's consent by making a copy of an image of them taken at any time on a camera system installed anywhere in the police station.

(c) Information to be given

5.16 When a person is searched, examined or photographed under the provisions as in *paragraph 5.1* and *5.12*, or their photograph obtained as in *paragraph 5.15*, they must be informed of the:

(a) purpose of the search, examination or photograph;

(b) grounds on which the relevant authority, if applicable, has been given; and

(c) purposes for which the photograph may be used, disclosed or retained. This information must be given before the search or examination commences or the photograph is taken, except if the photograph is:

(i) to be taken covertly;

(ii) obtained as in *paragraph 5.15*, in which case the person must be informed as soon as practicable after the photograph is taken or obtained.

(d) Documentation

5.17 A record must be made when a detainee is searched, examined, or a photograph of the person, or any identifying marks found on them, are taken. The record must include the:

(a) identity, subject to paragraph 2.18, of the officer carrying out the search, examination or taking the photograph;

(b) purpose of the search, examination or photograph and the outcome;

(c) detainee's consent to the search, examination or photograph, or the reason the person was searched, examined or photographed without consent;

(d) giving of any authority as in *paragraphs 5.2* and *5.3*, the grounds for giving it and the authorising officer.

5.18 If force is used when searching, examining or taking a photograph in accordance with this section, a record shall be made of the circumstances and those present.

(B) Persons at police stations not detained

5.19 When there are reasonable grounds for suspecting the involvement of a person in a criminal offence, but that person is at a police station voluntarily and not detained, the provisions of *paragraphs 5.1* to *5.18* should apply, subject to the modifications in the following paragraphs.

5.20 References to the 'person being detained' and to the powers mentioned in *paragraph 5.1* which apply only to detainees at police stations shall be omitted.

5.21 Force may not be used to:
(a) search and/or examine the person to:
(i) discover whether they have any marks that would tend to identify them as a person involved in the commission of an offence; or
(ii) establish their identity;
(b) take photographs of any identifying marks, see *paragraph 5.4*; or
(c) take a photograph of the person.

5.22 Subject to *paragraph 5.24*, the photographs of persons or of their identifying marks which are not taken in accordance with the provisions mentioned in *paragraphs 5.1* or *5.12*, must be destroyed (together with any negatives and copies) unless the person:
(a) is charged with, or informed they may be prosecuted for, a recordable offence;
(b) is prosecuted for a recordable offence;
(c) is cautioned for a recordable offence or given a warning or reprimand in accordance with the Crime and Disorder Act 1998 for a recordable offence; or
(d) gives informed consent, in writing, for the photograph or image to be retained as in *paragraph 5.6*.

5.23 When *paragraph 5.22* requires the destruction of any photograph, the person must be given an opportunity to witness the destruction or to have a certificate confirming the destruction provided they so request the certificate within five days of being informed the destruction is required.

5.24 Nothing in *paragraph 5.22* affects any separate requirement under the Criminal Procedure and Investigations Act 1996 to retain material in connection with criminal investigations.

6   Identification by body samples and impressions

(A) General

6.1   References to:
  (a) an 'intimate sample' mean a dental impression or sample of blood, semen or any other tissue fluid, urine, or pubic hair, or a swab taken from any part of a person's genitals or from a person's body orifice other than the mouth;

  (b) a 'non-intimate sample' means:
    (i) a sample of hair, other than pubic hair, which includes hair plucked with the root;

    (ii) a sample taken from a nail or from under a nail;

    (iii) a swab taken from any part of a person's body other than a part from which a swab taken would be an intimate sample;

    (iv) saliva;

    (v) a skin impression which means any record, other than a fingerprint, which is a record, in any form and produced by any method, of the skin pattern and other physical characteristics or features of the whole, or any part of, a person's foot or of any other part of their body.

(B) Action

(a) Intimate samples

6.2   PACE, section 62, provides that intimate samples may be taken under:
  (a) section 62(1), from a person in police detention only:
    (i) if a police officer of inspector rank or above has reasonable grounds to believe such an impression or sample will tend to confirm or disprove the suspect's involvement in a recordable offence and gives authorisation for a sample to be taken; and

    (ii) with the suspect's written consent;

  (b) section 62(1A), from a person not in police detention but from whom two or more non-intimate samples have been taken in the course of an investigation of an offence and the samples, though suitable, have proved insufficient if:
    (i) a police officer of inspector rank or above authorises it to be taken; and

    (ii) the person concerned gives their written consent.

6.3   Before a suspect is asked to provide an intimate sample, they must be warned that if they refuse without good cause, their refusal may harm their case if it comes to trial. If the suspect is in police detention and not legally represented, they must also be reminded of their entitlement to have free legal advice, see Code C, *paragraph 6.5*, and the reminder noted in the custody record. If *paragraph 6.2(b)* applies and the person is attending a station voluntarily, their entitlement to free legal advice as in Code C, *paragraph 3.21* shall be explained to them.

6.4   Dental impressions may only be taken by a registered dentist. Other intimate samples, except for samples of urine, may only be taken by a registered medical practitioner or registered nurse or registered paramedic.

(b) Non-intimate samples

6.5   A non-intimate sample may be taken from a detainee only with their written consent or if *paragraph 6.6* applies.

6.6   (a)   under section 63, a non-intimate sample may not be taken from a person without consent and the consent must be in writing

     (aa) A non-intimate sample may be taken from a person without the appropriate consent in the following circumstances:

        (i)   under section 63(2A) where the person is in police detention as a consequence of his arrest for a recordable offence and he has not had a non-intimate sample of the same type and from the same part of the body taken in the course of the investigation of the offence by the police or he has had such a sample taken but it proved insufficient.

        (ii)   Under section 63(3) (a) where he is being held in custody by the police on the authority of a court and an officer of at least the rank of inspector authorises it to be taken.

     (b)   under section 63(3A), from a person charged with a recordable offence or informed they will be reported for such an offence: and

        (i)   that person has not had a non-intimate sample taken from them in the course of the investigation; or

        (ii)   if they have had a sample taken, it proved unsuitable or insufficient for the same form of analysis; or

     (c)   under section 63(3B), from a person convicted of a recordable offence after the date on which that provision came into effect. PACE, section 63A, describes the circumstances in which a police officer may require a person convicted of a recordable offence to attend a police station for a non-intimate sample to be taken.

6.7   Reasonable force may be used, if necessary, to take a non-intimate sample from a person without their consent under the powers mentioned in *paragraph 6.6*.

6.8   Before any intimate sample is taken with consent or non-intimate sample is taken with, or without, consent, the person must be informed:

(a) of the reason for taking the sample;

(b) of the grounds on which the relevant authority has been given;

(c) that the sample or information derived from the sample may be retained and subject of a speculative search, unless their destruction is required.

6.9 When clothing needs to be removed in circumstances likely to cause embarrassment to the person, no person of the opposite sex who is not a registered medical practitioner or registered health care professional shall be present, (unless in the case of a juvenile, mentally disordered or mentally vulnerable person, that person specifically requests the presence of an appropriate adult of the opposite sex who is readily available) nor shall anyone whose presence is unnecessary. However, in the case of a juvenile, this is subject to the overriding proviso that such a removal of clothing may take place in the absence of the appropriate adult only if the juvenile signifies, in their presence, that they prefer the adult's absence and they agree.

(c) Documentation

6.10 A record of the reasons for taking a sample or impression and, if applicable, of its destruction must be made as soon as practicable. If force is used, a record shall be made of the circumstances and those present. If written consent is given to the taking of a sample or impression, the fact must be recorded in writing.

6.11 A record must be made of a warning given as required by *paragraph 6.3*.

6.12 A record shall be made of the fact that a person has been informed as in *paragraph 6.8(c)* that samples may be subject of a speculative search.

CIVIL PROCEDURE RULES 1998

PART 32
EVIDENCE

32.1   Power of court to control evidence

(1)   The court may control the evidence by giving directions as to —
- (a)   the issues on which it requires evidence;
- (b)   the nature of the evidence which it requires to decide those issues; and
- (c)   the way in which the evidence is to be placed before the court.

(2)   The court may use its power under this rule to exclude evidence that would otherwise be admissible.

(3)   The court may limit cross-examination(GL).

32.2   Evidence of witnesses – general rule

(1)   The general rule is that any fact which needs to be proved by the evidence of witnesses is to be proved —
- (a)   at trial, by their oral evidence given in public; and
- (b)   at any other hearing, by their evidence in writing.

(2)   This is subject —
- (a)   to any provision to the contrary contained in these Rules or elsewhere; or
- (b)   to any order of the court.

32.3   Evidence by video link or other means

The court may allow a witness to give evidence through a video link or by other means.

32.4   Requirement to serve witness statements for use at trial

(1)   A witness statement is a written statement signed by a person which contains the evidence which that person would be allowed to give orally.

(2)   The court will order a party to serve on the other parties any witness statement of the oral evidence which the party serving the statement intends to rely on in relation to any issues of fact to be decided at the trial.

(3)   The court may give directions as to —
- (a)   the order in which witness statements are to be served; and
- (b)   whether or not the witness statements are to be filed.

32.5   Use at trial of witness statements which have been served

(1)   If —
- (a)   a party has served a witness statement; and
- (b)   he wishes to rely at trial on the evidence of the witness who made the statement,

he must call the witness to give oral evidence unless the court orders otherwise or he puts the statement in as hearsay evidence.

(Part 33 contains provisions about hearsay evidence)

(2) Where a witness is called to give oral evidence under paragraph (1), his witness statement shall stand as his evidence in chief(GL) unless the court orders otherwise.

(3) A witness giving oral evidence at trial may with the permission of the court —
   (a) amplify his witness statement; and
   (b) give evidence in relation to new matters which have arisen since the witness statement was served on the other parties.

(4) The court will give permission under paragraph (3) only if it considers that there is good reason not to confine the evidence of the witness to the contents of his witness statement.

(5) If a party who has served a witness statement does not —
   (a) call the witness to give evidence at trial; or
   (b) put the witness statement in as hearsay evidence, any other party may put the witness statement in as hearsay evidence.

32.6 Evidence in proceedings other than at trial

(1) Subject to paragraph (2), the general rule is that evidence at hearings other than the trial is to be by witness statement unless the court, a practice direction or any other enactment requires otherwise.

(2) At hearings other than the trial, a party may, rely on the matters set out in —
   (a) his statement of case; or
   (b) his application notice, if the statement of case or application notice is verified by a statement of truth.

32.7 Order for cross-examination

(1) Where, at a hearing other than the trial, evidence is given in writing, any party may apply to the court for permission to cross-examine the person giving the evidence.

(2) If the court gives permission under paragraph (1) but the person in question does not attend as required by the order, his evidence may not be used unless the court gives permission.

32.8 Form of witness statement

A witness statement must comply with the requirements set out in the relevant practice direction.

(Part 22 requires a witness statement to be verified by a statement of truth)

32.9   Witness summaries

(1)   A party who —
   (a)   is required to serve a witness statement for use at trial; but
   (b)   is unable to obtain one, may apply, without notice, for permission to serve a witness summary instead.

(2)   A witness summary is a summary of —
   (a)   the evidence, if known, which would otherwise be included in a witness statement; or
   (b)   if the evidence is not known, the matters about which the party serving the witness summary proposes to question the witness.

(3)   Unless the court orders otherwise, a witness summary must include the name and address of the intended witness.

(4)   Unless the court orders otherwise, a witness summary must be served within the period in which a witness statement would have had to be served.

(5)   Where a party serves a witness summary, so far as practicable rules 32.4 (requirement to serve witness statements for use at trial), 32.5(3) (amplifying witness statements), and 32.8 (form of witness statement) shall apply to the summary.

32.10   Consequence of failure to serve witness statement or summary

If a witness statement or a witness summary for use at trial is not served in respect of an intended witness within the time specified by the court, then the witness may not be called to give oral evidence unless the court gives permission.

32.11   Cross-examination on a witness statement

Where a witness is called to give evidence at trial, he may be cross-examined on his witness statement whether or not the statement or any part of it was referred to during the witness's evidence in chief(GL).

32.12   Use of witness statements for other purposes

(1)   Except as provided by this rule, a witness statement may be used only for the purpose of the proceedings in which it is served.

(2)   Paragraph (1) does not apply if and to the extent that —
   (a)   the witness gives consent in writing to some other use of it;
   (b)   the court gives permission for some other use; or
   (c)   the witness statement has been put in evidence at a hearing held in public.

32.13   Availability of witness statements for inspection

(1) A witness statement which stands as evidence in chief(GL) is open to inspection during the course of the trial unless the court otherwise directs.

(2) Any person may ask for a direction that a witness statement is not open to inspection.

(3) The court will not make a direction under paragraph (2) unless it is satisfied that a witness statement should not be open to inspection because of —
    (a)   the interests of justice;
    (b)   the public interest;
    (c)   the nature of any expert medical evidence in the statement;
    (d)   the nature of any confidential information (including information relating to personal financial matters) in the statement; or
    (e)   the need to protect the interests of any child or protected party.

(4) The court may exclude from inspection words or passages in the statement.

32.14   False statements

(1) Proceedings for contempt of court may be brought against a person if he makes, or causes to be made, a false statement in a document verified by a statement of truth without an honest belief in its truth.

(Part 22 makes provision for a statement of truth)

(2) Proceedings under this rule may be brought only —
    (a)   by the Attorney General; or
    (b)   with the permission of the court.

32.15   Affidavit evidence

(1) Evidence must be given by affidavit(GL) instead of or in addition to a witness statement if this is required by the court, a provision contained in any other rule, a practice direction or any other enactment.

(2) Nothing in these Rules prevents a witness giving evidence by affidavit(GL) at a hearing other than the trial if he chooses to do so in a case where paragraph (1) does not apply, but the party putting forward the affidavit(GL) may not recover the additional cost of making it from any other party unless the court orders otherwise.

32.16   Form of affidavit

An affidavit(GL) must comply with the requirements set out in the relevant practice direction.

32.17   Affidavit made outside the jurisdiction

A person may make an affidavit(GL) outside the jurisdiction in accordance with —

(a)   this Part; or

(b)   the law of the place where he makes the affidavit(GL).

32.18   Notice to admit facts

(1)   A party may serve notice on another party requiring him to admit the facts, or the part of the case of the serving party, specified in the notice.

(2)   A notice to admit facts must be served no later than 21 days before the trial.

(3)   Where the other party makes any admission in response to the notice, the admission may be used against him only —
(a)   in the proceedings in which the notice to admit is served; and

(b)   by the party who served the notice.

(4)   The court may allow a party to amend or withdraw any admission made by him on such terms as it thinks just.

32.19   Notice to admit or produce documents

(1)   A party shall be deemed to admit the authenticity of a document disclosed to him under Part 31 (disclosure and inspection of documents) unless he serves notice that he wishes the document to be proved at trial.

(2)   A notice to prove a document must be served —
(a)   by the latest date for serving witness statements; or

(b)   within 7 days of disclosure of the document, whichever is later.

32.20   Notarial acts and instruments

A notarial act or instrument may be received in evidence without further proof as duly authenticated in accordance with the requirements of law unless the contrary is proved.

PRACTICE DIRECTION
EVIDENCE IN GENERAL

1.1

Rule 32.2 sets out how evidence is to be given and facts are to be proved.

1.2

Evidence at a hearing other than the trial should normally be given by witness statement (see paragraph 17 onwards). However a witness may give evidence by affidavit if he wishes to do so (and see paragraph 1.4 below).

1.3

Statements of case (see paragraph 26 onwards) and application notices may also be used as evidence provided that their contents have been verified by a statement of truth.

(For information regarding evidence by deposition see Part 34 and the practice direction which supplements it.)

1.4

Affidavits must be used as evidence in the following instances:

(1) where sworn evidence is required by an enactment, rule, order or practice direction,

(2) in any application for a search order, a freezing injunction, or an order requiring an occupier to permit another to enter his land, and

(3) in any application for an order against anyone for alleged contempt of court.

1.5

If a party believes that sworn evidence is required by a court in another jurisdiction for any purpose connected with the proceedings, he may apply to the court for a direction that evidence shall be given only by affidavit on any pre-trial applications.

1.6

The court may give a direction under rule 32.15 that evidence shall be given by affidavit instead of or in addition to a witness statement or statement of case:

(1) on its own initiative, or

(2) after any party has applied to the court for such a direction.

1.7

An affidavit, where referred to in the Civil Procedure Rules or a practice direction, also means an affirmation unless the context requires otherwise.

AFFIDAVITS

Deponent

2

A deponent is a person who gives evidence by affidavit or affirmation.

Heading

3.1

The affidavit should be headed with the title of the proceedings (see paragraph 4 of the practice direction supplementing Part 7 and paragraph 7 of the practice direction supplementing Part 20); where the proceedings are between several parties with the same status it is sufficient to identify the parties as follows:

	Number:
A.B. (and others)	Claimants/Applicants
C.D. (and others)	Defendants/Respondents (as appropriate)

3.2

At the top right hand corner of the first page (and on the backsheet) there should be clearly written:

(1) the party on whose behalf it is made,

(2) the initials and surname of the deponent,

(3) the number of the affidavit in relation to that deponent,

(4) the identifying initials and number of each exhibit referred to, and

(5) the date sworn.

Body of Affidavit

4.1

The affidavit must, if practicable, be in the deponent's own words, the affidavit should be expressed in the first person and the deponent should:

(1) commence 'I (*full name*) of (*address*) state on oath . . . . . .',

(2) if giving evidence in his professional, business or other occupational capacity, give the address at which he works in (1) above, the position he holds and the name of his firm or employer,

(3) give his occupation or, if he has none, his description, and

(4) state if he is a party to the proceedings or employed by a party to the proceedings, if it be the case.

4.2

An affidavit must indicate:

(1) which of the statements in it are made from the deponent's own knowledge and which are matters of information or belief, and

(2) the source for any matters of information or belief.

4.3

Where a deponent:

(1) refers to an exhibit or exhibits, he should state 'there is now shown to me marked '. . .' the (*description of exhibit*)', and

(2) makes more than one affidavit (to which there are exhibits) in the same proceedings, the numbering of the exhibits should run consecutively throughout and not start again with each affidavit.

Jurat

5.1

The jurat of an affidavit is a statement set out at the end of the document which authenticates the affidavit.

5.2

It must:

(1) be signed by all deponents,

(2) be completed and signed by the person before whom the affidavit was sworn whose name and qualification must be printed beneath his signature,

(3) contain the full address of the person before whom the affidavit was sworn, and

(4) follow immediately on from the text and not be put on a separate page.

Format of Affidavits

6.1

An affidavit should:

(1) be produced on durable quality A4 paper with a 3.5cm margin,

(2) be fully legible and should normally be typed on one side of the paper only,

(3) where possible, be bound securely in a manner which would not hamper filing, or otherwise each page should be endorsed with the case number and should bear the initials of the deponent and of the person before whom it was sworn,

(4) have the pages numbered consecutively as a separate document (or as one of several documents contained in a file),

(5) be divided into numbered paragraphs,

(6) have all numbers, including dates, expressed in figures, and

(7) give the reference to any document or documents mentioned either in the margin or in bold text in the body of the affidavit.

6.2

It is usually convenient for an affidavit to follow the chronological sequence of events or matters dealt with; each paragraph of an affidavit should as far as possible be confined to a distinct portion of the subject.

Inability of Deponent to read or sign Affidavit

7.1

Where an affidavit is sworn by a person who is unable to read or sign it, the person before whom the affidavit is sworn must certify in the jurat that:

(1) he read the affidavit to the deponent,

(2) the deponent appeared to understand it, and

(3) the deponent signed or made his mark, in his presence.

7.2

If that certificate is not included in the jurat, the affidavit may not be used in evidence unless the court is satisfied that it was read to the deponent and that he appeared to understand it. Two versions of the form of jurat with the certificate are set out at Annex 1 to this practice direction.

Alterations to Affidavits

8.1

Any alteration to an affidavit must be initialled by both the deponent and the person before whom the affidavit was sworn.

8.2

An affidavit which contains an alteration that has not been initialled may be filed or used in evidence only with the permission of the court.

Who may administer oaths and take Affidavits

9.1

Only the following may administer oaths and take affidavits:

(1) Commissioners for oaths,

(2) Practising solicitors,

(3) other persons specified by statute,

(4) certain officials of the Supreme Court,

(5) a circuit judge or district judge,

(6) any justice of the peace, and

(7) certain officials of any county court appointed by the judge of that court for the purpose.

9.2

An affidavit must be sworn before a person independent of the parties or their representatives.

Filing of Affidavits

10.1

If the court directs that an affidavit is to be filed, it must be filed in the court or Division, or Office or Registry of the court or Division where the action in which it was or is to be used, is proceeding or will proceed.

10.2

Where an affidavit is in a foreign language:

(1) the party wishing to rely on it —
    (a) must have it translated, and
    (b) must file the foreign language affidavit with the court, and

(2) the translator must make and file with the court an affidavit verifying the translation and exhibiting both the translation and a copy of the foreign language affidavit.

EXHIBITS

Manner of Exhibiting Documents

11.1

A document used in conjunction with an affidavit should be:

(1) produced to and verified by the deponent, and remain separate from the affidavit, and

(2) identified by a declaration of the person before whom the affidavit was sworn.

11.2

The declaration should be headed with the name of the proceedings in the same way as the affidavit.

11.3

The first page of each exhibit should be marked:

(1) as in paragraph 3.2 above, and

(2) with the exhibit mark referred to in the affidavit.

Letters

12.1

Copies of individual letters should be collected together and exhibited in a bundle or bundles. They should be arranged in chronological order with the earliest at the top, and firmly secured.

12.2

When a bundle of correspondence is exhibited, the exhibit should have a front page attached stating that the bundle consists of original letters and copies. They should be arranged and secured as above and numbered consecutively.

Other documents

13.1

Photocopies instead of original documents may be exhibited provided the originals are made available for inspection by the other parties before the hearing and by the judge at the hearing.

13.2

Court documents must not be exhibited (official copies of such documents prove themselves).

13.3

Where an exhibit contains more than one document, a front page should be attached setting out a list of the documents contained in the exhibit; the list should contain the dates of the documents.

Exhibits other than documents

14.1

Items other than documents should be clearly marked with an exhibit number or letter in such a manner that the mark cannot become detached from the exhibit.

14.2

Small items may be placed in a container and the container appropriately marked.

General provisions

15.1

Where an exhibit contains more than one document:

(1) the bundle should not be stapled but should be securely fastened in a way that does not hinder the reading of the documents, and

(2) the pages should be numbered consecutively at bottom centre.

15.2

Every page of an exhibit should be clearly legible; typed copies of illegible documents should be included, paginated with 'a' numbers.

15.3

Where affidavits and exhibits have become numerous, they should be put into separate bundles and the pages numbered consecutively throughout.

15.4

Where on account of their bulk the service of exhibits or copies of exhibits on the other parties would be difficult or impracticable, the directions of the court should be sought as to arrangements for bringing the exhibits to the attention of the other parties and as to their custody pending trial.

Affirmations

16

All provisions in this or any other practice direction relating to affidavits apply to affirmations with the following exceptions:

(1) the deponent should commence 'I (*name*) of (*address*) do solemnly and sincerely affirm . . . . . .', and

(2) in the jurat the word 'sworn' is replaced by the word 'affirmed'.

WITNESS STATEMENTS

Heading

17.1

The witness statement should be headed with the title of the proceedings (see paragraph 4 of the practice direction supplementing Part 7 and paragraph 7 of the practice direction supplementing Part 20); where the proceedings are between several parties with the same status it is sufficient to identify the parties as follows:

	Number:
A.B. (and others)	Claimants/Applicants
C.D. (and others)	Defendants/Respondents (as appropriate)

17.2

At the top right hand corner of the first page there should be clearly written:

(1) the party on whose behalf it is made,

(2) the initials and surname of the witness,

(3) the number of the statement in relation to that witness,

(4) the identifying initials and number of each exhibit referred to, and

(5) the date the statement was made.

Body of Witness Statement

18.1

The witness statement must, if practicable, be in the intended witness's own words, the statement should be expressed in the first person and should also state:

(1) the full name of the witness,

(2) his place of residence or, if he is making the statement in his professional, business or other occupational capacity, the address at which he works, the position he holds and the name of his firm or employer,

(3) his occupation, or if he has none, his description, and

(4) the fact that he is a party to the proceedings or is the employee of such a party if it be the case.

18.2

A witness statement must indicate:

(1) which of the statements in it are made from the witness's own knowledge and which are matters of information or belief, and

(2) the source for any matters of information or belief.

18.3

An exhibit used in conjunction with a witness statement should be verified and identified by the witness and remain separate from the witness statement.

18.4

Where a witness refers to an exhibit or exhibits, he should state 'I refer to the (*description of exhibit*) marked '. . .' '.

18.5

The provisions of paragraphs 11.3 to 15.4 (exhibits) apply similarly to witness statements as they do to affidavits.

18.6

Where a witness makes more than one witness statement to which there are exhibits, in the same proceedings, the numbering of the exhibits should run consecutively throughout and not start again with each witness statement.

Format of Witness Statement

19.1

A witness statement should:

(**1**) be produced on durable quality A4 paper with a 3.5cm margin,

(**2**) be fully legible and should normally be typed on one side of the paper only,

(**3**) where possible, be bound securely in a manner which would not hamper filing, or otherwise each page should be endorsed with the case number and should bear the initials of the witness,

(**4**) have the pages numbered consecutively as a separate statement (or as one of several statements contained in a file),

(**5**) be divided into numbered paragraphs,

(**6**) have all numbers, including dates, expressed in figures, and

(**7**) give the reference to any document or documents mentioned either in the margin or in bold text in the body of the statement.

19.2

It is usually convenient for a witness statement to follow the chronological sequence of the events or matters dealt with, each paragraph of a witness statement should as far as possible be confined to a distinct portion of the subject.

Statement of Truth

20.1

A witness statement is the equivalent of the oral evidence which that witness would, if called, give in evidence; it must include a statement by the intended witness that he believes the facts in it are true.

20.2

To verify a witness statement the statement of truth is as follows:

'I believe that the facts stated in this witness statement are true'.

20.3

Attention is drawn to rule 32.14 which sets out the consequences of verifying a witness statement containing a false statement without an honest belief in its truth.

(Paragraph 3A of the practice direction to Part 22 sets out the procedure to be followed where the person who should sign a document which is verified by a statement of truth is unable to read or sign the document.)

Alterations to witness statements

22.1

Any alteration to a witness statement must be initialled by the person making the statement or by the authorised person where appropriate (see paragraph 21).

22.2

A witness statement which contains an alteration that has not been initialled may be used in evidence only with the permission of the court.

Filing of witness statements

23.1

If the court directs that a witness statement is to be filed, it must be filed in the court or Division, or Office or Registry of the court or Division where the action in which it was or is to be used, is proceeding or will proceed.

23.2

Where the court has directed that a witness statement in a foreign language is to be filed:

(1) the party wishing to rely on it must —
   (a) have it translated, and
   (b) file the foreign language witness statement with the court, and
(2) the translator must make and file with the court an affidavit verifying the translation and exhibiting both the translation and a copy of the foreign language witness statement.

Certificate of court officer

24.1

Where the court has ordered that a witness statement is not to be open to inspection by the public or that words or passages in the statement are not to be open to inspection the court officer will so certify on the statement and make any deletions directed by the court under rule 32.13(4).

Defects in affidavits, witness statements and exhibits

25.1

Where:

(1) an affidavit,

(2) a witness statement, or

(3) an exhibit to either an affidavit or a witness statement,

does not comply with Part 32 or this practice direction in relation to its form, the court may refuse to admit it as evidence and may refuse to allow the costs arising from its preparation.

25.2

Permission to file a defective affidavit or witness statement or to use a defective exhibit may be obtained from a judge in the court where the case is proceeding.

STATEMENTS OF CASE

26.1

A statement of case may be used as evidence in an interim application provided it is verified by a statement of truth.

26.2

To verify a statement of case the statement of truth should be set out as follows:

> '[I believe][the *(party on whose behalf the statement of case is being signed)* believes] that the facts stated in the statement of case are true'.

26.3

Attention is drawn to rule 32.14 which sets out the consequences of verifying a witness statement containing a false statement without an honest belief in its truth.

(For information regarding statements of truth see Part 22 and the practice direction which supplements it.)

(Practice directions supplementing Parts 7, 9 and 17 provide further information concerning statements of case.)

AGREED BUNDLES FOR HEARINGS

27.1

The court may give directions requiring the parties to use their best endeavours to agree a bundle or bundles of documents for use at any hearing.

27.2

All documents contained in bundles which have been agreed for use at a hearing shall be admissible at that hearing as evidence of their contents, unless —

(1) the court orders otherwise; or

(2) a party gives written notice of objection to the admissibility of particular documents.

28.1   Penalty

(1) Where a party alleges that a statement of truth or a disclosure statement is false the party shall refer that allegation to the court dealing with the claim in which the statement of truth or disclosure statement has been made.

(2) the court may —
   (a) excercise any of its powers under the rules;
   (b) initiate steps to consider if there is a contempt of court and, where there is, to punish it;

   (The practice direction to RSC Order 52 (Schedule 1) and CCR Order 29 (Schedule 2) makes provision where committal to prison is a possibility if contempt is proved)

   (c) direct the party making the allegation to refer the matter to the Attorney General with a request to him to consider whether he wishes to bring proceedings for contempt of court.

28.2

(1) An application to the Attorney General should be made to his chambers at 9 Buckingham Gate London SW1E 6JP in writing. The Attorney General will initially require a copy of the order recording the direction of the judge referring the matter to him and information which —
   (a) identifies the statement said to be false; and
   (b) explains —
      (i) why it is false, and
      (ii) why the maker knew it to be false at the time he made it;
   and
   (c) explains why contempt proceedings would be appropriate in the light of the overriding objective in Part 1 of the Civil Procedure Rules.

(2) The practice of the Attorney General is to prefer an application that comes from the court, and so has received preliminary consideration by a judge, to one made direct to him by a party to the claim in which the alleged contempt occurred without prior consideration by the court.

An application to the Attorney General is not a way of appealing against, or reviewing, the decision of the judge.

28.3

Where a party makes an application to the court for permission for that party to commence proceedings for contempt of court, it must be supported by written evidence containing the information specified in paragraph 28.2(1) and the result of the application to the Attorney General made by the applicant.

28.4

The rules do not change the law of contempt or introduce new categories of contempt. A person applying to commence such proceedings should consider whether the incident complained of does amount to contempt of court and whether such proceedings would further the overriding objective in Part 1 of the Civil Procedure Rules.

VIDEO CONFERENCING

29.1

Guidance on the use of video conferencing in the civil courts is set out at Annex 3 to this practice direction.

A list of the sites which are available for video conferencing can be found on Her Majesty's Courts Service website at www.hmcourts-service.gov.uk.

ANNEX 1

Certificate to be used where a deponent to an affidavit is unable to read or sign it

Sworn at . . . . this . . . . . . day of . . . . Before me, I having first read over the contents of this affidavit to the deponent [*if there are exhibits, add* 'and explained the nature and effect of the exhibits referred to in it'] who appeared to understand it and approved its content as accurate, and made his mark on the affidavit in my presence.

Or; (after, *Before me*) the witness to the mark of the deponent having been first sworn that he had read over etc. (*as above*) and that he saw him make his mark on the affidavit. (*Witness must sign*).

Certificate to be used where a deponent to an affirmation is unable to read or sign it

Affirmed at . . . . this . . . . . . day of . . . . Before me, I having first read over the contents of this affirmation to the deponent [*if there are exhibits, add* 'and explained the nature and effect of the exhibits referred to in it'] who appeared to understand it and approved its content as accurate, and made his mark on the affirmation in my presence.

Or, (after, *Before me*) the witness to the mark of the deponent having been first sworn that he had read over etc. (*as above*) and that he saw him make his mark on the affirmation. (*Witness must sign*).

ANNEX 2

Omitted

ANNEX 3

VIDEO CONFERENCING GUIDANCE

This guidance is for the use of video conferencing (VCF) in civil proceedings. It is in part based, with permission, upon the protocol of the Federal Court of Australia. It is intended to provide a guide to all persons involved in the use of VCF, although it does not attempt to cover all the practical questions which might arise.

Video conferencing generally

1

The guidance covers the use of VCF equipment both (a) in a courtroom, whether via equipment which is permanently placed there or via a mobile unit, and (b) in a separate studio or conference room. In either case, the location at which the judge sits is referred to as the 'local site'. The other site or sites to and from which transmission is made are referred to as 'the remote site' and in any particular case any such site may be another courtroom. The guidance applies to cases where VCF is used for the taking of evidence and also to its use for other parts of any legal proceedings (for example, interim applications, case management conferences, pre-trial reviews).

2

VCF may be a convenient way of dealing with any part of proceedings: it can involve considerable savings in time and cost. Its use for the taking of evidence from overseas witnesses will, in particular, be likely to achieve a material saving of costs, and such savings may also be achieved by its use for taking domestic evidence. It is, however, inevitably not as ideal as having the witness physically present in court. Its convenience should not therefore be allowed to dictate its use. A judgment must be made in every case in which the use of VCF is being considered not only as to whether it will achieve an overall cost saving but as to whether its use will be likely to be beneficial to the efficient, fair and economic disposal of the litigation. In particular, it needs to be recognised that the degree of control a court can exercise over a witness at the remote site is or may be more limited than it can exercise over a witness physically before it.

3

When used for the taking of evidence, the objective should be to make the VCF session as close as possible to the usual practice in a trial court where evidence is taken in open court. To gain the maximum benefit, several differences have to be taken into account. Some matters, which are taken for granted when evidence is taken in the conventional way, take on a different dimension when it is taken by VCF: for example, the administration of the oath, ensuring that the witness understands who is at the local site and what their various roles are, the raising of any objections to the evidence and the use of documents.

4

It should not be presumed that all foreign governments are willing to allow their nationals or others within their jurisdiction to be examined before a court in England or Wales by means of VCF. If there is any doubt about this, enquiries should be directed to the Foreign and Commonwealth Office (International Legal Matters Unit, Consular Division) with a view to ensuring that the country from which the evidence is to be taken raises no objection to it at diplomatic level. The party who is directed to be responsible for arranging the VCF (see paragraph 8 below) will be required to make all necessary inquiries about this well in advance of the VCF and must be able to inform the court what those inquiries were and of their outcome.

5

Time zone differences need to be considered when a witness abroad is to be examined in England or Wales by VCF. The convenience of the witness, the parties, their representatives and the court must all be taken into account. The cost of the use of a commercial studio is usually greater outside normal business hours.

6

Those involved with VCF need to be aware that, even with the most advanced systems currently available, there are the briefest of delays between the receipt of the picture and that of the accompanying sound. If due allowance is not made for this, there will be a tendency to 'speak over' the witness, whose voice will continue to be heard for a millisecond or so after he or she appears on the screen to have finished speaking.

7

With current technology, picture quality is good, but not as good as a television picture. The quality of the picture is enhanced if those appearing on VCF monitors keep their movements to a minimum.

Preliminary arrangements

8

The court's permission is required for any part of any proceedings to be dealt with by means of VCF. Before seeking a direction, the applicant should notify the listing officer, diary manager or other appropriate court officer of the intention to seek it, and should enquire as to the availability of court VCF equipment for the day or days of the proposed VCF. The application for a direction should be made to the Master, District Judge or Judge, as may be appropriate. If all parties consent to a direction, permission can be sought by letter, fax or e-mail, although the court may still require an oral hearing. All parties are entitled to be heard on whether or not such a direction should be given and as to its terms. If a witness at a remote site is to give evidence by an interpreter, consideration should be given at this stage as to whether the interpreter should be at the local site or the remote site. If a VCF direction is given, arrangements for the transmission will then need to be made. The court will ordinarily direct that the party seeking permission to use VCF is to be responsible for this. That party is hereafter referred to as 'the VCF arranging party'.

9

Subject to any order to the contrary, all costs of the transmission, including the costs of hiring equipment and technical personnel to operate it, will initially be the responsibility of, and must be met by, the VCF arranging party. All reasonable efforts should be made to keep the transmission to a minimum and so keep the costs down. All such costs will be considered to be part of the costs of the proceedings and the court will determine at such subsequent time as is convenient or appropriate who, as between the parties, should be responsible for them and (if appropriate) in what proportions.

10

The local site will, if practicable, be a courtroom but it may instead be an appropriate studio or conference room. The VCF arranging party must contact the listing officer, diary manager or other appropriate officer of the court which made the VCF direction and make arrangements for the VCF transmission. Details of the remote site, and of the equipment to be used both at the local site (if not being supplied by the court) and the remote site (including the number of ISDN lines and connection speed), together with all necessary contact names and telephone numbers, will have to be provided to the listing officer, diary manager or other court officer. The court will need to be satisfied that any equipment provided by the parties for use at the local site and also that at the remote site is of sufficient quality for a satisfactory transmission. The VCF arranging party must ensure that an appropriate person will be present at the local site to supervise the operation of the VCF throughout the transmission in order to deal with any technical problems. That party must also arrange for a technical assistant to be similarly present at the remote site for like purposes.

11

It is recommended that the judge, practitioners and witness should arrive at their respective VCF sites about 20 minutes prior to the scheduled commencement of the transmission.

12

If the local site is not a courtroom, but a conference room or studio, the judge will need to determine who is to sit where. The VCF arranging party must take care to ensure that the number of microphones is adequate for the speakers and that the panning of the camera for the practitioners' table encompasses all legal representatives so that the viewer can see everyone seated there.

13

The proceedings, wherever they may take place, form part of a trial to which the public is entitled to have access (unless the court has determined that they should be heard in private). If the local site is to be a studio or conference room, the VCF arranging party must ensure that it provides sufficient accommodation to enable a reasonable number of members of the public to attend.

14

In cases where the local site is a studio or conference room, the VCF arranging party should make arrangements, if practicable, for the royal coat of arms to be placed above the judge's seat.

15

In cases in which the VCF is to be used for the taking of evidence, the VCF arranging party must arrange for recording equipment to be provided by the court which made the VCF direction so that the evidence can be recorded. An associate will normally be present to operate the recording equipment when the local site is a courtroom. The VCF arranging party should take steps to ensure that an associate is present to do likewise when it is a studio or conference room. The equipment should be set up and tested before the VCF transmission. It will often be a valuable safeguard for the VCF arranging party also to arrange for the provision of recording equipment at the remote site. This will provide a useful back-up if there is any reduction in sound quality during the transmission. A direction from the court for the making of such a back-up recording must, however, be obtained first. This is because the proceedings are court proceedings and, save as directed by the court, no other recording of them must be made. The court will direct what is to happen to the back-up recording.

16

Some countries may require that any oath or affirmation to be taken by a witness accord with local custom rather than the usual form of oath or affirmation used in England and Wales. The VCF arranging party must make all appropriate prior inquiries and put in place all arrangements necessary to enable the oath or affirmation to be taken in accordance with any local custom. That party must be in a position to inform the court what those inquiries were, what their outcome was and what arrangements have been made. If the oath or affirmation can be administered in the manner normal in England and Wales, the VCF arranging party must arrange in advance to have the appropriate holy book at the remote site. The associate will normally administer the oath.

17

Consideration will need to be given in advance to the documents to which the witness is likely to be referred. The parties should endeavour to agree on this. It will usually be most convenient for a bundle of the copy documents to be prepared in advance, which the VCF arranging party should then send to the remote site.

18

Additional documents are sometimes quite properly introduced during the course of a witness's evidence. To cater for this, the VCF arranging party should ensure that equipment is available to enable documents to be transmitted between sites during the course of the VCF transmission. Consideration should be given to whether to use a document camera. If it is decided to use one, arrangements for its use will need to be established in advance. The panel operator will need to know the number and size of documents or objects if their images are to be sent by document camera. In many cases, a simpler and sufficient alternative will be to ensure that there are fax transmission and reception facilities at the participating sites.

The hearing

19

The procedure for conducting the transmission will be determined by the judge. He will determine who is to control the cameras. In cases where the VCF is being used for an application in the course of the proceedings, the judge will ordinarily not enter the local site until both sites are on line. Similarly, at the conclusion of the hearing, he will ordinarily leave the local site while both sites are still on line. The following paragraphs apply primarily to cases where the VCF is being used for the taking of the evidence of a witness at a remote site. In all cases, the judge will need to decide whether court dress is appropriate when using VCF facilities. It might be appropriate when transmitting from courtroom to courtroom. It might not be when a commercial facility is being used.

20

At the beginning of the transmission, the judge will probably wish to introduce himself and the advocates to the witness. He will probably want to know who is at the remote site and will invite the witness to introduce himself and anyone else who is with him. He may wish to give directions as to the seating arrangements at the remote site so that those present are visible at the local site during the taking of the evidence. He will probably wish to explain to the witness the method of taking the oath or of affirming, the manner in which the evidence will be taken, and who will be conducting the examination and cross-examination. He will probably also wish to inform the witness of the matters referred to in paragraphs 6 and 7 above (co-ordination of picture with sound, and picture quality).

21

The examination of the witness at the remote site should follow as closely as possible the practice adopted when a witness is in the courtroom. During examination, cross-examination and re-examination, the witness must be able to see the legal representative asking the question and also any other person (whether another legal representative or the judge) making any statements in regard to the witness's evidence. It will in practice be most convenient if everyone remains seated throughout the transmission.

PART 33
MISCELLANEOUS RULES ABOUT EVIDENCE

33.1   Introductory

In this Part —

(a) 'hearsay' means a statement made, otherwise than by a person while giving oral evidence in proceedings, which is tendered as evidence of the matters stated; and

(b) references to hearsay include hearsay of whatever degree.

33.2   Notice of intention to rely on hearsay evidence

(1) Where a party intends to rely on hearsay evidence at trial and either —
   (a) that evidence is to be given by a witness giving oral evidence; or
   (b) that evidence is contained in a witness statement of a person who is not being called to give oral evidence;

that party complies with section 2(1)(a) of the Civil Evidence Act 19951 serving a witness statement on the other parties in accordance with the court's order.

(2) Where paragraph (1)(b) applies, the party intending to rely on the hearsay evidence must, when he serves the witness statement —
   (a) inform the other parties that the witness is not being called to give oral evidence; and
   (b) give the reason why the witness will not be called.

(3) In all other cases where a party intends to rely on hearsay evidence at trial, that party complies with section 2(1)(a) of the Civil Evidence Act 1995 by serving a notice on the other parties which —

(a) identifies the hearsay evidence;

(b) states that the party serving the notice proposes to rely on the hearsay evidence at trial; and

(c) gives the reason why the witness will not be called.

(4) The party proposing to rely on the hearsay evidence must —

(a) serve the notice no later than the latest date for serving witness statements; and

(b) if the hearsay evidence is to be in a document, supply a copy to any party who requests him to do so.

33.3 Circumstances in which notice of intention to rely on hearsay evidence is not required

Section 2(1) of the Civil Evidence Act 1995 (duty to give notice of intention to rely on hearsay evidence) does not apply —

(a) to evidence at hearings other than trials;

(aa) to an affadavit or witness statement which is to be used at trial but which does not contain hearsay evidence;

(b) to a statement which a party to a probate action wishes to put in evidence and which is alleged to have been made by the person whose estate is the subject of the proceedings; or

(c) where the requirement is excluded by a practice direction.

33.4 Power to call witness for cross-examination on hearsay evidence

(1) Where a party —

(a) proposes to rely on hearsay evidence; and

(b) does not propose to call the person who made the original statement to give oral evidence,

the court may, on the application of any other party, permit that party to call the maker of the statement to be cross-examined on the contents of the statement.

(2) An application for permission to cross-examine under this rule must be made not more than 14 days after the day on which a notice of intention to rely on the hearsay evidence was served on the applicant.

33.5 Credibility

(1) Where a party —

(a) proposes to rely on hearsay evidence; but

(b) does not propose to call the person who made the original statement to give oral evidence; and

(c) another party wishes to call evidence to attack the credibility of the person who made the statement, the party who so wishes must give notice of his intention to the party who proposes to give the hearsay statement in evidence.

(2) A party must give notice under paragraph (1) not more than 14 days after the day on which a hearsay notice relating to the hearsay evidence was served on him.

33.6 Use of plans, photographs and models as evidence

(1) This rule applies to evidence (such as a plan, photograph or model) which is not —
   (a) contained in a witness statement, affidavit (GL) or expert's report;
   (b) to be given orally at trial; or
   (c) evidence of which prior notice must be given under rule 33.2.

(2) This rule includes documents which may be received in evidence without further proof under section 9 of the Civil Evidence Act 19952.

(3) Unless the court orders otherwise the evidence shall not be receivable at a trial unless the party intending to put it in evidence has given notice to the other parties in accordance with this rule.

(4) Where the party intends to use the evidence as evidence of any fact then, except where paragraph (6) applies, he must give notice not later than the latest date for serving witness statements.

(5) He must give notice at least 21 days before the hearing at which he proposes to put in the evidence, if —
   (a) there are not to be witness statements; or
   (b) he intends to put in the evidence solely in order to disprove an allegation made in a witness statement.

(6) Where the evidence forms part of expert evidence, he must give notice when the expert's report is served on the other party.

(7) Where the evidence is being produced to the court for any reason other than as part of factual or expert evidence, he must give notice at least 21 days before the hearing at which he proposes to put in the evidence.

(8) Where a party has given notice that he intends to put in the evidence, he must give every other party an opportunity to inspect it and to agree to its admission without further proof.

33.7 Evidence of finding on question of foreign law

(1) This rule sets out the procedure which must be followed by a party who intends to put in evidence a finding on a question of foreign law by virtue of section 4(2) of the Civil Evidence Act 19723.

(2) He must give any other party notice of his intention.

(3) He must give the notice —
   (a) if there are to be witness statements, not later than the latest date for serving them; or

(b) otherwise, not less than 21 days before the hearing at which he proposes to put the finding in evidence.

(4) The notice must —
(a) specify the question on which the finding was made; and
(b) enclose a copy of a document where it is reported or recorded.

33.8 Evidence of consent of trustee to act

A document purporting to contain the written consent of a person to act as trustee and to bear his signature verified by some other person is evidence of such consent.

33.9 Human Rights

(1) This rule applies where a claim is —
(a) for a remedy under section 7 of the Human Rights Act 1998 in respect of a judicial act which is alleged to have infringed the claimant's Article 5 Convention rights; and
(b) based on a finding by a court or tribunal that the claimant's Convention rights have been infringed.

(2) The court hearing the claim —
(a) may proceed on the basis of the finding of that other court or tribunal that there has been an infringement but it is not required to do so, and
(b) may reach its own conclusion in the light of that finding and of the evidence heard by that other court or tribunal.

PART 34
WITNESSES, DEPOSITIONS AND EVIDENCE FOR FOREIGN COURTS

I WITNESSES AND DEPOSITIONS

I WITNESSES AND DEPOSITIONS

Scope of this Section

34.1

(1) This Section of this Part provides —
    (a) for the circumstances in which a person may be required to attend court to give evidence or to produce a document; and

   (b) for a party to obtain evidence before a hearing to be used at the hearing.

(2) In this Section, reference to a hearing includes a reference to the trial.

Witness summonses

34.2

(1) A witness summons is a document issued by the court requiring a witness to —

   (a) attend court to give evidence; or

   (b) produce documents to the court.

(2) A witness summons must be in the relevant practice form.

(3) There must be a separate witness summons for each witness.

(4) A witness summons may require a witness to produce documents to the court either —

   (a) on the date fixed for a hearing; or

   (b) on such date as the court may direct.

(5) The only documents that a summons under this rule can require a person to produce before a hearing are documents which that person could be required to produce at the hearing.

Issue of a witness summons

34.3

(1) A witness summons is issued on the date entered on the summons by the court.

(2) A party must obtain permission from the court where he wishes to —

   (a) have a summons issued less than 7 days before the date of the trial;

   (b) have a summons issued for a witness to attend court to give evidence or to produce documents on any date except the date fixed for the trial; or

   (c) have a summons issued for a witness to attend court to give evidence or to produce documents at any hearing except the trial.

(3) A witness summons must be issued by —

   (a) the court where the case is proceeding; or

   (b) the court where the hearing in question will be held.

(4) The court may set aside(GL) or vary a witness summons issued under this rule.

Witness summons in aid of inferior court or of tribunal

34.4

(1) The court may issue a witness summons in aid of an inferior court or of a tribunal.

(2) The court which issued the witness summons under this rule may set it aside.

(3) In this rule, 'inferior court or tribunal' means any court or tribunal that does not have power to issue a witness summons in relation to proceedings before it.

Time for serving a witness summons

34.5

(1) The general rule is that a witness summons is binding if it is served at least 7 days before the date on which the witness is required to attend before the court or tribunal.

(2) The court may direct that a witness summons shall be binding although it will be served less than 7 days before the date on which the witness is required to attend before the court or tribunal.

(3) A witness summons which is —
   (a)   served in accordance with this rule; and
   (b)   requires the witness to attend court to give evidence,
   is binding until the conclusion of the hearing at which the attendance of the witness is required.

Who is to serve a witness summons

34.6

(1) A witness summons is to be served by the court unless the party on whose behalf it is issued indicates in writing, when he asks the court to issue the summons, that he wishes to serve it himself.

(2) Where the court is to serve the witness summons, the party on whose behalf it is issued must deposit, in the court office, the money to be paid or offered to the witness under rule 34.7.

Right of witness to travelling expenses and compensation for loss of time

34.7

At the time of service of a witness summons the witness must be offered or paid —
   (a)   a sum reasonably sufficient to cover his expenses in travelling to and from the court; and
   (b)   such sum by way of compensation for loss of time as may be specified in the relevant practice direction.

Evidence by deposition

34.8

(1) A party may apply for an order for a person to be examined before the hearing takes place.

(2) A person from whom evidence is to be obtained following an order under this rule is referred to as a 'deponent' and the evidence is referred to as a 'deposition'.

(3) An order under this rule shall be for a deponent to be examined on oath before —
   (a) a judge;
   (b) an examiner of the court; or
   (c) such other person as the court appoints.

(Rule 34.15 makes provision for the appointment of examiners of the court)

(4) The order may require the production of any document which the court considers is necessary for the purposes of the examination.

(5) The order must state the date, time and place of the examination.

(6) At the time of service of the order the deponent must be offered or paid —
   (a) a sum reasonably sufficient to cover his expenses in travelling to and from the place of examination; and
   (b) such sum by way of compensation for loss of time as may be specified in the relevant practice direction.

(7) Where the court makes an order for a deposition to be taken, it may also order the party who obtained the order to serve a witness statement or witness summary in relation to the evidence to be given by the person to be examined.

(Part 32 contains the general rules about witness statements and witness summaries)

Conduct of examination

34.9

(1) Subject to any directions contained in the order for examination, the examination must be conducted in the same way as if the witness were giving evidence at a trial.

(2) If all the parties are present, the examiner may conduct the examination of a person not named in the order for examination if all the parties and the person to be examined consent.

(3) The examiner may conduct the examination in private if he considers it appropriate to do so.

(4) The examiner must ensure that the evidence given by the witness is recorded in full.

(5) The examiner must send a copy of the deposition —

   (a) to the person who obtained the order for the examination of the witness; and

   (b) to the court where the case is proceeding.

(6) The party who obtained the order must send each of the other parties a copy of the deposition which he receives from the examiner.

Enforcing attendance of witness

34.10

(1) If a person served with an order to attend before an examiner —

   (a) fails to attend; or

   (b) refuses to be sworn for the purpose of the examination or to answer any lawful question or produce any document at the examination,

   a certificate of his failure or refusal, signed by the examiner, must be filed by the party requiring the deposition.

(2) On the certificate being filed, the party requiring the deposition may apply to the court for an order requiring that person to attend or to be sworn or to answer any question or produce any document, as the case may be.

(3) An application for an order under this rule may be made without notice.

(4) The court may order the person against whom an order is made under this rule to pay any costs resulting from his failure or refusal.

Use of deposition at a hearing

34.11

(1) A deposition ordered under rule 34.8 may be given in evidence at a hearing unless the court orders otherwise.

(2) A party intending to put in evidence a deposition at a hearing must serve notice of his intention to do so on every other party.

(3) He must serve the notice at least 21 days before the day fixed for the hearing.

(4) The court may require a deponent to attend the hearing and give evidence orally.

(5) Where a deposition is given in evidence at trial, it shall be treated as if it were a witness statement for the purposes of rule 32.13 (availability of witness statements for inspection).

Restrictions on subsequent use of deposition taken for the purpose of any hearing except the trial

34.12

(1) Where the court orders a party to be examined about his or any other assets for the purpose of any hearing except the trial, the deposition may be used only for the purpose of the proceedings in which the order was made.

(2) However, it may be used for some other purpose —
   (a) by the party who was examined;
   (b) if the party who was examined agrees; or
   (c) if the court gives permission.

Where a person to be examined is out of the jurisdiction — letter of request

34.13

(1) This rule applies where a party wishes to take a deposition from a person who is —
   (a) out of the jurisdiction; and
   (b) not in a Regulation State within the meaning of Section III of this Part.

(1A) The High Court may order the issue of a letter of request to the judicial authorities of the country in which the proposed deponent is.

(2) A letter of request is a request to a judicial authority to take the evidence of that person, or arrange for it to be taken.

(3) The High Court may make an order under this rule in relation to county court proceedings.

(4) If the government of a country allows a person appointed by the High Court to examine a person in that country, the High Court may make an order appointing a special examiner for that purpose.

(5) A person may be examined under this rule on oath or affirmation or in accordance with any procedure permitted in the country in which the examination is to take place.

(6) If the High Court makes an order for the issue of a letter of request, the party who sought the order must file —
   (a) the following documents and, except where paragraph (7) applies, a translation of them —
      (i) a draft letter of request;
      (ii) a statement of the issues relevant to the proceedings;
      (iii) a list of questions or the subject matter of questions to be put to the person to be examined; and
   (b) an undertaking to be responsible for the Secretary of State's expenses.

(7) There is no need to file a translation if —
   (a) English is one of the official languages of the country where the examination is to take place; or
   (b) a practice direction has specified that country as a country where no translation is necessary.

Letter of request — Proceeds of Crime Act 2002

34.13A

(1) This rule applies where a party to existing or contemplated proceedings in —
   (a) the High Court; or
   (b) a magistrates' court,

   under Part 5 of the Proceeds of Crime Act 20023 (civil recovery of the proceeds etc. of unlawful conduct) wishes to take a deposition from a person who is out of the jurisdiction.

(2) The High Court may, on the application of such a party, order the issue of a letter of request to the judicial authorities of the country in which the proposed deponent is.

(3) Paragraphs (4) to (7) of rule 34.13 shall apply irrespective of where the proposed deponent is, and rule 34.23 shall not apply in cases where the proposed deponent is in a Regulation State within the meaning of Section III of this Part.

Fees and expenses of examiner of the court

34.14

(1) An examiner of the court may charge a fee for the examination.

(2) He need not send the deposition to the court unless the fee is paid.

(3) The examiner's fees and expenses must be paid by the party who obtained the order for examination.

(4) If the fees and expenses due to an examiner are not paid within a reasonable time, he may report that fact to the court.

(5) The court may order the party who obtained the order for examination to deposit in the court office a specified sum in respect of the examiner's fees and, where it does so, the examiner will not be asked to act until the sum has been deposited.

(6) An order under this rule does not affect any decision as to the party who is ultimately to bear the costs of the examination.

Examiners of the court

34.15

(1) The Lord Chancellor shall appoint persons to be examiners of the court.

(2) The persons appointed shall be barristers or solicitor-advocates who have been practising for a period of not less than three years.

(3) The Lord Chancellor may revoke an appointment at any time.

II EVIDENCE FOR FOREIGN COURTS

Scope and interpretation

34.16

(1) This Section applies to an application for an order under the 1975 Act for evidence to be obtained, other than an application made as a result of a request by a court in another Regulation State.

(2) In this Section —
   (a) 'the 1975 Act' means the Evidence (Proceedings in Other Jurisdictions) Act 1975(2); and
   (b) 'Regulation State' has the same meaning as in Section III of this Part.

Application for order

34.17

An application for an order under the 1975 Act for evidence to be obtained —
   (a) must be —
      (i)   made to the High Court;
      (ii) supported by written evidence; and
      (iii) accompanied by the request as a result of which the application is made, and where appropriate, a translation of the request into English; and
   (b) may be made without notice.

Examination

34.18

(1) The court may order an examination to be taken before —
   (a) any fit and proper person nominated by the person applying for the order;
   (b) an examiner of the court; or
   (c) any other person whom the court considers suitable.

(2) Unless the court orders otherwise —
   (a) the examination will be taken as provided by rule 34.9; and
   (b) rule 34.10 applies.

(3) The court may make an order under rule 34.14 for payment of the fees and expenses of the examination.

Dealing with deposition

34.19

(1) The examiner must send the deposition of the witness to the Senior Master unless the court orders otherwise.

(2) The Senior Master will —
   (a) give a certificate sealed with the seal of the Supreme Court for use out of the jurisdiction identifying the following documents —
      (i) the request;
      (ii) the order of the court for examination; and
      (iii) the deposition of the witness; and
   (b) send the certificate and the documents referred to in paragraph (a) to —
      (i) the Secretary of State; or
      (ii) where the request was sent to the Senior Master by another person in accordance with a Civil Procedure Convention, to that other person, for transmission to the court or tribunal requesting the examination.

Claim to privilege

34.20

(1) This rule applies where —
   (a) a witness claims to be exempt from giving evidence on the ground specified in section 3(1)(b) of the 1975 Act; and
   (b) That claim is not supported or conceded as referred to in section 3(2) of that Act.

(2) The examiner may require the witness to give the evidence which he claims to be exempt from giving.

(3) Where the examiner does not require the witness to give that evidence, the court may order the witness to do so.

(4) An application for an order under paragraph (3) may be made by the person who obtained the order under section 2 of the 1975 Act.

(5) Where such evidence is taken —
   (a) it must be contained in a document separate from the remainder of the deposition;
   (b) the examiner will send to the Senior Master —
      (i) the deposition; and
      (ii) a signed statement setting out the claim to be exempt and the ground on which it was made;

(6) On receipt of the statement referred to in paragraph (5)(b)(ii), the Senior Master will —

(a) retain the document containing the part of the witness's evidence to which the claim to be exempt relates; and

(b) send the statement and a request to determine that claim to the foreign court or tribunal together with the documents referred to in rule 34.17.

(7) The Senior Master will —

(a) if the claim to be exempt is rejected by the foreign court or tribunal, send the document referred to in paragraph (5)(a) to that court or tribunal;

(b) if the claim is upheld, send the document to the witness; and

(c) in either case, notify the witness and person who obtained the order under section 2 of the foreign court or tribunal's decision.

Order under 1975 Act as applied by Patents Act 1977

34.21

Where an order is made for the examination of witnesses under section 1 of the 1975 Act as applied by section 92 of the Patents Act 19771 the court may permit an officer of the European Patent Office to —

(a) attend the examination and examine the witnesses; or

(b) request the court or the examiner before whom the examination takes place to put specified questions to them.

III TAKING OF EVIDENCE – MEMBER STATES OF THE EUROPEAN UNION

Interpretation

34.22

In this Section —

(a) 'designated court' has the meaning given in the relevant practice direction;

(b) 'Regulation State' has the same meaning as 'Member State' in the Taking of Evidence Regulation, that is all Member States except Denmark;

(c) 'the Taking of Evidence Regulation' means Council Regulation (EC) No. 1206/2001 of 28 May 2001 on co-operation between the courts of the Member States in the taking of evidence in civil and commercial matters.

Where a person to be examined is in another Regulation State

34.23

(1) Subject to rule 34.13A, this rule applies where a party wishes to take a deposition from a person who is in another Regulation State—

    (a) outside the jurisdiction; and

    (b) in a Regulation State.

(2) The court may order the issue of a request to a designated court ('the requested court') in the Regulation State in which the proposed deponent is.

(3) If the court makes an order for the issue of a request, the party who sought the order must file —

    (a) a draft Form A as set out in the annex to the Taking of Evidence Regulation (request for the taking of evidence);

    (b) except where paragraph (4) applies, a translation of the form;

    (c) an undertaking to be responsible for costs sought by the requested court in relation to —

        (i) fees paid to experts and interpreters; and

        (ii) where requested by that party, the use of special procedures or communications technology; and

    (d) an undertaking to be responsible for the court's expenses.

(4) There is no need to file a translation if —

    (a) English is one of the official languages of the Regulation State where the examination is to take place; or

    (b) the Regulation State has indicated, in accordance with the Taking of Evidence Regulation, that English is a language which it will accept.

(5) Where article 17 of the Taking of Evidence Regulation (direct taking of evidence by the requested court) allows evidence to be taken directly in another Regulation State, the court may make an order for the submission of a request in accordance with that article.

(6) If the court makes an order for the submission of a request under paragraph (5), the party who sought the order must file —

    (a) a draft Form I as set out in the annex to the Taking of Evidence Regulation (request for direct taking of evidence);

    (b) except where paragraph (4) applies, a translation of the form; and

    (c) an undertaking to be responsible for the court's expenses.

Evidence for courts of other Regulation States

34.24

(1) This rule applies where a court in another Regulation State ('the requesting court') issues a request for evidence to be taken from a person who is in the jurisdiction.

(2) An application for an order for evidence to be taken —

    (a) must be made to a designated court;

    (b) must be accompanied by —

        (i) the form of request for the taking of evidence as a result of which the application is made; and

(ii) where appropriate, a translation of the form of request; and

(c) may be made without notice.

(3) Rule 34.18(1) and (2) apply.

(4) The examiner must send —

(a) the deposition to the court for transmission to the requesting court; and

(b) a copy of the deposition to the person who obtained the order for evidence to be taken.

PRACTICE DIRECTION — DEPOSITIONS AND COURT ATTENDANCE BY WITNESSES THIS PRACTICE DIRECTION SUPPLEMENTS CPR PART 34

WITNESS SUMMONSES

Issue of witness summons

1.1

A witness summons may require a witness to:

(1) attend court to give evidence,

(2) produce documents to the court, or

(3) both,

on either a date fixed for the hearing or such date as the court may direct.

1.2

Two copies of the witness summons should be filed with the court for sealing, one of which will be retained on the court file.

1.3

A mistake in the name or address of a person named in a witness summons may be corrected if the summons has not been served.

1.4

The corrected summons must be re-sealed by the court and marked 'Amended and Re-Sealed'.

Witness summons issued in aid of an inferior court or tribunal

2.1

A witness summons may be issued in the High Court or a county court in aid of a court or tribunal which does not have the power to issue a witness summons in relation to the proceedings before it.

2.2

A witness summons referred to in paragraph 2.1 may be set aside by the court which issued it.

2.3

An application to set aside a witness summons referred to in paragraph 2.1 will be heard:

(1) in the High Court by a Master at the Royal Courts of Justice or by a district judge in a District Registry, and

(2) in a county court by a district judge.

2.4

Unless the court otherwise directs, the applicant must give at least 2 days' notice to the party who issued the witness summons of the application, which will normally be dealt with at a hearing.

Travelling expenses and compensation for loss of time

3.1

When a witness is served with a witness summons he must be offered a sum to cover his travelling expenses to and from the court and compensation for his loss of time.

3.2

If the witness summons is to be served by the court, the party issuing the summons must deposit with the court:

(1) a sum sufficient to pay for the witness's expenses in travelling to the court and in returning to his home or place of work, and

(2) a sum in respect of the period during which earnings or benefit are lost, or such lesser sum as it may be proved that the witness will lose as a result of his attendance at court in answer to the witness summons.

3.3

The sum referred to in 3.2(2) is to be based on the sums payable to witnesses attending the Crown Court.

3.4

Where the party issuing the witness summons wishes to serve it himself, he must:

(1) notify the court in writing that he wishes to do so, and

(2) at the time of service offer the witness the sums mentioned in paragraph 3.2 above.

DEPOSITIONS

To be taken in England and Wales for use as evidence in proceedings in courts in England and Wales.

4.1

A party may apply for an order for a person to be examined on oath before:

(1) a judge,

(2) an examiner of the court, or

(3) such other person as the court may appoint.

4.2

The party who obtains an order for the examination of a deponent before an examiner of the court must:

(1) apply to the Foreign Process Section of the Masters' Secretary's Department at the Royal Courts of Justice for the allocation of an examiner,

(2) when allocated, provide the examiner with copies of all documents in the proceedings necessary to inform the examiner of the issues, and

(3) pay the deponent a sum to cover his travelling expenses to and from the examination and compensation for his loss of time.

4.3

In ensuring that the deponent's evidence is recorded in full, the court or the examiner may permit it to be recorded on audiotape or videotape, but the deposition must always be recorded in writing by him or by a competent shorthand writer or stenographer.

4.4

If the deposition is not recorded word for word, it must contain, as nearly as may be, the statement of the deponent; the examiner may record word for word any particular questions and answers which appear to him to have special importance.

4.5

If a deponent objects to answering any question or where any objection is taken to any question, the examiner must:

(1) record in the deposition or a document attached to it —

    (a) the question,

    (b) the nature of and grounds for the objection, and

    (c) any answer given, and

(2) give his opinion as to the validity of the objection and must record it in the deposition or a document attached to it.

The court will decide as to the validity of the objection and any question of costs arising from it.

4.6

Documents and exhibits must:

(1) have an identifying number or letter marked on them by the examiner, and

(2) be preserved by the party or his legal representative who obtained the order for the examination, or as the court or the examiner may direct.

4.7

The examiner may put any question to the deponent as to:

(1) the meaning of any of his answers, or

(2) any matter arising in the course of the examination.

4.8

Where a deponent:

(1) fails to attend the examination, or

(2) refuses to:

   (a) be sworn, or

   (b) answer any lawful question, or

   (c) produce any document,

the examiner will sign a certificate of such failure or refusal and may include in his certificate any comment as to the conduct of the deponent or of any person attending the examination.

4.9

The party who obtained the order for the examination must file the certificate with the court and may apply for an order that the deponent attend for examination or as may be. The application may be made without notice.

4.10

The court will make such order on the application as it thinks fit including an order for the deponent to pay any costs resulting from his failure or refusal.

4.11

A deponent who wilfully refuses to obey an order made against him under Part 34 may be proceeded against for contempt of court.

4.12

A deposition must:

(1) be signed by the examiner,

(2) have any amendments to it initialled by the examiner and the deponent,

(3) be endorsed by the examiner with —
    (a) a statement of the time occupied by the examination, and
    (b) a record of any refusal by the deponent to sign the deposition and of his reasons for not doing so, and

(4) be sent by the examiner to the court where the proceedings are taking place for filing on the court file.

4.13   *Rule 34.14 deals with the fees and expenses of an examiner*

Annex A Draft Letter of Request (where the Taking of Evidence Regulation does not apply)

To the Competent Judicial Authority of   in the   of

I [*name*] Senior Master of the Queen's Bench Division of the Supreme Court of England and Wales respectfully request the assistance of your court with regard to the following matters.

1   A claim is now pending in the Division of the High Court of Justice in England and Wales entitled as follows [*set out full title and claim number*] in which [*name*] of [*address*] is the claimant and [*name*] of [*address*] is the defendant.

2   The names and addresses of the representatives or agents of [*set out names and addresses of representatives of the parties*].

3   The claim by the claimant is for:-
    (a) [*set out the nature of the claim*]
    (b) [*the relief sought, and*]
    (c) [*a summary of the facts.*]

4   It is necessary for the purposes of justice and for the due determination of the matters in dispute between the parties that you cause the following witnesses, who are resident within your jurisdiction, to be examined. The names and addresses of the witnesses are as follows:

5   The witnesses should be examined on oath or if that is not possible within your laws or is impossible of performance by reason of the internal practice and procedure of your court or by reason of practical difficulties, they should be examined in accordance with whatever procedure your laws provide for in these matters.

6   Either/
    The witnesses should be examined in accordance with the list of questions annexed hereto.

Or/

The witnesses should be examined regarding [*set out full details of evidence sought*]

N.B. Where the witness is required to produce documents, these should be clearly identified.

7   I would ask that you cause me, or the agents of the parties (if appointed), to be informed of the date and place where the examination is to take place.

8   Finally, I request that you will cause the evidence of the said witnesses to be reduced into writing and all documents produced on such examinations to be duly marked for identification and that you will further be pleased to authenticate such examinations by the seal of your court or in such other way as is in accordance with your procedure and return the written evidence and documents produced to me addressed as follows:

Senior Master of the Queen's Bench Division
Royal Courts of Justice
Strand
London WC2A 2LL
England

PRACTICE DIRECTION — EXPERTS AND ASSESSORS THIS PRACTICE DIRECTION SUPPLEMENTS CPR PART 35

Part 35 is intended to limit the use of oral expert evidence to that which is reasonably required. In addition, where possible, matters requiring expert evidence should be dealt with by a single expert. Permission of the court is always required either to call an expert or to put an expert's report in evidence. There is annexed to this Practice Direction a protocol for the instruction of experts to give evidence in civil claims. Experts and those instructing them are expected to have regard to the guidance contained in the protocol.

Expert Evidence — General Requirements

1.1 It is the duty of an expert to help the court on matters within his own expertise: rule 35.3(1). This duty is paramount and overrides any obligation to the person from whom the expert has received instructions or by whom he is paid: rule 35.3(2).

1.2 Expert evidence should be the independent product of the expert uninfluenced by the pressures of litigation.

1.3 An expert should assist the court by providing objective, unbiased opinion on matters within his expertise, and should not assume the role of an advocate.

1.4 An expert should consider all material facts, including those which might detract from his opinion.

1.5 An expert should make it clear:
(a) when a question or issue falls outside his expertise; and
(b) when he is not able to reach a definite opinion, for example because he has insufficient information.

1.6 If, after producing a report, an expert changes his view on any material matter, such change of view should be communicated to all the parties without delay, and when appropriate to the court.

Form and Content of Expert's Reports

2.1 An expert's report should be addressed to the court and not to the party from whom the expert has received his instructions.

2.2 An expert's report must:
(1) give details of the expert's qualifications;
(2) give details of any literature or other material which the expert has relied on in making the report;
(3) contain a statement setting out the substance of all facts and instructions given to the expert which are material to the opinions expressed in the report or upon which those opinions are based;
(4) make clear which of the facts stated in the report are within the expert's own knowledge;
(5) say who carried out any examination, measurement, test or experiment which the expert has used for the report, give the qualifications of that person, and say whether or not the test or experiment has been carried out under the expert's supervision;
(6) where there is a range of opinion on the matters dealt with in the report —

(a) summarise the range of opinion, and

(b) give reasons for his own opinion;

(7) contain a summary of the conclusions reached;

(8) if the expert is not able to give his opinion without qualification, state the qualification; and

(9) contain a statement that the expert understands his duty to the court, and has complied and will continue to comply with that duty.

(10) An expert's report must be verified by a statement of truth as well as containing the statements required in paragraph 2.2(8) and (9) above.

2.4   The form of the statement of truth is as follows:

I confirm that insofar as the facts stated in my report are within my own knowledge I have made clear which they are and I believe them to be true, and that the opinions I have expressed represent my true and complete professional opinion.

2.5   Attention is drawn to rule 32.14 which sets out the consequences of verifying a document containing a false statement without an honest belief in its truth.

(For information about statements of truth see Part 22 and the practice direction which supplements it.)

Information

3   Under Rule 35.9 the court may direct a party with access to information which is not reasonably available to another party to serve on that other party a document which records the information. The document served must include sufficient details of all the facts, tests, experiments and assumptions which underlie any part of the information to enable the party on whom it is served to make, or to obtain, a proper interpretation of the information and an assessment of its significance.

Instructions

4   The instructions referred to in paragraph 2.2(3) will not be protected by privilege (see rule 35.10(4)). But cross-examination of the expert on the contents of his instructions will not be allowed unless the court permits it (or unless the party who gave the instructions consents to it). Before it gives permission the court must be satisfied that there are reasonable grounds to consider that the statement in the report of the substance of the instructions is inaccurate or incomplete. If the court is so satisfied, it will allow the cross-examination where it appears to be in the interests of justice to do so.

Questions to Experts

5.1 Questions asked for the purpose of clarifying the expert's report (see rule 35.6) should be put, in writing, to the expert not later than 28 days after receipt of the expert's report (see paragraphs 1.2 to 1.5 above as to verification).

5.2 Where a party sends a written question or questions direct to an expert, a copy of the questions should, at the same time, be sent to the other party or parties.

5.3 The party or parties instructing the expert must pay any fees charged by that expert for answering questions put under rule 35.6. This does not affect any decision of the court as to the party who is ultimately to bear the expert's costs.

Single Expert

6 Where the court has directed that the evidence on a particular issue is to be given by one expert only (rule 35.7) but there are a number of disciplines relevant to that issue, a leading expert in the dominant discipline should be identified as the single expert. He should prepare the general part of the report and be responsible for annexing or incorporating the contents of any reports from experts in other disciplines.

Orders

6A Where an order requires an act to be done by an expert, or otherwise affects an expert, the party instructing that expert must serve a copy of the order on the expert instructed by him. In the case of a jointly instructed expert, the claimant must serve the order.

Assessors

7.1 An assessor may be appointed to assist the court under rule 35.15. Not less than 21 days before making any such appointment, the court will notify each party in writing of the name of the proposed assessor, of the matter in respect of which the assistance of the assessor will be sought and of the qualifications of the assessor to give that assistance.

7.2 Where any person has been proposed for appointment as an assessor, objection to him, either personally or in respect of his qualification, may be taken by any party.

7.3 Any such objection must be made in writing and filed with the court within 7 days of receipt of the notification referred to in paragraph 6.1 and will be taken into account by the court in deciding whether or not to make the appointment (section 63(5) of the County Courts Act 1984).

7.4 Copies of any report prepared by the assessor will be sent to each of the parties but the assessor will not give oral evidence or be open to cross-examination or questioning.

CRIMINAL PROCEDURE RULES 2005

24.1   Requirement to disclose expert evidence

(1) Following –

   (a)   A plea of not guilty by any person to an alleged offence in respect of which a magistrates' court proceeds to summary trial;

   (b)   the committal for trial of any person;

   (c)   the transfer to the Crown Court of any proceedings for the trial of a person by virtue of a notice of transfer given under section 4 of the Criminal Justice Act 1987;

   (d)   the transfer to the Crown Court of any proceedings for the trial of a person by virtue of a notice of transfer served on a magistrates' court under section 53 of the Criminal Justice Act 1991;

   (e)   the sending of any person for trial under section 51 of the Crime and Disorder Act 1998;

   (f)   the preferring of a bill of indictment charging a person with an offence under the authority of section 2(2)(b) of the Administration of Justice (Miscellaneous Provisions) Act 1933; or

   (g)   the making of an order for the retrial of any person,

if any party to the proceedings proposes to adduce expert evidence (whether of fact or opinion) in the proceedings (otherwise than in relation to sentence) he shall as soon as practicable, unless in relation to the evidence in question he has already done so or the evidence is the subject of an application for leave to adduce such evidence in accordance with section 41 of the Youth Justice and Criminal Evidence Act 1999–

     (i)   furnish the other party or parties and the court with a statement in writing of any finding or opinion which he proposes to adduce by way of such evidence, and notify the expert of this disclosure, and

(ii) where a request in writing is made to him in that behalf by any other party, provide that party also with a copy of (or if it appears to the party proposing to adduce the evidence to be more practicable, a reasonable opportunity to examine) the record of any observation, test, calculation or other procedure on which such finding or opinion is based and any document or other thing or substance in respect of which any such procedure has been carried out.

(2) A party may by notice in writing waive his right to be furnished with any of the matters mentioned in paragraph (1) and, in particular, may agree that the statement mentioned in paragraph (1)(a) may be furnished to him orally and not in writing.

(3) In paragraph (1), "document" means anything in which information of any description is recorded.

Formerly rule 3 of the Magistrates' Courts (Advance Notice of Expert Evidence) Rules 1997 and rule 3 of the Crown Court (Advance Notice of Expert Evidence) Rules 1987. For the equivalent requirement in Crown Court proceedings under Part 2 of the Proceeds of Crime Act 2002 see rule 57.9. Part 33 contains rules about the duties of an expert and the content of an expert's report.

24.2 Withholding evidence

(1) If a party has reasonable grounds for believing that the disclosure of any evidence in compliance with the requirements imposed by rule 24.1 might lead to the intimidation, or attempted intimidation, of any person on whose evidence he intends to rely in the proceedings, or otherwise to the course of justice being interfered with, he shall not be obliged to comply with those requirements in relation to that evidence.

(2) Where, in accordance with paragraph (1), a party considers that he is not obliged to comply with the requirements imposed by rule 24.1 with regard to any evidence in relation to any other party, he shall give notice in writing to that party to the effect that the evidence is being withheld and the grounds for doing so.

Formerly rule 4 of the Magistrates' Courts (Advance Notice of Expert Evidence) Rules 1997 and rule 4 of the Crown Court (Advance Notice of Expert Evidence) Rules 1987. For the equivalent exception in Crown Court proceedings under Part 2 of the Proceeds of Crime Act 2002 see rule 57.10.

24.3 Effect of failure to disclose

A party who seeks to adduce expert evidence in any proceedings and who fails to comply with rule 24.1 shall not adduce that evidence in those proceedings without the leave of the court.

Formerly rule 5 of the Magistrates' Courts (Advance Notice of Expert Evidence) Rules 1997 and rule 5 of the Crown Court (Advance Notice of Expert Evidence) Rules 1987.

PART 25
APPLICATIONS FOR PUBLIC INTEREST IMMUNITY AND SPECIFIC DISCLOSURE

25.1   Public interest: application by prosecutor

(1) This rule applies to the making of an application by the prosecutor under section 3(6), 7A(8) or 8(5) of the Criminal Procedure and Investigations Act 1996.

(2) Notice of such an application shall be served on the court officer and shall specify the nature of the material to which the application relates.

(3) Subject to paragraphs (4) and (5) below, a copy of the notice of application shall be served on the accused by the prosecutor.

(4) Where the prosecutor has reason to believe that to reveal to the accused the nature of the material to which the application relates would have the effect of disclosing that which the prosecutor contends should not in the public interest be disclosed, paragraph (3) above shall not apply but the prosecutor shall notify the accused that an application to which this rule applies has been made.

(5) Where the prosecutor has reason to believe that to reveal to the accused the fact that an application is being made would have the effect of disclosing that which the prosecutor contends should not in the public interest be disclosed, paragraph (3) above shall not apply.

(6) Where an application is made in the Crown Court to which paragraph (5) above applies, notice of the application may be served on the trial judge or, if the application is made before the start of the trial, on the judge, if any, who has been designated to conduct the trial instead of on the court officer.

Formerly rule 2 of the Magistrates' Courts (Criminal Procedure and Investigations Act 1996) (Disclosure) Rules 1997 and rule 2 of the Crown Court (Criminal Procedure and Investigations Act 1996) (Disclosure) Rules 1997.

25.2   Public interest: hearing of application by prosecutor

(1) This rule applies to the hearing of an application by the prosecutor under section 3(6), 7A(8) or 8(5) of the Criminal Procedure and Investigations Act 1996.

(2) Where notice of such an application is served on the Crown Court officer, the officer shall on receiving it refer it—
   (a) if the trial has started, to the trial judge; or
   (b) if the application is received before the start of the trial either—
      (i)   to the judge who has been designated to conduct the trial, or
      (ii) if no judge has been designated for that purpose, to such judge as may be designated for the purposes of hearing the application.

(3) Where such an application is made and a copy of the notice of application has been served on the accused in accordance with rule 25.1(3), then subject to paragraphs (4) and (5) below—
   (a) the court officer shall on receiving notice of the application give notice to—
      (i)   the prosecutor,
      (ii) the accused, and
      (iii) any person claiming to have an interest in the material to which the application relates who has applied under section 16(b) of the 1996 Act4 to be heard by the court,

of the date and time when and the place where the hearing will take place and, unless the court orders otherwise, such notice shall be given in writing;
   (b) the hearing shall be inter partes; and
   (c) the prosecutor and the accused shall be entitled to make representations to the court.

(4) Where the prosecutor applies to the court for leave to make representations in the absence of the accused, the court may for that purpose sit in the absence of the accused and any legal representative of his.

(5) Subject to rule 25.5(4) (interested party entitled to make representations), where a copy of the notice of application has not been served on the accused in accordance with rule 25.1(3)—

   (a)   the hearing shall be ex parte;

   (b)   only the prosecutor shall be entitled to make representations to the court;

   (c)   the accused shall not be given notice as specified in paragraph (3)(a)(ii) of this rule; and

   (d)   where notice of the application has been served in the Crown Court in pursuance of rule 25.1(6), the judge on whom it is served shall take such steps as he considers appropriate to ensure that notice is given as required by paragraph (3)(a)(i) and (iii) of this rule.

Formerly rule 3 of the Magistrates' Courts (Criminal Procedure and Investigations Act 1996) (Disclosure) Rules 1997 and rule 3 of the Crown Court (Criminal Procedure and Investigations Act 1996) (Disclosure) Rules 1997.

25.3   Public interest: non-disclosure order

(1) This rule applies to an order under section 3(6), 7A(8) or 8(5) of the Criminal Procedure and Investigations Act 1996.

(2) On making an order to which this rule applies, the court shall state its reasons for doing so. Where such an order is made in the Crown Court, a record shall be made of the statement of the court's reasons.

(3) In a case where such an order is made following—

   (a)   an application to which rule 25.1(4) (nature of material not to be revealed) applies; or

   (b)   an application notice of which has been served on the accused in accordance with rule 25.1(3) but the accused has not appeared or been represented at the hearing of that application,

the court officer shall notify the accused that an order has been made. No notification shall be given in a case where an order is made following an application to which rule 25.1(5) (fact of application not to be revealed) applies.

Formerly rule 4 of the Magistrates' Courts (Criminal Procedure and Investigations Act 1996) (Disclosure) Rules 1997 and rule 4 of the Crown Court (Criminal Procedure and Investigations Act 1996) (Disclosure) Rules 1997.

25.4   Review of non-disclosure order: application by accused

(1) This rule applies to an application by the accused under section 14(2) or section 15(4) of the Criminal Procedure and Investigations Act 1996.

(2) Such an application shall be made by notice in writing to the court officer for the court that made the order under section 3(6), 7A(8) or 8(5) of the 1996 Act and shall specify the reason why the accused believes the court should review the question whether it is still not in the public interest to disclose the material affected by the order.

(3) A copy of the notice referred to in paragraph (2) shall be served on the prosecutor at the same time as it is sent to the court officer.

(4) Where such an application is made in a magistrates' court, the court officer shall take such steps as he thinks fit to ensure that the court has before it any document or other material which was available to the court which made the order mentioned in section 14(2) of the 1996 Act.

(5) Where such an application is made in the Crown Court, the court officer shall refer it–
   (a) if the trial has started, to the trial judge; or
   (b) if the application is received before the start of the trial either—
      (i) to the judge who has been designated to conduct the trial, or
      (ii) if no judge has been designated for that purpose, to the judge who made the order to which the application relates.

(6) The judge to whom such an application has been referred under paragraph (5) shall consider whether the application may be determined without a hearing and, subject to paragraph (7), may so determine it if he thinks fit.

(7) No application to which this rule applies shall be determined by the Crown Court without a hearing if it appears to the judge that there are grounds on which the court might conclude that it is in the public interest to disclose material to any extent.

(8) Where a magistrates' court considers that there are no grounds on which it might conclude that it is in the public interest to disclose material to any extent it may determine an application to which this rule applies without hearing representations from the accused, the prosecutor or any person claiming to have an interest in the material to which the application relates.

(9) Subject to paragraphs (10) and (11) of this rule and to rule 25.5(4) (interested party entitled to make representations), the hearing of an application to which this rule applies shall be inter partes and the accused and the prosecutor shall be entitled to make representations to the court.

(10) Where after hearing the accused's representations the prosecutor applies to the court for leave to make representations in the absence of the accused, the court may for that purpose sit in the absence of the accused and any legal representative of his.

(11) Subject to rule 25.5(4), where the order to which the application relates was made following an application of which the accused was not notified under rule 25.1(3) or (4), the hearing shall be ex parte and only the prosecutor shall be entitled to make representations to the court.

(12) The court officer shall give notice in writing to—

(a) the prosecutor;

(b) except where a hearing takes place in accordance with paragraph (11), the accused; and

(c) any person claiming to have an interest in the material to which the application relates who has applied under section 16(b) of the 1996 Act to be heard by the court, of the date and time when and the place where the hearing of an application to which this rule applies will take place and of any order which is made by the court following its determination of the application.

(13) Where such an application is determined without a hearing in pursuance of paragraph (6), the court officer shall give notice in writing in accordance with paragraph (12) of any order which is made by the judge following his determination of the application.

Formerly rule 5 of the Magistrates' Courts (Criminal Procedure and Investigations Act 1996) (Disclosure) Rules 1997 and rule 5 of the Crown Court (Criminal Procedure and Investigations Act 1996) (Disclosure) Rules 1997.

25.5 Public interest applications: interested persons

(1) Where the prosecutor has reason to believe that a person who was involved (whether alone or with others and whether directly or indirectly) in the prosecutor's attention being brought to any material to which an application under section 3(6), 7A(8), 8(5), 14(2) or 15(4) of the Criminal Procedure and Investigations Act 1996 relates may claim to have an interest in that material, the prosecutor shall—

(a) in the case of an application under section 3(6), 7A(8) or 8(5) of the 1996 Act, at the same time as notice of the application is served under rule 25.1(2) or (6); or

(b) in the case of an application under section 14(2) or 15(4) of the 1996 Act, when he receives a copy of the notice referred to in rule 25.4(2),

give notice in writing to—

(i) the person concerned of the application, and

(ii) (ii)the court officer or, as the case may require, the judge of his belief and the grounds for it.

(2) An application under section 16(b) of the 1996 Act shall be made by notice in writing to the court officer or, as the case may require, the judge as soon as is reasonably practicable after receipt of notice under paragraph (1)(i) above or, if no such notice is received, after the person concerned becomes aware of the application referred to in that sub-paragraph and shall specify the nature of the applicant's interest in the material and his involvement in bringing the material to the prosecutor's attention.

(3) A copy of the notice referred to in paragraph (2) shall be served on the prosecutor at the same time as it is sent to the court officer or the judge as the case may require.

(4) At the hearing of an application under section 3(6), 7A(8), 8(5), 14(2) or 15(4) of the 1996 Act a person who has made an application under section 16(b) in accordance with paragraph (2) of this rule shall be entitled to make representations to the court.

Formerly rule 6 of the Magistrates' Courts (Criminal Procedure and Investigations Act 1996) (Disclosure) Rules 1997 and rule 6 of the Crown Court (Criminal Procedure and Investigations Act 1996) (Disclosure) Rules 1997.

25.6   Disclosure: application by accused and order of court

(1) This rule applies to an application by the accused under section 8(2) of the Criminal Procedure and Investigations Act 1996.

(2) Such an application shall be made by notice in writing to the court officer and shall specify—
   (a) the material to which the application relates;
   (b) that the material has not been disclosed to the accused;
   (c) the reason why the material might be expected to assist the applicant's defence as disclosed by the defence statement given under section 5 or 6 of the 1996 Act; and
   (d) the date of service of a copy of the notice on the prosecutor in accordance with paragraph (3).

(3) A copy of the notice referred to in paragraph (2) shall be served on the prosecutor at the same time as it is sent to the court officer.

(4) Where such an application is made in the Crown Court, the court officer shall refer it—
   (a) if the trial has started, to the trial judge, or
   (b) if the application is received before the start of the trial–
      (i) to the judge who has been designated to conduct the trial, or
      (ii) if no judge has been designated for that purpose, to such judge as may be designated for the purposes of determining the application.

(5) A prosecutor receiving notice under paragraph (3) of an application to which this rule applies shall give notice in writing to the court officer within 14 days of service of the notice that—
   (a) he wishes to make representations to the court concerning the material to which the application relates; or
   (b) if he does not so wish, that he is willing to disclose that material,
   and a notice under paragraph 5(a) shall specify the substance of the representations he wishes to make.

(6) A court may determine an application to which this rule applies without hearing representations from the applicant or the prosecutor unless—

(a) the prosecutor has given notice under paragraph (5)(a) and the court considers that the representations should be made at a hearing; or

(b) the court considers it necessary to hear representations from the applicant or the prosecutor in the interests of justice for the purposes of determining the application.

(7) Subject to paragraph (8), where a hearing is held in pursuance of this rule—

(a) the court officer shall give notice in writing to the prosecutor and the applicant of the date and time when and the place where the hearing will take place;

(b) the hearing shall be inter partes; and

(c) the prosecutor and the applicant shall be entitled to make representations to the court.

(8) Where the prosecutor applies to the court for leave to make representations in the absence of the accused, the court may for that purpose sit in the absence of the accused and any legal representative of his.

(9) A copy of any order under section 8(2) of the 1996 Act shall be served on the prosecutor and the applicant.

Formerly rule 7 of the Magistrates' Courts (Criminal Procedure and Investigations Act 1996) (Disclosure) Rules 1997 and rule 7 of the Crown Court (Criminal Procedure and Investigations Act 1996) (Disclosure) Rules 1997.

25.7 Disclosure: application for extension of time limit and order of the court

(1) This rule applies to an application under regulation 3(2) of the Criminal Procedure and Investigations Act 1996 (Defence Disclosure Time Limits) Regulations 1997, including that regulation as applied by regulation 4(2).

(2) An application to which this rule applies shall be made by notice in writing to the court officer and shall, in addition to the matters referred to in regulation 3(3)(a) to (c) of the 1997 Regulations, specify the date of service of a copy of the notice on the prosecutor in accordance with paragraph (3) of this rule.

(3) A copy of the notice referred to in paragraph (2) of this rule shall be served on the prosecutor at the same time as it is sent to the court officer.

(4) The prosecutor may make representations to the court concerning the application and if he wishes to do so he shall do so in writing within 14 days of service of a notice under paragraph (3) of this rule.

(5) On receipt of representations under paragraph (4) above, or on the expiration of the period specified in that paragraph if no such representations are received within that period, the court shall consider the application and may, if it wishes, do so at a hearing.

(6) Where a hearing is held in pursuance of this rule—
   (a) the court officer shall give notice in writing to the prosecutor and the applicant of the date and time when and the place where the hearing will take place;
   (b) the hearing shall be inter partes; and
   (c) the prosecutor and the applicant shall be entitled to make representations to the court.

(7) A copy of any order under regulation 3(1) or 4(1) of the 1997 Regulations shall be served on the prosecutor and the applicant.

Formerly rule 8 of the Magistrates' Courts (Criminal Procedure and Investigations Act 1996) (Disclosure) Rules 1997 and rule 8 of the Crown Court (Criminal Procedure and Investigations Act 1996) (Disclosure) Rules 1997.

25.8   Public interest and disclosure applications: general

(1) Any hearing held under this Part may be adjourned from time to time.

(2) Any hearing referred to in paragraph (1) other than one held under rule 25.7 may be held in private.

(3) Where a Crown Court hearing, or any part thereof, is held in private under paragraph (2), the court may specify conditions subject to which the record of its statement of reasons made in pursuance of rule 25.3(2) is to be kept.

(4) Where an application or order to which any provision of this rule applies is made after the start of a trial in the Crown Court, the trial judge may direct that any provision of this rule requiring notice of the application or order to be given to any person shall not have effect and may give such direction as to the giving of notice in relation to that application or order as he thinks fit.

Formerly rule 9 of the Magistrates' Courts (Criminal Procedure and Investigations Act 1996) (Disclosure) Rules 1997 and rule 9 of the Crown Court (Criminal Procedure and Investigations Act 1996) (Disclosure) Rules 1997.

PART 26
CONFIDENTIAL MATERIAL

26.1   Application for permission to use or disclose object or information

(1) This rule applies to an application under section 17(4) of the Criminal Procedure and Investigations Act 1996.

(2) Such an application shall be made by notice in writing to the court officer for the court which conducted or is conducting the proceedings for whose purposes the applicant was given, or allowed to inspect, the object to which the application relates.

(3) The notice of application shall—
   (a) specify the object which the applicant seeks to use or disclose and the proceedings for whose purposes he was given, or allowed to inspect, it;
   (b) where the applicant seeks to use or disclose any information recorded in the object specified in pursuance of paragraph (3)(a), specify that information;
   (c) specify the reason why the applicant seeks permission to use or disclose the object specified in pursuance of paragraph (3)(a) or any information specified in pursuance of paragraph (3)(b);
   (d) describe any proceedings in connection with which the applicant seeks to use or disclose the object or information referred to in paragraph (3)(c); and
   (e) specify the name and address of any person to whom the applicant seeks to disclose the object or information referred to in paragraph (3)(c).

(4) Where the court officer receives an application to which this rule applies, the court officer or the clerk of the magistrates' court shall fix a date and time for the hearing of the application.

(5) The court officer shall give the applicant and the prosecutor at least 28 days' notice of the date fixed in pursuance of paragraph (4) and shall at the same time send to the prosecutor a copy of the notice given to him in pursuance of paragraph (2).

(6) Where the prosecutor has reason to believe that a person may claim to have an interest in the object specified in a notice of application in pursuance of paragraph (3)(a), or in any information so specified in pursuance of paragraph (3)(b), he shall, as soon as reasonably practicable after receipt of a copy of that notice under paragraph (5), send a copy of the notice to that person and inform him of the date fixed in pursuance of paragraph (4).

Formerly rule 2 of the Magistrates' Courts (Criminal Procedure and Investigations Act 1996) (Confidentiality) Rules 1997 and rule 2 of the Crown Court (Criminal Procedure and Investigations Act 1996) (Confidentiality) Rules 1997.

26.2 Prosecutor or interested party wishing to be heard

(1) This rule applies to an application under section 17(6)(b) of the Criminal Procedure and Investigations Act 1996.

(2) An application to which this rule applies shall be made by notice in writing to the court officer of the court referred to in rule 26.1(2) not less than 7 days before the date fixed in pursuance of rule 26.1(4).

(3) The applicant shall at the same time send to the person whose application under section 17(4) of the 1996 Act is concerned a copy of the notice given in pursuance of paragraph (2).

Formerly rule 3 of the Magistrates' Courts (Criminal Procedure and Investigations Act 1996) (Confidentiality) Rules 1997 and rule 3 of the Crown Court (Criminal Procedure and Investigations Act 1996) (Confidentiality) Rules 1997.

26.3 Decision on application for use or disclosure

(1) Where no application to which rule 26.2 applies is made in accordance with paragraph (2) of that rule, the court shall consider whether the application under section 17(4) of the Criminal Procedure and Investigations Act 1996 may be determined without hearing representations from the accused, the prosecutor or any person claiming to have an interest in the object or information to which the application relates, and may so determine it if the court thinks fit.

(2) Where an application to which rule 26.1 applies is determined without hearing any such representations the court officer shall give notice in writing to the person who made the application and to the prosecutor of any order made under section 17(4) of the 1996 Act or, as the case may be, that no such order has been made.

Formerly rule 4 of the Magistrates' Courts (Criminal Procedure and Investigations Act 1996) (Confidentiality) Rules 1997 and rule 4 of the

Crown Court (Criminal Procedure and Investigations Act 1996)
(Confidentiality) Rules 1997.

26.4   Unauthorised use or disclosure

(1) This rule applies to proceedings to deal with a contempt of court
under section 18 of the Criminal Procedure and Investigations Act
1996.

(2) In such proceedings before a magistrates' court the Magistrates' Courts
Act 1980 shall have effect subject to the modifications contained in
paragraphs (3) to (7) (being provisions equivalent to those in Schedule 3
to the Contempt of Court Act 1981 subject to modifications which the
Lord Chancellor considered appropriate after consultation with the rule
committee for magistrates' courts).

(3) Where proceedings to which this rule applies are taken of the court's own
motion the provisions of the 1980 Act listed in paragraph (4) shall apply
as if a complaint had been made against the person against whom the
proceedings are taken and subject to the modifications specified in
paragraphs (5) and (6).

(4) The provisions referred to in paragraph (3) are—
    (a) section 51 (issue of summons);
    (b) section 53(1) and (2) (procedure on hearing);
    (c) section 54 (adjournment);
    (d) section 55 (non-appearance of defendant);
    (e) section 97(1) (summons to witness);
    (f) section 101 (onus of proving exceptions etc);
    (g) section 121(1) and (3)(a) (constitution and place of sitting of court);
         and
    (h) section 123 (defect in process).

(5) In
    (a) section 55(1) for the words "the complainant appears but the
         defendant does not" there shall be substituted the words "the
         defendant does not appear"; and
    (b) section 55(2) the words "if the complaint has been substantiated on
         oath, and" shall be omitted.

(6) In section 123(1) and (2) the words "adduced on behalf of the prosecutor
or complainant" shall be omitted.

(7) Where proceedings to which this rule applies are taken by way of
complaint for an order
    (a) section 127 of the 1980 Act (limitation of time) shall not apply to
         the complaint;
    (b) the complaint may be made by the prosecutor or by any other
         person claiming to have an interest in the object, or in any

information recorded in an object, the use or disclosure of which is alleged to contravene section 17 of the 1996 Act; and

(c)   the complaint shall be made to the magistrates' court officer for the magistrates' court which conducted or is conducting the proceedings for whose purposes the object mentioned in paragraph (7)(b) was given or inspected.

(8)   An application to the Crown Court for an order of committal or for the imposition of a fine in proceedings to which this rule applies may be made by the prosecutor or by any other person claiming to have an interest in the object, or in any information recorded in an object, the use or disclosure of which is alleged to contravene section 17 of the 1996 Act. Such an application shall be made in accordance with paragraphs (9) to (20).

(9)   An application such as is referred to in paragraph (8) shall be made by notice in writing to the court officer at the same place as that in which the Crown Court sat or is sitting to conduct the proceedings for whose purposes the object mentioned in paragraph (2) was given or inspected.

(10)   The notice referred to in paragraph (9) shall set out the name and a description of the applicant, the name, description and address of the person sought to be committed or fined and the grounds on which his committal or the imposition of a fine is sought and shall be supported by an affidavit verifying the facts.

(11)   Subject to paragraph (12), the notice referred to in paragraph (9), accompanied by a copy of the affidavit in support of the application, shall be served personally on the person sought to be committed or fined.

(12)   The court may dispense with service of the notice under this rule if it is of the opinion that it is necessary to do so in order to protect the applicant or for another purpose identified by the court.

(13)   Nothing in the foregoing provisions of this rule shall be taken as affecting the power of the Crown Court to make an order of committal or impose a fine of its own motion against a person guilty of a contempt under section 18 of the 1996 Act.

(14)   Subject to paragraph (15), proceedings to which this rule applies shall be heard in open court.

(15)   Proceedings to which this rule applies may be heard in private where—

(a)   the object, the use or disclosure of which is alleged to contravene section 17 of the 1996 Act, is; or

(b)   the information, the use or disclosure of which is alleged to contravene that section, is recorded in, an object which is, or forms part of, material in respect of which an application was made under section 3(6), 7A(8) or 8(5) of the 1996 Act, whether or not the court made an order that the material be not disclosed:

Provided that where the court hears the proceedings in private it shall nevertheless, if it commits any person to custody or imposes a fine on him in pursuance of section 18(3) of the 1996 Act, state in open court the name of that person, the period specified in the order of committal or, as the case may be, the amount of the fine imposed, or both such period and such amount where both are ordered.

(16)   Except with the leave of the court hearing an application for an order of committal or for the imposition of a fine no grounds shall be relied upon at the hearing except the grounds set out in the notice referred to in paragraph (9).

(17)   If on the hearing of the application the person sought to be committed or fined expresses a wish to give oral evidence on his own behalf, he shall be entitled to do so.

(18)   The court by whom an order of committal is made may by order direct that the execution of the order of committal shall be suspended for such period or on such terms or conditions as it may specify.

(19)   Where execution of an order of committal is suspended by an order under paragraph (18), the applicant for the order of committal must, unless the court otherwise directs, serve on the person against whom it was made a notice informing him of the making and terms of the order under that paragraph.

(20)   The court may, on the application of any person committed to custody for a contempt under section 18 of the 1996 Act, discharge him.

Formerly rule 5 of the Magistrates' Courts (Criminal Procedure and Investigations Act 1996) (Confidentiality) Rules 1997 and rule 5 of the Crown Court (Criminal Procedure and Investigations Act 1996) (Confidentiality) Rules 1997.

26.5   Forfeiture of object used or disclosed without authority

(1)   Where the Crown Court finds a person guilty of contempt under section 18 of the Criminal Procedure and Investigations Act 1996 and proposes to make an order under section 18(4) or (7), the court may adjourn the proceedings.

(2)   Where the court adjourns the proceedings under paragraph (1), the court officer shall give notice to the person found guilty and to the prosecutor—
   (a)   that the court proposes to make such an order and that, if an application is made in accordance with paragraph (5), it will before doing so hear any representations made by the person found guilty, or by any person in respect of whom the prosecutor gives notice to the court under paragraph (3); and
   (b)   of the time and date of the adjourned hearing.

(3) Where the prosecutor has reason to believe that a person may claim to have an interest in the object which has been used or disclosed in contravention of section 17 of the 1996 Act he shall, on receipt of notice under paragraph (2), give notice of that person's name and address to the court office for the court which made the finding of guilt.

(4) Where the court officer receives a notice under paragraph (3), he shall, within 7 days of the finding of guilt, notify the person specified in that notice—

(a) that the court has made a finding of guilt under section 18 of the 1996 Act, that it proposes to make an order under section 18(4) or, as the case may be, 18(7) and that, if an application is made in accordance with paragraph (5), it will before doing so hear any representations made by him; and

(b) of the time and date of the adjourned hearing.

(5) An application under section 18(6) of the 1996 Act shall be made by notice in writing to the court officer not less than 24 hours before the time set for the adjourned hearing.

Formerly rule 6 of the Crown Court (Criminal Procedure and Investigations Act 1996) (Confidentiality) Rules 1997.

PART 27
WITNESS STATEMENTS

27.1 Witness statements in magistrates' courts

(1) Written statements to be tendered in evidence in accordance with section 5B of the Magistrates' Courts Act 1980 or section 9 of the Criminal Justice Act 1967 shall be in the form set out in the Practice Direction.

(2) When a copy of any of the following evidence, namely—

(a) evidence tendered in accordance with section 5A of the 1980 Act (committal for trial)3; or

(b) a written statement tendered in evidence under section 9 of the 1967 Act (proceedings other than committal for trial), is given to or served on any party to the proceedings a copy of the evidence in question shall be given to the court officer as soon as practicable thereafter, and where a copy of any such statement as is referred to in sub-paragraph (b) is given or served by or on behalf of the prosecutor, the accused shall be given notice by or on behalf of the prosecutor of his right to object to the statement being tendered in evidence.

(3) Where—

  (a) a statement or deposition to be tendered in evidence in accordance with section 5A of the 1980 Act; or

  (b) a written statement to be tendered in evidence under section 9 of the 1967 Act, refers to any document or object as an exhibit, that document or object shall wherever possible be identified by means of a label or other mark of identification signed by the maker of the statement or deposition, and before a magistrates' court treats any document or object referred to as an exhibit in such a statement or deposition as an exhibit produced and identified in court by the maker of the statement or deposition, the court shall be satisfied that the document or object is sufficiently described in the statement or deposition for it to be identified.

(4) If it appears to a magistrates' court that any part of any evidence tendered in accordance with section 5A of the 1980 Act or a written statement tendered in evidence under section 9 of the 1967 Act is inadmissible there shall be written against that part—

  (a) in the case of any evidence tendered in accordance with section 5A of the 1980 Act, but subject to paragraph (5) of this rule, the words "Treated as inadmissible" together with the signature and name of the examining justice or, where there is more than one examining justice, the signature and name of one of the examining justices by whom the evidence is so treated;

  (b) in the case of a written statement tendered in evidence under section 9 of the 1967 Act the words "Ruled inadmissible" together with the signature and name of one of the justices who ruled the statement to be inadmissible.

(5) Where the nature of the evidence referred to in paragraph (4)(a) is such that it is not possible to write on it, the words set out in that sub-paragraph shall instead be written on a label or other mark of identification which clearly identifies the part of the evidence to which the words relate and contains the signature and name of an examining justice in accordance with that sub-paragraph.

(6) Where, before a magistrates' court—

  (a) a statement or deposition is tendered in evidence in accordance with section 5A of the 1980 Act; or

  (b) a written statement is tendered in accordance with section 9 of the 1967 Act,

the name of the maker of the statement or deposition shall be read aloud unless the court otherwise directs.

(7) Where—
(a) under section 5B(4), 5C(4), 5D(5) or 5E(3) of the 1980 Act4; or
(b) under section 9(6) of the 1967 Act,

in any proceedings before a magistrates' court any part of the evidence has to be read out aloud, or an account has to be given orally of so much of any evidence as is not read out aloud, the evidence shall be read or the account given by or on behalf of the party which has tendered the evidence.

(8) Statements and depositions tendered in evidence in accordance with section 5A of the 1980 Act before a magistrates' court acting as examining justices shall be authenticated by a certificate signed by one of the examining justices.

(9) Where, before a magistrates' court—
(a) evidence is tendered as indicated in paragraph (2)(a) of this rule, retained by the court, and not sent to the Crown Court under rule 10.5; or
(b) a written statement is tendered in evidence as indicated in paragraph (2)(b) of this rule and not sent to the Crown Court under rule 43.1 or 43.2,

all such evidence shall, subject to any direction of the court in respect of non-documentary exhibits falling within paragraph (9)(a), be preserved for a period of three years by the magistrates' court officer for the magistrates' court.

Formerly rule 70 of the Magistrates' Courts Rules 1981. See also section 9 of the Criminal Justice Act 1967 and section 5A of the Magistrates' Courts Act 1980. On the editing of witness statements, see also direction III.24 in the Practice Direction.

27.2 Right to object to evidence being read in Crown Court trial

(1) The prosecutor shall, when he serves on any other party a copy of the evidence to be tendered in committal proceedings, notify that party that if he is committed for trial he has the right to object, by written notification to the prosecutor and the Crown Court within 14 days of being so committed unless the court in its discretion permits such an objection to be made outside that period, to a statement or deposition being read as evidence at the trial without oral evidence being given by the person who made the statement or deposition and without the opportunity to cross-examine that person.

(2) The prosecutor shall, on notifying a party as indicated in paragraph (1), send a copy of such notification to the magistrates' court officer.

(3) Any objection under paragraph 1(3)(c) or paragraph 2(3)(c) of Schedule 2 to the Criminal Procedure and Investigations Act 1996 to the reading out

at the trial of a statement or deposition without further evidence shall be made in writing to the prosecutor and the Crown Court within 14 days of the accused being committed for trial unless the court at its discretion permits such an objection to be made outside that period.

Formerly rule 4B of the Magistrates' Courts Rules 1981 and rule 22 of the Crown Court Rules 1982. On the coming into force of Schedule 3 to the Criminal Justice Act 2003 committal for trial will be abolished and cases will be sent for trial under sections 51 and 51A of the Crime and Disorder Act 1998.

PART 29
SPECIAL MEASURES DIRECTIONS

29.1   Application for special measures directions

(1) An application by a party in criminal proceedings for a magistrates' court or the Crown Court to give a special measures direction under section 19 of the Youth Justice and Criminal Evidence Act 1999 must be made in writing in the form set out in the Practice Direction.

(2) If the application is for a special measures direction –
   (a) enabling a witness to give evidence by means of a live link, the information sought in Part B of that form must be provided;
   (b) providing for any examination of a witness to be conducted through an intermediary, the information sought in Part C of that form must be provided; or

    (c)   enabling a video recording of an interview of a witness to be admitted as evidence in chief of the witness, the information sought in Part D of that form must be provided.

(3)   The application under paragraph (1) above must be sent to the court officer and at the same time a copy thereof must be sent by the applicant to every other party to the proceedings.

(4)   The court officer must receive the application –

    (a)   in the case of an application to a youth court, within 28 days of the date on which the defendant first appears or is brought before the court in connection with the offence;

    (b)   in the case of an application to a magistrates' court, within 14 days of the defendant indicating his intention to plead not guilty to any charge brought against him and in relation to which a special measures direction may be sought; and

    (c)   in the case of an application to the Crown Court, within 28 days of

        (i)   the committal of the defendant, or

        (ii)   the consent to the preferment of a bill of indictment in relation to the case, or

        (iii)   the service of a notice of transfer under section 53 of the Criminal Justice Act 1991, or

        (iv)   where a person is sent for trial under section 51 of the Crime and Disorder Act 1998, the service of copies of the documents containing the evidence on which the charge or charges are based under paragraph 1 of Schedule 3 to that Act, or

        (v)   the service of a Notice of Appeal from a decision of a youth court or a magistrates' court.

(5)   A party to whom an application is sent in accordance with paragraph (3) may oppose the application for a special measures direction in respect of any, or any particular, measure available in relation to the witness, whether or not the question whether the witness is eligible for assistance by virtue of section 16 or 17 of the 1999 Act is in issue.

(6)   A party who wishes to oppose the application must, within 14 days of the date the application was served on him, notify the applicant and the court officer, as the case may be, in writing of his opposition and give reasons for it.

(7)   Paragraphs (5) and (6) do not apply in respect of an application for a special measures direction enabling a child witness in need of special protection to give evidence by means of a live link if the opposition is that the special measures direction is not likely to maximise the quality of the witness's evidence.

(8)   In order to comply with paragraph (6) –

    (a)   a party must in the written notification state whether he –

(i) disputes that the witness is eligible for assistance by virtue of section 16 or 17 of the 1999 Act,

(ii) disputes that any of the special measures available would be likely to improve the quality of evidence given by the witness or that such measures (or a combination of them) would be likely to maximise the quality of that evidence, and

(iii) opposes the granting of a special measures direction; and

(b) where the application relates to the admission of a video recording, a party who receives a recording must provide the information required by rule 29.7(7) below.

(9) Except where notice is received in accordance with paragraph (6), the court (including, in the case of an application to a magistrates' court, a single justice of the peace) may –

(a) determine the application in favour of the applicant without a hearing; or

(b) direct a hearing.

(10) Where a party to the proceedings notifies the court in accordance with paragraph (6) of his opposition to the application, the justices' clerk or the Crown Court must direct a hearing of the application.

(11) Where a hearing of the application is to take place in accordance with paragraph (9) or (10) above, the court officer shall notify each party to the proceedings of the time and place of the hearing.

(12) A party notified in accordance with paragraph (11) may be present at the hearing and be heard.

(13) The court officer must, within 3 days of the decision of the court in relation to an application under paragraph (1) being made, notify all the parties of the decision, and if the application was made for a direction enabling a video recording of an interview of a witness to be admitted as evidence in chief of that witness, the notification must state whether the whole or specified parts only of the video recording or recordings disclosed are to be admitted in evidence.

(14) In this Part:

"an intermediary" has the same meaning as in section 29 of the 1999 Act; and

"child witness in need of protection" shall be construed in accordance with section 21(1) of the 1999 Act.

Formerly rules 1 and 2 of the Magistrates' Courts (Special Measures Directions) Rules 2002 and rules 1 and 2 of the Crown Court (Special Measures Directions and Directions Prohibiting Cross-examination) Rules 2002. See also chapter I of Part II of the Youth Justice and Criminal Evidence Act 1999.

29.2   Application for an extension of time

(1) An application may be made in writing for the period of 14 days or, as the case may be, 28 days specified in rule 29.1(4) to be extended.

(2) The application may be made either before or after that period has expired.

(3) The application must be accompanied by a statement setting out the reasons why the applicant is or was unable to make the application within that period and a copy of the application and the statement must be sent to every other party to the proceedings.

(4) An application for an extension of time under this rule shall be determined by a single justice of the peace or a judge of the Crown Court without a hearing unless the justice or the judge otherwise directs.

(5) The court officer shall notify all the parties of the court's decision.

Formerly rule 3 of the Magistrates' Courts (Special Measures Directions) Rules 2002 and rule 3 of the Crown Court (Special Measures Directions and Directions Prohibiting Cross-examination) Rules 2002.

29.3   Late applications

(1) Notwithstanding the requirements of rule 29.1 –
  (a) an application may be made for a special measures direction orally at the trial; or
  (b) a magistrates' court or the Crown Court may of its own motion raise the issue whether a special measures direction should be given.

(2) Where an application is made in accordance with paragraph (1)(a) –
  (a) the applicant must state the reasons for the late application; and
  (b) the court must be satisfied that the applicant was unable to make the application in accordance with rule 29.1.

(3) The court shall determine before making a special measures direction –
  (a) whether to allow other parties to the proceedings to make representations on the question;
  (b) the time allowed for making such representations (if any); and
  (c) whether the question should be determined following a hearing at which the parties to the proceedings may be heard.

(4) Paragraphs (2) and (3) do not apply in respect of an application made orally at the trial for a special measures direction –
  (a) enabling a child witness in need of special protection to give evidence by means of a live link; or
  (b) enabling a video recording of such a child to be admitted as evidence in chief of the witness,

if the opposition is that the special measures direction will not maximise the quality of the witness's evidence.

Formerly rule 4 of the Magistrates' Courts (Special Measures Directions) Rules 2002 and rule 4 of the Crown Court (Special Measures Directions and Directions Prohibiting Cross-examination) Rules 2002. An application to make or vary a special measures direction also may be made in the time allowed under rule 36.6.

29.4   Discharge or variation of a special measures direction

(1)   An application to a magistrates' court or the Crown Court to discharge or vary a special measures direction under section 20(2) of the Youth Justice and Criminal Evidence Act 1999 must be in writing and each material change of circumstances which the applicant alleges has occurred since the direction was made must be set out.

(2)   An application under paragraph (1) must be sent to the court officer as soon as reasonably practicable after the change of circumstances occurs.

(3)   The applicant must also send copies of the application to each party to the proceedings at the same time as the application is sent to the court officer.

(4)   A party to whom an application is sent in accordance with paragraph (3) may oppose the application on the ground that it discloses no material change of circumstances.

(5)   Rule 29.1(6) to (13) shall apply to an application to discharge or vary a special measures direction as it applies to an application for a direction.

Formerly rule 5 of the Magistrates' Courts (Special Measures Directions) Rules 2002 and rule 5 of the Crown Court (Special Measures Directions and Directions Prohibiting Cross-examination) Rules 2002.

29.5   Renewal application following a material change of circumstances

(1)   Where an application for a special measures direction has been refused by a magistrates' court or the Crown Court, the application may only be renewed ("renewal application") where there has been a material change of circumstances since the court refused the application.

(2)   The applicant must –
   (a)   identify in the renewal application each material change of circumstances which is alleged to have occurred; and

   (b)   send the renewal application to the court officer as soon as reasonably practicable after the change occurs.

(3)   The applicant must also send copies of the renewal application to each of the parties to the proceedings at the same time as the application is sent to the court officer.

(4) A party to whom the renewal application is sent in accordance with paragraph (3) above may oppose the application on the ground that it discloses no material change of circumstances.

(5) Rules 29.1(6) to (13), 29.6 and 29.7 apply to a renewal application as they apply to the application which was refused.

Formerly rule 6 of the Magistrates' Courts (Special Measures Directions) Rules 2002 and rule 6 of the Crown Court (Special Measures Directions and Directions Prohibiting Cross-examination) Rules 2002.

29.6 Application for special measures direction for witness to give evidence by means of a live television link

(1) Where the application for a special measures direction is made, in accordance with rule 29.1(2)(a), for a witness to give evidence by means of a live link, the following provisions of this rule shall also apply.

(2) A party who seeks to oppose an application for a child witness to give evidence by means of a live link must, in order to comply with rule 29.1(5), state why in his view the giving of a special measures direction would not be likely to maximise the quality of the witness's evidence.

(3) However, paragraph (2) does not apply in relation to a child witness in need of special protection.

(4) Where a special measures direction is made enabling a witness to give evidence by means of a live link, the witness shall be accompanied at the live link only by persons acceptable to the court.

(5) If the special measures directions combine provisions for a witness to give evidence by means of a live link with provision for the examination of the witness to be conducted through an intermediary, the witness shall be accompanied at the live link only by –
  (a) the intermediary; and
  (b) such other persons as may be acceptable to the court.

Formerly rule 7 of the Magistrates' Courts (Special Measures Directions) Rules 2002 and rule 7 of the Crown Court (Special Measures Directions and Directions Prohibiting Cross-examination) Rules 2002. As to the provision of support for witnesses giving evidence by live television link see also direction III.29 in the Practice Direction.

29.7 Video recording of testimony from witnesses

(1) Where an application is made to a magistrates' court or the Crown Court for a special measures direction enabling a video recording of an interview of a witness to be admitted as evidence in chief of the witness, the following provisions of this rule shall also apply.

(2) The application made in accordance with rule 29.1(1) must be accompanied by the video recording which it is proposed to tender in evidence and must include –

    (a) the name of the defendant and the offence to be charged;

    (b) the name and date of birth of the witness in respect of whom the application is made;

    (c) the date on which the video recording was made;

    (d) a statement as to whether, and if so at what point in the video recording, an oath was administered to, or a solemn declaration made by, the witness;

    (e) a statement that, in the opinion of the applicant, either –

        (i) the witness is available for cross-examination, or

        (ii) the witness is not available for cross-examination and the parties have agreed that there is no need for the witness to be so available;

    (f) a statement of the circumstances in which the video recording was made which complies with paragraph (4) of this rule; and

    (g) the date on which the video recording was disclosed to the other party or parties.

(3) Where it is proposed to tender part only of a video recording of an interview with the witness, the application must specify that part and be accompanied by a video recording of the entire interview, including those parts which it is not proposed to tender in evidence, and by a statement of the circumstances in which the video recording of the entire interview was made which complies with paragraph (4) of this rule.

(4) The statement of the circumstances in which the video recording was made referred to in paragraphs (2)(f) and (3) of this rule shall include the following information, except in so far as it is contained in the recording itself –

    (a) the times at which the recording commenced and finished, including details of interruptions;

    (b) the location at which the recording was made and the usual function of the premises;

    (c) in relation to each person present at any point during, or immediately before, the recording –

        (i) their name, age and occupation,

        (ii) the time for which each person was present, and

        (iii) the relationship, if any, of each person to the witness and to the defendant;

    (d) in relation to the equipment used for the recording –

        (i) a description of the equipment,

        (ii) the number of cameras used,

(iii) whether the cameras were fixed or mobile,

(iv) the number and location of the microphones,

(v) the video format used; and

(vi) whether it offered single or multiple recording facilities and, if so, which were used; and

(e) the location of the mastertape if the video recording is a copy and details of when and by whom the copy was made.

(5) If the special measures directions enabling a video recording of an interview of a witness to be admitted as evidence in chief of the witness with provision for the examination of the witness to be conducted through an intermediary, the information to be provided under paragraph (4)(c) shall be the same as that for other persons present at the recording but with the addition of details of the declaration made by the intermediary under rule 29.9.

(6) If the special measures directions enabling a video recording of an interview of a witness to be admitted as evidence in chief of the witness with provision for the witness, in accordance with section 30 of the Youth Justice and Criminal Evidence Act 1999, to be provided with a device as an aid to communication during the video recording of the interview the information to be included under paragraph (4)(d) shall include also details of any such device used for the purposes of recording.

(7) A party who receives a recording under paragraph (2) must within 14 days of its receipt, notify the applicant and the court officer, in writing –

(a) whether he objects to the admission under section 27 of the 1999 Act of any part of the video recording or recordings disclosed, giving his reasons why it would not be in the interests of justice for the recording or any part of it to be admitted;

(b) whether he would agree to the admission of part of the video recording or recordings and, if so, which part or parts; and

(c) whether he wishes to be represented at any hearing of the application.

(8) A party who seeks to oppose an application for a special measures direction enabling a video recording of an interview of a child witness to be admitted as evidence in chief of the witness must, in order to comply with rule 29.1(6), state why in his view the giving of a special measures direction would not be likely to maximise the quality of the witness's evidence.

(9) However, paragraph (8) does not apply if the witness is a child witness in need of special protection.

(10) Notwithstanding the provisions of rule 29.1 and this rule, any video recording which the defendant proposes to tender in evidence need not be sent to the prosecution until the close of the prosecution case at the trial.

(11)   The court may determine an application by the defendant to tender in evidence a video recording even though the recording has not, in accordance with paragraph (10), been served upon the prosecution.

(12)   Where a video recording which is the subject of a special measures direction is sent to the prosecution after the direction has been made, the prosecutor may apply to the court for the direction to be varied or discharged.

(13)   An application under paragraph (12) may be made orally to the court.

(14)   A prosecutor who makes an application under paragraph (12) must state –
   (a)   why he objects to the admission under section 27 of the 1999 Act of any part of the video recording or recordings disclosed, giving his reasons why it would not be in the interests of justice for the recording or any part of it to be admitted; and
   (b)   whether he would agree to the admission of part of the video recording or recordings and, if so, which part or parts.

(15)   The court must, before determining the application –
   (a)   direct a hearing of the application; and
   (b)   allow all the parties to the proceedings to be present and be heard on the application.

(16)   The court officer must notify all parties to the proceedings of the decision of the court as soon as may be reasonable after the decision is given.

(17)   Any decision varying a special measures direction must state whether the whole or specified parts of the video recording or recordings subject to the application are to be admitted in evidence.

Formerly rule 8 of the Magistrates' Courts (Special Measures Directions) Rules 2002 and rule 8 of the Crown Court (Special Measures Directions and Directions Prohibiting Cross-examination) Rules 2002. As to the use of video-recorded evidence in chief see also direction IV.40 in the Practice Direction.

29.8   Expert evidence in connection with special measures directions

Any party to proceedings in a magistrates' court or the Crown Court who proposes to adduce expert evidence (whether of fact or opinion) in connection with an application or renewal application for, or for varying or discharging, a special measures direction must, not less than 14 days before the date set for the trial to begin –
   (a)   furnish the other party or parties and the court with a statement in writing of any finding or opinion which he proposes to adduce by way of such evidence and notify the expert of this disclosure; and

(b) where a request is made to him in that behalf by any other party to those proceedings, provide that party also with a copy of (or if it appears to the party proposing to adduce the evidence to be more practicable, a reasonable opportunity to examine) the record of any observation, test, calculation or other procedure on which such finding or opinion is based and any document or other thing or substance in respect of which any such procedure has been carried out.

Formerly rule 9 of the Magistrates' Courts (Special Measures Directions) Rules 2002 and rule 9 of the Crown Court (Special Measures Directions and Directions Prohibiting Cross-examination) Rules 2002. Part 33 contains rules about the duties of an expert and the content of an expert's report.

29.9 Intermediaries

The declaration required to be made by an intermediary in accordance with section 29(5) of the Youth Justice and Criminal Evidence Act 1999 shall be in the following form:

> "I solemnly, sincerely and truly declare that I will well and faithfully communicate questions and answers and make true explanation of all matters and things as shall be required of me according to the best of my skill and understanding."

Formerly rule 9A of the Magistrates' Courts (Special Measures Directions) Rules 2002 and rule 9A of the Crown Court (Special Measures Directions and Directions Prohibiting Cross-examination) Rules 2002.

PART 30
USE OF LIVE TELEVISION LINK OTHER THAN FOR VULNERABLE WITNESSES

30.1 Evidence by live television link in the Crown Court where witness is outside the United Kingdom

(1) Any party may apply for leave under section 32(1) of the Criminal Justice Act 1988 for evidence to be given through a live television link by a witness who is outside the United Kingdom.

(2) An application under paragraph (1), and any matter relating thereto which, by virtue of the following provisions of this rule, falls to be determined by the Crown Court, may be dealt with in chambers by any judge of the Crown Court.

(3) An application under paragraph (1) shall be made by giving notice in writing, which shall be in the form set out in the Practice Direction.

(4) An application under paragraph (1) shall be made within 28 days after the date of the committal of the defendant or, as the case may be, of the giving of a notice of transfer under section 4(1)(c) of the Criminal Justice Act 1987, or of the service of copies of the documents containing the evidence on which the charge or charges are based under paragraph 1 of Schedule 3 to the Crime and Disorder Act 1998, or of the preferring of a bill of indictment in relation to the case.

(5) The period of 28 days in paragraph (4) may be extended by the Crown Court, either before or after it expires, on an application made in writing, specifying the grounds of the application. The court officer shall notify all the parties of the decision of the Crown Court.

(6) The notice under paragraph (3) or any application under paragraph (5) shall be sent to the court officer and at the same time a copy thereof shall be sent by the applicant to every other party to the proceedings.

(7) A party who receives a copy of a notice under paragraph (3) shall, within 28 days of the date of the notice, notify the applicant and the court officer, in writing—

   (a) whether or not he opposes the application, giving his reasons for any such opposition; and

   (b) whether or not he wishes to be represented at any hearing of the application.

(8) After the expiry of the period referred to in paragraph (7), the Crown Court shall determine whether an application under paragraph (1) is to be dealt with—

   (a) without a hearing; or

   (b) at a hearing at which the applicant and such other party or parties as the court may direct may be represented;

   (c) and the court officer shall notify the applicant and, where necessary, the other party or parties, of the time and place of any such hearing.

(9) The court officer shall notify all the parties of the decision of the Crown Court in relation to an application under paragraph (1) and, where leave is granted, the notification shall state

   (a) the country in which the witness will give evidence;

   (b) if known, the place where the witness will give evidence;

   (c) where the witness is to give evidence on behalf of the prosecutor, or where disclosure is required by section 5(7) of the Criminal Procedure and Investigations Act 1996 (alibi) or by rules under section 81 of the Police and Criminal Evidence Act 1984 (expert evidence), the name of the witness;

(d)   the location of the Crown Court at which the trial should take place; and

(e)   any conditions specified by the Crown Court in accordance with paragraph (10).

(10)   The Crown Court dealing with an application under paragraph (1) may specify that as a condition of the grant of leave the witness should give the evidence in the presence of a specified person who is able and willing to answer under oath or affirmation any questions the trial judge may put as to the circumstances in which the evidence is given, including questions about any persons who are present when the evidence is given and any matters which may affect the giving of the evidence.

Formerly rule 23B of the Crown Court Rules 1982. For the corresponding rule in the Court of Appeal see rule 68.19.

PART 31
RESTRICTION ON CROSS-EXAMINATION BY A DEFENDANT ACTING IN PERSON

31.1   Restrictions on cross-examination of witness

(1)   This rule and rules 31.2 and 31.3 apply where an accused is prevented from cross-examining a witness in person by virtue of section 34, 35 or 36 of the Youth Justice and Criminal Evidence Act 1999.

(2)   The court shall explain to the accused as early in the proceedings as is reasonably practicable that he –
    (a)   is prevented from cross-examining a witness in person; and
    (b)   should arrange for a legal representative to act for him for the purpose of cross-examining the witness.

(3)   The accused shall notify the court officer within 7 days of the court giving its explanation, or within such other period as the court may in any particular case allow, of the action, if any, he has taken.

(4)   Where he has arranged for a legal representative to act for him, the notification shall include details of the name and address of the representative.

(5)   The notification shall be in writing.

(6) The court officer shall notify all other parties to the proceedings of the name and address of the person, if any, appointed to act for the accused.

(7) Where the court gives its explanation under paragraph (2) to the accused either within 7 days of the day set for the commencement of any hearing at which a witness in respect of whom a prohibition under section 34, 35 or 36 of the 1999 Act applies may be cross-examined or after such a hearing has commenced, the period of 7 days shall be reduced in accordance with any directions issued by the court.

(8) Where at the end of the period of 7 days or such other period as the court has allowed, the court has received no notification from the accused it may grant the accused an extension of time, whether on its own motion or on the application of the accused.

(9) Before granting an extension of time, the court may hold a hearing at which all parties to the proceedings may attend and be heard.

(10) Any extension of time shall be of such period as the court considers appropriate in the circumstances of the case.

(11) The decision of the court as to whether to grant the accused an extension of time shall be notified to all parties to the proceedings by the court officer.

This rule derives in part from rule 24B of the Crown Court Rules 1982.

31.2 Appointment of legal representative

(1) Where the court decides, in accordance with section 38(4) of the Youth Justice and Criminal Evidence Act 1999, to appoint a qualified legal representative, the court officer shall notify all parties to the proceedings of the name and address of the representative.

(2) An appointment made by the court under section 38(4) of the 1999 Act shall, except to such extent as the court may in any particular case determine, terminate at the conclusion of the cross-examination of the witness or witnesses in respect of whom a prohibition under section 34, 35 or 36 of the 1999 Act applies.

This rule derives in part from rule 24C of the Crown Court Rules 1982.

31.3 Appointment arranged by the accused

(1) The accused may arrange for the qualified legal representative, appointed by the court under section 38(4) of the Youth Justice and Criminal Evidence Act 1999, to be appointed to act for him for the purpose of cross-examining any witness in respect of whom a prohibition under section 34, 35 or 36 of the 1999 Act applies.

(2) Where such an appointment is made –

(a) both the accused and the qualified legal representative appointed shall notify the court of the appointment; and

(b) the qualified legal representative shall, from the time of his appointment, act for the accused as though the arrangement had been made under section 38(2)(a) of the 1999 Act and shall cease to be the representative of the court under section 38(4).

(3) Where the court receives notification of the appointment either from the qualified legal representative or from the accused but not from both, the court shall investigate whether the appointment has been made, and if it concludes that the appointment has not been made, paragraph (2)(b) shall not apply.

(4) An accused may, notwithstanding an appointment by the court under section 38(4) of the 1999 Act, arrange for a legal representative to act for him for the purpose of cross-examining any witness in respect of whom a prohibition under section 34, 35 or 36 of the 1999 Act applies.

(5) Where the accused arranges for, or informs the court of his intention to arrange for, a legal representative to act for him, he shall notify the court, within such period as the court may allow, of the name and address of any person appointed to act for him.

(6) Where the court is notified within the time allowed that such an appointment has been made, any qualified legal representative appointed by the court in accordance with section 38(4) of the 1999 Act shall be discharged.

(7) The court officer shall, as soon as reasonably practicable after the court receives notification of an appointment under this rule or, where paragraph (3) applies, after the court is satisfied that the appointment has been made, notify all the parties to the proceedings –

(a) that the appointment has been made;

(b) where paragraph (4) applies, of the name and address of the person appointed; and

(c) that the person appointed by the court under section 38(4) of the 1999 Act has been discharged or has ceased to act for the court.

This rule derives in part from rule 24D of the Crown Court Rules 1982.

31.4   Prohibition on cross-examination of witness

(1) An application by the prosecutor for the court to give a direction under section 36 of the Youth Justice and Criminal Evidence Act 1999 in relation to any witness must be sent to the court officer and at the same time a copy thereof must be sent by the applicant to every other party to the proceedings.

(2) In his application the prosecutor must state why, in his opinion –

(a)   the evidence given by the witness is likely to be diminished if cross-examination is undertaken by the accused in person;

(b)   the evidence would be improved if a direction were given under section 36(2) of the 1999 Act; and

(c)   it would not be contrary to the interests of justice to give such a direction.

(3)   On receipt of the application the court officer must refer it –
(a)   if the trial has started, to the court of trial; or
(b)   if the trial has not started when the application is received –
   (i)   to the judge or court designated to conduct the trial, or
   (ii)   if no judge or court has been designated for that purpose, to such judge or court designated for the purposes of hearing that application.

(4)   Where a copy of the application is received by a party to the proceedings more than 14 days before the date set for the trial to begin, that party may make observations in writing on the application to the court officer, but any such observations must be made within 14 days of the receipt of the application and be copied to the other parties to the proceedings.

(5)   A party to whom an application is sent in accordance with paragraph (1) who wishes to oppose the application must give his reasons for doing so to the court officer and the other parties to the proceedings.

(6)   Those reasons must be notified –
(a)   within 14 days of the date the application was served on him, if that date is more than 14 days before the date set for the trial to begin;
(b)   if the trial has begun, in accordance with any directions issued by the court; or
(c)   if neither paragraph (6)(a) nor (b) applies, before the date set for the trial to begin.

(7)   Where the application made in accordance with paragraph (1) is made before the date set for the trial to begin and –
(a)   is not contested by any party to the proceedings, the court may determine the application without a hearing;
(b)   is contested by a party to the proceedings, the court must direct a hearing of the application.

(8)   Where the application is made after the trial has begun –
(a)   the application may be made orally; and
(b)   the court may give such directions as it considers appropriate to deal with the application.

(9)   Where a hearing of the application is to take place, the court officer shall notify each party to the proceedings of the time and place of the hearing.

(**10**)   A party notified in accordance with paragraph (9) may be present at the hearing and be heard.

(**11**)   The court officer must, as soon as possible after the determination of an application made in accordance with paragraph (1), give notice of the decision and the reasons for it to all the parties to the proceedings.

(**12**)   A person making an oral application under paragraph (8)(a) must –
   (a)   give reasons why the application was not made before the trial commenced; and
   (b)   provide the court with the information set out in paragraph (2).

This rule derives in part from rule 24E of the Crown Court Rules 1982.

PART 33
EXPERT EVIDENCE

Note. See rule 2.1(4) for the application of the rules in this Part. Part 24 contains rules about the disclosure of the substance of expert evidence. For the use of an expert report as evidence, see section 30 of the Criminal Justice Act 1988.

33.1   Reference to expert

A reference to an 'expert' in this Part is a reference to a person who is required to give or prepare expert evidence for the purpose of criminal proceedings, including evidence required to determine fitness to plead or for the purpose of sentencing.

Note. Expert medical evidence may be required to determine fitness to plead under section 4 of the Criminal Procedure (Insanity) Act 1964. It may be required also under section 11 of the Powers of Criminal Courts (Sentencing)

Act 2000, under Part III of the Mental Health Act 1983 or under Part 12 of the Criminal Justice Act 2003. Those Acts contain requirements about the qualification of medical experts.

33.2 Expert's duty to the court

(1) An expert must help the court to achieve the overriding objective by giving objective, unbiased opinion on matters within his expertise.

(2) This duty overrides any obligation to the person from whom he receives instructions or by whom he is paid.

(3) This duty includes an obligation to inform all parties and the court if the expert's opinion changes from that contained in a report served as evidence or given in a statement under Part 24 or Part 29.

33.3 Content of expert's report

(1) An expert's report must –
   (a) give details of the expert's qualifications, relevant experience and accreditation;
   (b) give details of any literature or other information which the expert has relied on in making the report;
   (c) contain a statement setting out the substance of all facts given to the expert which are material to the opinions expressed in the report or upon which those opinions are based;
   (d) make clear which of the facts stated in the report are within the expert's own knowledge;
   (e) say who carried out any examination, measurement, test or experiment which the expert has used for the report and –
      (i) give the qualifications, relevant experience and accreditation of that person,
      (ii) say whether or not the examination, measurement, test or experiment was carried out under the expert's supervision, and
      (iii) summarise the findings on which the expert relies;
   (f) where there is a range of opinion on the matters dealt with in the report –
      (i) summarise the range of opinion, and
      (ii) give reasons for his own opinion;
   (g) if the expert is not able to give his opinion without qualification, state the qualification;
   (h) contain a summary of the conclusions reached;
   (i) contain a statement that the expert understands his duty to the court, and has complied and will continue to comply with that duty; and
   (j) contain the same declaration of truth as a witness statement.

(2) Only sub-paragraphs (i) and (j) of rule 33.3(1) apply to a summary by an expert of his conclusions served in advance of that expert's report.

Note. Part 24 contains rules about the disclosure of the substance of expert evidence. Part 27 contains rules about witness statements. Declarations of truth in witness statements are required by section 9 of the Criminal Justice Act 1967 and section 5B of the Magistrates' Courts Act 1980. A party who accepts another party's expert's conclusions may admit them as facts under section 10 of the Criminal Justice Act 1967. Evidence of examinations etc. on which an expert relies may be admissible under section 127 of the Criminal Justice Act 2003.

33.4 Expert to be informed of service of report

A party who serves on another party or on the court a report by an expert must, at once, inform that expert of that fact.

33.5 Pre-hearing discussion of expert evidence

(1) This rule applies where more than one party wants to introduce expert evidence.

(2) The court may direct the experts to –
    (a) discuss the expert issues in the proceedings; and
    (b) prepare a statement for the court of the matters on which they agree and disagree, giving their reasons.

(3) Except for that statement, the content of that discussion must not be referred to without the court's permission.

33.6 Failure to comply with directions

A party may not introduce expert evidence without the court's permission if the expert has not complied with a direction under rule 33.5.

Note. At a pre-trial hearing a court may make binding rulings about the admissibility of evidence and about questions of law under section 7 of the Criminal Justice Act 1987; sections 31 and 40 of the Criminal Procedure and Investigations Act 1996; and section 45 of the Courts Act 2003.

33.7 Court's power to direct that evidence is to be given by a single joint expert

(1) Where more than one defendant wants to introduce expert evidence on an issue at trial, the court may direct that the evidence on that issue is to be given by one expert only.

(2) Where the co-defendants cannot agree who should be the expert, the court may –
    (a) select the expert from a list prepared or identified by them; or
    (b) direct that the expert be selected in such other manner as the court may direct.

33.8   Instructions to a single joint expert

(1) Where the court gives a direction under rule 33.7 for a single joint expert to be used, each of the co-defendants may give instructions to the expert.

(2) When a co-defendant gives instructions to the expert he must, at the same time, send a copy of the instructions to the other co-defendant(s).

(3) The court may give directions about –

    (a)   the payment of the expert's fees and expenses; and

    (b)   any examination, measurement, test or experiment which the expert wishes to carry out.

(4) The court may, before an expert is instructed, limit the amount that can be paid by way of fees and expenses to the expert.

(5) Unless the court otherwise directs, the instructing co-defendants are jointly and severally liable for the payment of the expert's fees and expenses.

PART 34
HEARSAY EVIDENCE

34.1   When this applies

This Part applies in a magistrates' court and in the Crown Court where a party wants to introduce evidence on one or more of the grounds set out in section 114(1)(d), section 116, section 117 and section 121 of the Criminal Justice Act 2003, and in this Part that evidence is called "hearsay evidence".

Section 114 of the 2003 Act provides that a statement not made in oral evidence in criminal proceedings is admissible as evidence of any matter stated only on certain conditions. This Part applies only to evidence that is admissible on one or more of the following grounds set out in the 2003 Act,

*namely where (a) it is in the interests of justice for it to be admissible (see
section 114(1)(d)), (b) the witness is unavailable to attend (see section 116),
(c) the evidence is contained in a business, or other, document (see section
117) or (d) the evidence is multiple hearsay (see section 121). The meaning of
"statements" and "matter stated" is explained in section 115 of the 2003 Act.
"Oral evidence" is defined in section 134(1) of that Act. For the introduction
of hearsay evidence in the Court of Appeal, see rule 68.20.*

34.2   Notice of hearsay evidence

The party who wants to introduce hearsay evidence must give notice in
the form set out in the Practice Direction to the court officer and all other
parties.

34.3   When the prosecutor must give notice of hearsay evidence

The prosecutor must give notice of hearsay evidence—

   (a)   in a magistrates' court, at the same time as he complies or purports
         to comply with section 3 of the Criminal Procedure and
         Investigations Act 1996 (disclosure by prosecutor); or

   (b)   in the Crown Court, not more than 14 days after –

         (i)   the committal of the defendant, or

         (ii) the consent to the preferment of a bill of indictment in relation
               to the case, or

         (iii) the service of a notice of transfer under section 4 of the Criminal
               Justice Act 19874 (serious fraud cases) or under section 53 of
               the Criminal Justice Act 1991 (certain cases involving children),
               or

         (iv) where a person is sent for trial under section 51 of the Crime
               and Disorder Act 19986 (indictable-only offences sent for trial),
               the service of copies of the documents containing the evidence
               on which the charge or charges are based under paragraph 1 of
               Schedule 3 to the 1998 Act.

34.4   When a defendant must give notice of hearsay evidence

A defendant must give notice of hearsay evidence not more than 14 days after
the prosecutor has complied with or purported to comply with section 3 of
the Criminal Procedure and Investigations Act 1996 (disclosure by
prosecutor).

34.5   Opposing the introduction of hearsay evidence

A party who receives a notice of hearsay evidence may oppose it by giving
notice within 14 days in the form set out in the Practice Direction to the court
officer and all other parties.

34.7   Court's power to vary requirements under this Part

The court may –
 (a) dispense with the requirement to give notice of hearsay evidence;
 (b) allow notice to be given in a different form, or orally; or
 (c) shorten a time limit or extend it (even after it has expired).

34.8   Waiving the requirement to give a notice of hearsay evidence

A party entitled to receive a notice of hearsay evidence may waive his entitlement by so informing the court and the party who would have given the notice.

PART 35
EVIDENCE OF BAD CHARACTER

35.1   When this Part applies

This Part applies in a magistrates' court and in the Crown Court when a party wants to introduce evidence of bad character as defined in section 98 of the Criminal Justice Act 2003.

For the introduction of evidence of bad character in the Court of Appeal see rule 68.21.

35.2   Introducing evidence of non-defendant's bad character

A party who wants to introduce evidence of a non-defendant's bad character or who wants to cross-examine a witness with a view to eliciting that evidence, under section 100 of the Criminal Justice Act 2003 must apply in the form set out in the Practice Direction and the application must be received by the court officer and all other parties to the proceedings–

    (a)   not more than 14 days after the prosecutor has –

        (i)   complied or purported to comply with section 3 of the Criminal Procedure and Investigations Act 1996 (initial disclosure by the prosecutor), or

        (ii)   disclosed the previous convictions of that non-defendant; or

    (b)   as soon as reasonably practicable, where the application concerns a non-defendant who is to be invited to give (or has given) evidence for a defendant.

Formerly rule 72A(1) of the Magistrates' Courts Rules 1981 and rule 23E(1) of the Crown Court Rules 1982.

35.3   Opposing introduction of evidence of non-defendant's bad character

A party who receives a copy of an application under rule 35.2 may oppose that application by giving notice in writing to the court officer and all other parties to the proceedings not more than 14 days after receiving that application.

Formerly rule 72A(2) of the Magistrates' Courts Rules 1981 and rule 23E(2) of the Crown Court Rules 1982.

35.4   Prosecutor introducing evidence of defendant's bad character

(1)   A prosecutor who wants to introduce evidence of a defendant's bad character or who wants to cross-examine a witness with a view to eliciting that evidence, under section 101 of the Criminal Justice Act 2003 must give notice in the form set out in the Practice Direction to the court officer and all other parties to the proceedings.

(2)   Notice under paragraph (1) must be given –

    (a)   in a case to be tried in a magistrates' court, at the same time as the prosecutor complies or purports to comply with section 3 of the Criminal Procedure and Investigations Act 1996; and

    (b)   in a case to be tried in the Crown Court, not more than 14 days after –

        (i)   the committal of the defendant, or

        (ii)   the consent to the preferment of a bill of indictment in relation to the case, or

(iii) the service of notice of transfer under section 4(1) of the Criminal Justice Act 1987 (notices of transfer) or under section 53(1) of the Criminal Justice Act 1991 (notices of transfer in certain cases involving children), or

(iv) where a person is sent for trial under section 51 of the Crime and Disorder Act 1998 (sending cases to the Crown Court) the service of copies of the documents containing the evidence on which the charge or charges are based under paragraph 1 of Schedule 3 to that Act.

Formerly rule 72A(3) of the Magistrates' Courts Rules 1981 and rule 23E(3) of the Crown Court Rules 1982.

35.5   Co-defendant introducing evidence of defendant's bad character

A co-defendant who wants to introduce evidence of a defendant's bad character or who wants to cross-examine a witness with a view to eliciting that evidence under section 101 of the Criminal Justice Act 2003 must give notice in the form set out in the Practice Direction to the court officer and all other parties to the proceedings not more than 14 days after the prosecutor has complied or purported to comply with section 3 of the Criminal Procedure and Investigations Act 1996.

Formerly rule 72A(4) of the Magistrates' Courts Rules 1981 and rule 23E(4) of the Crown Court Rules 1982.

35.6   Defendant applying to exclude evidence of his own bad character

A defendant's application to exclude bad character evidence must be in the form set out in the Practice Direction and received by the court officer and all other parties to the proceedings not more than 14 days after receiving a notice given under rules 35.4 or 35.5.

Formerly rule 72A(5) of the Magistrates' Courts Rules 1981 and rule 23E(5) of the Crown Court Rules 1982.

35.8   Court's power to vary requirements under this Part

The court may –
  (a) allow a notice or application required under this rule to be given in a different form, or orally; or
  (b) shorten a time-limit under this rule or extend it even after it has expired.

Formerly rule 72A(7) of the Magistrates' Courts Rules 1981 and rule 23E(7) of the Crown Court Rules 1982.

35.9   Defendant waiving right to receive notice

A defendant entitled to receive a notice under this Part may waive his entitlement by so informing the court and the party who would have given the notice.

Formerly rule 72A(6) of the Magistrates' Courts Rules 1981 and rule 23E(6) of the Crown Court Rules 1982.

PART 36
EVIDENCE ABOUT A COMPLAINANT'S SEXUAL BEHAVIOUR

Note. The rules in this Part derive in part from rule 23D of the Crown Court Rules 1982.

Section 41 of the Youth Justice and Criminal Evidence Act 1999 prohibits evidence or cross-examination about the sexual behaviour of a complainant of a sexual offence, subject to exceptions.

See also:

- section 42 of the 1999 Act, which among other things defines 'sexual behaviour' and 'sexual offence';
- section 43, which among other things, requires –
  - an application under section 41 to be heard in private and in the absence of the complainant,
  - the reasons for the court's decision on an application to be given in open court,
  - the court to state in open court the extent to which evidence may be introduced or questions asked;
- section 34, which prohibits cross-examination by a defendant in person of the complainant of a sexual offence.

36.1   When this Part applies

This Part applies in magistrates' courts and in the Crown Court where a defendant wants to (a) introduce evidence; or

(b)   cross-examine a witness

about a complainant's sexual behaviour despite the prohibition in section 41 of the Youth Justice and Criminal Evidence Act 1999.

36.2   Application for permission to introduce evidence or cross-examine

The defendant must apply for permission to do so –
  (a)   in writing; and
  (b)   not more than 28 days after the prosecutor has complied or purported to comply with section 3 of the Criminal Procedure and Investigations Act 1996 (disclosure by prosecutor).

Note. See Part 3 for the court's general powers to consider an application with or without a hearing and to give directions.

At a pre-trial hearing a court may make binding rulings about the admissibility of evidence and about questions of law under section 7 of the Criminal Justice Act 1987; sections 31 and 40 of the Criminal Procedure and Investigations Act 1996; and section 45 of the Courts Act 2003.

36.3   Content of application

The application must –
  (a)   identify the issue to which the defendant says the complainant's sexual behaviour is relevant;
  (b)   give particulars of –
    (i)   any evidence that the defendant wants to introduce, and
    (ii)   any questions that the defendant wants to ask;
  (c)   identify the exception to the prohibition in section 41 of the Youth Justice and Criminal Evidence Act 1999 on which the defendant relies; and
  (d)   give the name and date of birth of any witness whose evidence about the complainant's sexual behaviour the defendant wants to introduce.

36.4   Service of application

The defendant must serve the application on the court officer and all other parties.

36.5   Reply to application

A party who wants to make representations about an application under rule 36.2 must –
  (a)   do so in writing not more than 14 days after receiving it; and
  (b)   serve those representations on the court officer and all other parties.

36.6   Application for special measures

If the court allows an application under rule 36.2 then –

   (a) a party may apply not more than 14 days later for a special measures direction or for the variation of an existing special measures direction; and

   (b) the court may shorten the time for opposing that application.

Note. Special measures to improve the quality of evidence given by certain witnesses may be directed by the court under section 19 of the Youth Justice and Criminal Evidence Act 1999 and varied under section 20. An application for a special measures direction may be made by a party under Part 29 or the court may make a direction on its own initiative. Rule 29.1(6) sets the usual time limit (14 days) for opposing a special measures application.

36.7   Court's power to vary requirements under this Part

The court may shorten or extend (even after it has expired) a time limit under this Part.

PART 37
TRIAL AND SENTENCE IN A MAGISTRATES' COURT

Note. Part 3 contains rules about case management that apply at trial as well as during preparation for trial. The rules in this Part must be read in conjunction with those rules.

37.1   When this Part applies

(1) This Part applies in a magistrates' court where –
   (a)   the court tries a case; or
   (b)   the defendant pleads guilty.

(2) Where the defendant is under 18, in this Part –
   (a)   a reference to convicting the defendant includes a reference to finding the defendant guilty of an offence; and
   (b)   a reference to sentence includes a reference to an order made on a finding of guilt.

Note. A magistrates' court's powers to try an allegation of an offence are contained in section 2 of the Magistrates' Courts Act 1980 and, in relation to a defendant under 18, sections 45, 46 and 48 of the Children and Young Persons Act 1933, section 18 of the Children and Young Persons Act 196, section 47 of the Crime and Disorder Act 1998 and section 9 of the Powers of Criminal Courts (Sentencing) Act 2000.

The exercise of the court's powers is affected by –
   (a)   the classification of the offence (and the general rule, subject to exceptions, is that a magistrates' court must try –
       (i)   an offence classified as one that can be tried only in a magistrates' court (in other legislation, described as triable only summarily), and
       (ii)   an offence classified as one that can be tried either in a magistrates' court or in the Crown Court (in other legislation, described as triable either way) that has been allocated for trial in a magistrates' court); and
   (b)   the defendant's age (and the general rule, subject to exceptions, is that an allegation of an offence against a defendant under 18 must be tried in a magistrates' court sitting as a youth court, irrespective of the classification of the offence and without allocation for trial there).

Under sections 10, 14, 27A, 121 and 148 of the Magistrates' Courts Act 1980 and The Justices of the Peace (Size and Chairmanship of Bench) Rules 2005, the court –
   (a)   must comprise at least two but not more than three justices, or a District Judge (Magistrates' Courts) (but a single member can adjourn the hearing);
   (b)   must not include any member who adjudicated at a hearing to which rule 37.11(3)(e) applies (defendant's declaration of no knowledge of hearing);

    (c)   when reaching a verdict, must not include any member who was absent from any part of the hearing;

    (d)   when passing sentence, need not include any of the members who reached the verdict (but may do so).

Under The Youth Courts (Constitution of Committees and Right to Preside) Rules 2007, where the court is a youth court comprising justices –

    (a)   each member must be qualified to sit as a member of that youth court; and

    (b)   the members must include at least one man and one woman, unless –

        (i)   either is unavailable, and

        (ii)   the members present decide that the hearing will be delayed unreasonably if they do not proceed.

Under section 150 of the Magistrates' Courts Act 1980, where two or more justices are present one may act on behalf of all.

Section 59 of the Children and Young Persons Act 1933 requires that –

    (a)   the expressions 'conviction' and 'sentence' must not be used by a magistrates' court dealing with a defendant under 18; and

    (b)   a reference in legislation to a defendant who is convicted, to a conviction, or to a sentence, must be read as including a reference to a defendant who is found guilty of an offence, a finding of guilt, or an order made on a finding of guilt, respectively.

See also Part 44 (Breach, revocation and amendment of community and other orders in a magistrates' court). Rule 44.4 (Procedure on application by responsible officer) applies rules in this Part to the procedure with which that rule deals.

37.2   General rules

(1) Where this Part applies –

    (a)   the general rule is that the hearing must be in public; but

    (b)   the court may exercise any power it has to –

        (i)   impose reporting restrictions,

        (ii)   withhold information from the public, or

        (iii) order a hearing in private; and

    (c)   unless the court otherwise directs, only the following may attend a hearing in a youth court –

        (i)   the parties and their legal representatives,

        (ii)   a defendant's parents, guardian or other supporting adult,

        (iii) a witness,

     (iv) anyone else directly concerned in the case, and

     (v) a representative of a news-gathering or reporting organisation.

(2) Unless already done, the justices' legal adviser or the court must –

  (a) read the allegation of the offence to the defendant;

  (b) explain, in terms the defendant can understand (with help, if necessary) –

     (i) the allegation, and

     (ii) what the procedure at the hearing will be;

  (c) ask whether the defendant has been advised about the potential effect on sentence of a guilty plea;

  (d) ask whether the defendant pleads guilty or not guilty; and

  (e) take the defendant's plea.

(3) The court may adjourn the hearing –

  (a) at any stage, to the same or to another magistrates' court; or

  (b) to a youth court, where the court is not itself a youth court and the defendant is under 18.

Note. See sections 10, 27A, 29 and 121 of the Magistrates' Courts Act 1980 and sections 46 and 47 of the Children and Young Persons Act 1933.

Where the case has been allocated for trial in a magistrates' court, part of the procedure under rule 37.2(2) will have taken place.

The court's powers to impose reporting restrictions include those under –

(a) section 39 of the Children and Young Persons Act 1933 (identification of any defendant or witness under 18);

(b) section 4(2) of the Contempt of Court Act 1981 (information that may prejudice the administration of justice);

(c) section 11 of the 1981 Act (information about a matter withheld from the public); and

(d) section 46 of the Youth Justice and Criminal Evidence Act 1999 (identification of an adult witness).

Reporting restrictions that apply in all cases include those under –

(a) section 49 of the Children and Young Persons Act 1933 (identification of any defendant or witness under 18 involved in proceedings in a youth court);

(b) section 1 of the Sexual Offences (Amendment) Act 1992 (identification of the complainant of a sexual offence); and

(c) section 47 of the Youth Justice and Criminal Evidence Act 1999 (special measures direction or application for such a direction).

Under section 34A of the Children and Young Persons Act 1933, the court –

(a) may require the defendant's parents or guardian to attend court with the defendant, where the defendant is under 18; and

(b) must do so, where the defendant is under 16, unless satisfied that that would be unreasonable.

Part 7 contains rules about (among other things) the issue of a summons to a parent or guardian.

Part 2 contains rules allowing a parent, guardian or other supporting adult to help a defendant under 18.

37.3   Procedure on plea of not guilty

(1) This rule applies –

(a) if the defendant has –

   (i)   entered a plea of not guilty, or

   (ii) not entered a plea; or

(b) if, in either case, it appears to the court that there may be grounds for making a hospital order without convicting the defendant.

(2) If a not guilty plea was taken on a previous occasion, the justices' legal adviser or the court must ask the defendant to confirm that plea.

(3) In the following sequence –

(a) the prosecutor may summarise the prosecution case, identifying the relevant law and facts;

(b) the prosecutor must introduce the evidence on which the prosecution case relies;

(c) at the conclusion of the prosecution case, on the defendant's application or on its own initiative, the court –

   (i)   may acquit on the ground that the prosecution evidence is insufficient for any reasonable court properly to convict, but

   (ii) must not do so unless the prosecutor has had an opportunity to make representations;

(d) the justices' legal adviser or the court must explain, in terms the defendant can understand (with help, if necessary) –

   (i)   the right to give evidence, and

   (ii) the potential effect of not doing so at all, or of refusing to answer a question while doing so;

(e) the defendant may introduce evidence;

(f) a party may introduce further evidence if it is then admissible (for example, because it is in rebuttal of evidence already introduced);

(g) the defendant may make representations about the case; and

(h) the prosecutor may make representations about the relevant law and the defendant may respond.

(4) Where a party wants to introduce evidence or make representations after that party's opportunity to do so under paragraph (3), the court –
  (a) may refuse to receive any such evidence or representations; and
  (b) must not receive any such evidence or representations after it has announced its verdict.

(5) If the court –
  (a) convicts the defendant; or
  (b) makes a hospital order instead of doing so,
  it must give sufficient reasons to explain its decision.

(6) If the court acquits the defendant, it may –
  (a) give an explanation of its decision; and
  (b) exercise any power it has to make –
      (i)   a civil behaviour order,
      (ii) a costs order.

Note. See section 9 of the Magistrates' Courts Act 1980.

Under section 37(3) of the Mental Health Act 1983, if the court is satisfied that the defendant did the act or made the omission alleged, then it may make a hospital order without convicting the defendant.

Under section 35 of the Criminal Justice and Public Order Act 1994, the court may draw such inferences as appear proper from a defendant's failure to give evidence, or refusal without good cause to answer a question while doing so. The procedure set out in rule 37.3(3)(d) is prescribed by that section.

The admissibility of evidence that a party introduces is governed by rules of evidence.

See rule 37.10 for the procedure if the court convicts the defendant.

Part 50 contains rules about civil behaviour orders after verdict or finding.

37.4   Evidence of a witness in person

(1) This rule applies where a party wants to introduce evidence by calling a witness to give that evidence in person.

(2) Unless the court otherwise directs –
  (a) a witness waiting to give evidence must not wait inside the courtroom, unless that witness is –
      (i)   a party, or
      (ii) an expert witness;
  (b) a witness who gives evidence in the courtroom must do so from the place provided for that purpose; and
  (c) a witness' address must not be announced unless it is relevant to an issue in the case.

(3) Unless other legislation otherwise provides, before giving evidence a witness must take an oath or affirm.

(4) In the following sequence –

    (a) the party who calls a witness must ask questions in examination-in-chief;

    (b) every other party may ask questions in cross-examination;

    (c) the party who called the witness may ask questions in re-examination;

    (d) at any time while giving evidence, a witness may refer to a record of that witness' recollection of events, if other legislation so permits;

    (e) the party who calls a witness, in examination-in-chief may ask that witness to adopt all or part of such a record as part of that witness' evidence, but only if –

        (i) the parties agree, and

        (ii) the court so permits;

    (f) if the witness adopts any part of such a record –

        (i) that part must be read aloud, or

        (ii) with the court's permission, its contents may be summarised aloud.

(5) The justices' legal adviser or the court may –

    (a) ask a witness questions; and in particular

    (b) where the defendant is not represented, ask any question necessary in the defendant's interests.

Note. Section 53 of the Youth Justice and Criminal Evidence Act 1999 provides that everyone is competent to give evidence in criminal proceedings unless unable to understand questions put or give intelligible answers. See also section 1 of the Criminal Evidence Act 1898.

Sections 1, 3, 5 and 6 of the Oaths Act 1978 provide for the taking of oaths and the making of affirmations, and for the words that must be used. Section 28 of the Children and Young Persons Act 1963 provides that in a youth court, and where a witness in any court is under 18, an oath must include the words 'I promise' in place of the words 'I swear'. Under sections 55 and 56 of the Youth Justice and Criminal Evidence Act 1999, a person may give evidence without taking an oath, or making an affirmation, where that person (i) is under 14 or (ii) has an insufficient appreciation of the solemnity of the occasion and of the particular responsibility to tell the truth which is involved in taking an oath.

The questions that may be put to a witness –

    (a) by a party are governed by rules of evidence, for example –

        (i) the rule that a question must be relevant to what is in issue,

        (ii) the rule that the party who calls a witness must not ask that witness a leading question about what is in dispute, and

(iii) the rule that a party who calls a witness may contradict that witness only in limited circumstances (see section 3 of the Criminal Procedure Act 1865);

(b) by the justices' legal adviser or the court are in their discretion, but that is subject to –

(i) rules of evidence, and

(ii) rule 1.3 (the application by the court of the overriding objective).

Under sections 34, 35 and 36 of the Youth Justice and Criminal Evidence Act 1999, a defendant who is not represented may not cross-examine a witness where –

(a) the defendant is charged with a sexual offence against the witness;

(b) the defendant is charged with a sexual offence, or one of certain other offences, and the witness is a child; or

(c) the court prohibits the defendant from cross-examining the witness.

Part 31 contains rules relevant to restrictions on cross-examination.

Under section 139 of the Criminal Justice Act 2003, a witness may refresh his or her memory by referring to a record made before the hearing, either contained in a document made or verified by the witness, or in the transcript of a sound recording, if –

(a) the witness states that it records his or her recollection of events at that earlier time; and

(b) that recollection is likely to have been significantly better when the record was made than at the time of the hearing.

In some circumstances, a witness may give evidence in accordance with special measures directed by the court under section 19 of the Youth Justice and Criminal Evidence Act 1999, or by live link under section 32 of the Criminal Justice Act 1988 or section 51 of the Criminal Justice Act 2003. Parts 29 and 30 contain relevant rules.

37.5   Evidence by written statement

(1) This rule applies where a party introduces in evidence the written statement of a witness.

(2) The party introducing the statement must read or summarise aloud those parts that are relevant to the issues in the case.

Note. See section 9 of the Criminal Justice Act 1967. Part 27 contains rules about written statements. The admissibility of evidence that a party introduces is governed by rules of evidence.

37.6   Evidence by admission

(1) This rule applies where –

(a) a party introduces in evidence a fact admitted by another party; or

(b) parties jointly admit a fact.

(2) Unless the court otherwise directs, a written record must be made of the admission.

Note. See section 10 of the Criminal Justice Act 1967. The admissibility of evidence that a party introduces is governed by rules of evidence.

37.7   Procedure on plea of guilty

(1) This rule applies if –
- (a) the defendant pleads guilty; and
- (b) the court is satisfied that the plea represents a clear acknowledgement of guilt.

(2) The court may convict the defendant without receiving evidence.

Note. See section 9 of the Magistrates' Courts Act 1980.

37.8   Written guilty plea: special rules

(1) This rule applies where –
- (a) the offence alleged –
    - (i) can be tried only in a magistrates' court, and
    - (ii) is not one specified under section 12(1)(a) of the Magistrates' Courts Act 1980;
- (b) the defendant is at least 16 years old;
- (c) the prosecutor has served on the defendant –
    - (i) the summons or requisition,
    - (ii) the material on which the prosecutor relies to set out the facts of the offence and to provide information relevant to sentence,
    - (iii) a notice that the procedure set out in this rule applies, and
    - (iv) a notice for the defendant's use if the defendant wants to plead guilty without attending court; and
- (d) the prosecutor has served on the court officer –
    - (i) copies of those documents, and
    - (ii) a certificate of service of those documents on the defendant.

(2) A defendant who wants to plead guilty without attending court must, before the hearing date specified in the summons or requisition –
- (a) serve a notice of guilty plea on the court officer; and
- (b) include with that notice any representations that the defendant wants the court to consider on that date.

(3) A defendant who wants to withdraw such a notice must notify the court officer in writing before the hearing date.

(4) The court may accept such a guilty plea on the hearing date, and if it does so must take account only of –

(a)   the material served by the prosecutor on the defendant under this rule; and

(b)   any representations by the defendant.

(5)   With the defendant's agreement, the court may deal with the case in the same way as under paragraph (4) where the defendant –

(a)   is present; and

(b)   has served a notice of guilty plea under paragraph (2); or

(c)   pleads guilty there and then.

Note. The procedure set out in this rule is prescribed by sections 12 and 12A of the Magistrates' Courts Act 1980. Under section 12(1)(a), the Secretary of State can specify offences to which the procedure will not apply. None has been specified.

Under section 1 of the Magistrates' Courts Act 1980 a justice of the peace may issue a summons requiring a defendant to attend court to answer an allegation of an offence. Under section 29 of the Criminal Justice Act 2003 a public prosecutor listed in that section may issue a written charge alleging an offence and a requisition requiring a defendant to attend court. Part 7 contains relevant rules.

The Practice Direction sets out forms of notice for use in connection with this rule.

37.9   Application to withdraw a guilty plea

(1)   This rule applies where the defendant wants to withdraw a guilty plea.

(2)   The defendant must apply to do so –

(a)   as soon as practicable after becoming aware of the reasons for doing so; and

(b)   before sentence.

(3)   Unless the court otherwise directs, the application must be in writing and the defendant must serve it on –

(a)   the court officer; and

(b)   the prosecutor.

(4)   The application must –

(a)   explain why it would be unjust not to allow the defendant to withdraw the guilty plea;

(b)   identify –

(i)   any witness that the defendant wants to call, and

(ii)   any other proposed evidence; and

(c)   say whether the defendant waives legal professional privilege, giving any relevant name and date.

37.10 Procedure if the court convicts

(1) This rule applies if the court convicts the defendant.

(2) The court –
  (a) may exercise its power to require –
    (i) a statement of the defendant's financial circumstances,
    (ii) a pre-sentence report; and
  (b) may (and in some circumstances must) remit the defendant to a youth court for sentence where –
    (i) the defendant is under 18, and
    (ii) the convicting court is not itself a youth court.

(3) The prosecutor must –
  (a) summarise the prosecution case, if the sentencing court has not heard evidence;
  (b) identify any offence to be taken into consideration in sentencing;
  (c) provide information relevant to sentence; and
  (d) where it is likely to assist the court, identify any other matter relevant to sentence, including –
    (i) aggravating and mitigating factors,
    (ii) the legislation applicable, and
    (iii) any guidelines issued by the Sentencing Guidelines Council, or guideline cases.

(4) The defendant must provide information relevant to sentence, including details of financial circumstances.

(5) Where the defendant pleads guilty but wants to be sentenced on a different basis to that disclosed by the prosecution case –
  (a) the defendant must set out that basis in writing, identifying what is in dispute;
  (b) the court may invite the parties to make representations about whether the dispute is material to sentence; and
  (c) if the court decides that it is a material dispute, the court will –
    (i) invite such further representations or evidence as it may require, and
    (ii) decide the dispute.

(6) Where the court has power to order the endorsement of the defendant's driving licence, or power to order the disqualification of the defendant from holding or obtaining one –
  (a) if other legislation so permits, a defendant who wants the court not to exercise that power must introduce the evidence or information on which the defendant relies;
  (b) the prosecutor may introduce evidence; and

(c)   the parties may make representations about that evidence or information.

(7)   Before the court passes sentence –
    (a)   the court must –

        (i)   give the defendant an opportunity to make representations and introduce evidence relevant to sentence, and

        (ii)   where the defendant is under 18, give the defendant's parents, guardian or other supporting adult, if present, such an opportunity as well; and

    (b)   the justices' legal adviser or the court must elicit any further information relevant to sentence that the court may require.

(8)   If the court requires more information, it may exercise its power to adjourn the hearing for not more than –
    (a)   3 weeks at a time, if the defendant will be in custody; or
    (b)   4 weeks at a time.

(9)   When the court has taken into account all the evidence, information and any report available, the general rule is that the court will –
    (a)   pass sentence there and then;
    (b)   explain the sentence, the reasons for it, and its effect, in terms the defendant can understand (with help, if necessary); and
    (c)   consider exercising any power it has to make a costs or other order.

(10)   Despite the general rule –
    (a)   the court must adjourn the hearing if –

        (i)   the case started with a summons or requisition, and the defendant is absent, and

        (ii)   the court considers passing a custodial sentence, or

        (iii)   the court considers imposing a disqualification (unless it has already adjourned the hearing to give the defendant an opportunity to attend);

    (b)   the court may exercise any power it has to –

        (i)   commit the defendant to the Crown Court for sentence (and in some cases it must do so), or

        (ii)   defer sentence for up to 6 months.

[Note. See sections 9, 10 and 11 of the Magistrates' Courts Act 1980, and sections 143, 158, 164, 172 and 174 of the Criminal Justice Act 2003.

Under section 11(3A) of the 1980 Act, a custodial sentence passed in the defendant's absence does not take effect until the defendant is brought before the court.

Under sections 57D and 57E of the Crime and Disorder Act 1998, the court may require a defendant to attend a sentencing hearing by live link.

Under section 162 of the Criminal Justice Act 2003, the court may require a defendant who is an individual to provide a statement of financial circumstances if the defendant –

(a) serves notice of guilty plea, where rule 37.8 applies; or

(b) is convicted.

Under section 20A of the Criminal Justice Act 1991, it is an offence for a defendant knowingly or recklessly to make a false or incomplete statement of financial circumstances, or to fail to provide such a statement, in response to a request by a court officer on behalf of the court.

Under section 156 of the Criminal Justice Act 2003, the general rule (subject to exceptions) is that the court must obtain and consider a pre-sentence report –

(a) where it is considering a custodial sentence or a community sentence;

(b) where it thinks the defendant may pose a significant risk of causing serious harm to the public by further offending.

Under section 159 of the Criminal Justice Act 2003, where the court obtains a written pre-sentence report about a defendant who is under 18, it may direct that information in it must be withheld if it would be likely to create a risk of significant harm to the defendant.

For the circumstances in which a magistrates' court may (and in some cases must) remit the defendant to a youth court for sentence, see section 8 of the Powers of Criminal Courts (Sentencing) Act 2000.

The Sentencing Guidelines Council may issue sentencing guidelines under section 170 of the Criminal Justice Act 2003.

For the circumstances in which a court may (and in some cases must) order the endorsement of a defendant's driving licence, or the disqualification of a defendant from holding or obtaining one, see sections 34, 35 and 44 of the Road Traffic Offenders Act 1988. Under that legislation, in some circumstances the court has discretion not to make such an order.

The evidence that may be introduced is subject to rules of evidence.

In addition to the specific powers to which this rule applies, the court has a general power to adjourn a trial: see rule 37.2.

For the circumstances in which a magistrates' court may (and in some cases must) commit a defendant to the Crown Court for sentence, see sections 3, 3A, 3B, 3C, 4, 4A and 6 of the Powers of Criminal Courts (Sentencing) Act 2000.

Under section 1 of the 2000 Act, if (among other things) the defendant consents, the court may defer sentence for up to 6 months, for the purpose of allowing it to take account of the defendant's conduct after conviction, or any change in the defendant's circumstances.

37.11   Procedure where a party is absent

(1) This rule –
   (a) applies where a party is absent; but
   (b) does not apply where the defendant has served a notice of guilty plea under rule 37.8 (written guilty plea: special rules).

(2) Where the prosecutor is absent, the court may –
   (a) if it has received evidence, deal with the case as if the prosecutor were present; and
   (b) in any other case –
       (i) enquire into the reasons for the prosecutor's absence, and
       (ii) if satisfied there is no good reason, exercise its power to dismiss the allegation.

(3) Where the defendant is absent –
   (a) the general rule is that the court will proceed as if the defendant –
       (i) were present, and
       (ii) had pleaded not guilty (unless a plea already has been taken)
   and the court must give reasons if it does not do so; but
   (b) the general rule does not apply if the defendant is under 18;
   (c) the general rule is subject to the court being satisfied that –
       (i) any summons or requisition was served on the defendant a reasonable time before the hearing, or
       (ii) in a case in which the hearing has been adjourned, the defendant had reasonable notice of where and when it would resume;
   (d) the general rule is subject also to rule 37.10(10)(a) (restrictions on passing sentence in the defendant's absence); and
   (e) the hearing must be treated as if it had not taken place at all if –
       (i) the case started with a summons or requisition,
       (ii) the defendant makes a statutory declaration of not having found out about the case until after the hearing began, and
       (iii) the defendant serves that declaration on the court officer not more than 21 days after the date of finding out about the case, unless the court extends that time limit.

(4) Where the defendant is absent, the court –
   (a) must exercise its power to issue a warrant for the defendant's arrest, if it passes a custodial sentence; and
   (b) may exercise its power to do so in any other case, if it does not apply the general rule in paragraph (3)(a) of this rule about proceeding in the defendant's absence.

Note. See sections 11, 14, 15 and 16 of the Magistrates' Courts Act 1980.

Under section 27 of the 1980 Act, where a magistrates' court dismisses an allegation of an offence classified as one that can be tried either in a magistrates' court or in the Crown Court (in other legislation, described as triable either way), that dismissal has the same effect as an acquittal in the Crown Court.

Under section 14(3) of the 1980 Act, a single justice of the peace may extend the time limit for serving a declaration to which rule 37.11(3)(e) applies.

Under section 11 of the 1980 Act, the court may pass a custodial sentence in the defendant's absence if the case started with the defendant's arrest and charge (and not with a summons or requisition). Section 11(3A) requires that, in that event, the defendant must be brought before the court before being taken to a prison or other institution to begin serving that sentence. Under section 7(1) of the Bail Act 1976, the court has power to issue a warrant for the arrest of a defendant released on bail who has failed to attend court when due to do so.

Under section 13 of the 1980 Act, the court has power to issue a warrant for the arrest of an absent defendant, instead of proceeding, where –

(1) the case started with –

    (a) the defendant's arrest and charge, or

    (b) a summons or requisition, if –

        (i) the court is satisfied that that summons or requisition was served on the defendant a reasonable time before the hearing, or

        (ii) the defendant was present when the hearing was arranged; and

(2) the offence is punishable with imprisonment; or

(3) the defendant has been convicted and the court considers imposing a disqualification.

The Practice Direction sets out a form of declaration for use in connection with rule 37.11(3)(e)(ii).

37.12   Provision of documents for the court

(1) This rule applies where a party –

    (a) introduces in evidence any document; or

    (b) relies on any other document in the presentation of that party's case.

(2) Unless the court otherwise directs, that party must supply sufficient copies of such a document for –

    (a) each other party;

    (b) the court; and

    (c) the justices' legal adviser.

37.13   Place of trial

(1) Unless the court otherwise directs, the hearing must take place in a courtroom provided by the Lord Chancellor.

(2) Where the hearing takes place in Wales –

    (a)   any party or witness may use the Welsh language; and

    (b)   if practicable, at least one member of the court must be Welsh-speaking.

Note. See section 3 of the Courts Act 2003 and section 22 of the Welsh Language Act 1993.

In some circumstances the court may conduct all or part of the hearing outside a courtroom. The members of the court may discuss the verdict and sentence outside the courtroom.

37.14   Duty of justices' legal adviser

(1) A justices' legal adviser must attend, unless the court –

    (a)   includes a District Judge (Magistrates' Courts); and

    (b)   otherwise directs.

(2) A justices' legal adviser must –

    (a)   give the court legal advice; and

    (b)   if necessary, attend the members of the court outside the courtroom to give such advice; but

    (c)   inform the parties of any such advice given outside the courtroom.

(3) A justices' legal adviser must –

    (a)   assist an unrepresented defendant;

    (b)   assist the court by –

        (i)   making a note of the substance of any oral evidence or representations, to help the court recall that information,

        (ii)   if the court rules inadmissible part of a written statement introduced in evidence, marking that statement in such a way as to make that clear,

        (iii) ensuring that an adequate record is kept of the court's decisions and the reasons for them, and

        (iv) making any announcement, other than of the verdict or sentence.

(4) Where the defendant has served a notice of guilty plea to which rule 37.8 (written guilty plea: special rules) applies, a justices' legal adviser must read aloud to the court –

    (a)   the material on which the prosecutor relies to set out the facts of the offence and to provide information relevant to sentence (or summarise any written statement included in that material, if the court so directs); and

(b)   any written representations by the defendant.

Note. Section 28 of the Courts Act 2003 provides for the functions of a justices' legal adviser. See also section 12 of the Magistrates' Courts Act 1980.

37.15   Duty of court officer

The court officer must –

(a)   serve on each party notice of where and when an adjourned hearing will resume, unless

   (i)   the party was present when that was arranged, or

   (ii)   the defendant has served a notice of guilty plea to which rule 37.8 applies, and the adjournment is for not more than 4 weeks;

(b)   if the reason for the adjournment was to postpone sentence, include that reason in any such notice to the defendant;

(c)   unless the court otherwise directs, make available to the parties any written report to which rule 37.10 applies;

(d)   where the court has ordered a defendant to provide information under section 25 of the Road Traffic Offenders Act 1988, serve on the defendant notice of that order unless the defendant was present when it was made;

(e)   serve on the prosecutor –

   (i)   any notice of guilty plea to which rule 37.8 applies, and

   (ii)   any declaration served under rule 37.11(3)(e) that the defendant did not know about the case;

(f)   record in the magistrates' court register the court's reasons for not proceeding in the defendant's absence where rule 37.11(3)(a) applies; and

(g)   give the court such other assistance as it requires.

Note. See sections 10, 11 and 12 of the Magistrates' Courts Act 1980.

Under section 25 of the Road Traffic Offenders Act 1988, where the court does not know a defendant's sex or date of birth, then on convicting the defendant of an offence involving obligatory or discretionary disqualification, the court must order the defendant to provide that information.

Under Part 6, the magistrates' court officer must record in the court register details of a case and of the court's decisions.

PART 39
TRIAL ON INDICTMENT

39.1 Time limits for beginning of trials

The periods set out for the purposes of section 77(2)(a) and (b) of the
Supreme Court Act 1981 shall be 14 days and 8 weeks respectively and
accordingly the trial of a person committed by a magistrates' court—

(a) shall not begin until the expiration of 14 days beginning with the
date of his committal, except with his consent and the consent of the
prosecution; and

(b) shall, unless the Crown Court has otherwise ordered, begin not later
than the expiration of 8 weeks beginning with the date of his
committal.

Formerly rule 24 of the Crown Court Rules 1982.

39.2 Appeal against refusal to excuse from jury service or to defer attendance

(1) A person summoned under the Juries Act 1974 for jury service may
appeal in accordance with the provisions of this rule against any refusal
of the appropriate court officer to excuse him under section 9(2), or to
defer his attendance under section 9A(1), of that Act.

(2) Subject to paragraph (3), an appeal under this rule shall be heard by the
Crown Court.

(3) Where the appellant is summoned under the 1974 Act to attend before
the High Court in Greater London the appeal shall be heard by a judge of
the High Court and where the appellant is summoned under that Act to
attend before the High Court outside Greater London or before a county
court and the appeal has not been decided by the Crown Court before the
day on which the appellant is required by the summons to attend, the
appeal shall be heard by the court before which he is summoned to
attend.

(4) An appeal under this rule shall be commenced by the appellant's giving
notice of appeal to the appropriate court officer of the Crown Court or
the High Court in Greater London, as the case may be, and such notice
shall be in writing and shall specify the matters upon which the appellant
relies as providing good reason why he should be excused from attending
in pursuance of the summons or why his attendance should be deferred.

(5) The court shall not dismiss an appeal under this rule unless the appellant has been given an opportunity of making representations.

(6) Where an appeal under this rule is decided in the absence of the appellant, the appropriate court officer of the Crown Court or the High Court in Greater London, as the case may be, shall notify him of the decision without delay.

Note. Formerly rule 25 of the Crown Court Rules 1982.

39.3   Application to change a plea of guilty

(1) The defendant must apply as soon as practicable after becoming aware of the grounds for making an application to change a plea of guilty, and may only do so before the final disposal of the case, by sentence or otherwise.

(2) Unless the court otherwise directs, the application must be in writing and it must –
   (a) set out the reasons why it would be unjust for the guilty plea to remain unchanged;
   (b) indicate what, if any, evidence the defendant wishes to call;
   (c) identify any proposed witness; and
   (d) indicate whether legal professional privilege is waived, specifying any material name and date.

(3) The defendant must serve the written application on –
   (a) the court officer; and
   (b) the prosecutor.

PART 40
TAINTED ACQUITTALS

40.1   Time of certification

Where a person is convicted of an offence as referred to in section 54(1)(b) of the Criminal Procedure and Investigations Act 1996 and it appears to the court before which the conviction has taken place that the provisions of section 54(2) are satisfied, the court shall make the certification referred to in section 54(2) at any time following conviction but no later than –

(a)   immediately after the court sentences or otherwise deals with that person in respect of the offence; or

(b)   where the court, being a magistrates' court, commits that person to the Crown Court, or remits him to another magistrates' court, to be dealt with in respect of the offence, immediately after he is so committed or remitted, as the case may be; or

(c)   where that person is a child or young person and the court, being the Crown Court, remits him to a youth court to be dealt with in respect of the offence, immediately after he is so remitted.

Formerly rule 2 of the Magistrates' Courts (Criminal Procedure and Investigations Act 1996) (Tainted Acquittals) Rules 1997 and rule 2 of the Crown Court (Criminal Procedure and Investigations Act 1996) (Tainted Acquittals) Rules 1997.

40.2   Form of certification in the Crown Court

A certification referred to in section 54(2) of the Criminal Procedure and Investigations Act 1996 by the Crown Court shall be drawn up in the form set out in the Practice Direction.

Formerly rule 3 of the Crown Court (Criminal Procedure and Investigations Act 1996) (Tainted Acquittals) Rules 1997.

40.3   Service of a copy of the certification

(1)   Where a magistrates' court or the Crown Court makes a certification as referred to in section 54(2) of the Criminal Procedure and Investigations Act 1996, the court officer shall, as soon as practicable after the drawing up of the form, serve a copy on the acquitted person referred to in the certification, on the prosecutor in the proceedings which led to the acquittal, and, where the acquittal has taken place before a court other than, or at a different place to, the court where the certification has been made, on –

(a)   the clerk of the magistrates' court before which the acquittal has taken place; or

(b)   the Crown Court officer at the place where the acquittal has taken place.

This rule derives in part from rule 4 of the Magistrates' Courts (Criminal Procedure and Investigations Act 1996) (Tainted Acquittals) Rules 1997 and rule 4 of the Crown Court (Criminal Procedure and Investigations Act 1996) (Tainted Acquittals) Rules 1997.

40.4 Entry in register or records in relation to the conviction which occasioned certification

A clerk of a magistrates' court or an officer of a Crown Court which has made a certification under section 54(2) of the Criminal Procedure and Investigations Act 1996 shall enter in the register or records, in relation to the conviction which occasioned the certification, a note of the fact that certification has been made, the date of certification, the name of the acquitted person referred to in the certification, a description of the offence of which the acquitted person has been acquitted, the date of the acquittal, and the name of the court before which the acquittal has taken place.

Formerly rule 5 of the Magistrates' Courts (Criminal Procedure and Investigations Act 1996) (Tainted Acquittals) Rules 1997 and rule 5 of the Crown Court (Criminal Procedure and Investigations Act 1996) (Tainted Acquittals) Rules 1997. As to the requirement for a magistrates' court to keep a register, see rule 6.1.

40.5 Entry in the register or records in relation to the acquittal

The court officer of the court before which an acquittal has taken place shall, as soon as practicable after receipt of a copy of a form recording a certification under section 54(2) of the Criminal Procedure and Investigations Act 1996 relating to the acquittal, enter in the register or records a note that the certification has been made, the date of the certification, the name of the court which has made the certification, the name of the person whose conviction occasioned the making of the certification, and a description of the offence of which that person has been convicted. Where the certification has been made by the same court as the court before which the acquittal has occurred, sitting at the same place, the entry shall be made as soon as practicable after the making of the certification. In the case of an acquittal before a magistrates' court the entry in the register shall be signed by the clerk of the court.

Formerly rule 6 of the Magistrates' Courts (Criminal Procedure and Investigations Act 1996) (Tainted Acquittals) Rules 1997 and rule 6 of the Crown Court (Criminal Procedure and Investigations Act 1996) (Tainted Acquittals) Rules 1997. As to the requirement for a magistrates' court to keep a register, see rule 6.1.

40.6 Display of copy certification form

(1) Where a court makes a certification as referred to in section 54(2) of the Criminal Procedure and Investigations Act 1996, the court officer shall, as soon as practicable after the drawing up of the form, display a copy of

that form at a prominent place within court premises to which place the public has access.

(2) Where an acquittal has taken place before a court other than, or at a different place to, the court which has made the certification under section 54(2) of the 1996 Act in relation to the acquittal, the court officer at the court where the acquittal has taken place shall, as soon as practicable after receipt of a copy of the form recording the certification, display a copy of it at a prominent place within court premises to which place the public has access.

(3) The copy of the form referred to in paragraph (1), or the copy referred to in paragraph (2), shall continue to be displayed as referred to, respectively, in those paragraphs at least until the expiry of 28 days from, in the case of paragraph (1), the day on which the certification was made, or, in the case of paragraph (2), the day on which the copy form was received at the court.

Formerly rule 7 of the Magistrates' Courts (Criminal Procedure and Investigations Act 1996) (Tainted Acquittals) Rules 1997 and rule 7 of the Crown Court (Criminal Procedure and Investigations Act 1996) (Tainted Acquittals) Rules 1997.

40.7   Entry in the register or records in relation to decision of High Court

(1) The court officer at the court where an acquittal has taken place shall, on receipt from the Administrative Court Office of notice of an order made under section 54(3) of the Criminal Procedure and Investigations Act 1996 quashing the acquittal, or of a decision not to make such an order, enter in the register or records, in relation to the acquittal, a note of the fact that the acquittal has been quashed by the said order, or that a decision has been made not to make such an order, as the case may be.

(2) The court officer of the court which has made a certification under section 54(2) of the 1996 Act shall, on receipt from the Administrative Court Office of notice of an order made under section 54(3) of that Act quashing the acquittal referred to in the certification, or of a decision not to make such an order, enter in the register or records, in relation to the conviction which occasioned the certification, a note that the acquittal has been quashed by the said order, or that a decision has been made not to make such an order, as the case may be.

(3) The entries in the register of a magistrates' court referred to, respectively, in paragraphs (1) and (2) above shall be signed by the magistrates' court officer.

Formerly rule 8 of the Magistrates' Courts (Criminal Procedure and Investigations Act 1996) (Tainted Acquittals) Rules 1997 and rule 8 of the Crown Court (Criminal Procedure and Investigations Act 1996) (Tainted Acquittals) Rules 1997. As to the requirement on a magistrates' court to keep a register, see rule 6.1. As to the procedure to be followed in the High Court, see RSC Order 116 in Schedule 1 to the Civil Procedure Rules 1998.

40.8 Display of copy of notice received from High Court

(1) Where the court officer of a court which has made a certification under section 54(2) of the Criminal Procedure and Investigations Act 1996 or before which an acquittal has occurred to which such a certification refers, receives from the Administrative Court Office notice of an order quashing the acquittal concerned, or notice of a decision not to make such an order, he shall, as soon as practicable after receiving the notice, display a copy of it at a prominent place within court premises to which place the public has access.

(2) The copy notice referred to in paragraph (1) shall continue to be displayed as referred to in that paragraph at least until the expiry of 28 days from the day on which the notice was received at the court.

Formerly rule 9 of the Magistrates' Courts (Criminal Procedure and Investigations Act 1996) (Tainted Acquittals) Rules 1997 and rule 9 of the Crown Court (Criminal Procedure and Investigations Act 1996) (Tainted Acquittals) Rules 1997. As to the procedure to be followed in the High Court, see RSC Order 116 in Schedule 1 to the Civil Procedure Rules 1998.

PART 41
RETRIAL FOLLOWING ACQUITTAL FOR SERIOUS OFFENCE

41.1   Interpretation

In this Part:

> "business day" means any day other than a Saturday, Sunday, Christmas Day, Good Friday or a bank holiday under the Banking and Financial Dealings Act 1971, in England and Wales; and

> "section 76 application" means an application made by a prosecutor under section 76(1) or (2) of the Criminal Justice Act 2003.

41.2   Notice of a section 76 application

(1) A prosecutor who wants to make a section 76 application must serve notice of that application in the form set out in the Practice Direction on the Registrar and the acquitted person.

(2) That notice shall, where practicable, be accompanied by –
     (a) relevant witness statements which are relied upon as forming new and compelling evidence of guilt of the acquitted person as well as any relevant witness statements from the original trial;
     (b) any unused statements which might reasonably be considered capable of undermining the section 76 application or of assisting an acquitted person's application to oppose that application under rule 41.3;
     (c) a copy of the indictment and paper exhibits from the original trial;
     (d) copies of the transcript of the summing up and any other relevant transcripts from the original trial; and
     (e) any other documents relied upon to support the section 76 application.

(3) The prosecutor must, as soon as practicable after service of that notice on the acquitted person, file with the Registrar a witness statement or certificate of service which exhibits a copy of that notice.

41.3   Response of the acquitted person

(1) An acquitted person who wants to oppose a section 76 application must serve a response in the form set out in the Practice Direction on the Registrar and the prosecutor which –

(a) indicates if he is also seeking an order under section 80(6) of the Criminal Justice Act 2003 for –

    (i) the production of any document, exhibit or other thing, or

    (ii) a witness to attend for examination and to be examined before the Court of Appeal; and

(b) exhibits any relevant documents.

(2) The acquitted person must serve that response not more than 28 days after receiving notice under rule 41.2.

(3) The Court of Appeal may extend the period for service under paragraph (2), either before or after that period expires.

41.4 Examination of witnesses or evidence by the Court of Appeal

(1) Prior to the hearing of a section 76 application, a party may apply to the Court of Appeal for an order under section 80(6) of the Criminal Justice Act 2003 for –

(a) the production of any document, exhibit or other thing; or

(b) a witness to attend for examination and to be examined before the Court of Appeal.

(2) An application under paragraph (1) must be in the form set out in the Practice Direction and must be sent to the Registrar and a copy sent to each party to the section 76 application.

(3) An application must set out the reasons why the order was not sought from the Court when –

(a) the notice was served on the Registrar under rule 41.2, if the application is made by the prosecutor; or

(b) the response was served on the Registrar under rule 41.3, if the application is made by the acquitted person.

(4) An application must be made at least 14 days before the day of the hearing of the section 76 application.

(5) If the Court of Appeal makes an order under section 80(6) of the 2003 Act on its own motion or on application from the prosecutor, it must serve notice and reasons for that order on all parties to the section 76 application.

41.5 Bail or custody hearings in the Crown Court

(1) Rules 19.18, 19.22 and 19.23 shall apply where a person is to appear or be brought before the Crown Court pursuant to sections 88 or 89 of the Criminal Justice Act 2003 (with the modification as set out in paragraph (2)), as if they were applications under rule 19.18(1).

(2) Substitute the following for Rule 19.18:

"Where a person is to appear or be brought before the Crown Court pursuant to sections 88 or 89 of the Criminal Justice Act 2003, the prosecutor must serve notice of the need for such a hearing on the court officer."

(3) Where a person is to appear or be brought before the Crown Court pursuant to sections 88 or 89 of the 2003 Act the Crown Court may order that the person shall be released from custody on entering into a recognizance, with or without sureties, or giving other security before –

(a)   the Crown Court officer; or

(b)   any other person authorised by virtue of section 119(1) of the Magistrates' Courts Act 1980 to take a recognizance where a magistrates' court having power to take the recognizance has, instead of taking it, fixed the amount in which the principal and his sureties, if any, are to be bound.

(4) The court officer shall forward to the Registrar a copy of any record made in pursuance of section 5(1) of the Bail Act 1976.

41.6   Further provisions regarding bail and custody in the Crown Court

(1) The prosecutor may only apply to extend or further extend the relevant period before it expires and that application must be served on the Crown Court officer and the acquitted person.

(2) A prosecutor's application for a summons or a warrant under section 89(3)(a) or (b) of the Criminal Justice Act 2003 must be served on the court officer and the acquitted person.

41.7   Bail or custody orders in the Court of Appeal

Rules 68.8 and 68.9 shall apply to bail or custody orders made in the Court of Appeal under section 90 of the Criminal Justice Act 2003 as if they were orders made pursuant to an application under rule 68.7.

41.8   Application for restrictions on publication

(1) An application by the Director of Public Prosecutions, under section 82 of the Criminal Justice Act 2003, for restrictions on publication must be in the form set out in the Practice Direction and be served on the Registrar and the acquitted person.

(2) If notice of a section 76 application has not been given and the Director of Public Prosecution has indicated that there are reasons why the acquitted person should not be notified of the application for restrictions on publication, the Court of Appeal may order that service on the acquitted person is not to be effected until notice of a section 76 application is served on that person.

(3) If the Court of Appeal makes an order for restrictions on publication of its own motion or on application of the Director of Public Prosecutions, the Registrar must serve notice and reasons for that order on all parties, unless paragraph (2) applies.

41.9 Variation or revocation of restrictions on publication

(1) A party who wants to vary or revoke an order for restrictions on publication, under section 82(7) of the Criminal Justice Act 2003, may apply to the Court of Appeal in writing at any time after that order was made.

(2) A copy of the application to vary or revoke shall be sent to all parties to the section 76 application unless paragraph (3) applies.

(3) If the application to vary or revoke is made by the Director of Public Prosecutions and –
   (a) the notice of a section 76 application has not been given under rule 41.2; and
   (b) the Director of Public Prosecutions has indicted that there are reasons why the acquitted person should not be notified of an application for restrictions on publication, the Court of Appeal may order that service on the acquitted person is not to be effected until notice of a section 76 application is served on that person.

(4) If the Court of Appeal varies or revokes an order for restrictions on publication of its own motion or on application, it must serve notice and reasons for that order on all parties, unless paragraph (3) applies.

41.10 Powers exercisable by a single judge of the Court of Appeal

(1) The following powers under the Criminal Justice Act 2003 and under this Part may be exercised by a single judge in the same manner as they may be exercised by the Court of Appeal and subject to the same provisions, namely to –
   (a) order the production of any document, exhibit or thing under section 80(6)(a) of the 2003 Act;
   (b) order any witness who would be a compellable witness in proceedings pursuant to an order or declaration made on the application to attend for examination and be examined before the Court of Appeal under section 80(6)(b) of the 2003 Act;
   (c) extend the time for service under rule 41.3(2); and
   (d) delay the requirement of service on the acquitted person of an application for restrictions on publication under rules 41.8(2) and 41.9(3).

(2) A single judge may, for the purposes of exercising any of the powers specified in paragraph (1), sit in such place as he appoints and may sit otherwise than in open court.

(3) Where a single judge exercises one of the powers set out in paragraph (1), the Registrar must serve notice of the single judge's decision on all parties to the section 76 application.

41.11 Powers exercisable by the Registrar

(1) The Registrar may require the Crown Court at the place of original trial to provide the Court of Appeal with any assistance or information which it may require for the purposes of exercising its jurisdiction under Part 10 of the Criminal Justice Act 2003 or this Part.

(2) The following powers may be exercised by the Registrar in the same manner as the Court of Appeal and subject to the same provisions –
  (a) order the production of any document, exhibit or thing under section 80(6)(a) of the 2003 Act;
  (b) order any witness who would be a compellable witness in proceedings pursuant to an order or declaration made on the application to attend for examination and be examined before the Court of Appeal under section 80(6)(b) of the 2003 Act; and
  (c) extend the time for service under rule 41.3(2).

(3) Where the Registrar exercises one of the powers set out in paragraph (2) the Registrar must serve notice of that decision on all parties to the section 76 application.

(4) Where the Registrar has refused an application to exercise any of the powers referred to in paragraph (2), the party making the application may have it determined by a single judge by serving a renewal in the form set out in the Practice Direction within 14 days of the day on which notice of the Registrar's decision is served on the party making the application, unless that period is extended by the Court of Appeal.

41.12 Determination by full court

(1) Where a single judge has refused an application to exercise any of the powers referred to in rule 41.10, the applicant may have that application determined by the Court of Appeal by serving a notice of renewal in the form set out in the Practice Direction.

(2) A notice under paragraph (1) must be served on the Registrar within 14 days of the day on which notice of the single judge's decision is served on the party making the application, unless that period is extended by the Court of Appeal.

(3) If a notice under paragraph (1) is not served on the Registrar within the period specified in paragraph (2) or such extended period as the Court of Appeal has allowed, the application shall be treating as having been refused by the Court of Appeal.

41.13   Notice of the determination of the application

(1) The Court of Appeal may give its determination of the section 76 application at the conclusion of the hearing.

(2) If determination is reserved, the Registrar shall as soon as practicable, serve notice of the determination on the parties to the section 76 application.

(3) If the Court of Appeal orders under section 77 of the Criminal Justice Act 2003 that a retrial take place, the Registrar must as soon as practicable, serve notice on the Crown Court officer at the appropriate place of retrial.

41.14   Notice of application to set aside order for retrial

(1) If an acquitted person has not been arraigned before the end of 2 months after the date of an order under section 77 of the Criminal Justice Act 2003 he may apply in the form set out in the Practice Direction to the Court of Appeal to set aside the order.

(2) An application under paragraph (1) must be served on the Registrar and the prosecutor.

41.15   Leave to arraign

(1) If the acquitted person has not been arraigned before the end of 2 months after the date of an order under section 77 of the Criminal Justice Act 2003, the prosecutor may apply in the form set out in the Practice Direction to the Court of Appeal for leave to arraign.

(2) An application under paragraph (1) must be served on the Registrar and the acquitted person.

41.16   Abandonment of the application

(1) A section 76 application may be abandoned by the prosecutor before the hearing of that application by serving a notice in the form set out in the Practice Direction on the Registrar and the acquitted person.

(2) The Registrar must, as soon as practicable, after receiving a notice under paragraph (1) send a copy of it endorsed with the date of receipt to the prosecutor and acquitted person.

ALPHABETICAL INDEX

CHRONOLOGICAL INDEX

THEMATIC INDEX